UNDERSTANDING THE MEDIA

EOIN DEVEREUX

THIRD EDITION

Los Angeles | London | New Delhi
Singapore | Washington DC

Los Angeles | London | New Delhi
Singapore | Washington DC

SAGE Publications Ltd
1 Oliver's Yard
55 City Road
London EC1Y 1SP

SAGE Publications Inc.
2455 Teller Road
Thousand Oaks, California 91320

SAGE Publications India Pvt Ltd

B 1/I 1 Mohan Cooperative Industrial Area
Mathura Road
New Delhi 110 044

SAGE Publications Asia-Pacific Pte Ltd
3 Church Street
#10-04 Samsung Hub
Singapore 049483

Editor: Mila Steele
Editorial assistant: James Piper
Production editor: Vanessa Harwood
Copyeditor: Rosemary Campbell
Proofreader: Louise Harnby
Indexer: Elizabeth Ball
Marketing manager: Michael Ainsley
Cover design: Jen Crisp
Text design: Francis Kenney
Typeset by: C&M Digitals (P) Ltd, Chennai, India
Printed and bound in Great Britain by Ashford
Colour Press Ltd

Library of Congress Control Number: 2013942562

British Library Cataloguing in Publication data

A catalogue record for this book is available from
the British Library

ISBN 978-1-4462-4879-9
ISBN 978-1-4462-4880-5 (pbk)

For Liz, my rock chick ...

CONTENTS

ACKNOWLEDGEMENTS

Special thanks to my editor Mila Steele at Sage (London) for her kindness and understanding.

Thanks to James Piper and Vanessa Harwood at Sage (London) for their careful attention to detail.

In my own training as a Sociologist I have been very fortunate to have worked with some incredible teachers. In particular, I would like to record my debt of gratitude to the inspirational Michael D. Higgins (now President of Ireland) who launched the second edition of this book in 2007.

Thanks to the following colleagues at University of Limerick: Paul Boland, Eamonn Cregan, Brian Keary, Helen Kelly-Holmes, Adrienne Magliocco, Mairead Moriarty, Anne McCarthy, Patrick O'Connor and Tina O'Toole.

I would also like to remember the late Tony Mulrennan for all the lively conversations about books, ideas and rock music.

Special thanks to my close friends Michael Breen, Aileen Dillane, Amanda Haynes, Ger Fitzgerald, Joe Gervin, Sarah Moore, Martin Power and Mikey Ryan – 'There Is A Light...'

And finally... thanks to Liz, Gavin and Joe Devereux for their love and all the laughs.

ABOUT THE AUTHOR

Dr Eoin Devereux is Senior Lecturer in Sociology at University of Limerick in the Republic of Ireland. An award winning university teacher, he is widely recognized as an expert in media analysis and popular culture. Eoin's teaching is primarily focused on the Sociology of Media and on the Sociology of Media Audiences. His research interests lie in cultural and economic Sociology, publishing most recently on media constructions of stigmatised neighbourhoods. Media re-representations of class-based inequality is a consistent thread in his published research. He is the editor of *Media Studies: Key Issues and Debates* (Sage, 2007) and the co-editor (with Aileen Dillane and Martin Power) of *Morrissey: Fandom, Representations and Identities* (Intellect, 2011). Previous editions of his book *Understanding the Media* (Sage, 2003 and 2007) have been widely adopted as textbooks in classrooms around the world. Eoin has co-organized symposia on Morrissey, The Smiths, Oscar Wilde and the Riot Grrrl movement. In 2012 he co-organized the first ever academic symposium on David Bowie. Dr Devereux has published in many academic journals including *Media, Culture and Society*; *New Media and Society*; *Critical Discourse Studies* and *Journalism: Theory and Practice*. In his spare time he writes short fiction, DJs and listens to punk rock.

FOREWORD

Why study media? Why would we spend so much time and energy analysing complex systems of communication unless we thought they had some crucial role in our lives. This book explores that role and shows the relationship between mass communications and issues of power, inequality, the organization of economy, and crucially how all these are justified and legitimized.

We have recently witnessed an intense crisis in the international finance and banking systems. For a time, there was public outrage at bankers who had speculated with the wealth of the world while generating fortunes for themselves. Even the right wing media featured strong criticism, reflecting the views of their readers. The *Daily Mail*, with its middle-class readership whose pensions and saving were potentially threatened, thundered from its front page:

GREED THAT FUELLED A CRASH   (14 October 2008)

The *Sun* put it more succinctly:

SCUMBAG MILLIONAIRES

Shamed Banked Bosses 'Sorry' For Crisis (11 February 2009)

But among the sound and fury, there were no demands for alternative solutions, such as taking back the bonuses through a wealth tax, or transforming the financial sector by taking the bulk of it into public ownership. These are 'outside' acceptable media debate, so we can complain but in the end the existing system must remain. As the *Sun* explains in this editorial:

> Many will ask if it is right that tax payers are forced to subsidise irresponsible borrowers and greedy banks. But what was the alternative? Neither America nor Britain could stand by and watch their economies disintegrate. (20 September 2008)

This thought is then taken further by David Cameron who, as Prime Minister, argued that we must stop attacking the bankers. In the *Daily Telegraph* he was reported as saying:

David Cameron: stop seeking vengeance on bankers

Voters must stop seeking to 'take revenge' on banks and accept they are vital to economic recovery, David Cameron said yesterday.

(*Daily Telegraph* 15 January 2011)

A month later the *Independent* and the *Guardian* (9 February 2011) reported that the Conservative Party had received more than half its income from the City and property developers. In the face of such structures of power, the role of the mainstream media is largely to act as a forum for grumbles and discontent, but not to explore serious alternatives. As Mike Berry has shown, alternatives such as taking control of the financial system or nationalizing the banks to run them in the public interest are excluded from debate. The people most likely to be interviewed and asked about solutions and what was to be done were those closely associated with the area from which the problem came. He analysed coverage, on the BBC's flagship *Today* programme, of the banking bail-out in Britain in 2008, and found that 75% of interviewees were from city, business, or financial services community (2013).

And very quickly, new targets for public outrage are found and old favourites are revived. The politicians of the right and the conservative press tell us that 'Welfare scroungers' would now be forced back to work, as if the £67 a week which the unemployed received is the reason for the government deficit rather than the actions of the financial class. As the *Daily Express* put it:

WORKSHY LOSE BENEFITS

Britain's something-for-nothing benefits bonanza was declared extinct yesterday as David Cameron unleashed the greatest welfare shake-up for 60 years

(*Daily Express*, 18 February 2011)

We analysed the growth of these attacks on people claiming welfare, on disability benefits, and the long history of attacks migrants, refugees, and asylum seekers (Briant, Watson, and Philo, 2011; Philo, Briant, and Donald, 2013). A journalist from the *Daily Star* described to us how such stories were constructed: 'There is nothing better than the Muslim asylum seeker, that's sort of jackpot I suppose: all social ills can be traced to immigrants and asylum seekers flooding into this country.' Another from a broadsheet described how young, inexperienced reporters would be pressured "to put their conscience aside and go and monster an asylum seeker' (Philo, Briant, and Donald, 2013: 8-10).

The resulting coverage becomes part of the everyday language of our society and when we asked focus group members to think up typical headlines, they readily provided us with examples such as 'Migrants, how can we cope?', 'Britain getting flooded', 'Britain being invaded', 'Free homes', 'Crime rate increases: asylum' (Philo, Briant, and Donald, 2013: 52).

As social scientists analysing media, we need to understand both the social and economic processes which shape our world, which underpin the key movements of people, wealth and capital and also how the damaging effects of these movements are then reported in distorted and ideological ways. Two recent stories in the *Guardian* highlighted these central processes. They appeared on the same day and the first related to the climate of fear generated around migration, including a new government campaign and the second was about the rise in house prices ('"Go home" campaign denounced by human rights groups', 'Buy-to-let fuels property boom', both 9 August 2013). The house price rise, especially in London, was caused partly by the international movement of money as the wealthy seek to capitalize on speculative investment. At the same time those with access to money can borrow more and invest in buy-to-let properties, to profit from those who must rent. So this system works to move capital to where it will make more and to divide those who have it from those who don't. Wealth accumulates in fewer hands and its movement produces rapid, uneven developments. Writ large, that is the story of our world, and the free flow of capital is followed inevitably by the flow of labour, as people move from areas of forced decline to wherever there is a prospect of work. Employers benefit from cheaper labour but the migrants are blamed for displacing unskilled workers and competing for scarce resources in housing and health. To reverse these processes would require economic planning and wealth taxes to put accumulated private capital back towards social use; in the UK the £4.5 trillion owned by the top 10% could pay off the national debt four times or finance re-skilling, infrastructure, green technology and much else. It also requires politicians and media to stop blaming the migrants, refugees and other victims of the system, and to look instead at how to rebuild our world so it is more use to all who have to live in it.

But you will find little such analysis or alternative economic solutions in most popular media. To understand why, is a key issue in Media Studies and we can see that issues of power, ideology and control remain central concerns. Our world is profoundly unequal, and that inequality is sustained through the mass production of confusion and ignorance. This book will help you find your way through this towards something closer to the truth.

References

Berry, M. (2013) 'The *Today* programme and the banking crisis', in *Journalism,* 14: 253, DOI: 10.1177/1464884912458654, originally published online 27 September 2012.

Briant, E., Watson, N. and Philo, G. (2011) *Bad News for Disabled People: How the Newspapers are Reporting Disability.* Project Report. Strathclyde Centre for Disability Research and Glasgow Media Unit, University of Glasgow, Glasgow, UK. http://eprints.gla.ac.uk/57499/

Philo, G. Briant, E. and Donald, P. (2013) *Bad News for Refugees*, London: Pluto.

Greg Philo

KEY TO ICONS

Key Thinkers

Stop and
Think

Chapter Links

Case Studies

A Closer Look

Do It!

Chapter
Toolkit

Further
Reading

COMPANION WEBSITE

Understanding The Media's updated Companion Website contains a number of important features that will assist both student readers and their instructors. **www.sagepub.co.uk/devereux3e**

Divided into two resources, the companion website provides you with additional materials which are intended to complement the print edition of *Understanding The Media*, Third Edition. These supplementary materials are best used sequentially and will help students and their instructors to engage further with sometimes complex issues and debates in creative ways. The carefully selected materials are intended to deepen student knowledge and serve as an exciting starting point in developing a critical gaze concerning the media.

In the **Student Resources** you will find a toolkit comprising practical exercises. I have devised and applied these exercises in my own teaching. Pertinent online readings from SAGE Journals Online as well as key discussion points are also provided. Where relevant, there are additional case-studies and guidance in the useful web-links and further reading sections. These are intended as signposts to guide you in how you might go further in your quest to understand the media more critically. The materials will help you to compare and contrast evidence from a wide variety of contexts and perspectives. They will allow you to test your level of knowledge and above all, they will help you to realise the key goal of *Understanding The Media* which is to ask critical and sometimes *tricky* questions.

In the password protected **Instructor Resources** a range of tutorial exercises are provided. As in the Student Resources, these exercises have been tried and tested with positive results. They are intended to make learning fun as well as engaging. I offer some reflections from my own experiences as a university lecturer on how individual chapters are best taught. The Instructor Resources also contains sample exam/assessment questions which may be used as the basis of term papers or written assignments.

Introduction: Asking Awkward Questions

Dear Student,

Introductions to textbooks are usually skipped over. However, in order to get the most from this book, I would like you to read the following introduction closely. It is meant for you as a student reader rather than just something aimed at your lecturer.

We live in a time of unprecedented media saturation, so much so that it is very difficult to stand back and ask questions about how all of this has come about and the implications it has for how we make sense of, and behave or act in, the social world. How much of your personal media experience is shaped and determined by profit hungry multimedia **conglomerates**? To what extent do you have freedom and power as an audience member when audiences themselves are becoming increasingly fragmented? How free is your free choice regarding media consumption?

This book is largely informed by a critical sociological understanding of the media. Its hallmark is to ask important – and sometimes awkward – questions. It demands of you to think beyond your everyday experiences of Facebook, Twitter, the iPad and TV, for example, and to engage in the exciting and challenging prospect of 'defamiliarizing the familiar' by using the '**sociological imagination**' as elaborated by C. Wright Mills (1976). As you will see in greater detail in Chapter 1, this challenge requires you to stand back and examine your everyday, familiar and often mundane media experiences and pose *critical* questions. In doing so, this book takes a further cue from Todd Gitlin, who proposes that we:

> ... stop – and imagine the whole phenomenon freshly, taking the media seriously, not as a cornucopia of wondrous gadgets or a collection of social problems, but as a central condition of an entire way of life. Perhaps if we step away from the ripples of the moment, the week or the season, and contemplate the torrent in its entirety, we will know what we want to do about it besides change channels. (2002: 210)

In looking critically at our media saturated world, Gitlin's key phrase is that the media represent 'a central condition of an entire way of life'. His challenge to all of us, as students, as teachers and most importantly as *citizens*, is to engage critically with the everyday media world in which we live. Given the conditions – such as:

ongoing **media globalization**; the proliferation of **social media**; the reconfiguration of audiences as producers of media content; the re-structuring of media ownership; and rapid technological change – that have given rise to the historically unprecedented levels of media saturation and social transformation, this is by no means a simple task.

This textbook is *not* about asking questions just for the sake of asking questions. As well as casting a critical gaze on the media, *Understanding the Media* is concerned with the role of the media in contributing to and sustaining unequal power relationships in the social world (see Couldry, 2009). Thus, your textbook has a deliberate focus on the media's role in creating and perpetuating inequalities based upon **class**, **ethnicity** and **gender**, either singly or more usually in combination. While the intention of this book is not to detract from your enjoyment of the media as either a student or as an audience member, the book's one ambition is that you will begin to look at the media in a very different and critical light.

Asking questions about the media: an example

As a media student you need to look at the everyday and commonplace as if you were seeing it for the very first time. This book asks you to see past the hyperbole circulated by global multimedia conglomerates and to ask critical questions.

Let's consider briefly an example of the sorts of questions you might ask of a widely circulated media text. As a media student you might wish to undertake some research into the globally popular Harry Potter film series (see 'A closer look I.1 How does Harry Potter travel?') For example, in addition to examining the production values employed in making the eight films (the quality of the camera work, the faithfulness of the scripts and storylines to the original novels), your research might focus on the ownership, production and distribution of such a series. In this regard you might want to pay particular attention to the commodification of popular culture and examine how media products such as Harry Potter are a major source of profit for their owners. Profits are generated not only from selling the series throughout the world (in cinemas, on television, on DVD, online, etc.), but also through a wide variety of merchandising associated with the series. You might want to examine the diversity of personnel who are involved in the making of Harry Potter – the owners, the creator, the scriptwriters and the team who cast the films. You could focus on Harry Potter as a multimedia phenomenon by examining how it has crossed over into a range of media **genres** such as DVD, computer games, official and fan created websites as well as comics, soundtracks and magazines.

Alternatively, you might examine cross-cultural audience responses focusing on, for example, how the films represent the age-old struggles between 'good' and 'evil', power relationships or how corruption manifests itself. Might the reading or interpretation of Harry Potter vary according to the location of audience members in terms of region, age, gender and cultural contexts (such as religious beliefs or ethnicity)? Given the series emphasis on the many trials and tribulations associated with being an adolescent you might focus specifically on the meaning that teenage **fans** take from Harry Potter, comparing male and female fans for example. Do the narratives contained in the novels and films have a discernible **discourse** concerning power relationships? Do audiences across the world have equal access to Harry Potter in terms, for example, of being able to afford the texts themselves or the associated merchandise?

You might choose all or any of these approaches in analysing the series in question. In reading and using *Understanding the Media* you will learn about the implications of choosing one or other or all of these approaches in analysing a media text.

A CLOSER LOOK 1.1

How does Harry Potter travel?

Since the publication of *Harry Potter and the Philosopher's Stone* in 1997, the Harry Potter series of books and films have become global cultural phenomena (see Anatol, 2003; Gupta, 2009) and have understandably attracted much interest amongst the academic community (see Ciolfi and O'Brien, 2013). Focused primarily on the themes of death, power, corruption, goodness and evil and aimed initially at younger readers, J.K. Rowling's fantasy gothic novels have sold in excess of 450 million copies globally and have been translated into 67 languages (including Urdu and Vietnamese). The series is read by both younger and adult readers and has been praised for reviving an interest in reading among children in particular. While the novels were initially published by two independently owned publishing houses (Bloomsbury in the UK and Scholastic Press in the USA), the ownership and control of the eight films arising from the series rests with Warner Bros, part of the global multimedia conglomerate Time-Warner.

The Harry Potter 'brand' is worth 15 billion US dollars and generates significant revenues from merchandising, for example branded iPods and games such as 'The Harry Potter Quidditch World Cup' and 'Harry Potter Lego', as well as other commercial activities, for example 'The Wizarding World of Harry Potter' theme park in the USA (Florida) and a studio tour in the UK (Leavesden). Undertaking research on global phenomena such as Harry Potter can sometimes be problematic, however. For example, a request to reproduce an image from one of the Harry Potter films in this textbook resulted in the following response from the multimedia conglomerate which owns and controls the brand:

> Warner Bros. Entertainment Inc., together with the author and her agents, strive to avoid diluting the pure entertainment value of the Harry Potter

series by ensuring that it is used for entertainment only and *not for educational or other didactic/teaching purposes.* (Personal communication from Warner Bros 2011, emphasis added)

While the ownership and control of the Harry Potter brand is carefully controlled and has resulted in considerable earnings for the author, her publishers and for Warner Bros, the global popularity of Harry Potter raises perhaps equally interesting questions about media audiences. Launch dates for Harry Potter novels and films are best understood as being participatory (belonging to a fan community) and **performative** (e.g. fans dressing up and acting out roles as the characters). There is also an abundance of online activity, ranging from podcasts, fan discussion fora and news sites to sites focused on the practice of slash fiction. In addition to the official site (http://www.pottermore.com/), fan-administered sites such as http://www.mugglenet.com/ act as places where fans can participate in virtual Harry Potter fan communities. Researchers have examined the 'parasocial' or affective relationships that fans have formed with Harry Potter's character across different cultures (see Schmid and Klimmt, 2011). Fan creativity takes a further step in the shape of slash fiction activity. The website http://www.squidge.org/ states, for example, 'The characters do not belong to us but the stories do'.

Plate I.1   The Harry Potter fan website MuggleNet.com is an example par excellence of the participatory aspects of fan culture. Screengrab reproduced by kind permission of MuggleNet.

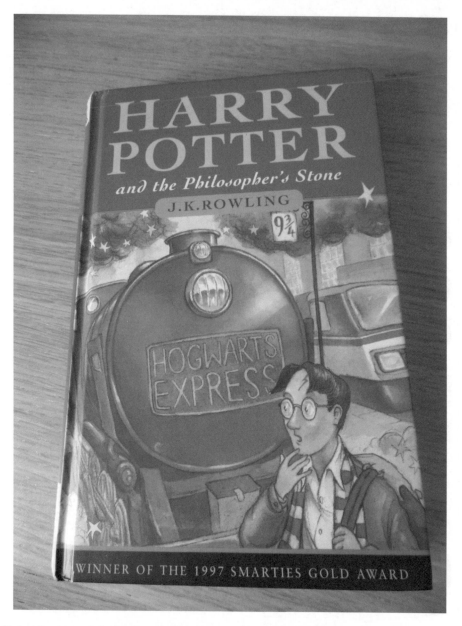

Plate I.2   As a global cultural phenomenon Harry Potter encapsulates the many complexities of twenty-first-century media culture. (Image of *Harry Potter and The Philosopher's Stone* (1997) by J.K. Rowling kindly reproduced with permission of The Blair Partnership and Bloomsbury Press ©, photo by Joe Devereux.)

Key features of your textbook

This book's main aim is to develop your understanding of the media through a mixture of theoretical discussion, **empirical** research findings and practical research exercises. To facilitate this, each of the main chapters contain the following features:

Chapter overviews	Provide an overview of the key debates which are covered in individual chapters.
Key concepts	Key concepts are listed at the start of each chapter. Key concepts appear in **bold** within the text and are given further elaboration in the book's glossary.
Key thinkers boxes	Attempt to bring key ideas and concepts to life by placing them in a wider set of contexts (biographical, historical and theoretical).
Stop and think	Intended as a series of 'quick questions' to test your understanding so far, they are highlighted throughout the text.
Case studies	Up-to-date case studies which illuminate a particular concept or approach.
A closer look	Directs you to research evidence on specific themes. Elaborates on theoretical discussions and provides relevant research findings.
Do it!	Short practical exercises which will help illuminate your understanding of specific topics.
Read on!	Extracted readings with accompanying quick questions are provided in each chapter.
Chapter summaries	A series of takeaway bullet points at the end of each chapter which will allow you to test your knowledge and understanding.
Further reading	A short annotated reading list which will direct you to useful and important articles, books and web content.
Online reading	Using *Sage Online*, you are directed to two or three readings per chapter in the book's companion website.
Chapter toolkit	In the book's companion website you will find practical exercises which aim to bring to life a key chapter theme. There is a strong emphasis in these practical exercises on applying theory and learning about research methods.
Chapter links	Useful links between chapters are signified by this icon.

To obtain the greatest benefit from this textbook it is best to read the individual chapters in the sequence in which they are presented here. *Understanding the Media* introduces you to some of the main approaches that you can follow in asking critical questions about the media. As a student reader you will gain most by engaging with the theoretical discussion, examples of research findings and the suggested practical research exercises contained in each chapter. For the purposes of introducing the variety of analytical approaches to the media, each approach is presented separately. However, you are encouraged to read the textbook in its entirety and consider the ways in which the approaches discussed here may be used either separately or in combination in order to significantly deepen your understanding of the media.

How should you approach this textbook?

Building on the success of two previous editions, *Understanding the Media* is an introductory text for first-time undergraduate media and communications students. This third edition has been significantly expanded and updated. Reflecting the rapidly evolving technological changes that surround all of our lives – and taking an explicit critical sociological slant informed by a political economy approach – this revised and extended edition places a firm focus on the role of social media in your everyday media life.

Using a variety of pedagogic devices, this book invites you to engage with a range of questions about the media in the early twenty-first century. It is intentionally student-friendly and is consciously written in an accessible and straightforward manner. Drawing upon a wide variety of examples, it will encourage you to think critically about recent changes and developments in the traditional and newer forms of media. With this in mind, a broad range of updated illustrative materials have been selected that will pertain to a maximum number of student readers. As an experienced university lecturer I have already used most of the practical exercises that form a core part of this book. In the light of these experiences, as well as feedback from other lecturers and students who have made use of the first and second editions of *Understanding the Media*, I devised them primarily to encourage greater **reflexivity** or critical reflection among media students (and their lecturers!). It is hoped that the exercises will be used as the basis of collective or individual assignments either at home or in the classroom and thus stimulate some lively and informative discussions and debates on the contemporary media. In my own experience as a lecturer I have found that these practical exercises have worked to bring (sometimes difficult and often vague) theoretical concepts – such as discourse, **hegemony**, **ideology**, **structure** or **agency**, for example – to life for undergraduate students, and for that reason a particular emphasis is placed upon them in this textbook.

Aims and objectives of your textbook

Understanding the Media's main aim is to familiarize first-time students with a variety of salient questions about the media. As well as introducing you to the theoretical debates that are taking place about specific issues, the structure of the book actively encourages you to go further in your quest for understanding and knowledge. Each chapter contains detailed case studies, boxes with further discussion of key concepts and theories, details on the key thinkers who have informed specific debates, critical questions for consideration, discussion points and questions for further consideration as well as signposts for further reading and research both in-text and online. The practical exercises contained in each chapter have an important role to play, not only in getting you to think more critically about your own (and others') experience of the media, but also to introduce you to some of the many methodological approaches that may be used in media analysis.

The term 'explosion' is sometimes used to describe both the expansion of the media themselves and the consequent rise of media studies. In reflecting the excitement typically associated with media analysis, *Understanding the Media* draws upon illustrative materials from a wide range of media and from diverse geographical territories, thus ensuring its broad appeal as a Level 1 undergraduate textbook. Its aim is to whet the appetite of the first-time media student and to nurture, in the longer term, a more critical interest in the analysis and study of the media.

Understanding the Media aims to equip you as a student reader with the appropriate theoretical and methodological tools in your initial efforts to deepen your understanding of the media. Although individual chapters are written as self-contained units, and may be read as such, the book – as is demonstrated in more detail in Chapter 1 – follows a deliberate organizational sequence. The over-arching organization of chapters in this book is based upon giving equal weighting to the 'trinity' of **production, content and reception**. *Understanding the Media* is therefore an unapologetically 'traditional' textbook in this regard. As is documented in Chapter 1, you are encouraged to think critically about **media texts** in terms of how they are created, their structure and content and their reception by audiences. All three aspects are crucial in taking what some might term a more holistic approach to media analysis in an age of media globalization. While the **postmodern** approach to media analysis may, on the face of it, seem tantalizing, this textbook takes the view that we need to continue to examine the production, content and reception of media texts in a *systematic* way. The media are changing with great rapidity but the old questions remain. These include questions about:

- the ownership and control of the global media industries
- the power of media content to disseminate dominant and other forms of ideology which shape audience attitudes and beliefs about the social world
- how the media represent and perpetuate social inequalities in terms of class, ethnicity gender and region
- the power of audiences to negotiate and renegotiate media texts
- the actual extent of audience power and agency, particularly in reference to the spread of social media such as Twitter and Facebook.

Having introduced you to the rudiments of media analysis, through a number of case studies and an examination of your own personal media use and exposure by means of keeping a media diary, *Understanding the Media* proceeds to examine the history of media analysis with particular reference to debates about: media power; media globalization; media ownership and **conglomeration**; media professionals and the production of media texts; media and the economy; media **regulation** and policy; media and ideology and discourse; media **representation** of class, gender and ethnicity; media audiences and reception; and **new media** and social media. The textbook also includes a new 'capstone' chapter focused on the how and why of undertaking critical media research. *Understanding the Media* concludes by restating the continued importance of the need to have a critical media studies focused on the question of unequal power relationships.

Understanding the Media online

A very useful companion website for this textbook may be found at http://www. uk.sagepub.com/devereux3e/. As outlined in Table I.1, the website contains important resources for both students and lecturers, including access to online journal articles and other readings, online exercises and assessment resources.

Table I.1   *Understanding the Media* online

Student Resources	Instructor Resources
Toolkit	Tutorial exercise(s)
Further reading and discussion points	How is the chapter best taught?
Additional case studies	Sample exam/assessment questions
Going further: weblinks and further reading	

How is the third edition different? (a.k.a. writing and thinking about a moving target)

This is a substantially revised textbook. In addition to many new individual features, three additional chapters, a more developed companion website and updated illustrative materials, the third edition of *Understanding the Media* is vastly different to its predecessors. Writing about the contemporary media is equivalent to writing about a moving target. That is its challenge and its appeal. There is a stronger emphasis throughout the text on political economy. Given my commitment to a critical sociology of media, further weight has been added to questions concerning unequal power relationships. Equally, examples involving new and social media are liberally sprinkled throughout the text and are also the focus of a new chapter. The book attempts to reflect the kinds of changes that have occurred/ are occurring in the field of media studies. A variety of new chapter features such as 'A closer look', 'Stop and think' and 'Do it!' invite students to engage with up-to-date research or key concepts and apply them to specific chapter themes.

And finally ... the need for critical eclecticism

Reflecting my own training as a sociologist and my experiences in teaching about the media at the University of Limerick and elsewhere, there is an obvious emphasis in this book on the importance of examining the media in a social context. Although not exclusively written from a sociological perspective, the importance of examining the media in this regard is clearly reflected in many of the themes chosen for discussion. This textbook recognizes the contribution that a sociological approach can give us in our analysis of the media in the form of tried and well-tested methodological and theoretical principles (see e.g. Berger, 2011; Carey, 2009; Croteau et al., 2012; Gamson, 2004; Hanson, 2005; Hodkinson, 2011; McCullagh, 2002). That said, sociology is not alone in having an interest in the significance of the media. Rather, *Understanding the Media*, as well as being heavily indebted to the sociological tradition, draws upon a range of illustrative materials that owe much to the diverse range of academic disciplines and approaches – such as, political economy, communications studies, cultural studies, feminist studies, journalism studies and media studies to name but six – that seek to make sense of the media. It is only through using what Halloran (1998: 19) terms a 'critical eclecticism' that we will further our appreciation of the complexities involved in studying the contemporary media. This complexity demands that we are far-reaching and open-minded in our overall approach in attempting to critically understand the media and its central role in everyday life. In endeavouring to do this we need to ask some awkward questions.

Eoin Devereux
University of Limerick, Ireland
December 2013

CHAPTER  1

Understanding the Media

Chapter overview

This chapter will help you appreciate:

- The critical questions which need to be addressed in order to develop more fully your understanding of the media
- How the study of media is eclectic in nature
- The importance of investigating the media in a social context
- The overall approach taken in this book
- The benefits of beginning to examine your own media use, consumption and exposure in a more critical light
- The necessity to focus on the production, content and reception of media texts. This is achieved through the use of case studies on the iPod, U2 and *The Simpsons*.

Key concepts

- Media saturation
- Media
- Mass media
- Social context
- Sociological imagination
- Media globalization
- Media texts
- Production–content–reception model of media analysis
- Audiences as participants and producers/produsers
- Theoretical and methodological tools
- Media use and media exposure
- Political economy

Introduction

It's just after 7 am in Auckland, New Zealand. **Media** and journalism student Emily Johnson wakes and thinks about the busy day ahead in college. Before she even gets out of bed, she reaches for her iPad and goes immediately to her Facebook page. Emily immediately sees that she has a new friend request, nine comments and 12 'likes'. Overnight, her Facebook friends have left replies to Emily's most recent postings about her favourite singer David Bowie. She reviews the news timeline and leaves a comment or two. Facebook reminds her that it is her friend Gavin's birthday and suggests that she post a birthday message to him. A banner advert asks Emily to think about local gym membership. She receives invites to a college party being held after her final exams. She tentatively answers with a 'Maybe'. Emily also replies to the comments left by her two sisters who have moved to London to further their studies. They have uploaded photographs taken at a punk t-shirt stall in Camden Market. By way of return, Emily posts the most recent picture of her cat Snowtoes. She thinks about how Facebook allows them to stay in contact every day so that they can catch up on family news and gossip. In doing so, Emily and her sisters are participating in the largest virtual or online community in human history. As of 2013, there were over 1 billion active users of Facebook which is an example of the unprecedented scale of media saturation that we now encounter.

It is also big business. On the first day of its stock market flotation in 2012 Facebook was valued at US$104.2 billion.

As a media and journalism student Emily thinks about how her use of Facebook stands in stark contrast to her grandparents' experience, and how, when they first migrated to New Zealand, they had to wait several weeks for a letter to arrive via ship from their families in Manchester in the UK.

Like Emily, you are presented every day with a plethora of images and messages about the social world. The vast array of images and messages you encounter – increasingly created and distributed by a handful of multimedia conglomerates – is unprecedented in human history. In addition to this, many audience members have themselves become producers of media content through their use of Facebook and YouTube. The minutiae of the lives of celebrities are dissected and re-circulated on Twitter. Social media allow for the illusion of familiarity between the ordinary and the famous by facilitating the development of para-social relationships. Ordinary people compete for stardom, celebrity and wealth on programmes like *X-Factor* where audience members at home vote to keep the prospective stars on or off the show. They are constantly reminded of the need to consume certain products and look a certain way. Celebrity chefs lecture the poor and unemployed on their eating habits. Print and other forms of media represent being 'fat' or 'overweight' as a disease in the shape of the so-called 'obesity epidemic' (see Saguy and Almeling, 2008). The covers of magazines aimed at a female readership mix the themes of celebrity gossip and the possibility of weight loss each week ('Lose 3 Stone before Christmas', 'How I Lost 100lbs …', 'The New Me …').

These are just few of the myriad of media contexts in which we all find ourselves. More importantly, there are fundamental questions to be addressed about the democratic nature of the media. The media saturation that shapes all of our lives is increasingly colonized by commercial interests that are driven not by altruism but by profit. The intention of this book is to allow you to unpick the complexities of these relationships by learning to ask critical questions, and to ask questions about the media and power in particular.

This book's starting point is your own vast experience as an audience member. From the outset you are encouraged to think critically and ask awkward questions about your own experience of the media, whether as a consumer or as a producer of media content. The chapter starts by looking at the main issues that you need to address in order to begin to more fully understand the ever-burgeoning media. Although the diverse nature of media analysis is acknowledged, a particular emphasis is placed in your textbook on the need to examine the media in a social context. A sociological approach – with a particular focus on **political economy** – to media analysis continues to offer a set of approaches that are both critical and fruitful. Starting with three detailed examples, the iPod, U2 and *The Simpsons* are used as case studies in order to demonstrate the kinds of critical questions you might raise about the contemporary media.

····(A CLOSER LOOK 1.1)··· ◉

Media saturation

The Kaiser Foundation has undertaken a number of detailed surveys of media use amongst 8–18-year-olds in the USA. In their study *Generation M2: Media Lives of the 8- to 18-Year-Olds*, Rideout et al. (2010) surveyed 2,002 students and also gathered data from 702 of the students who kept a media diary over seven days. The study found a significant increase in media use amongst students and especially amongst those from ethnic minorities. The study estimates that 8–18-year-olds spend an average of 7 hours and 38 minutes on entertainment media each day (in excess of 53 hours per week). The authors note that many of their respondents engage in what they term 'media multitasking', that is, using more than one form of media at the same time, resulting in 10 hours and 45 minutes of media content being used in the 7 hours and 38 minutes. In addition to the increasingly high levels of media use we can also think about the rapid expansion in the number of contexts in which audiences are exposed to media content.

Plate 1.1   24/7, Always On Media. It is next to impossible to avoid the media in a media saturated world. Image reproduced courtesy of The Kaiser Foundation 2010 ©.

Defining the media

McQuail (2010), in acknowledging the rapidly changing environment in which the media operate, offers us a useful set of criteria through which we can define the contemporary media. McQuail argues that these features have profound consequences for the cultural life and political and economic organization of contemporary societies. He says:

In respect of *politics*, the **mass media** provide:

An arena of debate and a set of channels for making policies, candidates, relevant facts and ideas more widely known as well as providing politicians, interest groups and agents of government with a means of publicity and influence. (2010: 4)

In the realm of *culture*, the mass media:

Are for most people the main channel of cultural representation and expression, and primary source of images of social reality and materials for forming and maintaining social identity. Everyday social life is strongly patterned by the routines of media use and infused by its contents through the way leisure time is spent, lifestyles are influenced, conversation is given its topics and models of behavior are offered for all contingencies. (2010: 4)

In addition:

The media have grown in economic value, with even larger and more international media corporations dominating the media market, with influence extending through sport, travel, leisure, food and clothing industries and with interconnections with telecommunications and all information-based economic sectors. (2010: 4–5)

Therefore, as well as allowing the communication of messages or texts between senders and receivers, the mass media need to be seen in terms of their public character and in respect of their political, cultural, social and economic importance. The extracted reading by McChesney (1999) below stresses the important role that the media can (and should) play in ensuring the existence of a democratic society. Media professionals working in the media industries produce media products, which are increasingly seen as commodities to be bought and sold in a globalized marketplace. Many of these products or texts have significance in the day-to-day lives of many audience members in different parts of the globe. The texts may be a primary source of information and knowledge about the social world and most significantly about relationships of power. **Media texts** have a further potency in the way in which cultural and political differences are constructed and defined. The experience of living in modern and postmodern societies is defined primarily by the very existence of the media. Our understanding of the media then has to go further than a narrow technical definition of the media as the medium of communication between senders and receivers.

Figure 1.1 summarizes the key ways in which the media can be conceptualized. Moving from the narrow technical definition of the media as the medium through which messages or texts may be sent between senders and receivers, a much broader understanding of the media suggests that they are understood as industries or organizations, where media texts are commodities as well as cultural products, where and when the media act as powerful agents of social change and transformation, and where audiences have the potential to be producers of media content. In short, this book is concerned with understanding the media in a social context. Such a concern will invariably be taken up with questions of power and unequal power relationships. As the case study of the iPod will shortly demonstrate, students of the media need to move beyond the novelty of the latest technological device or application and confront sometimes difficult questions about the twenty-first century media.

- Media as means of communication between 'senders' and 'receivers'
- Media texts as cultural products with social, cultural and political significance

Media as means of communication between 'senders' and 'receivers'	Media as industries or organizations.	Media texts as commodities produced by the media industries.
Media texts as cultural products with social, cultural and political significance.	Media as agents of social change and **globalization**.	Media as agents of **socialization** and powerful sources of social meaning.
		Media as content produced and disseminated by audiences.

Figure 1.1 **Conceptualizing the media.**

 Key thinker 1.1   C. Wright Mills (1916–1962)

Although he lived a relatively short life, the American sociologist C. (Charles) Wright Mills contributed significantly to the development of recent sociological thinking. From a young age, Wright Mills perceived himself to be an outsider, a fact which influenced his formation as a radical thinker. A motorcycle enthusiast, Wright Mills's views were also shaped by his extensive travels in Europe. Much of his work as a sociologist was concerned with applying ideas and concepts developed initially by Karl Marx and Max Weber which sought to understand more about power relationships and the growing problem of alienation in the twentieth century. C. Wright Mills is best known for his critically acclaimed book *The Sociological Imagination* (1976). This provocative text poses a challenge to all of us, as students of society, to look at our everyday 'run of the mill' familiar world, as if we were looking at it for the very first time as newcomers or strangers. In doing so, Wright Mills asks us to 'de-familiarize the familiar' and make use of a sociological lens or imagination. The 'sociological imagination' requires of us to think about why and how the social world is organized the way that it is. It asks us to think critically about our immediate personal experiences and situate them in a wider social context. By doing so, we will be able to best ask (and answer) questions about the social world and gain deeper insights into those larger forces that shape our personal experiences. For more go to: http://www.cwrightmills.org/

The media in a social context

Living as we do in a media-saturated society, we can run the very real risk of taking the social significance of the media for granted (see Hanson, 2005). However, the questions posed in this chapter about the role of the media in everyday life will remind you about the extent to which the media are an intrinsic part of the web of your day-to-day experience. Applying the 'sociological imagination' (see Key thinker 1.1 and Stop and think 1.1) to these commonplace experiences allows you to look on these phenomena as if you were seeing them for the very first time. In 'defamiliarizing the familiar' you will begin to appreciate how the media operate at both macro and micro levels.

Let's briefly consider one example. Imagine if you came from another planet and had never read a newspaper. If you arrived in the last 20 years you might notice that in many newspapers (and other media settings) journalists have increasingly expressed concerns about the reported levels of fatness in the **developed world**. As a stranger to our planet you might be forgiven for thinking that 'fatness' is something that can be transmitted from one person to another (rather like AIDS, HIV or influenza for example). Your mistake might be influenced by the fact that recent media constructions of fatness have seen it consistently framed as an 'obesity epidemic'. The reporting of this 'epidemic' citing evidence of a rise in 'morbid obesity' reproduces moral discourses which blame individuals (women, the poor, members of ethnic minority groups) for their fatness and lack of control with food. As a first-time user of the media you might also be struck by the irony that the media have successfully managed to construct a moral panic about fatness and yet carry considerable amounts of advertising or copy (adverts for McDonald's, restaurant reviews, lifestyle features focused on food or recipes, for example) which encourage more and more consumption (see Boero, 2007, 2012; Saguy and Almeling, 2008). By applying the sociological imagination to the media you can begin to think about the degree to which media representations of the world are socially constructed and about the extent to which media reproduce dominant discourses as if they were social facts.

···· **CHAPTER LINK** ··

As you will see in more detail in Chapters 6 and 7, the media continue to play an important ideological role in contemporary societies in terms of how they contribute to, or challenge unequal power relationships through the dissemination of hegemonic discourses.
··

? Stop and think 1.1

Using the sociological imagination

The media diary exercise in the 'Toolkit' in your book's companion website may surprise you as to the degree to which you are exposed

(Continued)

to the media in your everyday life. Because of their ubiquity, it is difficult for us to separate ourselves from our everyday, largely mass-mediated, experiences (see Gitlin, 2002). The challenge for media students is to stand back from this media saturation for a while and ask critical questions of what we otherwise take for granted in our day-to-day lives. In doing so, we have the potential to gain new and hopefully critical insights into an otherwise all too familiar world. By asking questions such as those just outlined you stand to gain much from your study of the media. Applying the concept of 'the sociological imagination', try to imagine how your everyday life would be without the media.

1. What sorts of differences would there be in a medialess society?

2. How would you find out about national and world events?

3. Where would you get your ideas and opinions about those who are 'different' from you?

4. How would you know about the views and opinions of the powerful?

5. Would your conversations with family and friends be any different?

6. In the absence of social media such as Facebook would your friendships and relationships be different?

7. How would you entertain yourself?

8. How would your use of time be different in your daily life?

At the macro level the media are an important agent of transformation and social change, they are inextricably bound up with the capitalist project and they play a centre-stage role in the reproduction and continuation of various kinds of social inequalities at local, national and global levels. The media have played – and continue to play – an important part in the transformation of societies from being traditional to modern and from being modern to postmodern. The experience of living in **modernity** and **postmodernity** is shaped significantly by mass mediation.

For most people the 'texture' of modernity and postmodernity is formed as a result of the very existence of the media in their everyday lives. More importantly, there are fundamental questions to be addressed about the democratic nature of the media. The media saturation that shapes your life is increasingly colonized by commercial interests who are not driven by altruism but by profit. The media play a central role in defining societies as traditional, modern or postmodern. The mainstream media industries – many of which in their own right are examples par excellence of global capitalist organizations – play a pivotal role in the continued spread of a consumer culture that drives and perpetuates global capitalism. One can find very obvious examples of consumerism within advertising across the media, but at a more general level the media promote certain kinds of lifestyles and taste cultures within a broad range of media genres as being more legitimate and desirable than others. The increasingly complex ownership structure of the media industries and their interconnections with other kinds of capitalist industries have in recent times reinforced these patterns even further.

Modern and postmodern societies continue to be marked by inequalities in terms of class, ethnicity and gender. The media's role in reproducing these inequalities may be seen on two main fronts. We can view the question of the media and inequality in terms of access to the media and we can and should ask questions about the extent to which the media either challenge or reproduce social inequality in their representation of the social world.

The much favoured illusion of the global community or 'global village' used repeatedly by the media industry itself needs to be balanced with a more realistic perspective that recognizes that not all social groups or societies have equal access to media technology or the increasing amount of media content being made available for purchase and consumption.

At a micro level the media act as agents of socialization, constitute a powerful source of social meaning and occupy a significant amount of people's leisure time. Writing about mediated childhoods and leisure in a comparative European context, Livingstone reminds us of the increasingly complex nature of the media environment in which many children now live (see Livingstone, 2002 for an elaboration). She begins with the following example to make the point that we need to recognize the importance of contextualizing the uses of 'new' and 'old' media in everyday life:

> Two eight-year-old boys play their favourite multimedia adventure game on the family PC. When they discover an Internet site where the same game could be played interactively with unknown others, this occasions great excitement in the household. The boys choose their fantasy personae and try diverse strategies to play the game, both co-operative and competitive, simultaneously 'talking' on-line (i.e. writing) to the other participants. But when restricted in their access to the Internet, for reasons of cost, the game spins off into 'real life'. Now the boys, together with their younger sisters, choose a character, don their battledress and play 'the game' all over the house, going downstairs to Hell, The Volcanoes and The Labyrinth, and upstairs to The Town, 'improving' the game in the process. The new game is called, confusingly for adult observers, 'playing the Internet'. (Livingstone, 1998: 436)

Attention also needs to be paid to the **agency** or creativity of both media professionals and media audiences when the media is considered at this micro level.

The media are important agents of socialization in that they reproduce dominant (and other) social norms, beliefs, discourses, ideologies and values.

Although sometimes media content may be constructed with the expressed aim of educating or duping audience members – as evidenced in anti-smoking advertising campaigns or in propaganda films, for example – most of the time the transmission of norms, beliefs, ideologies, discourses and values happens in an unconscious fashion. The mainstream media draw upon a wide range of taken-for-granted assumptions about the social world: assumptions that, more often than not, go unquestioned by media professionals and audiences alike.

One of the key aims of this book is to introduce you to the tools of analysis that you might use to interrogate the otherwise all too familiar media content of your daily life. Consider, for example, the array of messages within media content that you will encounter today about gender roles. Do these messages challenge or perpetuate what are currently viewed as the 'appropriate' gender roles in your specific social setting or cultural context? What do these messages tell you about masculinity and femininity? What sorts of assumptions are inherent in these media messages about being a 'man' or a 'woman' in the early twenty-first century? What aspects of being male or female are downplayed or ignored altogether in these media messages? What sorts of normative assumptions are made about sexuality? Is universal heterosexuality assumed? What sorts of discourses predominate about ideal body shapes and weight? Within the mainstream print and broadcast media how are these messages articulated at a symbolic level? Do you think that they alter in any way the understanding you have about the social world in terms of gender divisions and gender-based inequality? If you were to compare how these messages concerning gender politics vary with those reproduced in the media, say, twenty years ago, how would they differ? Why? Whose interests are served by the predominance of certain kinds of assumptions within media content and why (see Hesmondhalgh, 2013)?

Media content acts as a powerful source of social meaning. The media are centrally involved in the social construction of reality for audience members, giving them an understanding – however limited – of both their immediate and their more distant social contexts. Media audiences are informed and entertained by the media industries. A significant amount of people's leisure time is taken up with media consumption, and media content itself plays an important role in the day-to-day conversations and interactions in which members of society engage. Media content draws upon and contributes to the discourses or forms of knowledge that we have about the wider social world.

? Stop and think 1.2

Ask someone from an older generation in your family (a parent, guardian, grandparent, for example) to describe their media lives from when they were teenagers. What are the main differences between your media experiences and theirs? What shapes or determines these differences? Do these differences matter?

'Do it!' 1.1 Media and the construction of social reality

Go to the Toolkit section in the book's companion website and complete the short exercise on the Media Construction of Social Reality. Having done so, think about the role played by journalists and others in shaping our perception of social issues – particularly issues that prove to be contentious in society, for example immigration, class inequalities and poverty. In your opinion are powerful people (those with more economic or political power or a higher class status) treated differently than ordinary people in the media? Why do you think that this is?

Finally, it is important to remember that the media industries and media audiences are comprised of living, breathing people who shape and are shaped by media content as well as a wide range of other social forces. Given the centrality of the media in people's everyday lives, it is important to stress the capacity that audience members have to actively engage with media content. As you will see later on, an appreciation of the specific social contexts in which media consumption takes place is a crucial starting point in attempting to understand the power of the media over their audience and the circumstances in which audience members can exercise agency in their interactions with media texts. Similarly, it is this tension between structure and agency that frames our concerns in beginning to understand the world of the media professional.

Stop and think 1.3

It's a man's world

It is common practice for women to be portrayed in a narrow and sexist fashion in tabloid newspapers. They are, to use Tuchman's (1978) important phrase, 'symbolically annihilated'. Routinely, women are written about in terms of their beauty, their physical attributes or celebrity status. It is, of course, important to note that the tabloid press ignore significant numbers of women who owing to their age, class background, disability, ethnicity or physical shape or size, for example, do not fit in with received notions of glamour or attractiveness. Try to imagine a situation in which these roles

(Continued)

would be reversed. What do you think might happen if tabloid journalists wrote about men in the same way as they regularly do about women? How might male and female readers react? Would it be perceived as amusing or threatening? Why?

Case study 1.1   Asking questions: the iPod

The 'i' world and the digital divide

On 21 September 2012, queues formed overnight at Apple Stores throughout the world in order for Apple devotees to acquire the iPhone 5. Its launch attracted fever-pitch interest, bearing a strong resemblance to movie premieres or record releases in the recent past. It is hardly surprising as Apple products such as the iPod, iPhone and iPad have attained iconic status and have come to symbolize media **convergence** in an age of media globalization. They have radically altered the relationship between audiences and content in terms of the consumption and production of media content. Perceived by many as having a counter-cultural or an alternative image, the advertising strategies used to sell the aforementioned media products to the 'net generation' celebrate the values of individuality and networked individualism. However, behind the glitz and appeal of these clever technological devices lie some more problematic questions about their production and manufacture. Setting aside the ingenuity of the devices and their many applications, the hegemonic position achieved by Apple in a very competitive marketplace has arisen in no small measure from the company's dependency on cheap labour in Asia. Mulrennan (2010) demonstrates how Apple (and other global firms like Dell, Sony and Hewlett Packard) is directly implicated in the more exploitative aspects of digital capitalism.

The iPod, for example, sold 225 million units in 2009 and accounted for 78% of all digital media players (Mulrennan, 2010: 92). From its initial launch in 2001, the iPod saw Apple's shares rise from $9.43 to $203.00 in 2009. Mulrennan (2010) reminds us that we have to take the (usually invisible) exploitative dimensions of the manufacture of the iPod into account in order to fully understand Apple's dominant position in the global marketplace. While the iPod is manufactured in China, the components are sourced in the US or from **transnational** US companies who are present in countries like Japan and Taiwan. According to Linden et al. (2007) the cheapest aspect of the making of the 5th generation iPod is their assembly and testing in China. Estimated to be just $4, it accounts for 1.3% of overall costs. The bulk of profits revert to the US or to transnational US companies. In 2012, Apple paid just US$713 million in tax on its overseas profits of $36.8 billion – less than 2% (*The Irish Times*, 4 November 2012).

The iPod is assembled by a Taiwanese Company – Foxconn – based in China. Investigative journalists and others have repeatedly criticized the working and living conditions of the (mainly rural) workers who assemble and test the iPod. Mulrennan (2010) notes that the

Foxconn factory in Guandong province employs '... 200,000 people, most of whom live, 100 to a room, in dormitories that are free to employees ... a stipulation exists that should an employee live within the compound, they are forbidden visitors. Employees were found to work up to 15 hours per day for a wage of £27.00 per month' (Mulrennan, 2010: 97). The walled campus which has its own fire brigade and television service – Foxconn TV – is known locally as 'iPod City'. Perhaps the most concrete manifestation of serious problems in the workplace where the iPod is assembled is the presence of suicide prevention netting at the first floor level of the gigantic factory building. Despite Apple's subsequent claims that they are 'dedicated to ensuring that working conditions are safe and employees are treated with respect and dignity wherever Apple products are made' (Mulrennan, 2010: 98), criticisms of the working conditions at Foxconn have persisted. As further evidence of this, Apple asked the Fair Labour Association in 2012 to investigate further claims of mistreatment and exploitation of employees at the Foxconn factory.

Apple is not alone in the exploitative relationship that exists between the Western capitalist world and less developed emerging economies. However, the continued use of cheap labour is an essential part of the story of their success and their now dominant global position. Digital capitalism, like Apple, has to be understood not only at a surface level – that is, what the latest gadget can do – but in terms of *all* aspects of production, consumption and use, and especially so if the production involves exploitation.

 ## Stop and think 1.4

1. If you own an iPod, iPad or iPhone take a close look at it. Does it tell you where it is manufactured and by which company?

2. Apple's iTunes dominates the way in which we now download music. Do you think that is a good or a bad thing?

 ## Do it! 1.2   An apple a day ...

Listen to Leslie T. Chang's TED Talk on the experiences and perspectives of female Chinese workers who manufacture Apple and other products: http://www.ted.com/talks/leslie_t_chang_the_voices_of_china_s_workers.html

Read the online article on iPhones in China by Shi (2011) on your companion website.

Case study 1.2   I know it's only rock and roll
Asking questions about U2

In a remote South African village a group of teenage boys listen to the U2 song 'One' on a shared wind-up radio. Afterwards they talk about U2 and the fact that they find them appealing because of their meaningful lyrics. They usually listen to U2 on the radio or on cheap pirated cassette copies of the band's recordings. At the same time in Tokyo a female fan participates in an internet chat room discussion about the band's film *Rattle and Hum*. Using a pseudonym, she converses with other U2 fans in America, Australia, Germany and Sweden. A heated debate ensues about the overall quality of the film. The participants debate whether the film represents a high or low point in the band's journey through the roots of American rock-and-roll culture. Some of the fans argue that U2's reinvention of themselves as being postmodern and ironic in their 1990s recordings *Achtung Baby* and *Zooropa* was in fact the zenith of their creativity. Meanwhile in London a young man listens to the band's music on his recently purchased limited edition U2 branded iPod as he travels to work on the Tube. His passage to work is itself a media-rich environment. There are hundreds of adverts in the various underground stations in addition to the posters within his individual carriage. His fellow travellers read newspapers, books, magazines. Where possible, some work on their iPads. Like him, many of them are listening to music

Plate 1.2   'U2 image reproduced by kind permission of Principle Management © Deirdre O'Callaghan 2011.

on their phones. The young man is thinking about the fact that later that evening he will watch U2's '360 Degrees' tour in a 'pay per view' concert, live from Bucharest, via his recently purchased digital satellite television system. The latest technology will allow him to choose from a range of camera angles while watching the concert in his sitting room. The irony that one of the main themes of U2's 1992 'Zoo TV' tour was the subversive power of the audience is not lost on him. He watches the concert wearing a U2 t-shirt that he has bought from the official U2 website. As the concert is televised he posts tweets to his Twitter account on each song and on Bono's performance in particular. He also adds comments about U2 to his Facebook page. Afterwards he converses online in a forum with other U2 fans about the concert.

These fans all share a common interest in the globalized popular culture and multimedia phenomenon that is U2. However, they interact with and about U2 using different media and in clearly different social contexts. In spite of their shared interest in U2 they do not have equal access to the range of media settings in which U2 may now be found. The fans differ in terms of which of them can afford to pay for legitimate recordings, official band merchandise or live concert broadcasts by the band. Although U2 has an importance for all these fans we cannot presume anything about the meanings that these fans take from either U2's lyrics or the images contained within their promotional videos or films.

CHAPTER LINK

Fandom is discussed in detail in Chapter 8.

Asking questions about U2

What sorts of questions might you usefully ask about this specific example of media use? Depending on your chosen theoretical perspective or methodological approach you might have concerns, for example, about U2 being representative of a globalized (or Americanized) form of popular culture that now predominates over all other popular cultures. If you follow a **feminist** line of argument you might be interested in whom – in gender terms – U2 appeal to. Is their audience what is presumed to be a traditional male-dominated rock-and-roll audience or have they also significance for female fans? What differences, if any, emerge between male and female U2 fans? What other kinds of demographic factors such as age, class or ethnicity shape their fan base? Do U2 fans constitute a specific sub-culture as would many of the fans of Marilyn Manson, Morrissey or Nirvana? How do they differ from younger fans of 'manufactured' stars like Justin Bieber or Britney Spears?

CHAPTER LINK

Audience reception and rock music fandom are discussed in greater detail in Chapter 8.

A student taking a postmodern position might be interested in exploring to what extent U2's media products contribute towards creating what Baudrillard termed a '**hyperreality**' for their fans. She might ask to what extent their promotional videos, DVDs or films make use of **intertextuality**. To what extent do U2's audiences appropriate or localize the main themes of their songs in terms of either their own personal experience or their own cultural context?

Alternatively, you might focus on the band's use of new media technology and examine how it shapes the media texts that they produce for their fans.

You could decide to focus on the selling of music (and its related products) as a phenomenon in itself. You could also usefully ask questions about the ownership and control of the production and distribution of media products such as U2's recordings and associated merchandise. In U2's case they are signed to Interscope Records, which is owned and controlled by the multinational global corporation Vivendi-Universal – a global conglomerate with diverse interests ranging from music, games, pay TV, digital television and telephony.

You could possibly do an analysis of their records and videos to examine their content in terms of dominant themes and representations. U2 have already been a focus of attention for some musicologists and sociologists. The songs 'Sunday, Bloody Sunday' and 'Zoo Station' have, for instance, been examined as examples of discourses (Fast, 2000). On the other hand, you might also want to ask some questions about the meaning that U2 have for their audiences in the totality of markets in which their products are bought, sold and exchanged. In doing so you would need to acknowledge the fact that their audiences vary in terms of age, class, gender and ethnicity and location, for example. The contexts in which these fans are exposed to the variety of media products associated with the band – whether they are alone or in a group, for example – might also be of possible significance in your deliberations.

 Stop and think 1.5

Apply the questions posed above about U2 to your favourite recording artiste. What sorts of differences emerge and why?

Asking questions? Which questions?

The case studies of the iPod and U2 offer you some clues as to how you should approach understanding the media more generally. These examples suggest that in undertaking media analysis you need to ask fundamental questions about the media. These questions might be about the ownership, control and distribution of media products; they might be about the dynamics involved in the creation of media products, or equally they might be concerned with audience response(s) or activities. In approaching the media in this way we have the potential to gain deeper insights into what are increasingly multifaceted phenomena. This more broadly defined approach to understanding the media means that we must learn to choose between a wide range of theoretical and methodological models of media analysis.

The importance of theory and method

We use a variety of theories and methods in an attempt to add to our overall understanding or knowledge base. Our choice of theory and method not only provides the means of identifying 'truths' but also provides the context within which those 'truths' are reliable and valid. Theories allow us to move from the specific to the general. They permit us to think about 'facts' at a higher level. They help us to make connections between sometimes otherwise seemingly unrelated phenomena. One useful way to think about the use of theory in this context is to imagine that your overall subject area, discipline or approach is a camera. As a student of the media you have a range of lenses that you may place on the camera. These will allow you look at something in a variety of ways and perhaps result in you coming to a multiplicity of conclusions, depending upon your chosen lens or lenses. Theories work like a camera lens in this regard. They will help illuminate different aspects of the same phenomena. To extend the camera metaphor for a moment, **research methods** may be likened to the other techniques involved in camera work in that they allow you to zoom in or out of specific phenomena. Your choice of method will determine whether you go for the very detailed or the very general aspect of your **research question**. Research methods allow us to undertake research that is credible. Research should be carried out in a transparent and reputable way. A research design may be replicated in other contexts (in other cultures, societies or communities, for example) and this allows researchers to compare their findings and to test the theoretical implications of their results. Whether you are a student who prefers a qualitative to a quantitative approach, or you prefer to combine research approaches depending upon your particular research question, the overall aim is to engage in work that is trustworthy and rigorous. Your choice of theoretical perspective(s) and methodological approach(es) will have an important bearing on how you arrive at a position of understanding and knowledge.

Imagine that you were asked to undertake a short piece of observation-based research on the followers of punk music. If your interest is in the sociology of subcultures or countercultures you might concentrate on how punks invert the meanings of symbols that already have currency in wider society such as safety pins, the swastika or bin bags, for example. Alternatively, you might be interested in how individual punks conform to the norms and values of the subculture or counterculture to which they belong. If your interest is in gender politics your focus might be on whether punk culture replicates or challenges patriarchal relationships of power. The choices that you make about theory and method therefore have important implications for furthering your knowledge and understanding.

····**CHAPTER LINK**··

An extended discussion on research methods and media analysis is to found in Chapter 10, 'The How and Why of Media Analysis'.
···

 Key thinker 1.2   Jean Baudrillard (1929–2007)

The late, brilliant (and contentious) French thinker Jean Baudrillard looms large over recent thinking about the role of the media in everyday life. Influenced initially by Marxism and **semiotics** – and by Roland Barthes and Marshall McLuhan in particular – Baudrillard's writings have come to serve as *the* manifesto for adherents of postmodern theory. According to Baudrillard, the postmodern experience is defined by and through the 'ecstasy of communication'. In living media-saturated lives, the media texts which surround us simulate a 'hyper-reality' for audiences in which 'media reality' is more 'real' than 'reality' itself. Baudrillard's most controversial book is, arguably, *The Gulf War Did Not Take Place* (1995). Here, he examines the extent to which the (first) Gulf War took place in a virtual space, that is, on our television screens. This war was different from previous wars in that it was represented within some media coverage as a virtual reality game. The symbols and language used (e.g. a target-rich environment) were unprecedented in terms of war coverage. It is not surprising that Baudrillard's ideas have caused considerable controversy. He has been criticized for over-generalizing, for being politically disengaged and for not testing his ideas against any empirical research findings on how audience members actually experience media saturation and whether or not they engage critically with media content.

Read on! 1.1   A sociological approach to media analysis

Keith Tester (1994) *Media, Culture and Morality.* London: Routledge, pp. 4–5.

... There is much more to be said about the media than cultural studies can allow. Most of these additional things can be said if a sociological light is brought to bear on the media. This is because sociology holds out the possibility of a lively study of culture which is informed by a seriousness of moral and cultural purpose of a kind that is inconceivable from the point of view of cultural studies.

... Sociology might do this because, unlike cultural studies, if it is worth doing, sociology is not happy just to describe and explore what exists. Sociology ought to be driven by a sense of moral commitment and by a moral outrage at what presently passes for a good life; an outrage that cultural studies, with its increasing emphasis on things like clothes and shopping, can say absolutely nothing about.

Sociology ought to seek to know why things happen. In so doing it offers the chance that it will be possible to develop an argument for why things ought to have happened differently in the past or could be made to happen differently in the future. Consequently, a sociological approach can mean that we will refuse to take anything at all for granted. Certainly, we will be unable to take it for granted that something is 'good' or 'boring' simply because it is. Sociology can in principle rescue the media – and therefore the cultural and moral values – from the trivialization to which they are otherwise all too susceptible.

... If a sociological imagination is brought to bear on the question of the media and their impact on cultural and moral values, then it is potentially possible to encourage people to think about the media for themselves. People in principle will be able to develop their own attitudes towards the media rather than simply accept what they are told.

 Stop and think 1.6

1. How does Tester characterize a sociological approach to media analysis? How does it differ from a cultural studies approach?

2. Tester stresses the need to use the 'sociological imagination' – a term first coined by the sociologist C. Wright Mills and discussed in here in the introduction and this chapter – in our approach to the media. What sorts of benefits does its use bring?

Read on! 1.2   Asking the right questions

James Halloran (1998) 'Mass communication research: asking the right questions' in Anders Hansen, Simon Cottle, Ralph Negrine and Chris Newbold (eds) *Mass Communication Research Methods*. London: Macmillan, p. 19.

... Over the years there has been a growing appreciation that the whole communication process needs to be studied, and that includes those who provide (including their institutions) as well as the nature of what is provided, and those who receive what is provided. For example, the production of programmes in broadcasting fulfils functions for the institution, the broadcaster, the audience and society at large. This needs to be recognized and dealt with in research. Intentions, aims, purposes, policies, organizational frameworks, modes of operation, professional values, funding, general circumscriptions, external pressures and ideological considerations all need to be taken into account.

Ideally, the media should not be seen in isolation, but as one set of social institutions, interacting with other institutions within the wider social system. The failure to recognize the relevance of context and interaction between institutions has resulted in a neglect of the part played in the communication process by non-media institutions, and an underestimation of the importance of mediation, support factors, follow-up activities and the like. The other side of this coin is the problem of media-centredness. The media do not work in isolation, but in and through a nexus of mediating factors. What any medium can do on its own is probably quite limited.

Let it be repeated that, simply stated, this means that we should not be asking what the media do to people, or what they could do to people, but what will people, variously located in society, with different experiences, opportunities, skills, competencies and needs make of what the media and other sources provide, and which are available to them? This is really at the heart of the problem, and if we fail to get this question right, our research will be worthless.

 ## Stop and think 1.7

1. Do you understand what Halloran means by the term 'media-centredness'? What are the problems with taking a media-centred approach in media analysis?

2. Think of an example of how you would apply Halloran's model in attempting to understand more about the communications process. In doing so outline the various stages involved in undertaking such a piece of research.

Case study 1.3   Asking questions about *The Simpsons*

Let's consider one further example of how you might approach and critically understand the media. The cartoon series *The Simpsons* is a classic example of the globalization of popular culture. Phrases such as 'Doh' and 'Don't have a cow, man!' have entered everyday speech across the globe. Its importance, however, extends beyond its obvious popularity with younger and older audience members in different societies and cultures. *The Simpsons* also makes an interesting case study in the increasingly transnational nature of cultural production, given that the main animation of the series is undertaken in South Korea, while its distribution is owned and controlled by Twentieth Television (formerly known as Twentieth Century Fox) in North America (see Elber, 2001). Produced by Gracie Films for Twentieth Television – a media giant that is in turn owned by Rupert Murdoch's News Corporation – the programme is a valuable commodity for its owners and creators.

The Simpsons

The Simpsons began life as a short insert on the *Tracey Ullman Show* in 1989 and in 2011 it aired its 23rd season. The show's central protagonist was initially Bart but this soon gave way to a greater focus on Homer, who represents a latterday bungling but immensely popular 'Everyman'. In 1998 *The Simpsons* generated syndication sales of US$3 million per episode (Schlosser, 1998). In 2003 it was estimated that sales from Simpsons t-shirts in the US alone were worth $20 million with global syndication revenues estimated to be $1 billion (Bonné, 2003). The series has helped maximize audiences, advertising and sponsorship for a variety of television networks and it has generated additional profits for its owners and creators through the merchandising of toys, t-shirts, pyjamas, chocolate, breakfast cereals and PlayStation games, for example. In a range of territories such as Australia and Western Europe, *The Simpsons* series has played a pivotal role in the ratings war between publicly and privately owned television channels.

    The Simpsons is not just a television phenomenon, however. It has crossed over into other media settings such as film, video, DVD and the internet. There are many websites where dedicated fans dissect individual episodes of the series and discuss the meaning of specific storylines. As a complex media text about the lives and experiences

(Continued)

of America's most famous dysfunctional **blue-collar** family, the television programme attempts to engage with its audience on a wide variety of issues. Individual episodes of the programme are replete with intertextual references and parodies. The cartoon within the cartoon – *The Itchy and Scratchy Show* – is a clear send-up of the effects debate within media and communications studies about children and television violence. The decoding of *The Simpsons* requires of its readers a vast array of reference points from Western popular culture. The history of the Beatles, for example, was used as the basis of the storyline of Homer's barbershop quartet group 'The B-Sharps'. The storyline included a reference to barfly Barney Gumble's decision to marry a Japanese performance artist, based presumably on the John Lennon and Yoko Ono story. The Beatle's pilgrimage to India in search of knowledge and wisdom was parodied in an episode which saw Homer and Apu travel to India in order to speak to the founder of Kwik-E-Mart.

There is also – to a certain extent – evidence of reflexivity in that *The Simpsons* manages to critique many of the dominant ideologies at play in North America about class, ethnicity, gender and religiosity. Bad capitalism is personified in the programme through the character of Mr Burns – owner of, among other things, the local nuclear power plant. The hypocrisy of the media dropping in on the homeless on Thanksgiving while rendering them invisible for the rest of the year was satirized in an episode entitled 'Bart versus Thanksgiving'. Issues concerning ethnic differences and gender inequality in the United States are recurring themes.

There is also a sense in watching *The Simpsons* that it is consciously written as a multilayered text. One of the best examples of this might be the ongoing reference to the ambiguous nature of Mr Smithers's sexuality. Within a single episode the text can reproduce some of the slapstick humour traditionally associated with cartoons in combination with a discourse about being a closeted gay man. Many of the episodes contain a consciously 'camp' discourse (see Henry, 2004). Thus the programme manages to mix the usual ingredients of the cartoon genre – that presumably appeal to its younger fans – with other narratives that have more of an adult interest (see Mullen, 2004). *The Simpsons* has (rightly) been celebrated by many commentators for the way in which it has challenged racism and ethnic stereotypes – the one exception being its repeated representation of the Irish as being simian or ape-like and being particularly prone to being violent and/or drunk.

There is more to the series than its clever scripts, however. In a rare moment in one episode of *The Simpsons* viewers saw its news anchorman Kent Brockman reporting on location from a South Korean animation house where the animators were drawing and colouring at bayonet point (episode 9503: 1992). Although the programme has in the past parodied media mogul Rupert Murdoch and his dominance of the world's media, the 'moment' of Brockman's report was a defining one. While it did not contain any direct reference to its own production context, the parody struck an important chord. While some might see this as being just one more example of postmodern irony, it is also a very telling comment on the American animation industry that increasingly makes use of what it euphemistically refers to as 'overseas animation'. In an important essay, Cherniavsky gives us an account of how and where *The Simpsons* is produced:

> Film Roman subcontracts the labor-intensive aspects of production of the series, including the drawing and coloring of cells, to one of six 'animation houses' in South Korea. According to studio owner Phil Roman, underpriced Asian labor has become indispensable to the animation industry in the United States: 'If we had to do animation here,' Roman notes, 'it would cost a million dollars instead of $100,000 to $150,000 to produce a half-hour, and nobody could afford to do it except for Disney.' (1999: 141)

She argues that *The Simpsons*, in spite of its occasional reflexivity about capitalism, is:

> profoundly implicated in a system of global capital that requires and perpetuates the existence of a casual and chronically impoverished labor force – for example, at Akom, the largest of the South Korean animation houses, where *The Simpsons* is produced, 1,100 of the 1,200 employees are temporary workers, paid around $1.50 per cell for the tedious job of inking and painting – *The Simpsons* cannot reflect on its own transpacific origins. (1999: 153–4)

The Simpsons animation is sub-contracted to five animation houses in South Korea. Where Akom is concerned, for example, the current production arrangements for *The Simpsons* involve upwards of 120 animators working for Akom in Seoul, South Korea. Here, animators are paid less than one-third of what their North American counterparts would be paid for the same work. They work according to instructions sent from the US on the desired camera and colouring requirements. The wider political context of the relationship between the US and the South Korea should also be noted. In addition to availing itself of cheap labour, the US seems intent on bolstering the economic development of South Korea whilst it is in ideological conflict with communist North Korea.

By looking at *The Simpsons* in this way we have highlighted a number of important issues. *The Simpsons* can be seen as a well-constructed media text containing a range of meanings for its global audience which is in itself segmented into various groups depending on age, social status, geographical location, gender and ethnicity, for example. *The Simpsons* can also be viewed as a valuable commodity produced by one of the key players in the global media industry. Like many other commodities its overall production takes place in more than one country. The programme is a source of profit for its owners and creators as well as the television networks that buy the right

(Continued)

to broadcast the series. Animated television and film are more amenable to translation and therefore travel well in the globalized media marketplace. While at this juncture we can only speculate on the intentions of the programme's writers and producers, there is nonetheless some evidence to suggest that, as a text, *The Simpsons* reproduces an ideological viewpoint that may be considered to be liberal rather than critical in orientation.

Read on! 1.3   Playing the piano wearing mittens

Robert W. McChesney (2000) 'The political economy of communication and the future of the field', *Media, Culture & Society*, 22(1): 109–16, p. 115.

Communication scholars must play a central role in analyzing, debating and popularizing issues concerning the relationship of media and democracy. This is an area that conventional politicians and the corporate media have shown little inclination to pursue. Only communication scholars have the resources and institutional basis to move forward with honest independent scholarship and instruction, with a commitment first and foremost to democratic values. The field of communication needs to apply the full weight of its intellectual traditions and methodologies to the daunting questions before us. They desperately require scholarly attention … if the field of communication does not do it, nobody else will.

… Political economy and communication have a special relationship. Each of them is located uneasily but necessarily between capitalism and democracy; each deals with commercial and material issues and each is ultimately concerned with issues of social justice and political self-government. While one can be a political economist and have only a passing interest in communication issues, the need to at least have a passing interest has grown considerably in this, the so-called Information Age. And if one is a scholar of communication, it strikes me as highly questionable not to have a working knowledge of political economy, in order to understand how capitalism works. To approach communication without political economy is similar to playing the piano wearing mittens. If scholars are to move beyond description to explanation, political economy must be at the center of the enterprise. It is not only the necessary aspect of the field of communication, but it is one of the cornerstones.

Stop and think 1.8

1. What is the nature of the relationship between the media and democracy?

2. Why do students and scholars of the media have a special role to play in the analysis of the contemporary media?

Stop and think 1.9

Asking critical questions

You will gain most as a media student by asking critical questions. Critical thinking requires in all of us a healthy scepticism about what is presented as *fact*. In engaging with media content (a newspaper article, a website or TV news report, for example) or academic writing (a journal article, report or textbook, for example), a sharpening of the senses allows you to be critical of the information you are being presented with. What evidence does an author use? How convincing is it? Are there contrary arguments? Have any aspects been ignored in the **narrative**? Whose interests are served by the way in which the argument is presented? (See Browne and Keeley, 2011; Cottrell, 2008.)

Conclusion

The twenty-first-century media present the media student with an increasingly complex set of questions. Globalization, technological change and the restructuring of media ownership underscore many of the questions that have been asked about the media as well as raising new kinds of issues for all of us in our roles as students and citizens. There are clear tensions in the field of media analysis as to how we should approach a critical understanding of the media. While a sociological approach to media analysis would recognize the so-called 'pleasure(s) of the text' experienced by audience members, there is more to media analysis than a sole focus on the 'ecstasy of communication' which many postmodernists would hold as sacrosanct. A sociology of media informed by political economy stresses the need to examine these new media realities by reference to the increasingly concentrated nature of media ownership. It asks us to consider whose interests exactly are served by media conglomeration. In this chapter it has been suggested that we need to undertake media analysis in a critical and systematic way. By using a framework that gives equal recognition to the production, content and reception of media texts we can begin to make sense of the increasingly complex media environment in which we live our lives. It is within these parameters that we can now proceed to consider questions – both old and new – about the twenty-first-century media.

Chapter summary

In this chapter we stressed:

1. The importance of critically examining the media in a social context.
2. The variety of ways in which the media can be conceptualized.
3. The differences between a cultural studies and sociological approach to media analysis.
4. That while our experience of media saturation is historically specific, we need to ask critical questions about the media, especially in terms of its role in the reproduction and perpetuation of unequal power relationships.
5. The importance of giving equal recognition to the production, content and reception aspects of media texts.
6. That using tried and tested methodological approaches as well as theoretical perspectives helps you to deepen your understanding of the media.
7. The value of the political economy approach in engaging in a critical media studies, as highlighted in the case studies on Apple, U2 and *The Simpsons*. As students of the media we need to get behind the glitz of media texts and technologies and ask the hard questions about their production, content and reception.

Further reading

Branston, G. and R. Stafford (2006) *The Media Student's Handbook*, 4th edn. London: Routledge.

Croteau, D., W. Hoynes and S. Milan (2012) *Media Society: Industries, Images and Audiences*, 4th edn. London: Sage. This is a very thorough and student-friendly introduction to media analysis from a sociological perspective.

Deacon, D., M. Pickering, P. Golding and G. Murdock (1999) *Researching Communications*. London: Arnold. A very useful introduction to the key research methods needed for mass media analysis.

Ferguson, R. (2004) *The Media in Question*. Oxford: Oxford University Press. An important defence of media studies in the twenty-first century.

Long, P. and T. Wall (2012) *Media Studies: Texts, Production and Context*, 2nd edn. Harlow: Pearson Education.

MacNamara, J.R. (2010), *The 21st Century Media (R)evolution: Emergent Communication Practices*. New York: Peter Lang. MacNamara provides his readers, students and academics alike, with a thorough and thought-provoking text which is far-reaching in scope. An experienced practitioner in the media industry, MacNamara's book is written in an informative and entertaining style which will be of immense benefit to both postgraduate and undergraduate students as well as to their teachers. A particular strength of this book is the breadth of illustrative materials used.

Shi, Y. (2011) 'iPhones in China: the contradictory stories of media-ICT globalization in the era of media convergence and corporate synergy', *Journal of Communication Inquiry*, 35(2): 134–56. This article examines the official and unofficial reception of the iPhone in mainland China.

Tremayne, M. (2007) (ed.) *Blogging, Citizenship and the Future of Media*. London: Routledge. A collection of very interesting

(Continued)

essays on blogging and its implications for politics, citizenship and democracy, see in particular the chapters by Papacharissi on audiences as media producers and Bentley et al. on citizen journalism.

Online reading

Go to your book's companion website and read the following:

- Couldry, N. (2009) 'My media studies: thoughts from Nick Couldry', *Television and New Media*, 10(1).
- Morimoto, S.A. and L.A. Friedland (2011) 'The lifeworld of youth in the information society', *Youth & Society*, 43(2).

CHAPTER 2

Media Histories, Media Power

Chapter overview

In this chapter you will:

- Learn to situate your understanding of the media and media analysis in an historical context
- Gain an overview of the various academic disciplines and approaches that have attempted to make sense of the media
- Learn that power (in a range of guises) is the key unifying theme across the history of media analysis and debate
- Encounter an argument that makes the case for a *critical* analysis of media which draws upon sociological as well as other disciplines and approaches in order to focus on questions concerning power and the media
- Engage with the argument that makes the case for the continued use of a model of media analysis which combines analyses of production, content and reception.

Key concepts

- Paradigm
- Media studies 2.0
- Power
- Political economy
- Cultural studies
- Production/content/reception model

Introduction

In early 2007 a provocative essay was published by the media theorist David Gauntlett. 'Media studies 2.0' (2007 and 2011) called for a sweeping overhaul of how media analysis might be undertaken. The analysis and study of the media, he argued, as it had been traditionally constituted, could no longer engage with the radically altered mediascape resulting from media globalization. The traditional boundaries within media studies, Gauntlett suggested, with its focus on industry/institutions, content and reception had ceased to be (as) relevant in a world where media audiences could now become media producers or '**produsers**'. Understandably, Gauntlett's essay provoked a lively response from many in the field (see http://www.theory.org.uk/mediastudies2.htm) and whatever its many merits and demerits, its publication and the subsequent debate it provoked, it serves to remind us that approaches to media analysis are not fixed. They have been subject to much heated debate and controversy and have, like their subject matter, changed radically over time.

From the outset, it is instructive to locate our understanding of media analysis in an historical context. Our discussion therefore begins by noting some of the key moments within media history. An awareness of the historical specificity of the media and its development will allow us to think more critically about how and when it developed, as well as the kinds of questions asked by media theorists and others.

The chapter also introduces you to the key approaches in media analysis. It demonstrates how competing **paradigms** have used a range of theories and methodological approaches in their efforts to understand the media. The discussion will show how the history of media analysis is neither linear nor tidy. Reflecting many of the concerns also expressed within public discourse by politicians, journalists and other commentators, media analysis has seen claim and counterclaim about the media (for better and for worse) in its many forms. It is best described as a contested field.

Notwithstanding these conflicts, one particularly useful way to understand and to organize the multitude of approaches to media analysis is by specific reference to the concept of **power**. Questions concerning power (in a wide variety of manifestations) lie at the heart of media analysis. These range from thinking about the power (and effect) of media content; the relationships between the powerful and the media industries and the degree to which audiences are viewed as possessing power in their own right.

In introducing this book I wrote of the need to ask awkward questions. This, I argue, can only be achieved by maintaining a focus on unequal power relationships and by using an approach that continues to recognize the importance of understanding the *production*, *content* and *reception* of media texts. A critical approach to the analysis of media demands that we give equal consideration to each of these important areas. The chapter concludes by focusing on a set of key questions which will underpin the remaining chapters in *Understanding the Media*.

Media histories

1450	Gutenberg invents the printing press
1486	First book (in Armenian Letters) published
1620	The first English language newspaper in Europe – *Corrant Out of Italy, … Germany*, etc. is published
1690	The first North American newspaper *Publick Occurrences Both Foreign and Domestick* is published in Boston
1788	*The Times* of London newspaper begins publication
1837	Rudolphe Töpffer publishes the first comic book, *The Adventures of Obadiah Oldbuck*
1851	*New York Times* founded
1858	First transatlantic telegraph cable communication between North America and Europe (allows telegraphs to be sent between Newfoundland and Ireland and reduces communications time to minutes rather than several days)
1872	Eadweard Muybridge credited as creating the first moving film
1907	First commercial transatlantic radio communications service between North America and Europe
1923	First commercial 'talkie' – a film with accompanying sound – is screened in New York City
1926	Logie Baird demonstrates the first working television system
1928	WRGB (Schenertady, NY) lays claim to being the world's first TV station
1936	The BBC commences regular TV broadcasts
1949	The 7-inch single record (or 45) is introduced by RCA records
1950	The first ever network TV soap opera – *The First Hundred Years* – sponsored by Proctor and Gamble, is broadcast in the USA
1953	*Playboy* Magazine is first published
1954	First ever colour TV broadcast (in the USA)
1960	TV soap opera *Coronation Street* begins (in the UK)
1962	First satellite TV content transmitted via the Telstar Satellite (between the USA and France)
1963	First home VCR available to buy
1975	First portable or laptop computer
1979	Sony Walkman becomes commercially available
1983	Mobile or cell phone available to purchase
1989	Nintendo Game Boy on the market
1989	Sky News commences satellite news broadcasts from London

(Continued)

1992	First SMS text-message sent
1994	PlayStation goes on sale
1995	The DVD is unveiled
1995	Digital radio broadcasts begin (in the UK)
1996	Google search engine is created
1997	Blogs are first published
1999	Indymedia is founded
2001	Ipod launched by Apple
2001	Xbox launched
2004	Facebook commences
2005	YouTube created
2006	Start of the Twitter social network
2007	First iPhone revealed by Steve Jobs

Figure 2.1 **Some milestones in media history.**

Figure 2.1 reminds you just how recent (in historical terms) the media actually are. In reviewing this timeline note the main changes and developments over time with the media. In reading Figure 2.1, pay particular attention to changing media technologies, changing media genres and the increasing number of possibilities being presented to media audiences. Note also when you think media globalization (see Chapter 3) actually commences. In thinking about these changes and developments consider the following:

1. The rapid (and historically quite recent) pace of change in the media's development as well as the hastening of media saturation in the last two decades

2. The changes in media ownership and the degree to which media are increasingly owned and controlled by large corporations

3. How the media are centrally involved in communication concerning politics and the economy

4. The ways in which developments in media technologies have constituted and reconstituted media audiences as either groups or individuals

5. The degree to which the media are involved in explaining the social world to all of us. Think about the ways in which social relationships which are unequal (such as in the areas of class, gender and ethnicity) are explained in a media setting and the extent to which we rely upon second-hand media-based information and knowledge about the social world.

Do it! 2.1   Create a media timeline

Create a timeline for the milestones in your country's media history. To what extent, if any, does it differ from Figure 2.1 above? In reviewing your own timeline think about the many changes in evidence since the 1990s. What are the implications of these changes for media audiences?

Changing media histories: an Irish example

In the 1940s and 1950s it was common for Irish sports fans to gather at houses in local villages and towns whose owners were fortunate enough to own a radio. The broadcasts of match commentaries from Dublin (and from further afield) were the reason for such communal gatherings. Radios were sometimes placed outside such houses (usually on the windowsill or on the doorstep or stoop) for the ears of avid sports fans. The commentaries provided these sports fans with mental pictures of distant events and presumably lots of material for post-match discussion and analysis. Today, by contrast, Irish sports fans are more likely to meet in pubs or bars to view matches broadcast by global conglomerates, whilst wearing official team merchandise. Results and fixtures may be texted by mobile phone. Social media such as Facebook and Twitter may be used to meet up either virtually or in reality in order to discuss favourite sports teams. A return to outward migration in the second decade of the twenty-first century has witnessed more and more media traffic amongst the **diaspora** who wish to keep in contact with news and information about sport at 'home'. This brief example stresses the importance of understanding the media in a social context. It reminds you that media use is often bound up with bigger questions concerning leisure and identity (e.g. local, national or gender identities expressed through sport). It also serves to remind you about the degree to which experiences of media have radically changed and our growing dependence on multimedia conglomerates. And yet we also need to recognise just how new these and other experiences of media are in the overall scheme of human history. It has already been noted in Chapter 1 that we can't take these experiences for granted. They have arisen as a result of technological developments and particular sets of economic, political and social relationships.

A contested field

Fractures and factions: key paradigms and perspectives in media research

It is clear from the above discussion that the relatively young discipline known as media studies has been the subject of many hostile attacks by media commentators, amongst others. However the broader field of media analysis has involved a much wider range of academic disciplines, which have used a variety of theoretical and research approaches. While individual authors and members of particular 'schools' may be dedicated to a specific theoretical or methodological model, the practice of doing media analysis is clearly not the preserve of any single discipline or approach. Where actual research is concerned, authors vary not only in terms of their chosen theoretical position, research question(s) and research design but also in the extent to which their work may be described as being quantitative or qualitative in its orientation. An additional fault-line may rest on the degree to which individual examples of research are behaviourist or interpretative in focus.

Media analysis began in the first half of the twentieth century within established subject areas such as philosophy, political science, psychology and sociology. Early examples of empirical research on the media – such as those using the experimental design model most associated with social psychology – are usually described as following an '**effects**' model of media research in that they sought to examine the effects that the media content were reputed to have on the audience.

The last thirty years or so of the twentieth century witnessed more highly specialized media analysis with the emergence of a range of approaches – as opposed to particular academic disciplines – that are more specifically focused on particular aspects of the media. These approaches include, for example, communication studies, cultural studies, film studies, journalism, linguistics, media studies, new media, social media and social informatics. Such approaches have borrowed theories and methods of research from subject areas in the social sciences and humanities (e.g. critical theory, feminist theory, queer theory) as well as generating novel ways of approaching the analysis of media. **Ethnography**, for example, which has its roots within traditional anthropology and was originally applied to the study of 'primitive' societies, has been used to analyse the internal workings of media organizations and to understand more about the media audience. Its online variant – digital ethnography – is used to observe and sometimes participate in virtual audience spaces such as blogs, social media, etc. The textual orientation of a great deal of cultural studies research on the media has its roots within literary criticism and semiotics (the study of signs and symbols) in particular. These developments have given rise to a growing body of research literature, much of it concerned with popular forms of culture and especially those to be found on television and online.

Older academic disciplines such as sociology and psychology continue to have an interest in the media and it is also a well-established concern for the 'younger' and related subject areas and approaches such as **discourse analysis**, gender studies and postmodernism. The broad field of media analysis is not without its tensions, however. As the extracted reading by Tester (1994) in Chapter 1 illustrated, there have been hostile exchanges between the more established disciplines such as sociology and newer approaches like cultural studies as to the form and direction of media analysis. Lively debates have taken place, for example, between those who favour textual analysis and those who emphasize the importance of examining the structure of ownership and control of the media (e.g. Chomsky, McChesney). Others have concentrated their research energies on the sense that audiences are believed to make of media texts. All in all, the continuing growth and expansion of the media have been mirrored by the development of more sophisticated means of media analysis within both the older disciplines and the newer more recent approaches.

The robust nature of the debate amongst those interested in media analysis is testament to the vitality and health of the subject area. In many respects focusing on which academic discipline or approach is supposedly the 'best' one in undertaking media analysis is to miss the point. Such academic sectarianism runs the risk of losing sight of what is arguably more important. By this I mean that what matters more is to ask questions about what any one approach applied towards understanding the media tells us about the issue of unequal power relations.

Read on! 2.1   Media histories

T. O'Malley (2002) 'Media history and media studies: aspects of the development of the study of media history in the UK 1945–2000', *Media History*, 8(2): 155–73.

While it was 'only in the 1920s – according to the *Oxford English Dictionary* – that most people began to speak of "the media"' (Briggs and Burke, 2002), intellectual interest in mass communications goes back much further. In the UK there were widespread concerns about the spread of mass printed materials in the nineteenth century and the study of journalism had begun to develop in the UK and the USA by the late nineteenth and early twentieth centuries. Intellectual concerns about the 'mass media' in these years were linked to concerns about the emergence of 'mass society' and in the UK there were concerns about the impact of cinema on behaviour and attitudes. As Asa Briggs has noted, the development of audience research from the 1930s onwards 'sprang from an attempt on the part of organised communicators … to discover facts about their audience either for marketing or for programming purposes or both' (Briggs, 1991). In the UK the BBC began systematic audience research in the 1930s and the critical study of the press grew in vogue in the first 30 years of the century, culminating in 'the first empirical report on the British Press' in 1938 by the Political and Economic Planning group. In the USA empirical, industry and government funded research into the impact of the mass media was established in universities in the 1930s and 1940s. The impulses behind and the forms of research into mass communications were various, but in the UK in the 1940s and 1950s 'very general speculation remained in vogue' (Briggs, 1991). What was to prove a major influence on the academic study of media and culture in the UK was the work of tutors within the Workers Educational Association (WEA). In the 1930s and 1940s, the adult education movement, in which the economic historian R.H. Tawney and the émigré sociologist Karl Mannheim were involved, brought together concerns about the relationship between 'popular culture', literature and sociology. The structure of adult classes in which questions of social history, industrial relations or literature were discussed over extended periods by working people launched for one tutor, Richard Hoggart, 'implicit but powerful challenges to the definition of my subject—English literature' and led him 'to move out to an area I called contemporary cultural studies'. ...

The formative influence on early cultural studies was, indeed, English literary criticism, a tradition from which both Raymond Williams and Richard Hoggart came. Hoggart has described how the early impulses, applying 'the methods of literary criticism, very often Leavisite methods, close analysis, listening to a text, feeling a text and its texture' to 'the study of popular culture; and not just the words but the images too' (Corner, 1991). Hoggart brought this approach with him to the University of Birmingham where, in 1964, he founded the influential Centre for Contemporary Cultural Studies and where he hoped to maintain an interdisciplinary approach to the study of culture drawing on philosophy, literary criticism and history. Hoggart retained this stress on literary critical methods, and it became a pervasive form of analysis within media studies.

? Stop and think 2.1

1. What were the main concerns of intellectuals and others involved in mass media research in the pre-1950s period?

2. The extract stresses the important role of the Workers' Educational Association and of Richard Hoggart in particular in the development of media studies. What sorts of methods and approaches were used in cultural studies to understand media and other forms of culture?

Media and power

The concept of power is central to the discipline of sociology. Classical (e.g. Weber, Parsons) and contemporary (e.g. Giddens, Lukes) sociologists have understood the concept in a number of different ways. Bruce and Yearly (2006) state that Weber defined power as 'the probability that one person in a relationship will be able to carry out his will despite resistance' (2006: 241), while Parsons and Giddens, amongst other sociologists, conceptualize power '... as the transformational capacity of people: the ability to intervene in a given state of affairs so as to alter them if desired' (2006: 241). Other writers such as Wright Mills and Gramsci have examined how powerful positions are achieved and maintained by elite groups. Much of the time (unequal) power relationships are either invisible or presented as being 'natural' and 'inevitable' thus allowing them to continue. The concept of power is central to all social relationships. Power relationships are intertwined with competing ideologies and discourses (see Chapters 5 and 6). Unequal power relationships, whether framed in terms of class, ethnicity or gender, remain overarching themes within sociology and these concerns feature strongly within media analysis.

It is essential that the concept of power be at the heart of any serious attempt at understanding the media.

Over time, media theorists have concerned themselves with the determining or persuasive power of media content; the increasing economic and political power of the transnational media industries and the degree to which audiences can exercise power in the face of hegemonic and other forms of media discourse (see Devereux, 2005 for an elaboration). As will be apparent in later chapters of this book, significant differences exist between media theorists vis-à-vis the relative degree of power possessed by media audiences, the media industries and media texts themselves. The following discussion is meant as an overview, as many of the theories referred to will be explored in much greater detail later on in your textbook.

Power and media content

Several media theories have focused on the power of media content to shape or determine public beliefs or behaviours. Early versions of media effects theory were based on the assumption that audiences were generally passive and easily influenced by media content or by elite figures speaking about media content. The Frankfurt School, for example (most notably, Marcuse and Adorno), saw media content in largely negative terms. They had witnessed, at first hand, how the mass media in the shape of film, radio broadcasts and newspapers were used to disseminate propaganda in Nazi Germany. In addition to this, the Frankfurt School held that the mass media were pivotal to the spread of capitalist ideology. As will be discussed in greater detail in Chapter 5, other strains of **Marxist** theory (both classical and neo-Marxist varieties) also contend that media content contributes to the continued existence of unequal economic or class-based power relationships in capitalist society.

The role of the media in fostering unequal power relationships is further acknowledged by theorists working from feminist (van Zoonen, 1994) and queer perspectives (Dyer, 2001). Mainstream media content is understood as being a key site of patriarchal and heterosexist ideologies and discourses. Many writers, for example, have noted the invisibility of gays, lesbians, bisexuals and the transgendered in everyday media discourse (see Chapter 6). They have also stressed the ways in which women are misrepresented, underrepresented and objectified in a media setting.

As media analysis has become more sophisticated, the power of media content is best understood not in terms of the effect of individual media texts but rather in the repeated (and often uncontested) use of particular kinds of partial **media discourses**. Semiotic and discourse theory, for example (see Chapter 5), have each sought to explain how media content works to create meaning for media audiences. Van Dijk's (1991, 1998a) research on 'race'/ethnicity and ideology, for example, shows how media content (discourse) can have an impact upon public beliefs and social (in)action. Other approaches such as framing theory and agenda-setting theory (see Chapter 6) have been used to demonstrate how media content – often masquerading as 'commonsensical' explanations of the social world – come to occupy a position of dominance within media and public discourse. Media content clearly has power and influence. However, any serious engagement with media content needs to be systematic and thorough and recognize the complexities involved in such an undertaking.

Power and the media industries

The vast economic and political power of the media industries is the focus of political economy theory. The giantism of multimedia conglomerates; their control over the production and distribution of media content as well as their sheer political and economic weight has been widely debated (see Chapter 4). Political economy, feminist and liberal-pluralist theories have been applied towards understanding the internal dynamics of the media industries (see Chapter 5). While liberal-pluralists would question the degree to which media organizations are actually dominated by elite individuals (e.g. **media moguls**) or groups, those working from a **political economy perspective** point to the ways in which media content has been directly affected by the growing levels of ownership concentration and conglomeration. **Media imperialism** and globalization theories have also expressed concern about the homogenizing effect of media content emanating from the Anglo-American world (see Chapter 3).

Changes in ownership structures have significant economic, political and cultural implications. In spite of media saturation, writers like Mosco (1996) have expressed legitimate concerns about the narrowing of the range of voices and perspectives to be found within mainstream media content. Political economy theory stresses how an understanding of media ownership structures is essential in any engagement with media content and its power. McQuail (2000) notes how the restructuring of the media industries has, from a political economy perspective, meant:

> ... a reduction in independent media sources, concentration on the largest markets, avoidance of risks and reduced investment in less profitable media tasks (such as investigative reporting and documentary film-making). We also find neglect of smaller and poorer sections of the potential audience and often a politically unbalanced range of news. (2000: 82)

Power and media audiences

While the thorny issue of media effects can still be found within much media and public discourse, the media effects **paradigm** was largely supplanted by a number of theoretical perspectives that recognised the agency or creativity of audiences. Originating in the 1940s, **uses and gratifications** theory marked the initial break from the effects model, stressing as it did the ways in which audiences used a variety of media genres to gratify their needs for entertainment or information. **Reception analysis**, however, put the issue of audience agency centre stage (see Chapters 8 and 5). Although they might differ in the degree to which they concede audience agency, Marxist, feminist and postmodern accounts allow for audience **resistance**. Audiences are believed to have the potential to critically engage with media content in the form of using negotiated or oppositional codes; **reading against the grain** of dominant discourses or subverting them altogether. The possibility of agentic audience members resisting, critiquing and contesting dominant media discourses is fundamental to such accounts.

Towards a (more) critical media studies

The academic study of the media embraces a wide range of disciplines and research paradigms. In the midst of an ever-expanding body of media research, and in the light of the explicit emphasis upon social context in this textbook, nine interrelated concerns stand out as being the most salient in terms of attempting to explain recent changes and developments in the media. These are:

1. What is the extent and significance of media globalization?
2. Who owns and controls the media?
3. What sorts of forces inside and outside media organizations shape the creation of media products?

4. How is media content best analysed?

5. How do media texts represent the social world? What do they tell us about unequal social relationships concerning power?

6. How democratic are the media in terms of audience access and participation?

7. To what extent and in what circumstances are audiences active agents in the construction of meaning?

8. What is the real extent of audiences' power when they themselves act as producers of media content?

9. What is the impact of new forms of media technology upon society and more specifically how are they responsible for social change?

The above themes underscore the focus of the chapters that follow. These themes – all concerned with the concept of 'power' in one shape or another – point to the complexities involved in doing critical media analysis and also are indicative of why the study of the media with all its inherent complexities and contradictions is ultimately a fascinating and rewarding enterprise (see Devereux, 2005 for an elaboration).

The importance of theory and method

By learning to apply a range of theoretical perspectives to the media you will deepen your understanding of what you might otherwise take for granted. The use of theory will help you think more critically about the media. At the practical level of actually doing media-based research, this typically involves using a research design that draws upon the strengths of a number of research approaches. That the media play a central role in the social construction of reality is a key tenet of this book. This stance has important implications in terms of how we approach the analysis of the media and of society in general. How do we arrive at a position of knowledge and understanding? Ultimately through combining theory and method you will be able to ask critical questions, gather reliable empirical data and compare and contrast how the media work and are experienced by audiences in diverse social settings.

Model of media analysis: production, content and reception

These nine key questions about the media clearly all overlap and intersect with one another. Taken singly, and in combination, all these issues have the potential to throw further light on how we understand the media. This book, however, is concerned, in the main, with the analysis of mass-mediated texts that are circulated among large numbers of people. When we come to analyse such media texts we do so increasingly in the twin contexts of media

Media in social context	
Contexts	Focuses
Media globalization	Production, content and reception of media texts
The restructuring of media ownership	Media 're-presentations' of the social world
Technological change and especially the development of newer forms of media	Audiences are capable of agency
Unequal social structure in modern/ postmodern societies	Audiences' interpretation of media texts
	Audiences as producers (produsers) of media texts.

Figure 2.2 **Model of media analysis.**

globalization and technological change. Both are responsible for the shaping and reshaping of the media environment in which we operate as citizens, audience members and as students of the media.

In terms of an overall model of media analysis (see Figure 2.2), this book encourages you to think sequentially about media texts in the contexts of their production, content and reception. While there will be the inevitable variations between media and divergences in emphasis among individual media researchers, these are, arguably, the three zones of critical importance in doing media analysis.

The proposed model suggests that you begin by thinking initially about the production context of media texts. Here you might consider the various contexts – cultural, economic, legal, organizational, political, social and technological – in which a specific media text is created. This approach will help inform your understanding of the dynamics involved in the making of a particular media text and it may also be used as a backdrop towards furthering your understanding of its actual content and reception.

The second suggested stage in undertaking media analysis is to examine the content of the media text. In focusing on media content we are usually concerned with the potency (or not) of a media text in shaping people's understanding of social reality in some way. It might be used, for example, as the basis for investigating the ideological content of a media text concerning **patriarchy** or gender inequality. As before, this research strategy may be used in isolation or in combination with analyses of production or audience reception.

The power of both media organizations and media texts to shape perceptions of social reality hinges ultimately on their capacity to influence audiences. The media occupy a privileged position in the socialization of both young and old in society. While media texts have the potential to alter one's perception of the world they are not operating in a vacuum. Media texts are in competition with other media texts, and audiences, as we will see in Chapter 8, can accept, appropriate or reject media texts depending upon a wide range of sometimes complex circumstances.

Conclusion

In Chapter 1 you were asked to try to adopt the sociological imagination in beginning to cast your critical gaze on the media. Chapter 2 suggests that you can go further by thinking about the historical specificity of the media and by paying particular attention to the social, economic and political contexts which underlie such developments. The traditional sociological concept of power is essential in attempting to reach a critical understanding of the media. While a range of academic disciplines, theories and approaches have been applied towards understanding the media, this chapter argues for a focus on examining the media in the context of unequal power relationships in society. As noted in Chapter 1 and in the book's Introduction, *Understanding the Media* favours a political economy approach to media analysis. It will be apparent in the remaining chapters in this book that while a political economy of media is seen as key, other approaches and theories are not ruled out entirely. Explicit reference will therefore be made to other perspectives and approaches which are also focused on the media's role in unequal power relationships (e.g. feminist theory; queer theory). This chapter also argues for the retention of what some might refer to as a 'traditional' approach to media analysis. If we are to begin to make sense of the media's complexities we need to continue to focus on the production, content and reception of media texts. Whether those media texts are produced by large-scale institutions or by individual audience members we need to continue to examine their production, their content and how they are interpreted by audiences.

Chapter summary

1. This chapter has stressed the need to place our understanding of the media in an historical context. An appreciation of media history allows us to think not only about changes and developments in media technologies but also about who the key actors were in these changes (e.g. press barons; transnational multimedia conglomerates).

2. A focus on the history of media analysis itself demonstrates the many fractures and factions in the field. Like most other subject areas, researchers and writers have argued over the value of one approach over another.

3. Despite the many competing approaches adopted by different academic disciplines and paradigms, power is a unifying theme within media analysis.
4. A critical media studies, whilst eclectic, needs to be rooted in a political economy approach and maintain a necessary focus on the production, content and reception of media texts.

Further reading

Barlow, D.M. and B. Mills (2009) *Reading Media Theory: Thinkers, Approaches and Contexts*. London: Pearson/Longman. This is a comprehensive introduction to key thinkers and schools of thought (as well to how these various approaches have been applied by media theorists). The book includes extracted readings from a range of classic texts in the field, including Hall's *The Television Discourse: Encoding and Decoding* (1974), van Zoonen's *Feminist Media Studies* (1994) and Webster's *Theories of The Information Society* (1995).

Schlosberg, J. (2013) *Power Beyond Scrutiny: Media, Justice and Accountability*. London: Pluto Press. This book is a tour de force by media lecturer, researcher and activist Justin Schlosberg. He explains how and why limitations have been placed on public debate in a media setting in the UK.

Curran, J. (2002) *Media and Power*. London: Routledge. A lively and provocative account focused on media and power. See in particular Curran's first chapter on media history.

Howley, K. (ed.) (2013) *Media Interventions*. New York: Peter Lang and Associates. A collection of important essays which examines how 'media interventions' may be made by civil society and other groups in order to challenge hegemonic power relations. Included are considerations of how DIY media, cyberactivism, culture jamming and PR campaigns may be used to question and challenge existing power relations.

Online reading

Go to the companion website and read the following:

- McQuail, D. (2010) 'The rise of mass media', in *McQuail's Mass Communication Theory*. London: Sage, pp. 23–48.

- Fenton, N. (2007) 'Bridging the mythical divide: political economy and cultural studies approaches to the analysis of media', in E. Devereux (ed.), *Media Studies: Key Issues and Debates*. London: Sage.

CHAPTER 3

Media Globalization

Chapter overview

In this chapter you will discover:

- The main features of globalization and media globalization
- The pivotal role played by transnational media organizations in the more general globalization process
- That globalization is a problematic, complex and contested concept that defies simple definition
- The importance of examining the experiences of audiences in terms of their access to, consumption of and the meanings they derive from globalized media products
- That while the dominance or hegemony of the globalized media industry is of obvious significance in the twenty-first century, the ability of local media audiences to resist, appropriate or reconstruct globally distributed media messages should never be underestimated
- As you will see in more detail in later chapters, there are also hopeful signs that at least *some* citizens have begun to resist the hegemony or dominance of the global media through the creation of their own media texts and through the use of new media. Such developments however – while obviously very welcome – should not be overstated, and it would be naïve to ignore the sheer power of the global media giants and some governments
- Globalization is not a one-way street. One of the possible net results of globalization is **glocalization** – whereby *localizing* and *globalizing* forces merge to create new **hybrid** identities. There has been a particular focus in this regard on how **diasporic media audiences** engage with globalized and other media texts. Glocalization processes will also be examined in terms of their presence within popular culture and within music in particular.

Key concepts

- Globalization
- Media globalization
- Transnational media industries
- Media imperialism
- Homogenization
- Information rich and poor
- Digital divide
- Audience resistance
- Hybridization
- Localization
- Glocalization
- Diaspora/diasporic media audiences

Introduction

In writing your media diary you were asked to reflect on what portion of your regular media consumption is produced and distributed by media organizations that operate at a global level. In watching television news, going to the cinema, reading a book, surfing the net, downloading music, playing the latest computer game or listening to a new recording by your favourite band, DJ or singer, the chances are that you were using or consuming a media product created, controlled and distributed by the global media industry. The production, distribution and consumption of an increasing number of media products now take place in a transnational context. An understanding of what media globalization is all about is a crucial starting point in any attempt to come to terms with media in the twenty-first century. Media globalization has resulted in a radically changed media landscape for media audiences. It is in the context of this rapidly changing milieu that questions surrounding media ownership, technologies, production, content and reception will be addressed in this chapter.

So what is the real significance of media globalization? Is it responsible for unprecedented social change, a growing cosmopolitanism, the shrinkage of time and space, the perpetuation of global capitalism, the creation of a hierarchy of media 'haves' and 'have nots', the further hastening of cultural **homogenization** or sameness, or the intensification of local, ethnic and national identities?

Whatever its shortcomings (and there are many), as a process, media globalization represents one of the most complex, fascinating and dynamic questions facing all of us in the twenty-first century. It is at once both immensely powerful and laden with many contradictions and ambiguities. Media globalization is characterized by convergence. It has come about because of the convergence of old and new media technologies as well as the convergence of old and new media organizations to form immensely powerful transnational media conglomerates. It raises new possibilities and new (and not so new) questions for media audiences and media organizations. It poses important challenges for students of the media.

In seeking to further explain what media globalization is, this chapter takes the view that we need to fuse elements of both the macro theoretical accounts of media globalization with the emerging accounts of the workings of media globalization at the micro or local level (see Lull, 1995; Silverstone, 1999; Tomlinson, 1997). This second research approach draws upon a largely **ethnographic** research model that seeks to understand how audiences actively engage with and have the capacity to resist aspects of the globalized media.

Having introduced the phenomenon of globalization, this chapter outlines the key features of media globalization in particular. It is crucial that you engage critically with the hyperbole evident in a significant amount of the commentary on what the globalization project is all about. A special emphasis will be placed on the degree to which a great deal of the reported globalization of people's local lives is as a result of mass mediation. Finally, the chapter considers the relationship between audiences and the globalized media. The focus here will be on access to, the consumption of and the meanings that audiences make of globalized media products with particular reference to what is termed glocalization.

What is globalization?

Explaining the social changes associated with industrial capitalism has been a central preoccupation within sociology since its beginnings in the nineteenth century. Traditionally, sociologists explained concepts such as class, community, family and the emerging media in terms of how they operated within individual societies and nation states. This emphasis has now firmly shifted and, in recent decades, globalization has become arguably *the* core concept that sociologists and others use in order to explain the experience of living in modernity or postmodernity (see Scholte, 2000). There is no one agreed definition of globalization, and, as will be shown later on in this chapter, the concept is a problematic one – especially so when it comes to understanding the media.

 Do it! 3.1   The spectre of the global in everyday life

Starting with some examples from shopping for clothes or music, or your daily consumption of food and drink, draw up a list of examples of where global phenomena are present in your own day-to-day life. How many of these are a result of your exposure to and interaction with the media?

Read on! 3.1   A window on the world?

John Tomlinson (1994) 'A phenomenology of globalization? Giddens on global modernity', *European Journal of Communication*, 9(2): 149–72.

The point of maintaining this distinction between modes of experience is that it qualifies the claim about distanciated events being 'integrated into the frameworks of personal experience'. While the media provide the most obvious access to 'the world' for the majority of people, this experience is always, in a sense, contained within the lifeworld as 'mass-mediated experience'. To compare this with [Anthony] Giddens's claim about the 'provisional' sense in which we experience localities, we might think of mass-mediated experience as a very provisional sense of the global: instantly and ubiquitously accessible, but 'insulated' from the local quotidian by virtue of its very form. If this is so, it has implications for the idea that the world becomes 'open' to us via the mass media. Zygmunt Bauman is sceptical of the idea that television overcomes cultural distance by giving us insight into the lives of 'institutionally separated' others:

Contrary to widespread opinion, the advent of television, this huge and easily accessible peephole through which the unfamiliar ways may be routinely glimpsed, has neither eliminated the institutional separation nor diminished its effectivity. McLuhan's 'global village' has failed to materialize. The frame of a cinema or television screen staves off the danger of spillage more effectively than tourist hotels and fenced off camping sites; the one-sidedness of communication further entrenches the unfamiliars on the screen as essentially incommunicado (Bauman, 1990: 149).

... local exigencies maintain a certain priority even in a lifeworld opened up to the global. This derives from the sheer material demands of local routines tied to the satisfaction of basic needs. But it also derives from the distinctions people routinely make between an 'immediate' local world and the mass-mediated experience of the global, which is, for most people, the commonest way in which the world is opened to them. Clearly the media represent a highly significant linkage between local and global experience, and there is a lot of work to be done investigating the phenomenology of this linkage: the precise sense in which, for example, television can be said to bring the world into our living rooms. What I have tried to suggest is that this problematizing of mass-mediated experience is a necessary qualification for Giddens's claims about the 'intrusion of distant events into everyday consciousness'. (p. 160)

Stop and think 3.1

1. To what extent are people's local lives more 'open' to global phenomena as a result of mass mediatization?

2. Why is the globalized media *not* a window on the world?

The latest brand of colonialism?

The globalization of everyday life for a significant number of the world's citizens is a result of the restructuring of economic and cultural activities on global lines. It is intrinsically tied to the neo-liberal project.

CHAPTER LINK

Neo-liberalism is discussed in more detail in Chapter 6.

Globalization is founded upon increasing levels of rationality, and the hyper-rationality of transnational corporations in particular. While the media and communications industries are part and parcel of this more general restructuring of economic activity at a global level, it is they who are primarily responsible for the promotion of the notion of globalism as well as contributing to the qualitative shift in how modernity or postmodernity is experienced by an increasing number of social actors.

It is worthwhile thinking about this for a moment. The dominant players in the global media industry continue to represent globalization as an unproblematic given. They repeatedly (and cynically) reproduce the idea – first mooted by the late Canadian scholar Marshall McLuhan – of the 'global village' where it is assumed that all the planet's citizens can – if they want to – participate in a global society through their media use. This of course naïvely (or otherwise) presumes equal access to media technologies and products in all societies and cultures across the globe. It ignores the information deficit that exists between the **information rich** and **information poor** within the developed world and between the developed and **Third World**. It downplays the profit motives of the agents of globalization.

Globalization is responsible for the exploitation of people and resources on an unprecedented scale. It should be seen as the continuation of the colonization project which involved the process of exploitation (including people as well as raw materials) in the eighteenth and nineteenth centuries in particular. While the process of globalization is a reality, we need to be cautious of the ways in which it is heralded and celebrated by those interests that benefit most from it.

⚡ Key thinker 3.1   Marshall McLuhan 1911–1980

Born in Canada in 1911, Marshall McLuhan published his bestselling book *Understanding Media: The Extensions of Man* in 1964. McLuhan is celebrated by many media scholars for the far-seeing nature of his work on the contemporary mass media. He argued, somewhat controversially, that what mattered most was not media content but the effect the medium itself has on human beings. The act of watching television, reading a newspaper or novel or listening to the radio was of greater significance than the content involved *per se* and in McLuhan's much quoted words 'The medium is the message'. McLuhan's foresight on the potential of electronically based media to re-shape human experience is of major significance. He argued that the initial rise of print media resulted in the privatization of media activity, whereas electronic media had the potential to restore collective media experiences and lead to the creation of a global village. This utopian view has resulted in McLuhan being celebrated by many recent theorists who are interested in the capabilities of ICT in terms of how it can re-shape society.

Go to: http://www.marshallmcluhan.com/

Plate 3.1   **Marshall McLuhan argued that the medium is the message. With incredible foresight, McLuhan predicted both media globalization and the Internet. Image reproduced by kind permission of The Estate of Marshall McLuhan ©.**

A CLOSER LOOK 3.1

Competing definitions of globalization

Globalization is 'the compression of the world and the intensification of consciousness of the world as a whole' (Robertson, 1992: 8)	Globalization is 'the product of a changing economic and political order, one in which technology and capital have combined in a new multi-faceted imperialism' (Silverstone, 1999: 107)
Globalization is 'best considered a complex set of interacting and often countervailing human, material and symbolic flows that lead to diverse, heterogeneous cultural positionings and practices which persistently and variously modify established vectors of social, political and cultural power' (Lull, 1995: 150)	Globalization 'refers to the rapidly developing process of complex interconnections between societies, cultures, institutions and individuals world-wide. It is a social process which involves a compression of time and space, shrinking distances through a dramatic reduction in the time taken – either physically or representationally – to cross them, so making the world seem smaller and in a certain sense bringing them "closer" to one another' (Tomlinson, 1999: 165)
'Globalisation is a jargon term which journalists and politicians have made fashionable and which is often used in a positive sense to denote a "global village" of "free trade", hi-tech marvels and all kinds of possibilities that transcend class, historical experience and ideology' (Pilger, 1999: 61)	'Globalization means different things to different people. Some say it is the movement of people, language, ideas, and products around the world. Others see it as the dominance of multinational corporations and the destruction of cultural identities' (Peters and Peters, 2005)

As 'A closer look 3.1' indicates, there are a variety of definitions and interpretations of what constitutes globalization. It is, however, usually discussed in terms of the following key features:

1. The growing level of *connectedness* between individuals, societies and nation states at a global level.

2. The reduction in the distance between individuals, societies and nation states in terms of both time and space facilitated by technological developments such as the internet and other media. These are usually referred to as Information Communication Technologies (ICTs).

3. The development of ICTs has not only resulted in major changes in the workings of the media but also allows the rapid transfer of information, knowledge and capital.

4. Globalization involves not only the movement of capital and knowledge facilitated by technological developments within ICT, but also, crucially, the displacement and movement of people. Migration is a key feature of globalization.

5. Globalization is characterized by a series of flows; the flow of capital, knowledge, mass mediated symbols and people (see Appadurai, 1996).

6. An increased awareness of global phenomena in people's (local) lives.

7. The globalization of culture and economic activity as a direct result of the activities of powerful transnational capitalist organizations. It has also meant the disaggregation of economic activities through a process of deterritorialization. US PC manufacturers, for example, build computers in Eastern Europe or Asia using parts and labour in at least four different economies, thus taking advantage of a combination of cheap labour, low or no tax environments and non-unionized workers. A PC sold in Scandinavia or Australia may have its support network based in a call centre in India. Call centre workers in New Delhi, for example, are trained to speak 'American', follow set scripts and mask their actual location in dealing with First-World consumers (see Mirchandani, 2004).

8. Globalization tends to assume a decrease in the significance of other kinds of identities such as the ethnic, the local, the regional or the national in people's everyday lives. Globalization has increased the possibility of greater reflexivity among social actors. It offers the potential to human beings to become more critical of their immediate environment by allowing them to compare their experiences with those living in other societies or under different political arrangements. Media activities such as watching satellite television news or surfing the internet offer the potential for this kind of reflexivity in an unprecedented way (see Kit-Wai Ma, 2000). The restrictions imposed by the Chinese authorities in 2001 and 2002 on internet use are a concrete example of how powerful interests in that country are fearful of reflexivity among its citizens. In 2006, global capitalism and state communism reached an accord when Google agreed with the Chinese government to limit the extent of access afforded to Chinese citizens who use its search engines. It was reported that Google.cn would not allow its users to access information about the Tiananmen Square student massacre, Tibet or the outlawed Falun Gong organization (Sabbagh, 2006). China is not alone in the regard. Following the Arab Spring of 2011 a number of countries (including Egypt, Syria and Libya) sought to limit internet access (and access to social media sites in particular). It is currently illegal to own a satellite dish in Iran and while access to Gmail accounts was relaxed in late 2012, YouTube remains banned.

9. Critics of globalization argue that it has resulted in even more exploitation of the Third World. Those whom journalist John Pilger (2002) terms 'the new rulers of the world' exploit both the raw materials and the labour power of the world's poorest people in order to feed the insatiable consumer demand in the West. The use of child labour in the manufacture of well-known global

brands has been a particular focus of anti-globalization activists. Given its credo of marketization and privatization, advocates of globalization strongly support a de-regulated global economy in which ownership and control rests in the hands of powerful transnational conglomerates.

10. The stark realities behind much of the hype associated with globalization have been noted by many feminists. Far from being a utopian process which has smoothed out the power differentials between women and men, globalization has accentuated many inequalities. Globalization has witnessed an increase in the trafficking of women and children for the global sex industry as well as their exploitation in the workplace.

11. Resistance to economic and cultural globalization has taken many forms (see Webb, 2005). What has been termed the 'Anti-globalization' movement is in fact made up of various groups and alliances comprising of anarchists, anti-consumerists, communists, green activists, socialists and women's groups. Their protests have been in evidence in the Occupy Movement, at various G8 summits as well as in specific campaigns about McDonald's restaurants or Nike products, for example. Critics of 'McWorld' have argued that McDonaldization is responsible for increased levels of cultural homogenization and obesity; the destroying of the rain forest to make way for the ranching of cattle in order to supply the increased demand for cheaper beef; and also the exploitation of children in China who are a source of cheap labour in the manufacture of toys given away with 'Happy Meals'.

Proponents of globalization theory – especially those who follow either a Global Society or Global Culture approach – argue, perhaps predictably, that the experience of day-to-day living in the early twenty-first century is markedly different from that which has gone before. People's local lives are increasingly lived in the shadow of global phenomena. We can see the 'spectre of globalization' in our everyday experience and it is particularly evident in terms of our working lives, our consumption – especially in our shopping and eating – and our mass-media activities. The spaces and places of everyday life are awash with the images and messages of globalization. Everyday life has been Disneyfied, McDonaldized, Coca-Colonized and Starbuckized (see Ritzer, 2000). The iconography associated with global brands such as Apple, Microsoft, McDonald's, Nike or Pizza Hut transcends both space and language. In Tokyo, the phrase 'I'm Lovin' It' appears side by side with Japanese in adverts for McDonald's. On the main street in Warsaw, a giant Nike shoe sits on top of a small kiosk selling local and national newspapers in Polish. In Latin America the Microsoft logo appears on a PC screen whose on-screen language is Spanish. Globally, Ronald McDonald is as well known as Santa Claus.

A positive view of globalization would hold that the globalization process brings with it the possibility of creating a truly global society. A more critical perspective – best embodied in the political economy viewpoint – would argue that globalization is just Western capitalist imperialism under another guise. Both perspectives would be in broad agreement about the crucial role played in the globalization process by the media, and by television and the internet in particular.

A CLOSER LOOK 3.2

The language of globalism

'Think globally, act locally' (bumper sticker encouraging greater environmental awareness at local level)	'Reaching forty million people, in eighty different countries, twenty-four hours a day, this is Sky News!' (Sky News jingle)
The global telecommunications companies use an AAA paradigm: 'Anything, Anytime, Anywhere' (see Negroponte, 1995: 174)	'The world's largest mobile community' (Vodafone corporate website, 2006)
Time Warner's website speaks of engaging with 'Active Citizens in a Global Community' (Time Warner corporate website, 2006)	'Producing and distributing the most compelling news, information and entertainment to the furthest reaches of the globe' (News Corporation corporate website, 2002)
'We will help the people of the world to have fuller lives – both through the services we provide and through the impact we have on the world around us', 'Passion for the World Around Us', Vodafone's Business Principles (Vodafone corporate website, 2006)	'At the core of our business is a corporate philosophy that guides our conduct wherever we do business, which we call the Soul of Dell. Central to that philosophy is our commitment to global citizenship – understanding and respecting the laws, values and cultures wherever we do business; profitably growing in all markets; promoting a healthy business climate globally; and contributing positively in every community we call home, both personally and organizationally' (Dell corporate website, 2006)
'More than 70 percent of our income comes from outside the US, but the real reason we are a truly global company is that our products meet the varied tastes and preferences of customers everywhere' (Coca-Cola corporate website, 2006)	'This is what globalization is about: people. It's about confirming our shared humanity and simultaneously exploring our diversity. It is not about products. The Occupy Movement represents resistance against oppression, but it also signals the first truly globalized movement in history' (Occupy Movement website, 2012)
'Little Britain Anywhere in the World, £149.99' (PSP PlayStation advert 2006)	'The world in your back yard' (Australian Broadcasting Corporation corporate website, 2006)

Theories of globalization

There are a wide range of diverse theoretical positions that seek to explain the concept of globalization. Following Sklair (1999) these can be summarized under four main headings. They can be further subdivided in terms of the relative amount of stress they place on the cultural or economic aspects of globalization. One thing is certain – there is very little consensus as to what constitutes globalization.

The Global Society approach

Proponents of the Global Society approach emphasize the extent to which we all as citizens of the planet inhabit one society that has common concerns and possibilities. The Global Society position points to the increasing consciousness of the global that is said to exist in everyday life. People's local lives are becoming more and more affected by global phenomena. According to this perspective the global media industries play a key role in raising global awareness and in the extent to which global phenomena are said to impinge on everyday consciousness via media products. Environmental issues such as global warming might be an example of where the media have raised public awareness of the possible local implications of a global problem. The approach has been accused of seriously underplaying the continuing extent of global inequalities and of overstating the argument that we live in a 'global village'. According to the UN, 25,000 children die each day in the world from hunger or from hunger-related illnesses. The failure of the media in the Western world to report on Third-World poverty and famine in a sustained and critical way is an example of one of the contradictions of the Global Society approach. At a technological level it is now possible to beam stories back and forth across the globe in a matter of seconds. Standing in stark contrast to the general invisibility of the Third-World stories in the Western media, the 2004 Asian Tsumani received blanket media coverage (for upwards of four weeks) in the West – arguably because the catastrophe involved Western citizens and many of the areas affected were tourist destinations. The Asian Tsumani and the 2005 7/7 bombings in London were also noteworthy for the use by ordinary people of images captured on their mobile phones.

The Global Culture approach

Those who take a Global Culture standpoint see an increasing level of cultural homogenization taking place at a global level. Members of culturally and politically diverse societies participate in a global cultural experience never before witnessed in human history. Following the logic of this perspective, children in Belfast, Berlin and Budapest all play with the latest Digimon characters. They are likely to want to eat the same kinds of fast food in McDonald's, Burger King or Pizza Hut. Depending on their age and gender they are also likely to be fans of specific kinds of popular music such as 'boy bands' that are marketed on a global scale. There is, according to this perspective, an increasing amount of homogenization or 'sameness' in the cultural practices evident in the early twenty-first century. The Global Culture approach allows little room for either local resistance to or local appropriation and reinvention of globalized cultural products. A counter-argument to the homogenization thesis favoured by Global Culture theorists is the fact that global giants are adept at localizing their globalized products to suit local market conditions. The Indian McDonald's menu, for example, includes a Vegetable McMuffin and a McSpicy Paneer to cater for local tastes. Multimedia conglomerates also demonstrate the capacity to localize their products to suit local and regional market conditions.

The World System approach

Both the World System and Global Capitalism approaches are primarily concerned with explaining the continuing dominance of capitalism. While the World System position is not expressly concerned with explaining globalization *per se*, it provides us with a model that divides the world into **core, semi-peripheral and peripheral societies** and economies that are exploited by the capitalist system. The parts needed to assemble media hardware such as personal computers or digital television sets may be produced in peripheral or semi-peripheral societies to feed the consumer demand for such products in the core societies in the West. The production of certain media texts and products – the animation industry and the iPod were referred to in Chapter 1 as powerful examples of this phenomenon – takes place in peripheral and semi-peripheral societies in order to maximize profits for transnational multimedia conglomerates and to feed consumer demand in core and non-core countries.

The Global Capitalism approach

The Global Capitalism approach argues that the globalization of capitalism is at the heart of the globalization process. Its key actors are transnational corporations which in many instances are more powerful in economic and political terms than many of the countries they exploit, in terms of labour, raw materials or markets. At the heart of the Global Capitalism perspective is the viewpoint that globalization of this kind depends upon the promotion of the ideology of consumerism. The media industries relentlessly promote consumerism by emphasizing what is considered to be a desirable lifestyle. This is undertaken not only in the form of advertising, sponsorship and product endorsement, but also in the promotion of certain lifestyles as being more desirable than others within a wide range of media settings. Evidence of this desirable lifestyle is embodied, for example, in advertising, where specific kinds of body image for men and women are relentlessly promoted. There are implicit messages that if you buy this product (a car, after-shave, beer, running shoes to name but four examples) you will somehow be transformed and become more desirable to men or women. To paraphrase the noted French philosopher René Descartes (1596–1650), the watchword for many, in the age of globalization, has become 'I consume therefore I am.'

In spite of the overtones of globalism, Western and more particularly North American lifestyles are the ones given greatest prominence. As you will see in

Chapter 4, the increasingly complex ownership patterns of multimedia conglomerates or oligarchies means transnational media companies may not only be involved in the media industry *per se* but may also own or control other kinds of companies producing goods and services for sale in the global market.

Plate 3.2 'Mcnikecolasoft. Globalization is characterized by both the dominance and convergence of global capitalist organizations'. Reproduced with permission © Polyp/Paul Fitzgerald (2002) from *Big Bad World: Cartoon Molotovs in the Face of Corporate Rule*. Oxford: New Internationalist Publications.

? Stop and think 3.2

Theories of globalization

Which, if any, of the four theories discussed above best explain globalization? What are the respective strengths and weaknesses of each approach? What insights have they given you about the complexities and contradictions of globalization?

Key thinker 3.2   Naomi Klein

Canadian writer, journalist and social activist Naomi Klein (born 1970) has been central to the debate about globalization. Raised in a family which had a long history of social activism, Klein's work as a journalist, writer and documentary maker has brought many contentious issues concerning globalization, risk capitalism, the Israeli–Palestinian conflict, Iraq and environmental disasters to the forefront of public debate. In addition to a voluminous output as a journalist, Klein has made a documentary, *The Take*, which examines the experiences of a group of Argentinean workers who take control of their factory (which had been shut down by its owners) and run it on co-operative lines. Klein's writings have been particularly critical of late capitalism (see *The Shock Doctrine: The Rise of Disaster Capitalism* [2007]) and of globalization (see her collection of essays and articles in *Fences and Windows* (2002). She is best known, however, for her book *No Logo: Taking Aim at the Brand Bullies* (2001). *No Logo* is heavily critical of the rise of consumer culture. Such unparalleled consumption comes at a marked cost to workers in cheap labour economies who are exploited by transnational companies. Klein was particularly critical of Nike's work practices, so much so that the global firm published a formal response to her claims. *No Logo* has hugely influenced the debate concerning globalization being regularly cited by academics, journalists and social activists, amongst others. Perhaps somewhat ironically, the book's commercial and critical success and the fact that it was published by a multinational company has meant that this iconic book has in itself become a global brand. For more on Naomi Klein see http://www.naomiklein.org/ and her TED Talk on http://www.ted.com/talks/naomi_klein_addicted_to_risk.html

Read on! 3.2   'Culture jammers and semiotic resistance'

Owen Worth and Carmen Kuhling (2005) 'Counter-hegemony and anti-globalisation', *Capital & Class*, 84 (3): 31–42.

Klein's book *No Logo* (2001) focuses on the emergence of what she calls a new type of anti-consumerist activism, which challenges the intrusion of the commodity form into all avenues of public and private space. Some aspects of this anti-consumerist movement can be understood as subcultures of resistance to neoliberal globalisation, in the tradition of the Birmingham School of Cultural Studies. ...

Klein's 'culture jammers' express a 'semiotic resistance' to the hegemony of neoliberal globalisation, through a variety of strategies designed to transform and subvert advertising messages and, therefore, the ideological foundation of consumer society. 'Ad-busting', 'ad-bashing' and the other strategies of anti-globalisationists identified by Klein subvert the messages purveyed by advertisers, by exposing the various contradictions underlying advertising messages. For instance, the cynical targeting of vulnerable populations is exposed through the practice of 'skulling' or drawing skeletons, or writing 'Feed Me' on billboard models, in order to highlight the connection between advertising and eating disorders in teenage populations; the false equation of consumer 'choice' with agency is exposed by, for example, changing the Nike billboard slogan 'Just Do It' to 'Just Screw It'; the vacuousness of advertising messages is exposed through similar subversive interventions: for example, changing Absolut vodka slogans to 'Absolut Nonsense'.

While anti-consumerist activists engage in a wide variety of strategies of resistance at a micro-political level, many are members of 'virtual communities' with networks at local, regional, national and transnational levels. As Klein argues, the accessibility of new technologies makes the circulation of ad parodies much easier, and has facilitated the sharing of a variety of media technologies that have been used in such parodies. ...

These groups practice 'subvertising', combining adbusting with the publication of 'alternative' magazines, pirate radio broadcasts and the creation of independent videos, all with anticonsumerist messages. These jammers are joined by a global network of 'hacktivists', who break into corporate websites and leave their own messages behind.

 ## Stop and think 3.3

1. Naomi Klein's 'culture jammers' are examples of *some* audience members exercising agency. Can you think of other examples of where audience members exercise agency in the face of globalised media texts?

2. To what extent do new media technologies allow for greater audience agency?

3. Who do you think has the greater amount of power – audience members or the owners and producers of globalised media texts and why?

Media globalization

The pivotal role that the media play in the more general globalization process is now examined. The main features of recent media globalization raise important questions that we need to address as students and citizens. The anxieties about media imperialism and cultural homogenization raised initially by the late Herbert Schiller (1919–2000) and others concerning the dominant position assumed by the North American media industry in the post-war period has now given way to growing worries about the domination of the global media industry by a small number of powerful transnational vertically integrated media conglomerates. There are further well-founded anxieties about the extent to which access to the media is truly global and democratic. Having outlined the key features of media globalization we tease out more fully the concerns raised around technological change, ownership and access to the global media. The concerns that have been raised about the global media conglomerates mirror more general fears about the rise of global capitalism itself.

Main features

Media globalization is characterized by a number of distinct features (see Thompson, 1995). These are:

1. The emergence of a small number of transnational media conglomerates and their continued dominance of the global media industry.
2. The use by these media conglomerates of new information and communications technologies.
3. The increasingly deregulated environment in which these media organizations operate.
4. The globalization of media content has resulted in a greater amount of homogenization and standardization in certain media products produced and distributed by the global media industries.
5. The uneven flow of information and communication products within the global system and the different levels of access that global citizens have to global networks of communication.
6. Media globalization is inextricably linked with the promotion of the ideology of consumerism and is therefore bound up with the capitalist project.

Media ownership

Media globalization is also defined in terms of the restructuring of media ownership. The global media industry is dominated by a small number of powerful transnational media conglomerates that own and control a diverse range of traditional and newer forms of media (Bagdikian, 2004). Conglomerates such as Time Warner, Bertelsmann, Disney, Sony, Viacom and News Corporation operate at a global level in terms of the production, distribution and selling of their media products. While these companies are transnational in character they emanate from 'core societies' such as the United States, Australia, Japan or Western Europe. Unlike traditional publicly or privately owned media organizations, these conglomerates operate in an increasingly deregulated environment.

The structure of ownership of media conglomerates has become increasingly concentrated, and as convergence has taken place groups such as Bertelsmann (Europe) or Time Warner (North America) might be more accurately described as multimedia conglomerates. As we discuss in Chapter 4, a growing number of global media companies are engaged in cross-ownership. They are constituent parts of more general conglomerates with vested interests in companies that produce, among other things, armaments, cars and cigarettes. General Electric, for example, are involved in a number of areas, including the production of satellite systems, jet engines, electricity from nuclear power, the provision of financial services as well as television news. It co-owns (a 51% share) the multimedia conglomerate NBC-Universal with Comcast. Such monopolization raises serious questions about the extent to which media companies that are part of larger conglomerates can critically report on the activities of their sister companies.

···◖ CHAPTER LINK ◗···

The implications of heavily concentrated forms of media ownership (especially for democracy and citizenship) are discussed in Chapter 4.

···

As 'A closer look 3.3' demonstrates, the largest multimedia conglomerate Time Warner is characterized by its giantism, its economic (and political) power and its ability to dominate all aspects of the production, distribution and dissemination of both old and new media content throughout the world. Media representations circulated by the mainstream media are created by a handful of conglomerates – a development that raises important questions for all of us as audience members and as citizens.

···◖ A CLOSER LOOK 3.3 ◗···

An overview of Time Warner

- Time Warner's revenues in 2011 were $28.974 billion.
- In 2011 Time Warner Networks (including TBS and HBO) earned ($13.654 billion) or nearly half of the company's total revenues; Filmed Entertainment earned $12.638 billion and Publishing earned $3.677 billion.
- Key companies within its corporate structure include: CNN; Home Box Office; Time Inc.; Turner Broadcasting System; Warner Bros.
- Key global brands include: *Time Magazine*, Cartoon Network; CNN; Batman; Harry Potter; Lord of The Rings.

- Location: Although US-based (Delaware), Time Warner has a considerable number of joint venture activities in Asia, Europe and Latin America. Language is not a barrier to the conglomerates global domination. Filmed entertainment output is either dubbed or available in a number of languages (in the case of both home video and cinema based movies) and several of its radio and television channels use local languages such as Spanish, Polish or Japanese, for example CNN en Español.

- It projects itself as an agent of globalization with its 2011 Annual Report claiming that Time Warner are: 'Giving Millions A Voice and Connecting Billions'.

- It has made significant levels of political donations to the Democrat Party. It has donated less to the Republican party. According to OpenSecrets.Org Time Warner '… lobbies on a number of different issues, but right now its biggest concern is over the rules governing television ownership and net neutrality issues. The company wants the government to relax the rules prohibiting cable television stations from also owning broadcast stations in the same market'.

Sources: Time Warner corporate website, 2012 and Annual Report (2011); http://www.opensecrets.org/orgs/summary.php?id=d000000094

Access to the global media

One obvious counterpoint to those who herald media globalization as being unproblematic is to examine the question of access. A '**digital divide**' with 'information rich' and 'information poor' is in evidence both within societies in the developed world and between the northern and southern hemispheres (Van Dijk, 2005). The categories 'information rich' and 'information poor' refer to the degree of access that citizens have to both old and new media. One's ability to participate in a wired world is not a given. It is socially and economically determined. Utopian perspectives on media globalization and on the internet in particular need to be tempered by the growing body of empirical research which demonstrate that the digital divide (Norris, 2001) and/or digital inequalities (DiMaggio and Hargittai, 2001) are shaped by class, ethnicity, gender and location (see James, 2005; Korupp and Szydlik, 2005; Wilson et al., 2003). According to Internet World Stats, for example, in 2011 North America, which comprises just 5% of the world's population, had a 78.6% internet penetration rate. Africa, on the other hand, with 15.3% of the world's population, had an internet penetration rate of 13.5% (which in turn had considerable regional variations within Africa itself) (www.internetworldstats.com).

 Do it! 3.2   The globalization of news?

It has become commonplace for many transnational news and other media organizations to use symbols of globalization – usually symbolic representations of the globe itself – to suggest that their news coverage is truly global in its scope.

However, as Galtung and Ruge (1965) noted, what is usually considered to be newsworthy is framed by a range of criteria which place a strong emphasis on the degree to which the story being reported involves elite figures and/or elite nations. Write a brief report on this evening's news bulletin in terms of how it prioritizes certain kinds of stories as news items.

1. In doing this exercise it might be interesting to compare a national news broadcast with one from CNN or BBC World.

2. Of the total number of news items broadcast what proportion are concerned with local/national issues as opposed to international/global issues?

3. In what order are the stories broadcast?

4. How significant is proximity in determining the news value of the story?

5. If stories dealing with international/global issues are broadcast to what extent are they told from an elite nation's perspective?

6. Compare your findings with those of your fellow students and discuss the extent to which the 'spectre of the global' is truly evident in television news.

 ## Case study 3.1 *Big Brother* goes global?

The *Big Brother* television series has been one of the most talked-about media global phenomena in recent years. Created by John de Mol and broadcast for the first time in the Netherlands, it has attracted a considerable amount of attention from media researchers (see e.g, Chandler and Griffiths, 2004; Couldry, 2002; Griffen-Foley, 2004; Mathijs, 2002; Pecora, 2002; Scannell, 2002; Thomas, 2011; Van Zoonen and Aslama, 2006). Strong on active audience participation both in terms of viewing patterns, voting by telephone and email and the creation of fan-led websites, *Big Brother* is a potent illustration of media globalization (see http://www.welovebigbrother.com/).

As Figure 3.1 indicates, *Big Brother* and its localized variations have been produced in a variety of local and pan-regional settings.

The programme has given rise to several off-shoots such as *Celebrity Big Brother*, *Big Brother VIP*, *Das Dorf* (*The Village*), *Big Mother* and *Teen Big Brother* as well as an array of copy-cat programming, all of which share the essential *Big Brother* ingredients of engaging in the surveillance of 'ordinary people' who are challenged to survive either each other's company and to undertake specific tasks. With obvious Orwellian overtones (Big Brother features in George Orwell's futuristic novel *1984*), the series is fascinating in sociological terms.

(Continued)

Location:	Programme title	Spin-offs
Africa	*Big Brother Africa*	*Big Brother Africa: All Stars*
Albania/Kosovo	*Big Brother*	
Arab World	*Big Brother Al-Rais*	*Haya ma hawa*
Argentina	*Gran Hermano*	*Gran Hermano Famosos*
Australia	*Big Brother*	*Celebrity Big Brother*
Belgium	*Big Brother*	*Big Brother VIPs* *Big Brother All Stars*
Brazil	*Big Brother Brasil*	
Bulgaria	*Big Brother*	*Big Brother Family* *VIP Brother* *Big Brother All Stars*
Canada	*Big Brother Canada*	
Canada Quebec	*Loft Story* *Big Brother*	*Loft Story: La Revanche*
Netherlands	*Big Brother*	*Big Brother VIPs* *Secret Story*
Columbia	*Gran Hermano*	
Croatia	*Big Brother Veliki Brat*	*Celebrity Big Brother*
Denmark	*Big Brother*	*Big Brother VIP*
Germany	*Big Brother*	*Das Dorf* (The Village)
India	*Big Brother*	*Big Brother VIP* *Bigg Boss (Celebrity)*
Sweden	*Big Brother*	*Big Brother Stjarnveckan*
Indonesia	*Big Brother Indonesia*	
Israel	*HaAh HaGadol*	*VIP HaAh HaGadol*
Switzerland	*Big Brother*	
Slovakia	*Big Brother*	
Slovenia	*Big Brother*	*Big Brother Slavnih*
South Africa	*Big Brother*	*Celebrity Big Brother*
Thailand	*Big Brother*	
Finland	*Big Brother*	
Nigeria	*Big Brother Nigeria*	
Norway	*Big Brother Norge*	*Tilbake I Huset (VIP)*
Mexico	*Big Brother Mexico*	*Big Brother VIP*
Philippines	*Pinoy Big Brother*	*Pinoy Big Brother: Celebrity Edition* *Pinoy Big Brother: Teen Edition*

Pacific Region	Gran Hermano del Pacifico	
Paraguay	Gran Hermano	
Peru	La Casa de Los Sectretos	
Portugal	Big Brother	Big Brother Famosos
UK	Big Brother	Celebrity Big Brother Teen Big Brother Big Brother Panto Celebrity Hijack Ultimate Big Brother
USA	Big Brother	Big Brother All-Stars
Spain	Gran Hermano	Gran Hermano VIP Gran Hermano (All Stars) Gran Hermano: La Revuelta
Venezuela	Gran Hermano	
Ecuador	Gran Hermano	Big Brother Reality All Stars
Central America	Gran Hermano	
Colombia	Gran Hermano	
France	Loft Story	Secret Story
Middle East	Big Brother/Al Raiss	
Czech Republic	Big Brother/Velky Bratr	
Italy	Grande Fratello	
Poland	Big Brother/ Wielki Brat	Big Brother: Ty Wybierasz Big Brother VIP
Romania	Big Brother/Fratele Cel Mare	
Russia	Bol'shoy Brat	
Scandinavian Peninsula	Big Brother	
Serbia	Veliki Brat	Big Brother Veliki Brat
Greece/Cyprus	Big Brother	Big Mother The Wall
Hungary	Big Bother/Nagy Testver	
Ukraine	Big Brother Ykpaiha	

Figure 3.1 The *Big Brother* family.

In addition to the participants taking part in a public experiment in a media-free environment, *Big Brother* audiences can engage in sometimes intense parasocial relationships with people that they have never met or are likely to meet in real life. Social stratification is a key ingredient, with many *Big Brother* houses being divided between 'rich' and 'poor' (or 'Heaven' and 'Hell') areas. A further element involves the inclusion of characters who are

(Continued)

deemed likely to subvert dominant norms and values (especially around sexual orientation and gender roles). Although it is usually referred to as 'reality television', which implies that what you are seeing is in a raw natural state, *Big Brother* has a clearly identifiable 'script' with broadcast versions being edited and satellite feeds being delayed owing to fears about possible defamation or libel.

Big Brother is a multimedia phenomenon, being television-, telephone- and internet-based. The first UK series of *Big Brother* on Channel 4 attracted television audiences of up to 10 million viewers. Its associated website recorded over 200 million page impressions, while over 20 million phone votes were made. In addition, the second UK series on Channel 4 and E4 used a combination of interactive digital television, radio and mobile phone. More recent editions broadcast elsewhere have made use of live internet and satellite TV feeds.

Endemol Entertainment, which owns the *Big Brother* brand, is a European-based trans-national television production company. Endemol itself has a strong global presence and produces scripted and unscripted television formats (such as *Deal or No Deal* and *The Million Pound Drop*) which are sold around the world. Previously owned and controlled by the Spanish Telefonica conglomerate, the majority of share ownership of Endemol Entertainment now rests with Mediaset, which is in turn co-owned by the powerful Berlusconi family, the investment and securities firm Goldman Sachs and John de Mol's Cyrte Group.

The *Big Brother* series is transnational in the sense that the format has been success-fully sold to television networks around the globe. Its track record in terms of attracting large volumes of audience share appeals to programme makers. Hill (2002) observes that programmes like *Big Brother* '... indicates the economic success of selling a global format that is locally produced. ... Buying an established format such as BB reduces the costs of production and attenuates the risks associated with new programming' (2002: 324–5).

Some localizing has taken place in terms of the making of specific series. The homoge-neity of the *Big Brother* format has been altered by local context (see Frau-Miggs, 2006). Series differ, for example, in terms of their overall duration and in terms of what is deemed as permissible to viewers. Thus, in some locations, viewers have seen real or simulated sex scenes which would not be allowable in other contexts. Although *Big Brother* has been criticized by many for being exploitative (and in some instances for being boring!) its appeal seems to rest in the way that it allows us to engage in surveillance of an (artificially created) private sphere. Van Zoonen (2001: 672) summarizes the appeal to audiences of *Big Brother* in the words of one 17-year-old Dutch fan who stated:

If I could see what my sister is like with her girlfriends, how the maths teacher talks to his wife, how my parents behave among adults, I would not feel the need for a substitute for life. But I don't see all that. How do you learn how to read people if you only know three kinds: kids your age, teachers and parents? ... *Big Brother* is the only programme we watch and discuss everyday with the whole family. At last, we have common friends, [with] whom we can talk, think and gossip. (Woltz, 1999).

The *Big Brother* case study as outlined above is interesting on a number of levels. It is:

1. An illustration of the globalization of media culture and an example of how audiences and media companies across the world increasingly share homogenized media formats.

2. An example of how, in some instances, globalized media formats are localized to suit to local/regional markets and cultural contexts.

3. Evidence of the involvement of transnational conglomerates (and not just those from the media industries) in the cross-ownership and control of the media.

4. Proof of the increasingly rational mind-set of the global media industries whose primary aim is to maximize profits for their investors and shareholders. For Endemol, this means being able to devise and sell a format across as many broadcast territories as possible. For media companies it means less risk in terms of having to create and engage in market research on new programme formats (see Hill, 2002). Tie-in merchandising means that the Big Brother brand is a further source of income for its creators.

Globalization and media audiences

The cultural imperialism and political economy perspectives, referred to earlier, have many merits, especially in terms of how they have critically examined the dominant global market position of media conglomerates. However, insufficient attention has been paid by both perspectives to the diverse experiences of globalized media audiences in their day-to-day lives as users and consumers of local, globalized and 'glocalized' media texts. The **hermeneutic** dimension which focuses on the meanings derived in the context of consuming globally circulated media texts has been largely ignored (see e.g., Machin and Van Leeuwen, 2004; Oliveira, 1993; Thompson, 1995; Tomlinson, 1999).

········ **CHAPTER LINK** ··

Audience agency or creativity is discussed in detail in Chapter 8.
···

Media globalization resulting from the dominant position and the activities of media conglomerates using new technologies has radically transformed the media landscape, but it is not a one-way process. Developments within ICT have created space for audiences to exercise agency and to be the creators of **counter-hegemonic** media texts, and, as is discussed shortly, the recent focus by researchers on diasporic media audiences highlights the extent to which media audiences (both diasporic and non-diasporic) now experience an increasingly complex globalized media environment.

Recognizing this, the pluralist perspective holds that audiences shape and are shaped by media globalization (see e.g., Lull, 1995). This position argues that while media audiences now exist in an unalterably changed media environment, they continue to possess considerable agency. They possess the power to appropriate, localize and hybridize globally distributed media messages, resulting in 'glocalization' (see e.g., Husband, 1998). In this context Silverstone (1999) reminds us that globalization is an active dynamic process, stressing that 'cultures form and reform around the different stimuli that global communications enable' (1999: 111–12). In everyday life 'The topic may be global, but it becomes a resource for the expression of local particular interests and identities' (1999: 112).

Media globalization has resulted in globalized diffusion of media texts but it has also resulted in local appropriation and **hybridization** (see e.g., Liebes and Katz, 1993; Sreberny-Mohammadi and Mohammadi, 1994). In a fascinating anthropological study of media use amongst Moroccan adolescents Davis and Davis (1995) argue that:

> … much of the content of Western media images is hard to reconcile with traditional Moroccan values rooted in Islam and a strong extended family. While the young people we interviewed and observed often seemed acutely aware of the apparent contradictions between traditional and modern ways – between the Mosque and the satellite – they did not typically see these contradictions as irreconcilable and most seemed eager to preserve core traditional values while hoping to reap the benefits of the affluent and exciting society promised by the media. (1995: 578–9)

And they also note that:

> for television viewing, about half of both boys and girls said they preferred both Arab and Western programs. Many of both sexes seem to want to see what is going on all over the world. The visual character of television makes language differences less important. (1995: 590)

There is also some evidence to suggest that, in the face of media globalization and the threat of cultural homogenization, other forms of local identities actually intensify. **Localization**, however, is not just restricted to media audiences. As our earlier account of Time Warner's activities demonstrates, the global media giants localize many of their products to ensure global market domination and profits (see e.g., Herman and McChesney, 1999; Machin and van Leeuwen, 2003). While media globalization is a powerful process it is not a one-dimensional homogenizing force. The reception or hermeneutic model would suggest that audiences retain considerable power in terms of how globalized media texts are received, consumed, interpreted and even resisted, a phenomenon recognized in the emergence of a distinct strand of media analysis focused on diasporic media audiences.

Read on! 3.3   Media glocalization

Marwan M. Kraidy (1999) 'The global, the local, and the hybrid: a native ethnography of glocalization', *Critical Studies in Mass Communication* 16(4): 456–76.

Young Maronites articulated the discourse of individual freedom primarily with American television programs, with *The Cosby Show* and *Beverly Hills 90210* mentioned the most. Young Maronites liked *90210* because they connected their personal lives with the characters'. Maha and Karine emphasized that the television series showed a higher degree of freedom and openness in intimate relationships than they had personally experienced, and Peter and Antoun told me that they used the program in their daily lives, drawing on its events to articulate their social identity. *The Cosby Show*, broadcast in Lebanon in the eighties and early nineties, also emerged as a major text. Interlocutors indicated that they watched it with their families. Marianne told me how she 'exploited' *The Cosby Show* to gain more freedom from her parents: She would discuss the relationship between the parents on *The Cosby Show* and their daughters, arguing that although the parents were socially conservative, they allowed their daughters to go out on dates because they trusted them. Marianne strongly believed that the show helped her reduce parental restrictions.

In contrast to that favourable reading of *The Cosby Show*, most interlocutors criticized 'many' American movies and television programs for containing 'cheap, purely commercial, sexual scenes' (Elham, Maha), or to portray 'excessive promiscuity between teenagers' (Serge, Rima). Whereas Adib argued that such scenes were 'OK because, to an extent, they [reflected] real life,' Antoun and Peter recognized that some movies, such as *Basic Instinct*, effectively used sexuality for dramatic and aesthetic values. When I probed them about their own social and sexual freedom, interlocutors pointed out that they enjoyed less freedom than American youth, but believed that they endured less restrictions than Arab Muslim youth, thus positioning themselves, again, between the contrapuntal 'Western' and 'Arab' discourses.

Television emerged as my interlocutors' medium of choice. They adopted and rejected elements from both Arab and Western programs, underscoring symbolic leakage between the two worldviews, and speaking at their point of contact. As a general strategy, this hybrid enunciative posture harnessed three everyday life tactics: a propinquity towards consuming ostensibly hybrid texts, quotidian acts of mimicry, and nomadic reading strategies. Consumption, mimicry and nomadism thus enacted hybridity as the daily condition of Maronite youth identity. (pp. 466–7)

Stop and think 3.4

1. In Kraidy's account of this example of glocalization how does 'hybridity' manifest itself?

2. Discuss how Kraidy's respondents exhibit varying degrees of agency in their encounters with globalized media texts.

A CLOSER LOOK 3.4

Between the mosque and the satellite

> We were struck by the pervasiveness and manifest similarity of adolescents' media experience across developing countries. English speaking Inuit (Eskimo) youth 300 miles north of the Arctic circle were sitting with their Inuktitut speaking parents watching *The Love Boat* or southern Canadian hockey; young men in an Aboriginal settlement in northern Australia were dressing like Afro-American teens and listening to reggae; and Moroccans were discovering Dolly Parton and arguing over who shot J.R. Ewing. (Davis and Davis, 1995: 578)

Stop and think 3.5

We have already noted that powerful economic and political interests construct globalization in an unproblematic way.

1. How would critics of globalization such as environmentalists, green activists or members of the Occupy Movement, for example, interpret the globalization process?

2. In your experience how are critics of globalization portrayed in a media setting?

Diasporic media audiences

Earlier in this chapter the movement of people (as asylum seekers, refugees or as migrant workers) as an intrinsic part of the overall process of globalization was noted. The flow of people raises important questions concerned with identity formation and belonging and integration or segregation, especially in the context of the existence of discourses which either 'other', racialize, or problematize the migrant within mainstream media content or render them invisible.

The recent emergence of diasporic media audience research brings a number of important questions into focus (see Karim, 2003, 2007). In acknowledging the complexities involved in being part of the diaspora, this research has concentrated on four key issues which have developed within these new 'mediascapes' (Appadurai, 1996), namely: the consumption and reception of transnational media (such as satellite television, radio and film genres such as 'Bollywood'); the consumption and reception of mainstream media content that is available to both diasporic and non-diasporic audiences in the so-called 'host' country; the production and consumption of locally based media such as newspapers, magazines and newsletters; and the use of media technologies such as the VCR or DVD and ICT based media such as websites, discussion boards and blogs. There has been a particular focus on the degree to which diasporic audience members exercise agency in their media lives and on the emergence of glocalized hybrid identities given that many of the diaspora live somewhere 'between' the host society and their homeland.

The technological developments which are responsible for media globalization have created new contexts in which the diaspora can consume media texts emanating from their countries of origin (see Naficy, 2003). In addition to media content produced and/or disseminated by media conglomerates (such as Telemundo in the USA), diasporic satellite and cable-based television and radio channels allow for immediate contact with media content from the 'homeland' (also referred to as 'home' or the 'motherland'). A growing number of satellite and cable-based radio and television channels produced within the host society (many of which are based upon very modest budgets and of variable quality in terms of production values) are also available. Since 9/11, for example, Al Jazeera (now broadcasting in both Arabic and English) is arguably the best known satellite television channel broadcast to the transnational Arabic world and has a viewership of 50 million (see Georgiou, 2005). Zee TV, similarly, is consumed by a growing number of the Asian diaspora (see 'A closer look 3.5'). The significance of Bollywood films amongst the latter in places such as the UK and Australia has also been examined in terms of their construction of Indian identities within an epic romance genre (see Dudrah, 2002b, 2006; Ray, 2003). As was noted earlier in this chapter, the consumption and reception of media texts that are more widely available, such as globally circulated television and film, has been explored in terms of the emergence new hybrid identities (see Punathambekar, 2005). Hybridity is also in evidence in the way in which the diaspora communicate with one another online. Tsaliki (2003, 167) has demonstrated how some members of the Greek diaspora make use of a hybrid language, which she terms 'Greenglish', in communicating with one another. Gillespie's (1995) research on young Punjabi youth in South London also notes the ways in which diasporic audience members appropriate and hybridize elements of widely circulated popular culture such as soap operas (see also Davis and Davis, 1995; Kraidy, 1999; Ray, 2003). The production of newspapers, magazines and newsletters by and for diasporic consumers is also a feature. In addition to this use is made of new media spaces such as blogs, websites and discussion forums. Media research concerned with the diaspora reminds us that in spite of (and sometimes because of) media globalization, audiences have more possibilities in terms of communicating with one another and countering the dominant or hegemonic discourses which are part of the overall globalization process. Media technologies which are central to the spread of a homogenizing (Western) culture also enable the circulation of other cultural forms which often result in the cementing of other cultural identities and/or the creation of newer hybrid forms.

 A CLOSER LOOK 3.5 ....

Zee TV and diasporic media audiences

The BBC is arguably the world's best known **public service broadcasting** organization. It is also a global player in terms of the dissemination of media content through its online platforms, satellite television (BBC World, BBC 24) and radio (BBC Radio World Service, BBC Russian, BBC Mundo, BBC Persian) and a growing number of digital radio channels such as Asian Radio). In the context of a changing and multicultural Britain, the state broadcaster has been accused of articulating both monolithic and hegemonic discourses about nationhood and identity. In 2001 its own director general described the BBC as being 'Hideously White' (Helen, 2001 cited in Creeber, 2004: 32) and it was conceded that the organization was not accurately reflecting the increasing ethnic diversity within British society. One particular response to this issue has been the rise of new satellite and cable-based television stations which are aimed at diasporic media audiences. Owned by the Mumbai (formerly Bombay) based Zee Telefilms India, Zee TV is perhaps the best known of the diasporic media. It broadcasts to the South Asian diaspora in over 120 countries and has an annual viewership of 500 million. Creeber argues that:

> For many Asian viewers, this channel provides their main source of non-English programming, broadcasting in languages such as Hindi, Urdu, Punjabi, Bengali and Tamil. As well as screening Bollywood films, the channel provides several movie quiz shows and celebrity gossip about film stars and directors. It also transmits 'high quality' Pakistani

dramas while making its own 'lifestyle' and children's programs. ... This sort of TV clearly plays an important role in cementing relations between Asian families and communities, providing a 'common culture' for those viewers who do not fit easily into any neat definition of British citizenship. (2004: 33)

Channels like Zee TV attract diasporic audiences because they reflect more accurately the particularities of being Asian in a British context. Commenting, for example, on the hybridity evident within a children's television programme aired on Zee TV, one viewer stated that:

It's a guy sitting there, and he's talking in Urdu and then he changes to English. ... Like a lot of us if we were sort of talking amongst each other, we wouldn't be talking pure English. We would be talking English and Urdu and Punjabi, sort of everything mixed, you know. That is what he does. (Qureshi and Moores, 2000: 133, cited in Creeber, 2004: 33)

The larger Zee TV network broadcasts to the South Asian diaspora using a combination of free and pay television. May argues that Zee TV has positioned itself as ' ... a halfway house between the transnational (Asian) Star TV brand and traditional Hindi film, creating a hybrid genre that refers strongly to Western-style music and dance' (2003: 29) (see also Dudrah, 2002a, 2002b, 2005).

See also http://www.zeetv.com/

A CLOSER LOOK 3.6

Diasporic media audiences: Gillespie's (1995) Television, Ethnicity and Cultural Change

Marie Gillespie's fascinating ethnographic work (1989, 1993, 1995, 2002) has examined the interplay between the globalization and the localization of culture. As a member of the second-generation Irish community in the UK, her work research has focused on migration and media. She has examined the first-generation Indian diaspora in terms of their media use and the 'television talk' of Punjabi teenagers. Globalization has resulted in the movement of people and the circulation of media texts on a transnational basis. But what are its implications for local cultures? She contends that while the consumption of a growing number of transnational television programmes and films has affected cultural change among London Punjabi families she argues that 'Punjabi cultural "traditions" are just as likely to be reaffirmed and reinvented as to be challenged and subverted by television and video viewing experiences' (1995: 76).

Her earlier research on the importance of the video cassette recorder in Indian homes in the United Kingdom stressed:

> how the VCR enables families to maintain strong cultural ties with their countries of origin through the consumption of popular film and television exported from the Indian sub-continent. It pointed to the ways in which a 'new' communications technology is being mobilized for the purposes of maintaining and reinventing traditions, showing how it is implicated in the construction of 'ethnic' identities in the Indian diaspora. (1995: 49)

In *Television, Ethnicity and Cultural Change* (1995) she uses an ethnographic approach in her analysis of ethnicity and identity among Punjabi teenagers in Southall, south London. Gillespie is interested in the formation of British Asian identity in an era of media globalization. The research focuses on the media consumption and the 'television talk' of some members of the Punjabi diaspora and involved over 100 interviews. Gillespie argues that young Punjabis are 'shaped by but at the same time reshaping the images and meanings circulated in the media and in the market' (1995: 2). She argues that in Southall 'the redefinition of ethnicity is enacted in young people's collective reception and appropriation of television. Transnational and diasporic media representing several cultures are available in Southall homes, offering a range of choices of symbolic identification' (1995: 206).

Gillespie (1995) observes that in Southall 'a transnational media product is locally appropriated in ways in which encourage people to refine their conceptions of their own local culture, and at the same time redefine their collective identity in relation to representations of "others"' (1995: 207). 'Gossip' is singled out by Gillespie's informants as that which characterizes the culture of the Southall Punjabi diasporic community. The ethnography reveals that the Punjabi teenagers have appropriated the main gossip character of the Australian soap *Neighbours* (broadcast on BBC), 'Mrs Mangel'. According to Gillespie 'Among young people the term "Mangel" has entered everyday usage as a term of abuse for anyone who gossips: "Oh! She's a right Mangel!" can be heard commonly' (1995: 152). Gillespie (1995) underscores the need to understand media audiences as cultural actors.

 A CLOSER LOOK 3.7

1. Glocalization: Cantopop in Hong Kong

As we have already noted globalization is not a one-way street (see Grixti, 2006). Cultural and economic globalization as exemplified by the activities of the decreasing number of multimedia conglomerates has resulted in developments and changes, not all of which are negative in the production of popular culture.

Ho's (2003) research on the Hong Kong popular music industry is a powerful example. The music industry in Hong Kong was for a long time on the receiving end of Western globalizing forces. The emergence (and popularity) of pop music sung in Cantonese (as opposed to English or Mandarin) is shown to be a concrete example of cultural hybridization or glocalization. Many local singers who previously sang in English or Mandarin now record and perform in Cantonese only. Localization of global popular culture is however far from being seamless. Ho (2003) notes for example that 'five cover versions of Wham's [sic] 'Careless Whisper' were released simultaneously, each with different Cantonese lyrics' (2003: 149). Globalizing forces – in the shape of the global recording industry as well the availability of cheaper forms of technology (synthesizers, samplers, etc.) have all helped in the growth and development of a vibrant local music scene. He concludes that:

> Despite movements of popular artists, capital and technologies across national boundaries, nation-states still constitute the nexus of global-local exchange. Global localization involves the adaptation of global products to suit the local Hong-Kong conditions. Whilst the development of Hong Kong pop has been enabled by the development of multinational media industries such as EMI, Warner and Sony, the growth of the local Emperor Entertainment Group (EEG) Limited has injected new energy into the Hong Kong music business. Nonetheless, the 'international success' of Hong Kong artists is still almost exclusively within the Chinese diaspora in Southeast Asia, Canada and the USA and the UK, with more modest success in Japan, and very little inroad into mainstream English-speaking markets in the West (although top local popular artists have performed there). (2003: 154–5)

2. Glocalization: 'Hip Life' in Ghana

Hip Life has come about as a result of Ghanian contemporary music artists re-appropriating US rap music and mixing it with a popular local genre called 'High Life'. The latter is in fact itself a hybrid, combining as it does elements of African, American, European and African diasporic musical styles. Oduro-Frimpong (2009) demonstrates how Ghanian musicians localize a globally circulated cultural form through the processes of verbal indirection and naming practices. The end result is the creation of an indigenized musical genre which is strongly reflective of local Ghanian culture, thus reminding us that cultures are not static things. They are made and re-made.

CHAPTER LINK

Glocalization as evidenced by the emergence of the Chicano/Latino Morrissey fan subculture is discussed in detail in Chapter 8.

Conclusion

Media globalization is a very complex issue and needs to be approached with some caution. Students of the media should be critical of the way in which the agents of globalization and of media globalization in particular describe their project. Globalization has resulted in the creation of a series of interconnected but unequal global villages. While the global has become more prominent in people's local lives, other forms of identity – the ethnic, the local, the regional, the national, the subcultural – clearly remain potent. They are especially powerful in determining how audiences read media texts. The restructuring of the media industry along global lines has resulted in the creation of a very small number of transnational conglomerates with immense power and control whose *raison d'être* is profit. So far, media globalization has proved itself to be more amenable to particular forms of media such as television, film and popular music recordings. While the almost insatiable demands of television have resulted in a diet of re-runs and copycat programming – what the influential late French sociologist Pierre Bourdieu refers to as cultural fast food – we cannot take the arguments about cultural homogenization for granted. Audiences, as will be discussed in greater detail later in this book, possess considerable agency when encountering either locally or globally produced media texts.

Chapter summary

1. Globalization and media globalization have radically transformed the world in which we live. While globalization is celebrated by many (usually from those who benefit most) it also has its critics, who see it as being harshly exploitative.
2. Globalization is regularly portrayed as having 'shrunk' the world in terms of how it has managed to compress time and space. A critical view of the media's role in the overall globalization process would adopt a sceptical position on the degree to which media globalization acts as a window on the world.
3. A variety of theories help us to understand globalization (Global Society; Global Capitalism; Global Culture and World System approaches) They differ significantly in the degree to which they present a critical view on globalization.
4. The restructuring of media ownership (and **deregulation**) has been pivotal in the rise of global media giants.

5. Glocalization processes suggest to us that, in some instances, audiences exercise agency in the face of media globalization (e.g. diasporic audiences).

6. The agents of media globalization are powerful transnational multimedia conglomerates who have taken advantage of technological developments to control the production and distribution of media content. However, these technologies also allow for dissent amongst media audiences – some of whom have used new media technologies to circulate ideas and opinions that are critical of the globalization project.

Further reading

Cunningham, S. and J. Sinclair (eds) (2002) *Floating Lives: The Media and Asian Diasporas.* St Lucia, Queensland: Queensland University Press and Lanham, MD: Rowman and Littlefield Publishers. A critical examination of the Asian diaspora in an Australian context, combining political economy, reception and content analysis approaches.

Collins, R. (2002) *Media and Identity in Contemporary Europe: Consequences of Global Convergence.* Intellect Books: Bristol, UK. A critical examination of the European media landscape in the face of the global dominance of the US media industry.

Van Dijk, J.A.G.M. (2005) *The Deepening Divide: Inequality in the Information Society.* Sage: London. This text situates the digital divide in it social and political contexts and gets beyond technocentric accounts of the issues involved in information inequalities.

von Feilitzen C. and U. Carlsson (eds) (2002) *Children, Young People and Media Globalisation.* The Unesco/Nordicom/ Goteburg University. This collection of essays examines,

(Continued)

amongst other themes, the reception and appropriation by children and young people of globally circulated media texts such as animation (Pikachu) and online games.

Rantanen, T. (2004) *The Media and Globalization*. London: Sage Publications. An accessible student-friendly introduction to the complexities of media globalization.

Mirchandani, K. (2004) 'Practices of global capital: gaps, cracks and ironies in transnational call centres in India', *Global Networks*, 4(4): 355–73. This is a fascinating study of the resistive practices employed by Indian call centre workers in New Delhi who work for many of the global giants such as AOL, British Airways and Dell Computers.

Online reading

Go to the book's companion website and read the following:

- Breen, M.J. (2007) 'Mass media and new media technologies', in E. Devereux (ed.), *Media Studies: Key Issues and Debates*. London: Sage.

- Curran, J. and T. Witschge (2010) 'Liberal dreams and the internet', in N. Fenton (ed.), *New Media, Old News, Journalism and Democracy in the Digital Age*. London: Sage.

- Karim, K. (2007) 'Media and diaspora', in E. Devereux (ed.), *Media Studies: Key Issues and Debates*. London: Sage.

CHAPTER  4

Media Ownership: Concentration, Conglomeration and Regulation

Chapter overview

The ownership, control and regulation of the media are the focus of this chapter. The discussion concentrates on the following issues:

- The changing patterns of media ownership and control in an age of media globalization
- The explanatory power of the political economy perspective in terms of understanding these changes
- The social, cultural and political implications of the increased concentration of media ownership and control
- The increasingly powerful role of media conglomerates and media moguls in the global media industry
- The implications for media content and media audiences arising from the increased concentration of media ownership
- The degree to which the media industry can be regulated and controlled by state and other agencies.

Key concepts

- Ownership and control
- Vertical integration
- Horizontal integration
- Conglomeration
- Media monopolies
- Media oligopolies

(Continued)

- Media moguls
- Synergies
- The public sphere
- Deregulation
- Regulation
- Public service broadcasting

Introduction

In this chapter the question of media ownership is examined. It begins by outlining the shift towards concentration and **conglomeration** evident within the overall structure of the media industries. The political economy perspective is explained in detail. In the context of examining whether the increased concentration of media ownership has in fact resulted in a narrowing of the range of voices heard in a media setting, the important concept of the **public sphere** is outlined. In recent years a number of global media conglomerates have attempted to monopolize the ownership and distribution of cultural events (such as cricket, rugby, football, soccer, for example), many of which were once freely available to media audiences. It is particularly striking that since the first edition of this textbook was published (in 2003), the pace of change amongst the media conglomerates in terms of both corporate structure and areas of concentration has hastened with greater rapidity. Several of the conglomerates have radically re-structured themselves and have shifted away from older forms of media activities such as book publishing and the more traditional means of distributing popular music, for example. The further colonization of everyday media experience by private commercial interests continues unabated, adding to concerns raised by some about the continued debasement of media content as well as the ideological significance of a narrowing ownership base, especially at a time of renewed ideological conflicts. The important issues raised in this chapter are at the core of many of the overall themes raised in this book.

Why should we be bothered about media ownership?

Structures of ownership, whether non-profit, public or private, are seen to have a direct bearing upon media content. Interest in the issue of the changing structure of media ownership and its relationship to media content has focused upon a number of critically important questions, concerning:

1. The progressively more concentrated nature of media ownership by a small number of transnational multimedia conglomerates

2. The fact that many of these transnational conglomerates own, control or have substantial interests in both media and non-media companies

3. The continued shrinkage of the media's public sphere role arising from greater concentration and conglomeration

4. The negative consequences, in particular, for news, current affairs and investigative journalism given the macro shift towards entertainment, populism and '**infotainment**'

5. The redefinition of audiences as consumers rather than citizens

6. The commodification of media content and media audiences themselves

7. Unequal access to both media content and media technologies

8. The political and economic power of individual media moguls, and their reported political influence in particular.

At the heart of media conglomeration are the twin aims of reducing risk and maximizing profits. Legitimate concerns have been voiced about the negative relationship between concentrated ownership and the diversity of opinions evident within media content. Both liberal and Marxist commentators have expressed fears in relation to the threat that increased concentration poses for democratic dialogue and debate in society. Concentration of ownership and conglomeration, it is argued by proponents of political economy theory and others, means less pluralism within media content and closer links and involvement with the larger project of global capitalism. While media saturation and the convergence of media ownership are taking place simultaneously, more media do not necessarily mean more choice for audiences. Given the increasingly privatized nature of media ownership and the predominance of multimedia conglomerates focused primarily on profit-making, it is essential that we ask: whose version of the world do we hear about in media content?

As we noted in Chapter 3 in our discussion of the internet's public sphere role, significant information inequalities persist in an age of media globalization. All human societies continue to be divided into 'media haves' and 'media have nots' (see Van Dijk, 2005), and while audience agency in the form of **citizen journalism** and other forms of user generated content (Twitter, Tumblr, Facebook, blogs, for example) gives us some grounds for hope, the sheer power (ideological and economic) of multimedia conglomerates holds sway.

 ## Stop and think 4.1

More media/fewer viewpoints?

In an era of media saturation and conglomeration, does more media in our daily lives actually mean that we are exposed to a narrower range of viewpoints/opinions?

If you agree with the contention that the greater concentration of media ownership has resulted in a narrowing of viewpoints/opinions, where is this most in evidence and what are its implications?

Media ownership

Along the continuum of media ownership we can differentiate between community/not for profit media, public or state-owned media and privately owned (and increasingly transnational) media organizations. A further axis might be the degree to which media organizations are part of a larger conglomerate with interests in both media and non-media sectors.

Community-based media such as local radio (whether licensed or pirate), **e-zines**, blogs or newsletters are usually organized on a non-profit basis by specific interest groups, such as a women's collective or an ethnic minority group, for example. Attracting relatively small audiences, they are run typically on a modest budget and they aim to serve the needs and interests of a clearly defined community such as the students in a university or the inhabitants of a small town. A further example might be an online blog aimed at a diasporic audience in the blogosphere. While many community-based media depend upon small amounts of advertising and sponsorship from commercial interests, they are relatively independent of such interests. Depending upon specific circumstances, such media may have greater editorial freedom in terms of content and style.

State ownership and control of newspapers, television and radio remain a key aspect of communist societies such as China, Cuba and North Korea. State control has an obvious ideological role to play in attempting to secure hegemony among citizens. In spite of trends towards liberalization and deregulation in liberal democratic political systems, the state continues to have an involvement in the regulation of media such as radio and television. In the Republic of Ireland, for example, radio and television broadcasting (whether public, private or community owned) is controlled by the Broadcasting Authority of Ireland. The commission regulates radio, for example, in a number of key ways. It controls the issuing of broadcast licences; it determines how much air time should be given over to 'public interest' broadcasting; and it regulates how much air time can be expended on advertising or sponsorship. It also adjudicates on complaints from audience members on media content they may have found to be offensive or biased. This pattern is repeated elsewhere. In Sweden, local and neighbourhood radio is licensed by the Radio and Television Authority, whilst programming content is controlled by the Swedish Broadcasting Commission. Similarly, in the Netherlands the Commission for the Media controls the public system of television and radio broadcasting.

In liberal democratic political systems such as those of Western Europe or Australia, public ownership of television and radio has long been a feature of the social landscape, although one that is now under real threat from both deregulation and the rise of transnational multimedia conglomerates. Publicly owned media may be funded from direct and indirect taxation, a licence fee, and revenue generated from advertising, sponsorship or other commercial activities, such as the production and selling of content to other media organizations. These publicly owned media organizations operate in a mixed public–private marketplace

Not-for-profit media organizations, e.g. Wiki-leaks The Big Issue Public Broadcasting Service (USA)	Public/state owned media organizations, e.g. BBC (UK) Korean Central Television (North Korea) CCTV (China)	Privately owned media organizations Owned/controlled by individuals Owned/controlled by families Owned by media conglomerates, e.g. HBO owned by Time Warner e.g. Some conglomerates have been dominated by family dynasties such as the Murdochs in News Corporation

Figure 4.1 **Media ownership.**

and many are involved in co-production work with privately owned media companies in the film, radio and television sectors, for example. Public service broadcasters such as ABC (Australia), BBC (United Kingdom) or RTÉ(Ireland), for example, have traditionally had a strong focus on news, current affairs and documentaries in their overall mix of programming content (see Cushion, 2012). While not wishing to over-idealize the public sphere role of public service media, many have had a distinguished history of catering for a wide range of audience (and some minority) interests and tastes. In this regard we can find many examples of programming targeted at linguistic or ethnic minorities, but other minorities (gays, lesbians, bisexuals or transgendered, those with an intellectual or other disability, for example) are often ignored or relegated to off-peak times in broadcast schedules. The arrival of digital media, however, presents a vast new array of possibilities for public service broadcasters to cater for cultural diversity in a more committed way.

Media may be privately owned by companies controlled by individuals, families, shareholders or holding companies. Historically, many newspapers were owned, controlled and even edited by individual media entrepreneurs. In the nineteenth century, for example, many of the so-called press barons wielded considerable editorial power and allied themselves with the interests of the capitalist class. The vast majority of privately owned media companies are now owned and controlled by multimedia conglomerates. These organizations have immense economic and political power. They generate vast revenues for their owners and shareholders. While conglomeration is not by any means risk-free – as evidenced in the collapse of several media companies and in our later discussion of Vivendi – the fact is that more and more cultural production and distribution is controlled by a small number of privately owned players. One of the most telling aspects of this change is that entertainment is prioritized over information and knowledge. Critical journalism, while not by any means moribund, is under increased pressure in a world where, in Postman's (1986) words, we are 'Amusing Ourselves to Death'.

? Stop and think 4.2

Ownership and constraints on media work

What sorts of constraints do you think exist for media professionals who work for privately owned media organizations, given their dependence on advertising and sponsorship and the fact that their owners have other vested interests in other sectors of the economy?

How do think these might compare with the experiences of media professionals and other media activists who work within publicly or community owned media organizations?

Conglomeration, concentration and content

As a result of mergers, take-overs, deregulation, privatization, globalization and technological change, a substantial amount of mainstream media ownership increasingly rests in fewer hands. The growing concentration of media ownership, the formation of alliances, the merging of media and other companies into larger (and increasingly global) conglomerates raises serious concerns for many media scholars. Increased concentration, it is believed, has important implications for the media industry, media workers, media content and media audiences. There are additional worries about the power of individual media moguls regarding the capacity they may have to influence editorial decisions: to shape overall media output and to wield considerable political power.

Those who are critical of these changes in the structure of media ownership are concerned, in the main, about the ideological implications of such developments. They see a clear link between increased media ownership concentration and the narrowing, as they perceive it, of the range of voices heard within a media setting. The contraction of the public sphere, the rise of 'infotainment', the decline of critical investigative journalism, the casualization of much media work, the growing pressures on journalists, for example, to generate content across a number of media platforms, the homogenizing tendencies inherent in media globalization and the so-called 'dumbing down' of much media content (and of news and current affairs in particular) are all seen as resulting directly from this increased concentration.

In this new era of concentrated media ownership, O'Sullivan et al. (1994: 191) argue that 'The search for profit is seen as the key arbiter of what is produced in the media, first in the economic sense of achieving surplus revenue and secondly in the ideological sense of the values and beliefs which support capitalism'. As you will see shortly in this chapter the radical political economy perspective has been to the fore in raising these and other important issues.

Read on! 4.1 'The Big Five'

Ben H. Bagdikian (2004) *The New Media Monopoly*, 7th edn. Boston, MA: Beacon Press, pp. 3–6.

Five global-dimension firms, operating with many of the characteristics of a cartel, own most of the newspapers, magazines, book publishers, motion picture studios, and radio and television stations in the United States. Each medium they own, whether magazines or broadcast stations, covers the entire country, and owners prefer stories and programs that can be used everywhere and anywhere. Their media products reflect this. The programs broadcast in the six empty stations in Minot, N. Dak., were simultaneously being broadcast in New York City.

These five conglomerates are Time Warner, by 2003 the largest media firm in the world; The Walt Disney Company; Murdoch's News Corporation, based in Australia; Viacom; and Bertelsmann, based in Germany. Today, none of the dominant media companies bother with dominance merely in a single medium. Their strategy has been to have major holdings in all the media, from newspapers to movie studios. This gives each of the five corporations and their leaders more communications power than was exercised by any despot or dictatorship in history. ...

No imperial ruler in past history had multiple media channels that included television and satellite channels that can permeate entire societies with controlled sights and sounds. The leaders of the Big Five are not Hitlers and Stalins. They are American and foreign entrepreneurs whose corporate empires control every means by which the population learns of its society. And like any close-knit hierarchy, they find ways to cooperate so that all five can work together, to expand their power, a power that has become a major force in shaping contemporary American life. ...

The Big Five 'competitors' engage in numerous such cartel-like relations. News Corporation, for example, has a joint venture with the European operations of Paramount Pictures, which belongs to Viacom, another of its 'competitors' in the Big Five. According to American securities agencies, Vivendi, the disintegrating French media conglomerate, had agreed to place $25 million worth of advertising in AOL media in return for AOL giving the French firm a share of one of its operations in France.

▶

Some competition is never totally absent among the Big Five media conglomerates. The desire to be the first among many is as true for linked corporations as it is for politicians and nations. It was true two decades ago when most big media companies aspired to command market control in only one medium, for example, Gannett in newspapers; Time Incorporated in magazines; Simon and Schuster in books; the three TV networks in radio; CBS in television; Paramount in motion pictures. But the completion of that process fed an appetite for expansion toward a new and more powerful goal, a small group of interlocked corporations that now have effective control over all the media on which the American public says it depends.

Stop and think 4.3

1. What are the dangers inherent in conglomeration and concentration?

2. The Big Five: competitors or cartel?

3. What implications do conglomeration and concentration have for news production in particular and by extension for democracy?

4. How have ownership patterns changed since Bagdikian published his book in 2004?

Much media ownership is now increasingly characterized by both concentration and conglomeration. Individual media companies may be owned and controlled by conglomerates that concentrate exclusively on media activities or by conglomerates that have a wider range of commercial activities within their specific portfolios (see 'A closer look' 4.1 on Vivendi and 4.2 on General Electric, for example). Conglomerations operate at the local, regional, national and increasingly at the transnational levels. There has been a particular focus on how media conglomerates are controlled. Murdock (1982) has suggested that the control of media conglomerates is best understood in terms of a distinction between 'allocative control' and 'operational control'. The owners and those in senior management possess allocative control in that they determine the overall direction of the media organization(s) in question. They decide whether to concentrate on particular forms of programming over others, for example.

Decisions are taken in terms of how much money will be allocated to news and current affairs programming as opposed to 'reality' or entertainment based shows. Those with allocative control may decide to invest in other media companies who are in the business of producing or distributing media content through the use of new media technologies, for example. Operational control exists at a much lower level in the media organization. An editor or a series producer, for example, will exert operational control in the making of a particular television or radio programme. She will decide on content and on how a budget is spent during production. Operational control is constrained by the allocative control exerted by those at a more senior level in the media organization.

 Stop and think 4.4

Ownership and cross-promotion

A standard criticism levelled at media conglomerates is that they engage in cross-promotion of their various media products. A television news programme, for example, might feature a report on a storyline concerning a soap opera produced by a sister media company without ever referring to a possible conflict of interest. What are the implications (if any) for media professionals and for audiences arising from this practice?

A CLOSER LOOK 4.1

Vivendi

Vivendi (formerly Vivendi Universal) is an example of a transnational conglomerate which has had interests in both media and non-media sectors. Its parent company, Compagnie Générale des Eaux, was originally established to supply water in Lyons (France) in 1853. In recent years, Vivendi retreated from its activities in the non-media sectors and chose to concentrate on music (recording, publishing and distribution), telephony and telecommunications, and gaming and interactive entertainment. It acquired the formerly independent company MP3.com. Such rationalization has also meant that it has disengaged from more traditional media activities such as book publishing. In its guise as a multimedia conglomerate Vivendi has had mixed fortunes and has generated considerable losses. In 2001, for example, the conglomerate sold the publishing house Houghton Mifflin. Until 2011, Vivendi was a part owner with General Electric of NBC Universal (now

NBC Universal Media). It owns or has an interest in the following companies: Activation Blizzard (gaming and interactive media); the Universal Music Group (music publishing and distribution); the Canal+ Group (pay TV); SFR (mobile telephony and internet); Maroc Telecom (mobile telephony, internet and fixed line telephony in Morocco); and GVT (mobile telephony, internet and fixed line telephony in Brazil).

For a detailed account see: http://www.vivendi.com/

Source: Vivendi Annual Report (2011)

A CLOSER LOOK 4.2

General Electric

Vivendi's former dominant partner in NBC Universal Media was General Electric. The General Electric conglomerate is comprised of six divisions that have interests in commercial and consumer finance, healthcare, and industrial and domestic appliances, as well as mass media production and distribution. The group also has interests in nuclear power and in the armaments industry. It owns the film company Universal Pictures and a range of television news and entertainment channels such as Bravo, NBC News and Telemundo. This last channel is aimed at the Hispanic community. NBC Universal's recent successes include the films *Brokeback Mountain* (2005) and *Nanny McPhee* (2005) as well as the US version of the hit BBC series *The Office*.

For a detailed account see http://www.ge.com/

Vertical and horizontal integration

Concentration is usually described as being either vertical or horizontal. (For a variation on these definitions see Doyle, 2002.) According to Croteau and Hoynes (2003: 40) 'vertical integration refers to the process by which one owner acquires all aspects of production and distribution of a single type of media product'. **Horizontal integration**, conversely, 'refers to the process by which one company buys different kinds of media, concentrating ownership across differing types of media rather than "up and down" through one industry'. Media conglomerates that engage in horizontal integration own and control a diverse range of media companies involved in the print, broadcast and ICT sectors, for example.

Vertically integrated media conglomerates usually own and control a number of companies, all of which are involved in various stages in the production and distribution of a specific kind of media product. **Vertical integration** or concentration occurs when, for example, a conglomerate owns and controls the companies that print, publish, distribute and sell a women's magazine (see Figure 4.2a). A vertically integrated conglomerate in the field of television involved in making a drama serial might, in turn, own and control the production company, the television station and the cable network that broadcasts the programme in question.

Media organization X owns and control *all* of the companies involved in the production and distribution of a magazine aimed at a female readership:

Company 1: Produces all written content for the magazine.
Company 2: Is responsible for the photography, design and layout of the magazine.
Company 3: Sells advertising and sponsorship for the magazine.
Company 4: Prints the magazine.
Company 5: Distributes the paper copies of the magazine.
Company 6: Generates the online version of the magazine and its associated web portal, Facebook page and Twitter presence.
Company 7: Syndicates and sells on features and content from the magazine to other media companies.

Figure 4.2a   **Vertical integration of media ownership.**

A growing number of media conglomerates are horizontal in structure (see Figure 4.2b). Global media conglomerates such as Bertelsmann, Vivendi or Time Warner own and control a wide variety of media companies in the 'old' and 'new' media sectors (as well as other forms of economic activity). Their horizontal character may extend to owning companies that produce and sell merchandise associated with their media products.

Media organization Y owns and controls companies in a wide variety of media sectors:			
Company 1 Interactive media & gaming	Company 2 Internet service provision	Company 3 Radio station network	Company 4 Newspaper production

Figure 4.2b   **Horizontal integration of media ownership.**

There are clear strategic reasons why media (and other) firms engage in both horizontal and vertical integration. Doyle notes that horizontal expansion allows for greater economies of scale. In the case of a conglomerate involved in the television sector, for example, its ability to produce, sell or distribute a television programme in more than one territory means that once production costs have been met, in the United States, for example, they increase the likelihood of generating even greater profits in other territories.

Furthermore, she writes that:

> Vertically integrated media firms may have activities that span the creation of media output (which brings ownership of copyright) through to distribution

or retail of that output in various guises. Vertical expansion generally results in reduced transaction costs for the enlarged firm. Another benefit, which may be of great significance for media players, is that vertical integration gives firms some control over their operating environment and it can help them to avoid losing market access in important 'upstream' or 'downstream' phases. (Doyle, 2002: 4)

The term synergy has become the watchword of media conglomerates and a core part of their strategy in maintaining a position of power or dominance. Turow (1992: 683) defines synergy as: 'the co-ordination of parts of a company so that the whole actually turns out to be worth more than the sum of its parts acting alone, without helping one another'. In the face of increasing audience and media fragmentation conglomerates have used synergies in their endless search for profits.

The rationale for such an approach is quite clear. Turow (1992: 688) remarks that, from the perspective of those who own and control media conglomerates, 'Power would accrue to those who could use them synergistically to play out materials across a gamut of holdings for the most value possible'. Playing as they do on a global stage, media conglomerates try to maximize profits on the cultural products that they produce. The latest Hollywood movie, for example, produced by one of the studios owned and controlled by one of the global players, will maximize profits through the film itself and its subsequent release on DVD and video. In many instances the studios that make the film also own the distribution companies and cinemas where the movies are shown. This form of vertical integration gives the larger media organizations considerable

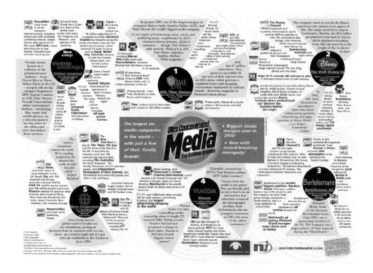

Plate 4.1   Ultra Concentrated Media. Reproduced by kind permission, New Internationalist Publications, Mediachannel.org & Granville Williams © 2001. First published in April 2001.

leverage. Their considerable power is manifest in their ability to keep smaller players out of the mainstream (and more profitable) market. Their influence goes further, however. There may be a wide range of promotional 'tie-ins' at the local McDonald's. 'Happy Meals' will come with a cheaply produced toy associated with the film. Toy shops will sell toys produced in a Third World country made under licence from the media conglomerate. More profits may be generated in the form of merchandising, such as hats, t-shirts, folders, pencil cases and posters, for example. There may be further promotion across the range of media owned by the conglomerate in question. The blurring of the distinction between the ownership and control of the culture industries and other types of economic production raises a number of important issues. Do the ownership and control of the media by conglomerates have a direct bearing on media content? How objective can a news organization be on the armaments industry if its parent company has a vested interest in the latter? Have concentration and conglomeration created new kinds of constraints for media professionals?

 ## Do it! 4.1 The scale and scope of conglomerate activities

Do an internet search on any of the following media giants in order to establish the range of companies that they own and control. Choose from Disney, General Electric, Bertelsmann and Sony. Is your selected media conglomerate engaged exclusively in media activities or does it also have other economic interests? To what extent is it intertwined with other media conglomerates? Would you characterize it as being either horizontally or vertically integrated or a mixture of these ownership structures? From what you have discovered, should we be concerned about the increasingly complex and concentrated nature of media ownership?

A CLOSER LOOK 4.3

Synergies and conglomeration: a media industry perspective

D. Elliman, Jr, executive at *Time Magazine*, speaking on Time Inc.'s decision to merge with Warner Communications, quoted in Turow (1992: 688–9).

A media company that intended to compete successfully in this environment would have to be big enough to be heard and big enough to hold consumer attention. It would have to propose products and synergies that only a large, versatile organization could offer. It'd have to be able to move its products through the emerging global marketplace and amortize its costs over as many distribution networks as possible. Advertisers would be demanding more speed, responsiveness, flexibility and teamwork. Time Inc. was big and strong and successful, but not big enough or strong enough for the challenges we saw on the fast approaching horizon. Long-term, we saw the world accommodating perhaps a half-dozen global media companies. And we intended to be one of them. Bigness for bigness's sake didn't interest us very much. We certainly didn't want to be caught up in an old Gulf & Western or ITT type of diversified conglomerate where the core business can get lost along the way. What we wanted was solid vertical integration so we could offer synergies that would bring together magazines, publishing ventures, studios, cable channels and other activities into a coherent operation. We wanted to be able to offer more than the Murdochs and Maxwells of the world.

The political economy perspective

Political economy theory has been to the fore in attempting to understand and critique the implications of media concentration and conglomeration. There are a variety of strands of political economy theory, which have been influenced by both Marxism and critical theory (see e.g. Bagdikian, 2004; McChesney, 1999; Semetko and Scammell, 2012; Wasko et al., 2011). The political economy perspective is concerned with investigating how the capitalist class promote and ensure their dominant or hegemonic position. It is first and foremost a theory about unequal power relations (see e.g. Mosco, 1996). In its more recent formulation it has been preoccupied with explaining the media's central role in the rise of global capitalism and the consequences of concentration and conglomeration for the public sphere.

In terms of its application in a media setting, McQuail provides us with a useful definition of political economy theory. It is, he writes:

> a socially critical approach that focuses primarily on the relation between the economic structure and dynamics of media industries and the ideological content of media. It directs research attention to the empirical analysis of the structure of ownership and control of media and to the way media market forces operate. From this point of view, the media institution has to be considered as part of the economic system, with close links to the political system. The predominant character of what the media produce can largely be accounted for by the exchange value of different kinds of content, under conditions of pressure to expand markets and by the underlying economic interests of owners and decision makers (Garnham, 1979). These interests relate to the need for profit from media operations and to the relative profitability of other branches of commerce as a result of monopolistic tendencies and processes of vertical and horizontal integration (such as into or from oil, paper, telecommunications, leisure, tourism and property. (2000: 82)

McQuail summarizes the implications of changes in the ownership structures of the media industries from a political economy perspective as being:

> [a] reduction in independent media sources, concentration on the largest markets, avoidance of risks, and reduced investment in less profitable media tasks (such as investigative reporting and documentary film-making). We also find neglect of smaller and poorer sections of the potential audience and often a politically unbalanced range of news media. (2000: 82)

Concentration and conglomeration, according to this perspective, have serious implications for media content (especially factual genres such as news, current affairs and documentaries) and media audiences. Audiences are constructed primarily as consumers rather than as citizens who have a right to be informed. Concentration and conglomeration also have implications for media workers. Casualization of media work has increased and the greater economies of scale demanded by the **media oligopolies** has also resulted in job losses.

The political economy perspective holds that if we wish to understand media content, and especially its ideological character, then we must begin by examining the ownership and control of the media industries. We need to examine both the ownership structure of the media industries and their relationship to other political and economic elite groups in society. If cultural production is driven predominantly by the relentless search for profit and is increasingly undertaken by media organizations that have a wide range of economic interests, then the political economy perspective would lead us to conclude that one of the first casualties tends to be media content which directly challenges the prevailing capitalist interests.

A CLOSER LOOK 4.4

The marketization of news

Devereux, Haynes and Power (2012) in a study of media representations of a stigmatized neighbourhood hold that commodification or marketization of news has adversely affected the practice of journalism and results in less critical coverage (see Bagdikian, 2004; Guyot, 2009; McChesney, 1999; Picard, 1989). In a detailed investigation of print and broadcast media, they argue that news is now primarily defined as a commodity. McManus (2009) sees the marketization of news as '... any action intended to boost profit that interferes with a journalist's or news organization's best effort to maximize public understanding of those issues and events that shape the community they claim to serve' (2009: 219). The increased marketization of news has radically reduced the possibility that the mass media can function as a public sphere informing *all* citizens about important social, economic and political issues that may affect their lives. This in turn has ideological implications in that existing power structures are rarely questioned (see Deuze, 2005).

'Follow the money ...'

In a world where an increasing amount of media activity (production, distribution and access) is being privatized, the political economy perspective is of critical importance. In attempting to understand the relationship between media ownership and media content the political economy perspective demands that we critically examine the profit-driven motives of media organizations that commodify both cultural production and audiences (McQuail, 2000). Media products, be they cartoons, DVDs or computer software, are primarily commodities produced to generate maximum profit. McQuail (2000: 82) notes that one strand of political economy theory holds that in an age of media globalization it is audiences that are being commodified. We can see evidence of this, for example, in the radio industry, where some media conglomerates speak of 'delivering key demographic groups' to advertisers and sponsors. Furthermore, social media companies have not been slow to engage in data mining in order to build profiles of their users and to attempt to profit from this. This is why when you use popular platforms such as Gmail or Google, you are often presented with pop-up adverts pertaining to your particular interests or are presented with a hierarchy of search findings which are more than likely paid for by companies such as Amazon. The challenge for all of us as media students and as citizens is to begin to see the likely links between the media oligopolies and the implications of their hegemonic position.

The political economy perspective illuminates our understanding of the media both historically and contemporaneously. Changes within the media industry would seem to add further weight to the political economy thesis. McQuail (2000) cites the work of Golding and Murdock (1996), who argue for the continued relevance of this theoretical perspective. They hold that the political economy perspective has two key tasks, namely the examination of cultural production and cultural consumption.

First, it must examine the relationship between structures of ownership (both private and public) and cultural production. As we will see in the next part of this chapter, political economists (and others) argue that the rise of the media oligopolies has resulted in a significant change in media content and a consequent contraction in the media's public sphere role. This perspective helps us understand why there is now a greater concentration on entertainment and infotainment within media content. Entertainment sells. In the USA, for example, changes in the ownership structure of local television stations resulting in the creation of 'duopolies' – whereby a media conglomerate such as General Electric owns more than one television station – has been shown to have had a negative impact in terms of the overall level of educationally based programming aimed at younger viewers. The Children Now organization found that in Los Angeles there was a significant reduction in the amount and diversity of children's programming between 1998 and 2003 – a fact explained by the shrinkage in ownership terms of the local television networks (Children Now, 2003).

Do it! 4.2 Media ownership and control – who owns Facebook?

Do a search on the ownership and control of the social media network Facebook. List its top 10 shareholders. What sorts of companies (media and otherwise) and individuals predominate? What strategic reasons may have guided their decision to invest in the company? Were you surprised in any way by what you found?

Read on! 4.2 Will the internet set us free?

Robert W. McChesney (1999) *Rich Media, Poor Democracy*, Champaign, IL: University of Illinois Press, pp. 182–3.

By 1999 notions of the Internet providing a new golden age of competitive capitalism were quickly fading from view in the business press. The *New York Times* argued that the lesson of the Internet was 'The big get bigger and the small fade away.' Indeed, as the newspaper noted, the Internet, rather than having a competitive bias, may in fact stimulate monopoly and oligopoly. 'At first glance, the Internet seems to favor David over Goliath, as any upstart can open an on-line store or an electronic publication. But it appears that the first capable pipsqueak to shoot a slingshot in any given area may grow to a giant size so quickly tha[t] any new challengers have been kept at bay.' The prospect for new giants emerging was even more remote in the area of 'content.' Despite its much ballyhooed 'openness', to the extent that it becomes a visible mass medium, it will likely be dominated by the usual corporate suspects. Certainly a few new commercial content players will emerge, but the evidence suggests that the content of the digital communication world will appear quite similar to the content of the pre-digital commercial media world. In some ways the Web has even extended commercial

▶

synergies and the role of advertising and selling writ large to new dimensions. This does not mean that the Internet will not be a major part in reconfiguring the way we lead our lives; it almost certainly will. Some aspects of these changes will probably be beneficial whereas others may be detrimental. Nor does this mean that there will not be a vibrant, exciting and important noncommercial citizen sector in cyberspace open to all who veer off the beaten path. For activists of all political stripes, the Web increasingly plays a central role in organizing and educational activities. But from its once lofty perch, this nonprofit and civic sector has been relegated to the distant margins of cyberspace; it is nowhere near the heart of the operating logic of the dominant commercial sector. In a less dubious political environment, the Internet could be put to far greater democratic use than it is or likely will be in the foreseeable future. But the key point is simply that those who think the technology can produce a viable democratic public sphere by itself where policy has failed to do so are deluding themselves.

 ## Stop and think 4.5

1. Where the internet is concerned, why is 'David' not really favoured over 'Goliath'?

2. Why is McChesney pessimistic about the possibility of creating an Internet-based public sphere?

3. Do you agree with his perspective?

Second, access to the growing number of cultural products in daily life is increasingly privatized. Access to the array of cultural products and media technologies now available is not equal, thus creating media haves and have-nots. Media conglomerates define their (potential) audiences primarily as consumers. Accessing much of the media is predicated upon one's ability to pay. Media conglomerates have managed to privatize a wide range of media activities by, for example, charging for cable television, selling pay-per-view movies and accessing the internet.

Do it! 4.3   Media moguls

Selecting any one of the better-known media moguls, try to establish the range and extent of their media ownership and control around the globe. In terms of either the print or the broadcast media organizations owned or controlled by your selected mogul, do these media organizations, in your opinion, share a common ideological view of the world?

A CLOSER LOOK 4.5

Media mogul Silvio Berlusconi

- Born in Italy in 1936

- Estimated to be worth US$6.2 billion (*Forbes Magazine*, 2013: http://www.forbes.com/profile/silvio-berlusconi/)

- A highly controversial politician, he served as Italian Prime Minister in 1994 (for nine months) from 2001 to 2006 and from 2008 to 2011. He is avowedly opposed to left-wing ideas

- Began his business career in construction and subsequently shifted to owning and controlling diverse media companies as well as companies in other sectors

- Has a controlling interest in Mediaset and Fininvest. Mediaset controls three TV channels and Publitalia (an advertising and PR company)

- Has financial interests in the insurance and banking sectors as well as construction, food production and a department store – Standa

- Founder of the political party Forza Italia (Go Italy)

- Owns the Italian soccer club AC Milan

- Has been criticized by many because of his direct and indirect control of the Italian media – a factor which his critics say has helped his rise to political power

- Convicted of tax fraud in 2012

- Sought re-election in 2013 as leader of The People of Freedom alongside several right-wing allies.

A CLOSER LOOK 4.6

Media mogul Rupert Murdoch

- Born in Australia in 1931 (has had US citizenship since 1985)
- Estimated to be worth US$11.2 billion (Forbes, 2013: http://www.forbes. com/profile/rupert-murdoch/)
- Founder, chairman and CEO of global media giant News Corporation, the second largest media conglomerate in the world (estimated worth US$60 billion)
- Has referred to his media empire as 'freedom's greatest messenger'
- Media interests lie in film, television, broadcasting delivery systems (cable, digital and satellite), print media (newspapers and magazines in the US, Australasia and the UK), book publishing and internet-based services. Buying sports teams as well as controlling the broadcasting rights to key sporting events has been a key part of his overall strategy in the USA, Australasia, the UK and India, for example
- Key media brands include Fox News, Twentieth Television, Sky television, Star television (China), Myspace.com, HarperCollins, a range of tabloid and broadsheet newspapers including the now defunct *News of The World*, the *Sun*, the *Sun on Sunday* and the London *Times* (UK); the *Daily Telegraph* (Australia) and the *New York Post* (USA)
- Like Berlusconi, Murdoch has been very controversial in political terms. Avowedly anti-trade union, his newspapers have openly supported political parties in favour of deregulation and liberalization. In the UK, for example, he has openly supported both the Conservatives and (New) Labour. Despite his own ideological commitment to free-market capitalism he has managed to hammer out an arrangement with state communist China in order to facilitate the spread of his Star TV network. He removed the BBC World Service TV from that network when Chinese authorities expressed alarm at the critical tone of the public service broadcasters coverage of world (and Chinese) affairs (see Wheen, 2004: 231–3 and Pilger, 1999).

Like his Italian counterpart, Murdoch has been no stranger to legal and political controversy. In 2011 it was revealed that Murdoch's *News of The World* was engaged in hacking the phones of ordinary citizens such as the late Millie Dowler, celebrities and members of the British Royal Family. The controversy led to Murdoch resigning from the board of News International and the resignation of the paper's editor Rebekah Brooks as well as the setting up of the Leveson Inquiry.

Jürgen Habermas and the public sphere

The concept of the public sphere as developed by the German sociologist Jürgen Habermas (1962) has been the subject of much debate and criticism (see e.g. Benhabib, 1992). Although not without its conceptual difficulties, it continues to inform thinking on how media organizations should operate. In his original study *Strukturwandel der Öffentlichkeit* (translated as *The Structural Transformation of the Public Sphere*) Habermas (1962) distinguishes between three types of sphere in society. These are the private sphere (consisting of family and economy), the sphere of public authority (consisting of state and judiciary) and the bourgeois public sphere.

For Habermas the coffee houses and salons of Enlightenment Europe represent the beginnings of a bourgeois public sphere. Within this sphere (bourgeois) citizens could debate matters of political importance. The development of the print media (newspapers, books, journals and pamphlets, etc.) allowed further growth in the public sphere. In Habermas's account the decline of the public sphere begins in the late nineteenth and early twentieth centuries once the print media become commercialized media. There is less room for the media to operate as a public sphere facilitating political discourse. In a critical essay, Verstraeten (1996: 348) identifies three key dimensions to Habermas's conceptualization of the public sphere:

1. The public sphere requires a 'forum' that is accessible to as many people as possible and where a large variety of social experiences can be expressed and exchanged.

2. In the public sphere, various arguments and views are confronted through rational discussion. This implies that 'rational' political choice is possible only if the public sphere first offers a clear insight into the alternatives from which one can choose. At the same time, the media should offer the widest possible range of interpretation frames so that the citizen is also aware of what he did not choose (Murdock, 1992: 17–41).

3. Systematically and critically checking on government policies is the primary task of this public sphere.

While recognizing the continuing importance of the concept, Verstraeten (1996) argues against the interpretation (held by Habermas and many others) that the public sphere has undergone a rise and subsequent fall. He suggests that, in practice, the public sphere has yet to be achieved. Furthermore, in examining the contemporary media, a focus on political economy remains necessary. As Verstraeten states:

> When studying the public sphere, especially as it is more and more mediatized, one should always bear in mind the following question: whose public sphere are we talking about and whose political or socio-economic interest is it? For it would be extremely naïve to assume that in our conflict-laden and dual society, an ideal typical neutral public sphere, belonging as it were to everyone, would emerge. It is therefore necessary always to examine and re-examine critically whose public sphere we are dealing with. (1996: 357–8)

While they recognize its limitations, the Goldsmiths Media Group are also supportive of the retention of Habermas's idea of the public sphere. Stressing its ethical significance, they argue that: 'It provides an indispensable perspective on the operations of media organisations, since it insists that we continually evaluate the media for what they contribute to our lives as citizens, as active participants in the public sphere' (2000: 43).

In summary, then, Habermas's notion of the public sphere stresses the importance of political discourse among citizens. Ideally, a public sphere has a crucial role to play in ensuring the continuation of a civic and democratic society. It allows rational discussion, debate and the exchange of information. Its key function is to facilitate debate and argument about the behaviour and performance of the powerful in society.

The proposition that the contemporary media operate as a public sphere is difficult to sustain. It is problematic because of increased ownership concentration and conglomeration. A major constraint on the media realizing their public sphere role arises from the fact that a growing amount of cultural production is in the hands of powerful media organizations whose sole *raison d'être* is profit. While certain kinds of media genres may have a public sphere dimension (talk radio, letters to the editor or internet bulletin boards, for example) there is now, arguably, less scope for a broadly based public sphere to be realized. In the context of greater media complexity it may be more appropriate to think in terms of a range of public spheres that appeal to different kinds of audience members rather than a single public sphere. Such public spheres may operate both inside and outside dominant discourse. From a neo-Marxist position, one could argue that the public sphere is a new opiate for the people, allowing them the illusion of democracy in a capitalist-controlled society.

 Key thinker 4.1   Jürgen Habermas

Born in Düsseldorf in 1929, Jurgen Habermas has contributed hugely to how we understand modernity, democracy, power relationships and the role of the media in particular. A major figure within critical theory and a critic of postmodernism, Habermas is best described as eclectic in terms of the range of disciplinary influences he has drawn upon in his many writings. He mixes ideas and concepts from philosophy, political science and sociology in order to understand and explain modern civil society. As is noted in this chapter, his most important (and most contentious) contribution rests in the ideas he has developed around the concept of the public sphere. As a major intellectual figure he has been embroiled in many controversies. As a graduate student, Habermas's supervisors (Horkheimer and Adorno of the Frankfurt School; see Chapter 6) vehemently disagreed over the direction his

PhD research was taking. Later in his career, Habermas himself was to have a very public row with the French theorist Derrida. As a public intellectual he has argued against attempts by some revisionist historians to lessen the significance of the Nazi regime in Germany. His concept of the public sphere has as many detractors as it has supporters, yet it remains an important lens through which we can evaluate whether or not the media contributes to the further development of civil society.

Read on! 4.3   'Mapping internet inequalities'

Korinna Patelis (2000) 'The political economy of the Internet', in James Curran (ed.), *Media Organisations in Society*. London: Arnold, pp. 92–3.

In 1997 Network Wizards figures showed only fifteen countries in the world with more than 100,000 hosts registered under their own domain name. ... All of those are in the West, which leaves 128 countries with fewer than 100 computers connected. Similarly the OECD Communication Outlook places 92 per cent of all Internet hosts in the OECD area. From Network Wizard statistics one can deduce that at least 60 per cent of these hosts are in the US. ... There were no host computers in the Honduras in 1995 and merely 400 in 1997. Today there are 45,000 users in Jamaica. ... There are 500 hosts in Morocco, none in some central African countries. Basic indicators also show that Europe is far behind in cyberspace. There were a total of 4.38 million hosts in the EU at the end of 1997, an increase of 140 per cent from the previous years, but still very low if one considers the total estimated number of hosts worldwide. Discrepancies between EU countries are dramatic. There were 2.7 hosts per 1000 habitants in Greece and only 0.2 domain names; 17.0 per 1000 in the UK – both countries being far from Finland's 95 per 1000. ... Such discrepancies show the exact opposite of what Internetphilac claims: the geo-economic periphery is not centred in the virtual world.

Profiles of the average user reconfirm these inequalities. CommerceNet Nielsen found that Internet access in the US and Canada was up by 50 per cent, from 23 million users in August–September 1996 to 34 million by April 1997. A Find/SVP and Jupiter Communication survey found that

▶

14.7 million households were on-line (a figure that had doubled from previous years), while International Data Corp. estimated that 20 per cent of American households in the US were on-line. ... Jupiter estimates that 3.7 million households are on the Net in Europe and 3.4 in the Asia Pacific Rim. ... The Internet is like a tree out of whose trunk branches keep growing all the time. The way this tree grows is not accidental; it is dictated by international economico-political structures. ... There is a main Internet backbone, a central intercontinental network to which smaller networks are connected. The US is at the centre of the majority of these connections.

Stop and think 4.6

1. Having considered Patelis's findings, do you think that we all share equally in the global village?

2. What determines access to the internet?

3. Apply the political economy perspective discussed in this chapter to Patelis's account of the internet. Does this illuminate your understanding of internet inequalities?

 A CLOSER LOOK 4.7 ....

Ownership and media content

A growing body of evidence clearly demonstrates the relationship between changing media ownership structures and media content. Moving beyond the concerns repeatedly expressed by many media scholars on the apparent dumbing down of media content, a number of studies have demonstrated how news in particular has been negatively affected. Dunaway's (2013) study examines election campaign news coverage in the United States. It concludes that media owned and controlled by large chain and corporate media organizations are more likely to produce coverage that is negative in tone in contrast to single-owned companies. Mao et al. (2012) examined three Canadian newspapers' coverage of homelessness. Informed by agenda-setting theory and adopting a detailed **content analysis** approach in terms of research method, their study compared regional and national newspaper coverage of homelessness in Canada. In addition to political and cultural contexts, they found that corporate ownership (in this instance a major multimedia conglomerate) was of significance in that such newspapers had less coverage of the complex issue of homelessness than their singly owned counterparts. (The advent of new media has also had important repercussions for media coverage of important social issues. See Chapter 9 for an elaboration of this theme.)

Media and regulation

It should already be apparent to you that the media are not just another industry (see McQuail, 2010: 218). Their cultural, economic, political and social significance raise the important, though sometimes problematic, issue of how they might be regulated. The 9 pm 'watershed' on television; advertising standards regarding the claims being made for specific products; the classification of movies and games in terms of age suitability (e.g. PG, 15+, 18+); the use of Parental Advisory stickers on music CDs; and the establishment of self-regulatory press councils in certain countries to adjudicate on complaints concerning individual journalists or newspapers are just some examples of how media are currently regulated (see also 'A closer look 4.9 The Leveson Inquiry – who guards the guardians?').

While we can think about how print, broadcast and online media continue to be tightly controlled in totalitarian political systems such as North Korea or China (see Chapter 3), our primary concern here is with how regulation issues currently play out in liberal democratic systems. Such debates are focused on whether media regulation by the state or other interest groups is necessary, desirable or even practical and the sorts of challenges that conglomeration, corporatization and technological change pose for the regulation of media content and its distribution.

While they may vary from country to country, debates concerning media regulation or governance have been a key feature of the history of the media (see McQuail, 2010: 232). As this book has already demonstrated, technological changes and the rise of powerful transnational media conglomerates (and individual media moguls) pose particular challenges for governments and others in terms of how regulation can take place in practice. How can governments guard against vested corporate media interests? Have nation states now been so overtaken by technological developments that meaningful regulation has in fact become impossible in practical terms? As part of a wider societal health strategy, a government, for example, might wish to regulate fast food advertising specifically aimed at children, but the television channel which is most watched by younger viewers is broadcast via satellite and its corporate headquarters are in another jurisdiction. Equally, it might wish to combat the rise of cyber-bullying amongst teenagers but face legal difficulties in pursuing the defendants when the internet site they are using is in fact hosted in a different country.

While regulation of the media is seen by many people as being desirable, it is also something that is contested and is often laden with contradictions. Powerful media conglomerates who would favour a heavily de-regulated environment with little or no state interference in which to operate have sought help in trying to regulate or sanction those Internet Service Providers who have assisted in the hosting of file-sharing sites which freely distribute music, games and movies, for example.

Although those holding a Libertarian political persuasion might argue that the principle of freedom of speech and expression should mean *no* regulation whatsoever, in reality most people, whether on the left or the right of the political spectrum, accept that some form of regulation is, in fact, necessary.

Media regulation is usually characterized as being either *external* or *internal*. External regulation refers to regulation from above. A government might create laws or regulations concerning public service television; it may create a licensing system for commercial and community based radio stations or curtail media ownership in broadcast or print media or the carving up bandwidth for broadband or mobile/cell phones. Internal regulation or regulation from within refers broadly to how the media industries regulate themselves. In the UK, arguments over whether the press should regulate itself or be regulated by means of a statutory body were at the centre of the contentious reaction to the Leveson Inquiry Report (The Right Honourable Lord Justice Leveson, 2012). As will be discussed in more detail in Chapter 5, self-regulation is a key feature of everyday media work. Those working in the media industries are constrained by internal rules, regulations, norms and routines of production. The need to maximize profit, the fear of offending advertisers or other commercial interests, as well as the threat of losing audiences, may in fact be more powerful forms of regulation than any formal external law or regulation.

Attempts at media regulation have revolved around questions concerning *press freedom*, *freedom of speech* and *the public interest*. The focus of public interest concerns have ranged from worries about the influence of certain forms of media content (e.g. pornography, gratuitous violence, hate speech) to the apparent shrinkage of the media's public sphere role owing to conglomeration and increased privatization. The desire to ensure the universality of reach of certain types of media has also been a focus.

Models of media regulation

In explaining the range of regulatory practices which have governed the media industries to date, three main models are usually discussed. These are (1) the Free Press Model; (2) the Broadcasting Model; and (3) the Common Carrier Model (see Croteau et al., 2012; McQuail, 2010). It should be noted that there exist significant variations from country to country and that these models represent a set of general patterns of regulation. Technological changes (most notably in the form of the internet) have resulted in many new pressures being brought to bear on state and other interests who wish to regulate the media. The idea of a free press is widely recognized as being at the heart of truly democratic societies. The Free Press Model assumes a press free from political interference and very little if any state regulation. The Free Press Model is of course potentially problematic in that the press assumes itself to be politically neutral and imagines itself to have a neutral surveillance function with respect to the politically and economically powerful. In reality, some state regulation of the press does take place. This may be in the shape of the state legislating to ensure diversity of ownership in the marketplace (ideally to safeguard the public sphere), in the establishment of statutory or self-regulatory bodies to oversee the behaviour of the newspaper industry, or in devising laws concerning libel and defamation.

A CLOSER LOOK 4.8

Media regulation: three examples

1. **Finland:** The Council for Mass Media is a self-regulating body whose membership is comprised of journalists and publishers. It is responsible for print, broadcast and internet based media. Go to http://www.jsn.fi/en/

2. **Australia:** Print media are regulated by the Australian Press Council – a self-regulating body – while broadcast and online media are regulated by the statutory Australian Communications and Media Authority. Go to http://www presscouncil.org.au/ and http://www.acma.gov.au

3. **The Netherlands:** Print media are self-regulated through The Netherlands Press Council (Raad voor de Journalistiek). Go to http://www.presserecht.de

Historically, the some states have taken a much stronger role in the regulation of broadcasting. The Broadcasting Model of media regulation was devised to ensure that television would reach as many citizens as possible. In licensing radio and television companies, governments control the use of the broadcast spectrum. In a European context, in particular (most notably in the form of the BBC), the advent of public service television and radio saw individual states create legislation concerning news and current affairs coverage, language policies, and the amount (if any) of advertising and sponsorship which public service stations might broadcast. Deregulation of media ownership, increased transnational competition, technological changes and the changing role of many public service broadcasters themselves (e.g. their involvement in partnerships with privately owned media companies) means that the Broadcasting Model is now under serious pressure. It is increasingly difficult to regulate media content when it is delivered from elsewhere using technologies that are difficult if not impossible to control.

The Common Carrier Model emerged in order to regulate postal, telephone and telegraph services. The desire to regulate these forms of communication stemmed from the need to ensure universal reach. Technological and other developments (e.g. social media, mobile/cell telephony, Skype, Facebook) mean that the Common Carrier Model is in serious decline. McQuail (2010) and

Croteau et al. (2012) acknowledge the state of flux that is now apparent in terms of media regulation. Technological developments have rendered many forms of regulation obsolete. Given the vast power of many media conglomerates it is interesting to note that many liberal democratic governments have now opted for a light-touch approach. Internet Service Providers, for example, are expected to regulate themselves.

So, do we need media regulation?

Media regulation is necessary and inevitable. The arguments in favour of media regulation stem from a need to protect the public interest. External regulation, however, is becoming more problematic owing to increased corporatization and technological change. The globalized mediascape presents nation states with a new set of challenges. How can the state ensure that the democratic health of an individual society be protected in the face of a narrowing array of voices and ideological perspectives within a media setting? Does state regulation result in press/media freedom being compromised? Can it ever really regulate online media such as Facebook or Twitter? How might internet bullying, defamation or identity theft issues be resolved in the case of either social media? There is a strong consensus that self-regulation by the media industries themselves is the most realistic way to ensure certain standards are adhered to amongst the older media. While self-regulation by some online communities has already emerged, online media generally present serious challenges concerning the likelihood of regulation.

 A CLOSER LOOK 4.9 ··

The Leveson Inquiry – who guards the guardians?

The publication in the UK of the Leveson Inquiry Report (The Right Honourable Lord Justice Leveson, 2012) (see http://www.levesoninquiry.org.uk/) brings many of the tensions involved in debates about media regulation into sharp focus. Should print and other forms of media regulate themselves or should they be governed by an independent (statutory) body? Does the radically altered media landscape mean that we should have more or less regulation of the print and other forms of media?

The Leveson judicial inquiry was set up to investigate the culture, practices and ethics of the UK press following revelations that the mobile phone of murdered teenager Millie Dowler had been hacked, in addition to other allegations of possible illegal behaviour by journalists and editors. As discussed earlier in this chapter, these and other events led to the closure of the *News of The World* newspaper and much criticism of the Murdoch-controlled News International conglomerate. The inquiry called many high-profile witnesses (such as J.K. Rowling, Steve Coogan,

Dr Gerry McCann (the father of Madeleine McCann)) to investigate the relationship between the press and the public; the relationship between the press and the police; and the relationship between the press and politicians. At its core the Leveson Inquiry was concerned with four things – media ethics; data protection; public confidence in the press; and the close relationship between the press and the powerful.

The Leveson Inquiry concluded that the existing Press Complaints Commission should be abolished. While it accepted the principle of self-regulation by the press, it proposed the establishment of a new industry-led Press Standards Body which would in turn create a new code of conduct for the print media. Such a body would be underpinned by statutory legislation in order to ensure its independence. Membership of the proposed Press Standards Body would be voluntary, carrying with it a number of incentives for the print media (specifically regarding how costs might be awarded in the event of libel/defamation to members and non-members).

There were a variety of reactions to this proposal. The Free Speech Network (representing the interests of many editors and journalists) argued that there could be no state involvement in press regulation and suggested that this would interfere with the print media's surveillance function over the politically powerful. Hacked Off, however, representing those whose phones had been illegally hacked, accepted Leveson's proposals regarding regulation.

The findings were also politically divisive, with Labour and the Liberal Democrats accepting its conclusions while the Conservatives were more reticent about implementing its recommendations. Many of the print media were also damning of Leveson's conclusions regarding the future regulation of the press.

 Stop and think 4.7

1. What are the arguments in favour of/against press regulation?

2. Why do you think the owners of newspapers are likely to be opposed to regulation?

3. Is the regulation of print and other forms of media purely aspirational?

Conclusion

As an antidote to the emphasis placed by the cultural studies approach on both media texts and media reception, researchers interested in the economics of the media industry argue that we must begin our analysis with a thorough appreciation of the ownership structures within which cultural production initially takes place. Perhaps the most critical change within the structure of media ownership patterns, identified by this chapter, is the growing overlap, in ownership terms, of companies involved in cultural as well as other forms of production, such as car manufacturing, nuclear power, or the armaments industry, for example. We can speculate as to the implications for media content that might arise from such cross-ownership. A majority of media organs in the nineteenth century were allied with the interests of the capitalist class. In the twenty-first century a growing number of media organizations are part of more general media conglomerates that have a wide range of media and other economic interests. What are the overall implications for media content? How real is the pressure on media professionals to cross-promote products, goods or services owned and controlled by the larger conglomerate to which their media organization belongs? Does this pressure mean that there is now a greater likelihood of interference in the daily work of media professionals? What sorts of tensions emerge between those who have allocative control and those who exercise managerial control in a media setting?

That the orientation of mainstream media content is changing as a result of greater concentration and conglomeration cannot be disputed. There is clear evidence that media genres of a more critical orientation (such as news, current affairs or documentary programmes) are coming under increasing pressure in the battle for resources and audiences. The shift towards 'reality' television and infotainment generally has to be understood in terms of the decisions taken by media companies to maximize audiences (and profits). In many respects this chapter has painted a bleak scenario – especially in its discussion of the political economy perspective and the likelihood (or not) of a public sphere emerging in the current context of largely privatized media ownership. Within public discourse there is a tendency to personalize the complex state of affairs regarding contemporary media ownership in terms of the activities of individual media moguls. While these well-known individuals have significant amounts of economic and political clout, the reality is that the key players in terms of the restructuring of media ownership are large-scale transnational conglomerates. Their dominant position has clear implications for stand-alone media organizations, for the practice of journalism and even for individual nation states. The increased concentration and conglomeration evident within the media industries is of major ideological significance. This restructuring has a direct bearing on the macro changes evident in terms of media content and in terms of how unequal relationships of power are portrayed – themes that we will discuss further in Chapters 5 and 6. The increase in conglomeration means that media space is being further colonized by commercial interests. We can see this within everyday media content where, in addition to advertising, sponsorship, product placement and cross-promotion are becoming even more significant features.

Chapter summary

1. This chapter has stressed the importance of understanding the relationship between ownership structures and media content.
2. It has investigated the implications of increased conglomeration and concentration of ownership for the public sphere.
3. It has demonstrated how the political economy perspective illuminates our understanding of the key changes in media ownership patterns.
4. The question of whether more media really means a greater range of voices and perspectives was raised.
5. Media ownership was examined with reference to horizontal and vertical structures and the rise of powerful media moguls.
6. The inherent difficulties in regulating the media were also discussed with particular reference to the Leveson Inquiry (The Right Honourable Lord Justice Leveson 2012).

Further reading

Bagdikian, B.H. (2004) *The New Media Monopoly*, 7th edn. Boston, MA: Beacon Press. This classic text has been radically revised and updated. It is a 'must' for all students who wish to understand the implications of the recent consolidation of media ownership.

Bettig, R.V. and J.L. Hall (2012) *Big Media, Big Money: Cultural Texts and Political Economics*, 2nd edn. Lanham MD: Rowan and Littlefield. The second edition of this engaging text examines the growing nexus between the media and big business. The authors discuss convergence and conglomeration in many media sectors including the music industry. See in particular their discussion of 'Ad Creep' – the increasing presence of advertising in places such as schools and universities.

(Continued)

Croteau, D. and W. Hoynes. (2006) *The Business of Media: Corporate Media and the Public Interest*, 2nd edn. Thousand Oaks, CA: Pine Forge Press. An accessible text that demystifies the complexities of media ownership with reference to public sphere and market models of the media industry. See in particular Chapter 5, 'How business strategy shapes media content', and Chapter 7, 'Choosing the future: citizens, policy and the public interest'.

Cushion, S. (2012) *The Democratic Value of News: Why Public Service Media Matter*. London: Palgrave. An essential read for those of you wishing to understand more about the challenges faced by, and the possibilities open to, public service media. In the light of the discussion in this chapter concerning the democratic deficit resulting from the marketization of news, see Chapter 7, in particular 'Protecting the democratic value of news: why public service media matter'.

Deacon, D., M. Pickering, P. Golding and G. Murdock (1999b) *Researching Communications: A Practical Guide to Methods in Media and Cultural Analysis*. London: Arnold. In a subsection of their chapter entitled 'Dealing with documentation' (pp. 34–8) the authors outline how you might map the complex web of ownership and control of the media industries.

Doyle, G. (2013) *Understanding Media Economics*, 2nd edn. London: Sage Publications. This book provides a thorough introduction to the economic bases of the contemporary media industries.

Hargittai, E. (2004) 'Internet access and use in context', *New Media and Society*, 6(1): 137–43. This is a succinct review essay on the question of media 'haves' and 'have nots'.

Thomas, P.N. and Z. Nain (2004) (eds) *Who Owns The Media? Global Trends and Local Resistance*. London: Zed Books. Fifteen essays on the political economy of contemporary media ownership in a wide range of settings including Africa, Asia, Latin America and China.

Wasko, J., G. Murdock and H. Sousa (2011) *The Handbook of Political Economy of Communications*. Oxford: Wiley-Blackwell. This is an essential text for students of media ownership and conglomeration. A weighty book in terms of its size, scope and importance, Murdock et al.'s *Handbook* brings together an array of scholars and classic studies which explain the political economy of communication both historically and in terms of more recent trends. See in particular Chapter 2 and Chapter 4, which deal with political economy and the cultural industries respectively.

Online reading

Go to your companion website and read the following:

- Croteau, D. and W. Hoynes (2007) 'The media industry: structure, strategy and debates', in E. Devereux (ed.), *Media Studies: Key Issues and Debates*. London: Sage.
- Fenton, N. (2007) 'Bridging the mythical divide: political economy and cultural studies approaches to the analysis of media', in E. Devereux (ed.), *Media Studies: Key Issues and Debates*. London: Sage.

CHAPTER  5

Media Professionals and Media Production

Chapter overview

This chapter introduces you to the following:

- The production research approach
- The rationale for and research methodologies employed in doing research on media production and media professionals
- The significance of understanding the contexts in which media professionals operate and in which media texts are initially created
- The concepts of structure and agency in understanding media professionals and media production
- The emergence of new forms of independent media production where alternative or counter-hegemonic voices may be heard
- The reconfiguration of audiences as produsers or prosumers.

Key concepts

- Production research
- Media professionals
- Cultural industries
- Sociology of organizations
- Structure and agency
- Qualitative media analysis
- Encoding and decoding
- Ethnography
- Participant observation
- Citizen journalism
- Prosumers/produsers

Introduction

Media globalization and the restructuring of media ownership have very real implications for media audiences, media content, media organizations and the day-to-day working lives of media professionals. In this chapter attention is placed on understanding the media at a micro level by examining the organizational or institutional contexts in which media professionals operate in the initial 'making' of media texts. Research on media professionals has been traditionally orientated towards understanding news journalism (see Ekstrom, 2002; Esser, 1998), and most recently the spotlight has been thrown upon the many challenges (and opportunities) that technological changes and convergence present (see Deuze, 2004; Dupagne and Garrison, 2006; Huang et al., 2006). While genuine concerns have been raised about the contraction of the mainstream media's public sphere role, technological developments have resulted in the emergence of hopeful signs in the shape of alternative media such as Indymedia and Freespeech as well as an array of citizen journalism circulated via social media. As a counterbalance to the kinds of changes already discussed in Chapters 3 and 4 (such as homogenization and the decline and contraction of a critical journalism), media production engaged in by activists of all kinds represents a critically important development, particularly in the context of attempting to ensure the democratic health of late modern societies. In this chapter, however, the focus is largely on those forces which shape the making of media content in an institutional or organizational setting.

Production research

Consider for a moment any mainstream media text that you may have encountered in the last few days. The text, in all likelihood, has come about as a result of the interaction of a large number of media professionals working within a specific organizational context. The front page of this morning's newspaper whether in print or online will, in all likelihood, have involved the interaction of the editor, journalists, sub-editors, advertising copywriters, photographers and printers, to name but a few. Media professionals such as those involved in bringing you the main stories on last night's main news bulletin will have engaged in a certain amount of agency or creativity in attempting to tell audience members a particular story about the world. The media texts that they created will have been based upon agreed and invariably unspoken notions of 'newsworthiness' and audience interest. Their activities, however, are also shaped and constrained by a large range of forces both inside and outside their individual media organization. They are in direct competition with other media organizations for the eyes and ears of audience members and may be dependent on other media organizations such as one of the international news agencies like Reuters, the Press Association or Agence France-Presse in order to bring the news story to your screen. Depending upon particular circumstances, the media professionals in question may or may not reproduce dominant ideological discourses within their media texts.

Production research has the potential to reveal much about the experiences of media professionals, the constraints within which they operate and the intended meanings that they encode into media texts. A legitimate stand-alone research strategy in its own right, production research may be used on its own, or as a constituent part of a wider approach that seeks to understand media production, content, reception and effects in one or other combination (see e.g. Deacon et al., 1999b).

The interplay between the agency or creativity of media professionals and the structures or constraints under which they operate is at the heart of what production research is all about. These tensions, however, are not confined to those working in the mainstream **cultural industries**, but, as is noted later in this chapter, are also evident in other forms of media production produced by members of the alternative or counter-hegemonic media.

As you will discover, in spite of the recent dominance within media studies of textual and reception analysis, there is in fact a long-standing research tradition of investigating the culture of media organizations and the activities, experiences and ideologies of media professionals. Researchers have examined news media organizations (and the culture of newsrooms in particular) with a view to understanding more about the workings of agenda setting, the use of particular sources in writing news stories and the increasing importance of other media professionals such as PR experts who attempt to generate a 'spin' on specific stories (see e.g. Davis, 2000: Iyengar and Kinder, 1987).

Interest in the cultural industries is once again attracting the attention of media scholars. This is both timely and necessary given the radical changes that are occurring within the media industries (see e.g. Hesmondhalgh, 2013, who combines a political economy and cultural studies approach in his attempt to understand the dynamics of the cultural industries). Bourdieu's (1996) writings on journalism in which he applies the concept of 'field' in order to understand more about the world of the journalist have resulted in a further revival of research interest in the media professional (see e.g. Ito, 2006).

This chapter begins by tracing the theoretical and methodological roots of production research. The main methodological choices facing researchers interested in understanding more about media professionals and media production are outlined. Hall's (1974) seminal **encoding/decoding** model is described. Its significance lies in the fact that it stresses the need to understand the media message or text in terms of both production and reception. Just how this model has been applied towards understanding media coverage of false-memory syndrome and cloning is discussed. Two case studies from Irish and North American television are used as illustrations of how the broader production research model has been utilized to learn more about the workings of the media. The production research approach underlines the significance of understanding *context* as much as *text* in undertaking even rudimentary media analysis.

By examining the production context of media texts, their contents and how audiences subsequently read media texts, we have the potential to understand more fully the dynamics involved in both media production as a result of the activities of media professionals and in the production of meaning through audience interpretation. An appreciation of the production research approach will also be of significance when the media's role in the reproduction of dominant and other ideologies is discussed in Chapter 6. The approach suggests that we place our investigative gaze on the kinds of discourses employed by media professionals in their efforts to communicate with audiences in an increasingly diverse range of regional and cultural settings.

Two traditions

Two main and often overlapping strands of production research can be identified. The first concentrates on the media professional in terms of constraints, professional ideologies and work practices. The second is of a more textual orientation in that it attempts to combine an understanding of the former concerns with an in-depth analysis of a specific media text or texts. Thus, in many instances, researchers have 'worked backwards' from the 'finished media product' or text to investigate the internal and external forces on the media professional that may have shaped its content (see e.g. Devereux, 1998; Elliot, 1979; Shoemaker and Reese, 1996).

The production research approach is primarily concerned with understanding more about how the creativity or agency of the media professional is constrained by both organizational and external factors. The organizational factors might be, for example, the specific routines of production, ownership structure, editorial line, culture or ethos of a particular media organization. External factors might be, for example, the economic power of advertisers or sponsors, the laws and regulations imposed by the nation state concerning libel or defamation, or the willingness (or not) of the politically or economically powerful to cooperate in the production of certain kinds of media texts such as news reports, investigative documentaries or current affairs programmes. Negative audience response might also be considered to be a possible constraint. In the production research tradition that is more textual in orientation, there are strong echoes of the 'author–text' tradition in literary criticism and the attempts within media studies to understand the relationship between the media professional and his or her text.

Theoretical underpinnings of production research

Production research aims to understand more about media production and media professionals. Four main theoretical perspectives have predominated in the field, namely political economy, critical theory/neo-Marxism, feminism and liberal pluralism. All four inform our understanding of media production in different but complementary ways.

The political economy approach emphasizes the extent to which media production and media professionals are constrained by powerful political and economic forces. An increasing amount of media production is now undertaken in media organizations that are owned and controlled by global media conglomerates. While the globalization of media production may have a direct impact on the autonomy of individual media professionals, the qualitative shift evident in much media content and its commercialization has created new kinds of pressures and constraints. In the context of increased competition for audiences in the television sector, for example, one concrete example might be the pressure on media professionals to 'dumb down' the content of (or indeed replace altogether with lighter entertainment-focused programming) programme areas that might traditionally have been more critical or investigative in orientation. The practice of doing the 'And finally ...' story at the end of news bulletins means that even news bulletins on more 'serious' networks have embraced news values that emphasize the importance of celebrity, at the expense presumably of harder news. Increased competition and the need to deliver larger audiences in order to satisfy commercial interests are among the key underlying reasons for the increased amount of 'infotainment' and 'newzak' evident on mainstream television (see Franklin, 1997). Those within the political economy camp have also raised concerns about the restructuring of media production in terms of the day-to-day working conditions of media professionals. Changes in the ownership structure of media organizations and an increase in the casualization of media work have created a less stable and more pressurized environment for media workers. Technological changes and convergences in terms of ownership structures have also radically altered the way in which day-to-day media work is undertaken.

The critical theory or neo-Marxist approach to production research has a related set of concerns. The emphasis here is on the extent to which media professionals knowingly (or otherwise) engage in the production of **dominant ideology** in support of the ruling class or other dominant social groups. As you will see in Chapter 6, while there has been some degree of slippage in the traditional critical theory perspective – conceding that both media professionals and audiences can exercise some amount of agency in the production and reception of media texts – there remains a strong sense that, while alternative ideologies are evident within some media texts, the mainstream media tend to reproduce ideologies that are favourable to the politically and economically powerful in society. One way in which media professionals might be seen to do this is in the way that certain ideological positions are given privileged space within specific media texts, thus being accorded greater legitimacy. While audiences and media professionals are clearly capable of agency, the question of how and why dominant ideologies and discourses such as patriarchy, racism or homophobia continue to surface in many media texts and the role of media professionals in sustaining or challenging these ideologies remains a central question worthy of further study and debate.

The last quarter of the twentieth century witnessed a growing amount of production research written from a feminist perspective. In a large range of geographical territories, feminist media researchers have examined the experiences of female journalists working in the print and broadcast news media (Chambers et al., 2004; Van Zoonen, 1998). A starting point for this research has been how female journalists cope with working in what has traditionally been a male-dominated environment. Although an increasing number of women are working in the print and broadcast news media, there remains anxiety, for example, about the extent to which news values are still driven by what are perceived to be male concerns. Drawing upon the Dutch experience, the renowned feminist media scholar van Zoonen (1998) notes that more women are ending up in news journalism because the genre itself is changing in orientation, developing a stronger 'human interest' focus. Feminist research has restated the importance of examining the socialization of media professionals, their work practices and ideological positions.

The liberal pluralist perspective in contrast to both political economy and critical/Marxist approaches argues that media professionals are evidently not slaves to the demands of the ruling class or other dominant social groups. What we see in media content is a vast array of media messages, some of which are supportive of the status quo while others question it directly. The liberal pluralist point of view recognizes the complexity of media organizations and the agency or creativity of the media professionals who work in such organizations.

 A CLOSER LOOK 5.1 ....

What is production research?

Although media studies has been dominated in recent years by analyses of content (discourse) and audience reception, there is a long-standing tradition within media sociology of examining the world of the media professional and of the activities of news journalists in particular (Cottle, 2007; Grossberg et al., 2006; Hesmondhalgh, 2006; Tuchman, 1991). Historically, sociologists such as Weber and Park recognized the pivotal role played by journalists and editors in shaping our understanding and perceptions of the social world (Devereux, 1995). What has come to be known as the production research paradigm places the spotlight on the initial 'making' of media texts or messages. Drawing upon a range of ethnographic research methods, including interviews and **participant observation**, it investigates the culture of media organizations, the dynamics involved in 'gate-keeping', and the activities, experiences and ideologies of journalists and other media professionals (Gitlin, 1994; Philo, 2008). The paradigm seeks to explain how and why particular discourses, ideologies, templates or frames come to predominate within media coverage. Influenced, in the main, by organizational sociology and by theories of political economy (Fenton, 2007; Mosco and Wasko, 1988) in particular, the production research paradigm carries with it the promise of revealing more about the realities of doing media work; the constraints within which journalists and other media professionals operate and the intended meanings that are encoded into media texts (Hall, 1974). The production research paradigm acknowledges that the creativity or agency of media professionals such as journalists and reporters is constrained by a wide range of factors internal and external to their respective media organizations. Internal constraints might include the routines of production, ownership structure, editorial line, and the culture or ethos of a particular media organization. External constraints might include the economic power of advertisers or sponsors, the laws and regulations imposed by the state concerning libel or defamation, the willingness (or not) of the politically and economically powerful to cooperate in the production of certain kinds of media texts, and the potential for negative reaction from audience members (Shoemaker and Reese, 1996). The production research paradigm underlines the importance of understanding the conscious and unconscious practices that shape media work, and by extension how an insight into media practices has an importance in terms of how we ultimately understand the content and reception of media texts.

Methodological basis

Production research is usually described as being ethnographic. In terms of its methodological basis, the production research approach is predominantly qualitative. It has borrowed much from social anthropology, the sociology of organizations, the sociology of occupations and the sociology of art in seeking to understand more about the realities of media production. To date, researchers have largely concentrated upon the experiences of media professionals in the shape of journalists and reporters engaged in the making of news for the broadcast and print media. A smaller body of work – but by no means of any less significance – has examined the making of other types of television programmes such as drama and documentary series (see e.g. Newcomb, 1991). When researchers engage in production research they usually make use of a number of **qualitative research** methodologies. It is fair to describe the production research model as being a hybrid. The terms 'participant observation' and 'ethnography' are the ones most likely to be used in reference to this kind of research strategy (see Deacon et al., 1999b). In reality, production research typically involves the use of a wide range of research methodologies, such as observation, participant observation, interviews, case studies, archival research and detailed analyses of public and private documents. This research model is reliant upon achieving access to and cooperation from media professionals and media organizations. Depending on the research question, media professionals and media organizations can sometimes be reticent in allowing themselves to be observed or questioned by academic or student researchers. So, in line with other kinds of ethnographic research, once access is achieved, the building of trust between the researcher and those researched is crucial. The greatest strengths of production research are its flexibility and the potential it holds for shedding light on an otherwise hidden world. Production research may be demanding in terms of the amount of time spent doing fieldwork, but it has the promise to be one of the most rewarding kinds of media research. Those following this research path have, for example, observed television and news reporters in their everyday work situations; they have undertaken participant observation through working as junior reporters themselves; they have used formal, informal and retrospective interviewing techniques in order to see the world from the point of view of the media professional and especially as a means of gaining further insights into the content of 'finished' media products. Production research can be illuminating in that it can reveal much about the day-to-day realities of media production. Because it situates the media professional in an organizational context, it can shed light on the internal and external pressures and constraints that prevail upon media production. It can be useful in explaining why certain decisions were made and why certain production values pertain.

A CLOSER LOOK 5.2

Creativity and constraint: explaining structure and agency

Our behaviour as human beings takes place in a social context. All of us are influenced by the dynamic generated between what sociologists term 'structure' and 'agency'. As members of society our viewpoints, attitudes, opinions and ultimately our behaviour are shaped by both **structure and agency**. The tension between both is at the core of what sociology is all about and is of vital importance in terms of understanding the workings of the mass media. Bilton et al. (1997) define structures as 'constructed frameworks and patterns of organization which in some way, constrain or direct human behaviour' (1997: 8), while agency, on the other hand, 'implies that actors have the freedom to create, change and influence events' (1997: 13). We are constrained by the social context in which we find ourselves but we are also capable of independent action as a result of reflection and growing self-awareness. Family, schooling and the media have undoubtedly shaped your understanding of gender roles, for example. You are not, however, a prisoner to the kinds of roles laid out for you in the social context in which you find yourself. You can exercise agency when you resist or reject the 'script' as laid out in the patriarchal view of the social world. Our task is to recognize the duality of both structure and agency in human behaviour. While we are constrained by social structures we are also clearly capable of transcending these constraints through independent agency or action. Within media analysis the relationship between structure and agency is especially important when we come to examine media professionals and media audiences. Media professionals such as print or broadcast journalists work in specific organizational contexts, each of which has its own constraints in terms of how media work is shaped. Audiences in turn may be influenced by media content but are quite capable of exercising considerable agency in their interpretation of media texts.

? Stop and think 5.1

Structure and agency

Apply the concepts of structure and agency to your immediate experience. What sorts of things constrain you? When do you have agency? Do you think that it is possible to ever really overcome those things (e.g. norms, values, attitudes, laws, rules) that constrain us?

Plate 5.1   **The production research approach invites us to examine the initial 'making' of media texts. It suggests that we need to go behind the scenes in order to understand more fully the tension between 'structure' and 'agency' evident in the creation of media texts such as news programming. Photograph reproduced by kind permission of Sky News (London) 2006 ©.**

Read on! 5.1   Alienation and exclusion in journalism

Kyung-Hee Kim (2006) 'Alienation and exclusion mechanisms in production' from 'Obstacles to the success of female journalists in Korea', *Media, Culture & Society*, 28(1): 124–41, pp. 126–7 and 130.

The alienation of female journalists can be investigated either at the level of the news organization or at the personal level. First, when investigating it from the organizational level, the marginalization of female journalists is the best example to show how they are alienated in a patriarchal and capitalist society. This ... defines the marginalization of females as the state in which they are put at the margin, far away from the power that decides on the strategic direction of an organization, while men are put at the centre of the organization. Generally, power is defined as an agent's potential influence over the attitudes and behavior of one or more designated target persons (Yukl, 1994). When considering the social meaning of the news, the most important power in the newsroom is the power to decide editorial direction, and to influence the course of editorial direction. ...

At the personal level, the alienation of females appears as a form of dissatisfaction with their work, or a low level of the sense of belonging to their organization. The most fundamental reason for the alienated state of females is the capitalist patriarchal structure. That is, the capitalist patriarchies make the mechanisms of exclusion work, which cause the alienation of females in the news production process. ...

The exclusion mechanisms within the news organization are those that alienate female journalists from the organization they belong to, that is, the mechanisms that derive from working in a male-centred system within the newsroom. The exclusion mechanisms in news gathering are external, and reject females in contexts outside the newsroom. Communication occurs through social networks and there is a tendency to ignore females in Korean society, so that some areas are not so easy for female journalists to report on as for male reporters. The exclusion mechanisms in the private area are those deriving from family issues which prevent females from living the life of a journalist. These exclusion mechanisms can function as the source of alienation of female journalists from the public area. ...

Informal communication is defined as communication that takes place between journalists and sources in an informal setting. In Korea, much important information is shared in a bar or a public bath rather than in an office. Since most of the news sources are male, it is difficult for female journalists to participate in male public baths or late night meetings in bars in order to obtain information. Informal communication, therefore, plays a central role as a mechanism that excludes females from the news production process.

▶

Stop and think 5.2

1. According to Kim (2006) what sorts of factors work to exclude women working in the field of journalism?

2. Kim's (2006) work is focused on Korea. To what extent would her arguments apply to female journalists working in your home country?

3. Kim's (2006) approach is to go beyond the personal and to examine how the wider organizational context works to exclude female journalists. Are you convinced by the evidence presented in this extract as to how unequal power relationships manifest themselves in an organizational setting?

Hall's encoding/decoding model

Stuart Hall's (1974) celebrated and highly influential essay 'The television discourse: encoding and decoding' suggests that we examine both the production and the reception of media messages. The encoding/decoding model as described by Hall argues that in the communicative exchange we need to pay attention to the production of media message(s) by media professionals and examine the subsequent readings that audiences place upon such messages. For as Hall says: 'the symbolic form of the message has a privileged position in the communicative exchange: and ... the moments of "encoding" and "decoding", though "relatively autonomous" in relation to the communicative process as a whole, are determinate moments' (1974: 8).

Hall's model runs counter to both effects and content analysis models of media research and instead situates the communicative exchange in a broader set of cultural, economic, historical, ideological, organizational, political and social contexts. If we wish to understand, for example, how a media message works or doesn't work at an ideological or at a discursive level we have to explore the codes and conventions employed by media professionals in the initial making of the media message and its subsequent decoding by audience members.

Hall's model allows for a certain amount of 'openness' in the media message. However, the reading or decoding of the message takes place in a social context where individual audience members occupy unequal positions of power and have the capacity to accept, adapt or reject media messages.

The encoding/decoding model outlines four main codes that are utilized in the production of meaning by media professionals and media audiences. These are the dominant/hegemonic code, the professional code, the negotiated code, and the oppositional code.

Media professionals encode a preferred or intended meaning into a media message such as a television news report or current affairs programme. If audience members interpret or decode the message in accordance with the intended or preferred meaning they are said in Hall's terms to be 'operating inside the dominant code' (1974: 10). The professional code refers to the conventions that media professionals use in order to encode meaning within the media message. Hall is referring here to the production techniques that are employed to tell a story in a particular way whilst remaining within the confines of the dominant code. Typically, audience members use a negotiated code when making sense of media messages. According to Hall:

> Decoding within the negotiated version contains a mixture of adaptive and oppositional elements: it acknowledges the legitimacy of the hegemonic definitions to make grand significations, while, at a more restricted level, it makes its own ground-rules, it operates with 'exceptions' to the rule. It accords the privileged position to the dominant definition of events, whilst reserving the right to make a more negotiated application to 'local conditions', to its own more corporate situation. (1974: 14)

An audience member operating within the negotiated code might accept the broad thrust of a specific media message and yet either adapt or reject elements of the overall message because it does not fit with their own immediate experience of the world. Finally, the oppositional code refers to the capacity of audience members to reject outright the preferred or intended meaning of a media message. Audience members who engage in an oppositional decoding recognize but ultimately reject the preferred or intended meaning as signified through the use of the dominant or hegemonic code.

 ## Do it! 5.1 Applying Hall's encoding/decoding model

Record a television news report on a subject of your own choice. See if you can identify its professional and dominant codes. In examining the text closely do you think that there is much scope within the text to allow for a negotiated reading? What role does the text (and by extension its creators) play in allowing for a negotiated position to be adopted?

Key thinker 5.1 Stuart Hall

Stuart Hall was born in Kingston, Jamaica in 1932 and emigrated to Britain in 1951. He has made a major contribution to intellectual and public life in Britain and beyond. Hall served as Director of the now defunct Centre for Contemporary Cultural Studies at the University of Birmingham and as Professor of Sociology at The Open University. More recently, Hall has been involved with the Runnymede Trust, which is concerned with examining the shape of a multi-ethnic Britain. His professional life has been characterized by serious engagement with questions surrounding unequal power relationships in terms of class, ethnicity/race and gender. Renowned as the person who coined the phrase 'Thatcherism', as a neo-Marxist, Hall has been equally critical of the British Conservative Party and Blair's 'New' Labour project. Hall's scholarly output has been voluminous. His writings on media and ideology, ethnicity, race and racism, and multiculturalism, as well as the concept of moral panic, have been highly influential. His most cited work within media and cultural studies is his famous essay 'Encoding and decoding in the media discourse' (1974). As we note in this chapter, Hall's work reminds us that the media do not simply *reflect* 'reality'; they are actively involved in *constructing* it. Such construction is never neutral, reflecting as it does the ideas of the dominant social class or group. Foremost in Hall's work is the contention that ideological struggle is real and in evidence within media discourse. Hall's key publications include *The Hard Road to Renewal* (1988) and *Resistance Through Rituals* (with T. Jefferson) (1993) (see Davis, 2004; Proctor, 2004).

Applying Hall's encoding/decoding model (1)

'From inception to reception: the natural history of a news item' by David Deacon, Natalie Fenton and Alan Bryman (Deacon et al., 1999a) is an important example of media research that seeks to combine the analysis of production and reception. Restating the significance of Hall's (1974) encoding/decoding model of media analysis, the authors examine the 'natural history' of a British broadsheet newspaper article concerning the phenomenon of 'false memory' in cases of sexual and other forms of abuse (see, *Guardian*, 13 January 1995, 'Psychologists guarded on "false memory" of abuse'). This research project is a telling example of 'the benefits that can accrue from a research focus that isn't solely fixated with the distinctiveness of decoding and which retains the holism of the original encoding/decoding formulation' (Deacon et al., 1999a: 6). The case study examines the production, content and reception of the newspaper article. It begins by investigating the inception and production of the article, focusing on the interactions that took place between a range of individual and institutional sources with news professionals. The authors discuss the article's content as well as its decoding by a wide range of social groups. The author of the article in question was interviewed and audience reception was examined by means of holding 14 focus group interviews. The audience groups discussed a wide range of news items as well as the specific article.

The authors argue that the 'preferred reading' of the text 'wasn't created by the journalist, but constituted by the source given most privileged access' (i.e. the British Psychological Society) (Deacon et al., 1999a: 25). Furthermore, they argue that their research:

> adds further support to those who argue that there are dangers in overstating the interpretative freedom of the audience from textual confines (see, for example, Murdock, 1989). The details reveal a marked consistency between intended meaning at the point of production and audience understanding and interpretation of the text. This is not to say that audience members passively deferred to the text – on the contrary, we found substantial evidence of independent thought and scepticism. However, the 'distinctiveness of decoding' in this instance occurred at the evaluative rather than interpretative level. Resistance to the message did not lead to a renegotiation of it. It was interrogated not expanded. (1999a: 26)

Applying Hall's encoding/decoding model (2)

In February 1997 the print and broadcast media in Britain reported that the Scottish-based Roslin Institute had successfully cloned a Finn Dorset sheep from a somatic cell. Reputedly called after the country and western singer Dolly Parton, 'Dolly the Sheep' became the focus of intense news media coverage in which specific concerns were raised about the implications this development might have for human cloning. The Dolly story was one of a number of instances of cloning which attracted media interest in the late 1990s and represents an important example of media coverage of scientific and ethical matters. In an exemplary study, Holliman (2004) examines the production, content and reception of media coverage of cloning. His research is governed by three interrelated questions. How was cloning represented within media coverage? What sources were used? What memories and understandings do audience members have of the coverage? His detailed study combines quantitative and **qualitative content analysis** of print and broadcast media and semi-structured interviews with media professionals and a representative of the Roslin Institute, as well as **focus group** interviews with audience members. Holliman's (2004) detailed content analysis is based upon a sample from television news and broadsheet, tabloid and 'mid-market' newspapers over a two-year period. The media professionals involved in covering the story were identified and interviewed. In addition to exploring how scientific issues were covered by individual media professionals, the interviews focused specifically on their use of sources. A representative from the Roslin Institute was also interviewed in order to understand more about the organization's own media strategy in attracting media interest in the issue of cloning. The reception analysis was based upon six group interviews which were subdivided in terms of gender, geographical region and knowledge of science. The group interviews used a combination of research strategies in order to understand more about the participants and their memory of media coverage of cloning. The participants were asked to complete a short questionnaire and to write headlines in order to demonstrate how they thought the media represented cloning. They then took part in the news game exercise in which they were asked to write a news bulletin. The focus groups concluded with a semi-structured discussion and a second questionnaire. Holliman's (2004) findings show how cloning was represented by the media through the use of specific frames and templates. He notes that:

> The coverage made regular use of science fiction references, associating Aldous Huxley's novel *Brave New World*, Mary Shelley's *Frankenstein* and the film *The Boys from Brazil* with cloning experiments. As previous researchers have suggested … by drawing on these dystopian visions, these cultural references framed the coverage in a negative light. (2004: 118)

Holliman's reception analysis demonstrates a clear link between media coverage of cloning and audience understandings of the issues. Furthermore, he provides a convincing example of how analyses of production, content and reception can be usefully combined in order to reach a more thorough understanding of the mass media's role in the social construction of reality.

 Stop and think 5.3

The changing world of media work

Conglomeration and technological developments have radically altered how media work is now undertaken. Why is it more important than ever that we have a critical understanding of the constraints being imposed upon media professionals?

? Stop and think 5.4

News journalists and 'objectivity'

News journalists often describe their professional activities as being 'objective' and 'neutral' in terms of how they report on events (see Skovsgaard et al., 2013). Many describe their work as being merely a mirror of what is going on in the wider world or as being a first draft of history. In your own experience of print, broadcast and online news journalism are these realistic assessments? Can news journalism ever be value-free? How might a production research approach deepen your understanding of the professional ideologies and work practices of media professionals?

Read on! 5.2   From Buerk to Band Aid

Greg Philo (1993) 'From Buerk to Band Aid', in John Eldridge (ed.), *Getting the Message*. London: Routledge, pp. 113–14.

News organizations

A good reason for covering a story is that someone else might do it before you. There were strong suggestions in 1984 that such concerns had influenced the BBC's decision to go into Ethiopia. ... Competition between channels can mean that they will all suddenly pursue a story if it is judged to be sufficiently important, or in different circumstances it can mean that some organizations will reject the story if they decide that it has already been covered by their competitors. Television is so competitive that even bulletins on the same channel compete with each other over the treatment of specific stories. Michael Buerk told us how this had affected the treatment of his second report from Ethiopia. The *Six O'Clock News* on the BBC had led with the story as a six-minute piece, giving it maximum impact. By contrast, the *Nine O'Clock News* had downgraded the story to fourth position and led with a story on the continuing British miners' strike, which was then in its seventh month. Buerk commented to us that:

> The *Nine O'Clock News* began on some minor accretion in the miners' strike of no consequence and [the Ethiopian report] was the fourth story

on the *Nine O'Clock News*. The *Six O'Clock News* was intended to be a programme rather than simply a bulletin – so their instinct was that if they had a big story, to go to town on it. There are rivalries between the bulletins and possibly [the *Nine O'Clock News* editor] thought that he had better be different.

Even with the *Six O'Clock News*, the decision to use the Buerk/Amin piece first was not immediate. By chance, it was a slack news day, but even then there was a discussion about whether to use other possible lead stories. John Simpson of the BBC … commented that 'We could have led with any of a handful of fairly substantial stories … in the end it was decided to try an imaginative lead' (cited in Magistead, 1986). Mike Wooldridge's radio report fared worse. He had filed it while the team was still in Ethiopia. It was a strong report but was not even given peak time exposure as it did not receive the necessary support in London (Harrison and Palmer, 1986: 121).

 ## Stop and think 5.5

1. How important are both inter- and intra-media competitiveness in reaching a better understanding of how editorial decisions are made?

2. From the perspective of media organizations the Third World appears to be less newsworthy. What factors might explain this?

Ethnographic research on media production and media professionals

Devils and Angels by Eoin Devereux

In *Devils and Angels* Devereux (1998) examines how the Irish radio and television public service broadcasting organization Radio Telefís Éireann (RTÉ) portrays poverty on its two television networks. Drawing upon a neo-Marxist theoretical position, the study uses a combination of qualitative content analysis and an ethnography – undertaken over a period of two years – in investigating how RTÉ's news, current affairs, serialized drama and telethon programmes construct poverty stories. In addition to content analysis, the study makes extensive use of the views, opinions and perspectives of media professionals involved in the production of television texts about Irish poverty. Observation, participant observation and a variety of interviewing styles are used to gain insights into the thinking of media professionals and the constraints both inside and outside the media organization under which they operate. The study uses a range of explanations – biographical, economic, ideological, organizational and production value oriented – in arguing that the television coverage in question reproduces a dominant ideological account of poverty.

Access to the media organization and to individual departments had to be negotiated and trust had to be established with those being studied. The researcher was given permission to observe all the weekly planning meetings in current affairs and the daily planning meetings in news, as well as being allowed to actively participate in the television station's biannual fund-raising telethon programme. Semi-structured and informal interviews were undertaken with media professionals at all levels of the production process. Devereux recalls:

> In my observation and unstructured interviews I had discovered evidence of intra-organizational conflict over the content of particular poverty stories. The semi-structured interviews were used to gain further information on these disputes and to compare the accounts of individual informants. These interviews helped in constructing a deeper understanding of the production processes which surrounded the making of poverty texts. They helped in validation and clarification of data gathered through both observation and participant observation. (1998: 153)

The participant observation dimension of the ethnography proved to be particularly fruitful. Covert participant observation was used in order to understand the background production processes of the People in Need telethon. The researcher worked as a volunteer (along with approximately 100 other volunteers) for the station's Variety Department, which was responsible for the programme's production. He adopted two potentially conflicting roles in undertaking participant observation. Devereux (1998) states that:

> From past knowledge of previous Telethons I correctly anticipated that there would be protests from an unemployment action group at the gates of RTÉ. During a two-hour break from my role as a runner on the Telethon programme, I managed to join the protestors to hear about their perspective on the event. As a protester, I witnessed how the police treated those on the picket line as well as gathering first hand information about their views. My main role however was that of runner for the event itself. This task involved the collection and delivery of faxes donating money to the programme's fund. It allowed me direct access to the broadcast and production studios. Even in the context of a busy fourteen-hour programme I found that this type of covert observation was useful in terms of furthering my understanding of the making of the Telethon programme. (1998: 154)

The close critical reading of specific media texts undertaken in the qualitative content analysis was strengthened further through regular contact with those who created the texts in the first place. The production research approach allowed the author to ask questions about the many constraints involved in covering what is potentially a controversial social and political issue. It provided insights into the use of particular kinds of production values and it shed light on how the media professionals in question viewed audience perceptions of poverty and other social problems. The study highlights the interplay between structure and agency in the creation of media texts from a variety of television genres. Ethnography of this kind allows the media professional to explain his or her intentions and may tell us much about how they perceive the media audience. One of the interviewees in the study who produced a contentious television documentary about Irish poverty argued that his documentary was: 'designed to do something dangerous ... it was designed to make people uncomfortable' (1998: 58). In the producer's words: 'The intention was to fling it at the audience and say, "You, there! Are you sitting comfortably? And if so, should you be thinking about what is going on around you, and why are you sitting comfortably when others aren't?"' (1998: 58).

As an illustration of the production research approach Devereux's (1998) study attempts to explain ideological content by reference to how media professionals structure meaning. The study is quite traditional in its orientation in that it does not consider how television audiences variously decode stories about poverty.

Inside Prime Time by Todd Gitlin

The controversial decision by the CBS television network to axe the critically acclaimed *Lou Grant* series in 1982 is the starting point for Gitlin's (1994) classic production research study *Inside Prime Time*. CBS's decision typified for Gitlin the interplay between power, politics and decision making within prime-time network entertainment television. Gitlin tells us that he embarked upon this ambitious project with:

> a question – or rather a curiosity – about how much a show's commercial success depended on its 'fit' with social trends abroad in the land. I also started with the notion that what sometimes gives commercial television its weird vitality, perhaps even its profitability, is its ability to borrow, transform – and deform – the energy of social and psychological conflict. Sometimes network television seemed to succeed in packaging images that drew upon unresolved tensions in the society. Cramming these tensions into the domesticated frame of the sitcom and the action-adventure, television whether 'realist' or 'escapist' clearly bore some relation to the real world of popular desire and fear. (1994: 12)

Gitlin starts out with the intention of examining closely how American prime-time network television fares in its treatment of social issues. Although some media analysts might question the wisdom of concentrating on popular television and its representation of social reality, Gitlin defends his decision by saying that:

network television did seem to track some version of social reality. But whose? It began to dawn on me that I could not hope to understand why network television was what it was unless I understood who put the images on the small screen and for what reasons. (1994: 13)

What follows is a hugely detailed analysis of the ideological role of the television entertainment industry in capitalist society. The work has been hailed by many as one of the most comprehensive production research studies ever undertaken (see Newcomb, 1991). Gitlin combines detailed textual analysis of prime-time entertainment television with secondary data in the form of television ratings alongside extensive primary data drawn from hundreds of interviews with network executives, producers, writers, agents, actors and others.

Given his interest in the ideological aspects of popular media representations of social reality, Gitlin tells us that he 'wanted to see whether the industry "knew" what "it" was doing when it came up with these images' (1994: 13). How do media professionals and media organizations come to agree on what is an 'acceptable' representation of race, class or poverty issues, for example, in a television series like *Hill Street Blues*? What happens when there are disagreements? What sorts of commercial and other pressures are brought to bear on scriptwriters, producers and directors, for example? Gitlin's decision to take a production research approach allows him the opportunity to attempt to answer these questions, and at the very least it allows him to document the kinds of tensions involved in the making of prime-time television.

Gitlin's fieldwork was based upon creating an opportunity sample among a wide range of media professionals. He was allowed to observe the production of specific series on the set and he witnessed at first-hand how scripts changed and developed in response to industry and other pressures. Gitlin reports that those interviewed spoke freely to him and a majority of his interviewees spoke 'on the record'. It was his intention to give a detailed ethnography of the media industry 'as it is lived' by media professionals. At an early stage of his fieldwork he quickly realized that it was a mistake to compartmentalize how media professionals treat 'social issues', as their views on these questions are inseparable from how they see anything else.

At a methodological level the strength of this study is its sheer depth of analysis. By choosing the ethnographic path Gitlin was able to check for consistencies and inconsistencies in his interview data. It allowed him to witness events as they happened on set and to have a fuller picture of the outcomes of specific controversies concerning programme content.

In three parts, *Inside Prime Time* begins by examining how the television industry attempts to control both the supply of and the demand for its products. Part one examines how networks try to achieve a maximum audience through an investigation of programme testing, audience ratings, demographic and schedule calculations, and self-imitation. Part two examines how the networks depend on major suppliers and agents for products. Gitlin describes the activities of networks and producers in the creation of television 'docudrama' movies, focusing specifically on how they deal with political controversy. Part three illustrates how network decision making about prime-time television series is shaped by politics. Here, Gitlin considers 'national political trends (both badly and well understood), the crusade of the fundamentalist right, and the normal political weight of advertisers' (1994: 15).

In the light of these concerns *Inside Prime Time* concludes with a thorough analysis of the hit television series *Hill Street Blues*. We get an extraordinarily detailed account of the creation of the series. Gitlin documents the tensions between the NBC television network and those involved in the conception and actual making of *Hill Street Blues*. As if to contradict the television industry's 'rational system of production' approach as described in the study's first section, *Hill Street Blues* bucked the usual trends in terms of prime-time television programme structure. It had a larger than usual number of central characters and its script structure was atypical. Gitlin recalls the many pressures that were brought to bear on the programme's creators, such as the attempts to curtail the sex scenes between two of the principal characters. (1994: 299) The internal constraints on the programme makers are amply demonstrated. Gitlin writes that:

> Sometimes, for example, someone in NBC's Current Programming department might object to something in the rough cut, which is the first stage of the assembled film. The producers could finesse such objections by counting on the inefficiency of the organization. 'It's amazing how much they don't know about film,' said Michael Kozoll. 'You say to them, you know, "That's just the rough cut; it will be smoothed and fixed." By the time they see the [late-stage] answer print, they don't remember any more.' There were simply too many shows and not enough time to police them. The network's desire to control the show was defeated by organizational overload, by inefficiency, and also by ignorance. 'They didn't know what they wanted,' said a delighted and relieved Kozoll. 'You'd go to meetings and say, Yeah, yeah, yeah, and go off and do what you want. If you did everything they wanted you'd end up in Cedars of Sinai – do they have a psychiatric ward?' (1994: 304)

Gitlin's conclusions are quite bleak. At best, one witnesses the prevalence of a liberal rather than a critical ideological framework within the content of popular television entertainment series such as *Hill Street Blues*. Many of his informants believe that there are no easy solutions to social problems and this viewpoint is shown to be reproduced within media content. As Newcomb (1991) comments: 'For Gitlin, television entertainment is a debased form of expression growing from, and contributing to, a social and political world already debased by consumer capitalism. The result in the television industry is a non-critical, indeed celebratory acceptance of "recombinative" art suggesting "cultural exhaustion"' (1991: 97).

? Stop and think 5.6

How do media professionals 'know' their audiences?

The era of media globalization poses new questions about the relationship(s) between media professionals and media audiences. Other than ratings or sales figures, or perhaps audience response through email, Facebook, Twitter, texting or interactive satellite television, how do media professionals who produce globally distributed media texts gauge audience interest and response to their texts?

Read on! 5.3   Media organization roles

Pamela J. Shoemaker and Stephen D. Reese (1996) *Mediating the Message: Theories of Influences on Mass Media Content.* Boston, MA: Longman, pp. 151–3.

Institutional position greatly determines the power vested in a role, although this power does not stem entirely from one's position in the organization chart. Lower ranking employees may have special expertise or other means to thwart directives from the top, often making negotiation and compromise necessary.

Media Organization Structure

Given this basic outline, there are any number of variations in the ways these roles can be combined and structured with organizations. The power associated with organization roles and the relationships between them vary both across and within media. Organization structure has a pervasive, if not readily identifiable, effect on media content.

In a typical newspaper organization a publisher runs the entire organization, which comprises the news, editorial, advertising, circulation and production departments. A glance at the masthead of most papers reveals their top management. At the *New York Times*, for example, Publisher Arthur Ochs Sulzberger oversees the editor of the paper and the president, who in turn oversees the vice-presidents in charge of operations, production, advertising, finance/human resources, systems, and circulation. ...

Regardless of the medium, the ultimate power lies in ownership. In most companies, stock ownership entitles one to vote for directors on the board that runs the company. Top management is either part of the board or accountable to it. That stock may be broadly owned or controlled by one family or a few large investors. The *New York Times* is a good example of how ownership can be structured to ensure the autonomy and control of a media organization. The *Times* is part of the New York Times Company, a $1.7 billion enterprise, which also owns other newspapers, magazines and broadcasting companies. The paper has remained in the hands of descendants of Adolph S. Ochs, who purchased the paper in 1891, earning for itself a strong reputation as an independent and leading voice among the news media. Recognizing the importance of ownership, Ochs distributed company stock such that voting rights and control remain within the family (the Sulzbergers), and thus management is not subject to pressures from outside stockholders and threats of corporate takeovers. Furthermore, a stockholders' agreement among the trustees prevents them from selling, merging or giving up control of the company.

 ## Stop and think 5.7

1. In your opinion how do ownership structures relate to media content?

2. What do Shoemaker and Reese (1996) understand by the relationship between organizational roles and views or perspectives?

3. Compare Shoemaker and Reese (1996) with Kim (2006) ('Read on! 5.1') – are both extracts in agreement about the importance of understanding power relationships within media organizations as a precursor to understanding the content produced?

···(A CLOSER LOOK 5.3)··

Citizens as producers: the case of Indymedia

Indymedia is the best-known recent example of citizen journalism (see Atton, 2002; Downing, 1988, 2001; Rodriguez, 2001). It follows in the footsteps of a much longer tradition of counter-hegemonic or radical journalism (Atton, 2002) and is best understood in terms of the wider context of what Carroll and Hackett (2006) refer to as 'democratic media activism'.

Founded in Seattle in 1999, as a global network of independent media centres, Indymedia was comprised of 190 affiliated groups by 2006. Coyer (2005) describes Indymedia as a '… global online network' which is made up of 'local autonomous Indymedia organisations around the world offering "grassroots non-corporate coverage" of major protests and issues relevant to the anti-capitalist, peace and social justice movements' (2005: 34).

It is no accident that Indymedia has most presence in the USA, where many community-based activists have raised concerns about the ideological orientation of media content produced by the mainstream multimedia conglomerates. The core philosophy of Indymedia is one of participatory democracy whereby activists and ordinary citizens can themselves become the producers of media content that is freely available. Constituent media organizations should ideally be democratic and non-hierarchical in structure (Platon and Deuze, 2003: 345).

The independent media centres that make up this global network are involved in the production of audio, video, print and web-based content (see http://www.indymedia.org/). Independently produced content is disseminated via public access television and radio networks, video and newsletters as well as the internet. Indymedia use an open-publishing system whereby activists and ordinary citizens can contribute and/or edit content. Blogs, email and discussion forums are also used to highlight particular events or issues.

Indymedia has been a phenomenal success, with many elements of the mainstream media relying upon it for information during the various G8 summits held since its foundation in 1999. Indymedia has had a particular interest in monitoring the World Trade Organization as well as the (non)implementation of the Kyoto protocol concerning emissions that are damaging to the environment. As an indication of its success, Platon and Deuze (2003) note that 'During the 1999 protests, the IMC site in Seattle had an average of two and a half million viewers every two hours. This high figure doubled during the protests in Genoa in 2002' (2003: 339).

Indymedia has understandably attracted an amount of attention from media scholars. Following in the path of previous researchers interested in media production, Coyer (2005) interviewed participants in a community-based media project. She also drew upon her own involvement with an Indymedia project. Eliasoph (1988), similarly, engaged in participant observation in a US-based radio station that produced counter-hegemonic content, a research strategy replicated by Platon and Deuze (2003), who participated in the generation of web-based news content for an alternative news organization.

Two key issues come to mind when considering Indymedia. Given its commitment to open publishing, how is content controlled? What editorial guidelines are in place and how are these administered? What happens, for example, if racist, homophobic or sexist content is posted to the Indymedia open source newswire site? Is Indymedia any different from the mainstream in terms of how content is controlled?

Platon and Deuze's (2003) ethnographic study of Indymedia suggests that clear tensions exist between the network's technical personnel and its editorial team. One of their informants stated:

> … in the beginning there was a kind of editorial group … Although the word 'editorial' was kind of forbidden (laughs, coughs). But it is simply an editorial team. Because the big shameful secret now about IMC is that the tech guys are running the show. And we have these editorial boards and these editorial practices and shit. And very few of tech guys actually know what the editorial team has decided, and feels … feels like implementing it. (2003: 347)

Indymedia's editorial guidelines disallow postings to its newswire which incite hatred, are fascist, racist, sexist or homophobic in orientation. Platon and Deuze's (2003) account of Indymedia's editorial practices suggests that content propagating hate against specific individuals or groups is discussed by the editorial team and 'hidden'. Content is hidden by removing it from Indymedia's newswire service and placing it on another part of the Indymedia website with an editorial disclaimer.

CHAPTER LINK

See Chapter 9 for an insight into the debate concerning new media and social media.

A CLOSER LOOK 5.4

Free Speech TV

Based in Boulder, Colorado, Free Speech TV is an interesting example of independent media production focused on the coverage of issues that are considered 'alternative' by the mainstream media. Founded in 1995, Free Speech TV broadcasts to a potential audience of 37 million homes. It is available online, on satellite (on the Dish Network) and via 177 community cable stations in the USA. Its programming content deals with a variety of issues concerning, for example, the war in Iraq, AIDS/HIV, the gay/lesbian/bisexual/transgendered community and immigrant, workers and women's rights, etc. While production values can be variable, the channel's programming content serves as a powerful example of counter-hegemonic media activism. It is worth noting that the decision to allow community groups access to between 4% and 7% of airtime on satellite channels was as a result of a ruling by the state body, the Federal Communications Commission. See https://www.freespeech.org/

Plate 5.2   **Free Speech TV: an example of alternative media production.**
Reproduced with kind permission Free Speech TV © 2013.

Conclusion

Although not as prominent in recent times as reception or content analyses of
the mass media, production research remains a dynamic, exciting and essential
area of media research. The emergence of new forms of media production
whereby activists (and ordinary audience members) become media producers
(or **prosumers**) in their own right raises interesting questions for production
research. What sorts of constraints operate within the alternative media
movement? To what extent do independent producers have greater agency
than their counterparts who typically work full-time in the media industry
(see Platon and Deuze, 2003)? While it has been noted in this chapter that
this research approach has focused heavily on news journalists as a discrete
category of media professional – and by extension the research literature
has been dominated by analyses of news production and the newsroom –
production research retains the potential to reveal a great deal about media
professionals and media production in general. By adopting, as this textbook
does, an approach that examines the totality of the communicative exchange,
we need to pay sufficient attention to the production context of media texts.

The production research approach, with its emphasis on the tensions between the creativity of media professionals and the constraints under which they operate, is an important first step in this regard. Analyses of the content and reception of a wide range of media genres informed by a production research approach hold the potential for a more truly holistic and critical understanding of the media, perhaps even more so at a time of radical change within the media industries.

Chapter summary

1. This chapter emphasizes the continued importance of understanding media production and media organizations. It suggests that we need to examine the forces which shape the initial making of a media text, whether by media professionals or by citizen journalists and others.

2. Understanding the interplay between structure and agency is at the core of understanding media production and the resultant media texts.

3. Stuart Hall's encoding/decoding model continues to represent an important paradigm in furthering our understanding of the relationship between the producers of media content and audience reception. Hall's model proposes a number of codes which help explain audience reception, namely the dominant code, the oppositional code and the negotiated code.

4. Media production in the alternative media sector is not free of constraints.

5. A range of qualitative methods broadly defined as ethnographic are used in researching media production.

6. Some theorists have re-framed audiences as produsers or prosumers. While the possibilities now afforded to (some) audience members is obviously to be welcomed – especially in terms of radical political activism – the reconfiguration of audiences as produsers or prosumers is also an unprecedented source of free labour for transnational media conglomerates – a theme which we will address in detail in Chapter 9 on new media/social media.

Further reading

Davis, H. (2004) *Understanding Stuart Hall*. London: Sage Publications. Davis's book provides an accessible introduction to Stuart Hall.

Domingo, D. and C. Paterson (eds) (2011) *Making Online News: Newsroom Ethnographies in the Second Decade of Internet Journalism*. New York: Peter Lang. This fascinating book contains a dozen ethnographic essays from a wide variety of geographical locations (including Asia, Europe, the USA and Africa) which illuminate the realities of newsmaking in a digitally converged media environment.

Hesmondhalgh, D. (2013) *The Cultural Industries*, 3rd edn. London: Sage Publications. Hesmondhalgh's book is *essential* reading for students of media. It critically examines changes and continuities within the cultural industries. With a particular focus on unequal power relationships, Hesmondhalgh convincingly shows how the cultural industries '... make and circulate products that influence our knowledge, understanding and experience (texts); their role as systems for the management of creativity and knowledge; and their effects as agents of economic, social and cultural change' (2013: 4).

Howley, K. (2005) *Community Media: People, Places and Communications Technologies*. Cambridge: Cambridge University Press. Howley investigates the emergence of grassroots media, focusing on street newspapers, radio and cable television.

Kitty, A. (2005) *Don't Believe It! How Lies Become News*. New York: The Disinformation Company. This highly entertaining book takes you behind the scenes of everyday journalism. It firmly debunks the myths of journalistic neutrality and objectivity.

Online reading

Go to the companion website and read the following:

- Usher, N. (2013) '*Marketplace* public radio and news routines reconsidered: between structures and agents'. *Journalism*, 14(6): 807–22.
- Willig, I. (2013) 'Newsroom ethnography in a field perspective', *Journalism*, 14(3): 372–87.

CHAPTER 6

Media, Ideology and Discourse

Chapter overview

This chapter introduces you to the following:

- The key concepts of ideology, dominant ideology, hegemony and discourse
- How these concepts have been applied towards furthering our understanding of the media's ideological role in contemporary societies
- The debate between those who favour and those who oppose the continued use of the concepts of ideology and dominant ideology in undertaking media analysis
- A tripartite methodological approach to ideological analysis of the media that gives equal recognition to the production, content and reception of media texts.
- An approach to ideological analysis that sees the concepts of ideology and discourse working together in a complementary way, thus furthering our understanding of the mass media's role in perpetuating unequal power relationships
- The importance of language and its use in a media setting
- The significance of media language (in all its guises) in reproducing and perpetuating ideologies.

Key concepts

- Ideology
- Hegemony
- Dominant ideology
- Asymmetrical or unequal relations of power
- Counter-hegemonic

(Continued)

- Content analysis
- Discourse
- Discursive formation
- Linguistic
- Hermeneutic
- 'Reading against the grain'
- Audience resistance
- Neo-liberalism

Introduction

The social world continues to be characterized by the persistence of unequal relations of power, especially in terms of class, ethnicity and gender. Inequalities between men and women, between the social classes and between different ethnic groups – either singly or more usually in one or other combination – are just a few of the many kinds of inequalities that currently exist. Added to these are numerous material inequalities that exist on a global scale between the so-called 'developing' and 'developed' worlds that result in absolute poverty, hunger, suffering and death. The question as to what role the media play in either sustaining or challenging these and other unequal relations of power through the reproduction of ideology has had a long and difficult history within social theory generally and within media studies in particular. When media sociologists and others investigate the media's ideological role they are essentially interested in the degree to which media content shapes **public knowledge** concerning unequal power relationships.

In this chapter you will be introduced to the sometimes contentious concept of ideology and to the debate concerning its continued usefulness in doing critical media analysis. In recent years the concept of ideology has come under increasing pressure from post-structuralism and postmodernism as well as from an ongoing critique within media studies itself, most notably from those following a reception analysis model of research (see Devereux, 1998: 17–23; 2005).

Following Thompson (1990), this textbook argues for the continued use of a revised definition of ideology within media analysis based upon a tripartite methodological approach that pays sufficient attention to the hermeneutic aspect of media texts. By this is meant that the analysis of dominant and other ideologies within the media needs to pay sufficient attention not only to media organizations or institutions, the content or structure of the **text(s)**, but also – and crucially – to the *meanings* that the text(s) have for audience members.

This approach has the capacity to make up for the shortcomings of the two research traditions that have, until recently, predominated within ideological analysis of the mass media, namely the political economy and content analysis approaches. The political economy approach has been criticized for being overly deterministic in explaining why the media reproduce an ideological slant that is favourable to the ruling class and other dominant groups. The content analysis approach has been criticized for being too narrow in terms of the kinds of media genres it has chosen to analyse and, in many instances, for making simplistic assumptions about the ideological effect on audiences based on analysis of content alone.

This chapter starts by briefly outlining the history of the concept of ideology, sketching its key 'moments' within its Marxist heritage. Beginning with Marx and then considering how the Frankfurt school, Althusser and Gramsci developed the concept of ideology, you will see a gradual move from an initial 'closed/materialist' conceptualization of ideology towards a more 'open/relaxed' understanding of the term. Thompson's (1990) attempt to rescue the concept of ideology from its many opponents is then considered. The chapter concludes by examining the more recent (and welcome) emphasis on the concept of discourse within ideological media analysis. The twin concepts of discourse and discursive formation underpin the recent attempts by media and communications scholars to understand the workings of ideology more fully by focusing on the power of media language (in all its forms) in explaining the social world.

It is somewhat ironic that many postmodernist scholars have called for the abandonment of the concept of ideology altogether, given that in the post 9/11 world we have seen an even greater focus on competing ideologies. As we have already noted in Chapter 3, one key outcome of the globalization process – which is itself founded upon the ideology of neo-liberalism – is the intensification of local and ethnic identities. Globalization and the reflexivity that it inculcates have, if anything, placed a greater emphasis on nationalist and other forms of ideology. In addition to the many residual ideological differences between left and right (as evidenced in the ongoing tensions between Cuba and the USA, for example) the early twenty-first century has witnessed a variety of ideological clashes between Islamic and Western viewpoints, as well as the re-appearance of fundamentalism of both the Christian and Islamic varieties. Ethnic conflicts, such as those between Palestine and Israel for example, have meant a continued war of attrition between competing worldviews. The shift to the right in many countries, debates over the causes of and possible solutions to the global economic crises, the persistence of patriarchal, classed and homophobic ideologies, and the re-emergence of anti-immigrant ideologies are further evidence of the ongoing ideological battles that are occurring.

Perhaps the most obvious recent example of the need to continue with a critical media studies lies in the so-called 'war on terror' campaigns in the Middle East. Media organizations on both sides of these conflicts have played a pivotal role in disseminating disinformation and propaganda about the United States, the West and the Islamic world. Ideologically loaded terms such as 'the civilized world', 'the democratic world', 'the free world', 'let the market decide', 'global terrorism', 'America at war', 'fighting back' and 'weapons of mass destruction' have been used by many media professionals in an unreflective way. The emergence of the 'embedded journalist' is a stark reminder of just how illusory the notion of journalistic objectivity actually is (see Kumar, 2006; Tumber and Palmer, 2004). These conflicts have presented media professionals in the Western world, and in the United States in particular, with a new set of challenges on how the practices of journalistic 'neutrality' and 'objectivity' might otherwise be observed. The coverage of the 'war on terror' and the images and language used to define 'the enemy' are obvious examples of where the ideological role played by the media comes into sharp focus. More often than not, however, the bulk of ideological activity that takes place in the context of media discourse happens unwittingly.

Our main challenge is to consider how ordinary, everyday media content performs an ideological role in narrating stories about power relationships. In *Devils and Angels*, for example, Devereux (1998: 15, 139) demonstrates how media coverage resorts to dissimulation in order to underpin a hegemonic or dominant ideological understanding of poverty. Many television news reports on charitable acts by elite figures resort to using a discourse that stresses the 'human interest' angle in the relationship between the well-off and the poor. The poverty and exclusion experienced by the poor are framed in terms of their individual case histories. Structural context referring to the causes of poverty and inequality is, more often than not, ignored. Fund-raising or telethon television is a good example of where this process takes place. The fact that telethons are needed at all is indicative of need and inequality in society. Telethons, however, typically concentrate on how the activities of (usually well-off) celebrities and the heroic deeds of 'ordinary people' help to alleviate poverty. The ideological work takes place in individualizing and personalizing poverty stories.

What precisely is meant by the term ideology?

In using the term 'ideology' in this textbook it is taken to mean the ideas that legitimize the power of a dominant social group or class (see Creeber, 2006; Devereux, 1998: 19–23; van Dijk, 1998a, for a more detailed overview). This interpretation of the term with its particular emphasis on ideology as dominant ideology is in broad alignment with the neo-Marxist tradition, but it is not solely confined to explaining class relations. Ideological analysis of the twenty-first century media might very well be concerned with discourses about class relations, but it might also be applied to, among other things, analyses of heterosexism, homophobia, disability, neo-liberalism, patriarchy, racism or 'terrorism'. It need not be restricted to analysing hegemonic ideology. It should also examine the workings of **counter-hegemonic** ideologies circulating, for example, among oppressed groups such as ethnic minorities, sexual minority groups or the colonized.

This chapter focuses on examining the interrelations of meaning and power, and more specifically with how meaning serves to maintain relations of domination by using a 'relaxed' rather than a 'closed' definition of the term. In practice when ideological analysis is undertaken we are often confronted with competing ideologies rather than a single monolithic 'thing' called ideology. The challenges facing us as students of the media are to examine the workings of and sometimes the tensions between dominant and counter-hegemonic ideologies that audiences are exposed to in an increasingly complex media setting. The media play an immensely powerful part in the production and circulation of ideologies. In *The Whole World is Watching* Gitlin explains this complex process as follows: 'everyday, directly or indirectly, by statement and omission, in pictures and in words, in entertainment and news and advertising, the media produce fields of definition and association, symbol and rhetoric, through which ideology becomes manifest and concrete' (1980: 2).

While it may be tempting to identify – usually through one or other kind of content analysis – certain media texts as having dominant and other ideologies, analysis based on content alone is not sufficient in undertaking ideological analysis. Content analysis, as we will see in greater detail in Chapter 7, is typically used to identify the intentions and other characteristics of communicators, detect the existence of latent propaganda or ideology, reflect cultural patterns of groups, reveal the foci of organizations and describe trends in communication content. However, content analysis should be seen as only one important part in our overall attempts at examining the operation of dominant and other ideologies in a media setting. If the media have an ideological role, then their job is to help perpetuate or sustain unequal relationships of power among real people in the real world. Ultimately what is at stake is whether existing (dominant) ideas and discourses surrounding unequal power relationships between men and women, between the social classes or between ethnic groups, for example, are reinforced or challenged and whether audiences accept, reject or appropriate these ideas or discourses. Ideological and discursive analysis of media content asks us to concentrate on the relationship between media language (in its broadest sense) and audience beliefs about the social world.

Communication with and between audiences could not exist without ideology and discourse. Media organizations engage in ideological work all of the time, so much so that the use of many ideas and assumptions about the social world are simply taken for granted by media professionals and others. However, when conflicts arise in society (involving, for example, challenges to patriarchy or institutional racism by the state or the police) then the mass media's ideological role becomes more apparent and the possibility of the hegemony or dominant ideology being challenged can arise for some audience members.

Stop and think 6.1

Unequal power relationships and the mass media

1. Think of three recent examples of media coverage concerning class, ethnicity, gender and sexual orientation.

2. What sorts of discourses (forms of knowledge), in your opinion, do these examples contain?

3. Can these discourses be considered to be ideological? Are they working to uphold unequal power relationships? How is this achieved?

4. Is there more than one kind of ideological position/perspective evident within the media content you have selected?

5. As an audience member were you in agreement or disagreement with the overall message contained in the report?

The terms ideology/ideological are often used within public discourse in a negative or a pejorative way. A politician, for example, might accuse an opponent of being ideological in supporting a particular point of view. The use and meaning of the term, as the following definitions demonstrate, has changed considerably over time.

Defining ideology

'The science of ideas' (Destutt de Tracy, 1817)

'The ideas of the ruling class are in every epoch the ruling ideas, i.e. the class which is the ruling material force of society, is at the same time its ruling intellectual force' (Marx and Engels, 1846)

'Ideology, broadly speaking, is meaning in the service of power' (Thompson, 1990)

'The ideas which legitimise the power of a dominant social group or class' (Eagleton, 1991)

'An interest linked perspective i.e. a way of explaining or describing the world which legitimizes the interests of a social group' (Philo, 2007)

A CLOSER LOOK 6.1

Changing definitions of ideology

Defining ideology

Closed/materialist definitions of ideology: Early attempts at defining what is meant by ideology are usually characterized as being restricted or closed. Karl Marx and more latterly the Frankfurt School developed a negative and largely deterministic understanding of ideology (see Figure 6.1).

In Marx's work the ruling classes in capitalist society not only control the means of material production but they also control the production of ideas. Ideas perform an ideological function when they either mask the exploitative nature of capitalism or present these kinds of exploitative economic relationships as being natural and inevitable. In this understanding of the term, ideology can serve to create false consciousness among the exploited and only when it is recognized as such will there be a revolution and a new social order.

Theorist	Definition of ideology	Mass media's ideological role	Conceptualization of audience
Karl Marx (1818–83)	Closed/materialist Negative	Only indirectly concerned with this issue. Nineteenth-century newspapers supportive of capitalism. Marx in his role as a journalist and commentator critiqued the capitalist system within the print media	The working class or proletariat have 'false consciousness'
The Frankfurt School. Various members, including Theodore Adorno (1903–69) and Herbert Marcuse (1898–1979)	Closed/materialist Negative	Media are a powerful source of propaganda. Specifically concerned with propaganda within radio and film in Nazi Germany	Audiences are duped by emerging mass media
Antonio Gramsci (1891–1937)	Increasingly open	Media play a central role in the creation of hegemony in the interests of the capitalist class	Applications of Gramsci's ideas see a continuous struggle within media texts in order to achieve hegemony
Louis Althusser (1918–90)	Increasingly open	Mass media's role as an ideological state apparatus is to legitimize the capitalist system	The media have the appearance of being relatively independent of the powerful capitalist class. The media manage to give greater legitimacy to certain kinds of ideas over others

(Continued)

Theorist	Definition of ideology	Mass media's ideological role	Conceptualization of audience
John B. Thompson	Open/relaxed Emphasis on dominant and other counter-hegemonic ideologies	A tripartite ideological analysis of the media is required to take account of the production context, the content of the text and the agency of audience members	Audiences are active and capable of considerable agency. The effect dominant ideology does or doesn't have is based upon taking a depth hermeneutic approach
Noam Chomsky (1928–)	Propaganda model	Ideological domination is achieved through the use of propaganda. According to Herman and Chomsky (1988) 'propaganda is to a democracy what the bludgeon is to a totalitarian state'	Powerful interests (e.g. big business, government) play a significant role in filtering what audiences encounter in media coverage of issues of social, economic and political importance

Figure 6.1 **Key thinkers on ideology, hegemony and dominant ideology.**

The Frankfurt school's attempts to apply Marx's understanding of ideology to the emerging twentieth-century media are a further example of a closed definition of ideology. In writing about the persistence of capitalism and the destruction brought about by two world wars, the Frankfurt school were critical of and pessimistic about the mass media. As an economic system, capitalism had gone from strength to strength in the post-war era because capitalists controlled the mass media. Writing about this theme in his famous study, *One Dimensional Man*, Marcuse (1964) argued that the media create products that 'indoctrinate and manipulate; they promote a false consciousness which is immune against its falsehood' (1964: 12).

Both Marx and the Frankfurt School emphasized the relationship, as they saw it, between the economic base and dominant ideas of capitalist society. Their understanding of the term is negative in that both imply passivity on the part of those who receive the ideas via the media or other ideological agencies. **Active audience** theorists, as you will see in Chapter 8, would firmly reject such blanket assertions of audience passivity.

Open/relaxed definitions of ideology: Louis Althusser and Antonio Gramsci are justifiably credited with broadening out the parameters of how we should understand ideology. In their work we can see the beginnings of a more open or relaxed definition of the term.

The French theorist Louis Althusser was concerned with explaining how the media created ideological meaning for audiences. In writing about ideology Althusser developed the concept of the ideological state apparatus. By this he meant that institutions such as the media or the educational system reproduced ideology in such a way as to represent capitalism as being natural, inevitable and indeed desirable.

Althusser's understanding of the term 'ideology' carried with it the concept of relative autonomy. To allow the continuation of class domination in capitalist society the media must be perceived by their audience as being relatively autonomous from the direct control of the ruling class. Althusser's notion of relative autonomy allowed for dissenting voices to be heard within the media but the ideas that legitimized and facilitated the continuation of capitalism remained dominant.

Ideology and hegemony

The Italian Marxist Antonio Gramsci also added much to our understanding of ideology through his development of the concept of hegemony. Gramsci wanted to know more about how the capitalist class achieved and maintained a position of dominance in modern society. Hegemony or domination may be achieved through the use or threat of force or more typically through the creation of consensus. Domination of the latter kind in capitalist society comes about by means of the powerful being able to fashion a consensus between those with power and those with little or no power. From Gramsci's perspective the media create a 'common-sense' view of the world that portrays capitalism as being natural and inevitable. In accepting this viewpoint the powerless allow themselves to be dominated by the ruling class through consent.

Do it! 6.1   Ideology and discourse

Go to the book's companion website and read Philo's (2007) discussion on the concepts of ideology and discourse.

Key thinker 6.1   Karl Marx

Born in Germany, Karl Marx (1818–1883) was one of the founding fathers of contemporary sociology. His voluminous work focused on explaining the workings (and contradictions) of capitalist society. Drawing from his analyses of economics, politics, philosophy and history, Marx outlined his vision for a socialist society. He combined his work as a social theorist with an intermittent career in journalism, as well as an involvement in communist politics. Owing to his revolutionary activities, Marx and his family lived in a variety of locations in Continental Europe and the UK (see Wheen, 1999).

Key thinker 6.2   Antonio Gramsci

Like Marx, the Italian theorist Antonio Gramsci (1891–1937) was a committed political activist and journalist. Imprisoned in 1926 for his political activism, Gramsci spent much of the following 10 years writing what have become known as the Prison Notebooks. The Italian theorist grappled with the failure of the socialist project, and in doing so he began to write about how consent is achieved in a society in which inequalities are in evidence. It was in this context that Gramsci developed his thinking about the concept of hegemony. He theorized as to how domination was achieved by the capitalist class, who used, he argued, either consent, force or the threat of force in order to dominate the social order. The work of both Gramsci and Louis Althusser (1918–1990) represent attempts to develop further the ideas first circulated by Marx in the nineteenth century.

For more go to: http://www.internationalgramscisociety.org/

Key thinker 6.3   Louis Althusser

Louis Althusser (1918–1990) was a French theorist who like his predecessors was a committed political activist. He attempted to combine Marxist thinking with the ideas being developed within structuralism. In doing so he was interested in understanding more about the deep structures which were said to underlie all texts. In contributing to the Marxist analysis of modern society Althusser developed the concept of the Ideological State Apparatus. Of the three theorists, Althusser had perhaps the most tragic life. He was incarcerated in a psychiatric hospital in 1980 for the murder of his wife.

Key thinker 6.4   Noam Chomsky

Noam Chomsky was born in New York in 1928. As an activist, commentator and multi-talented academic (with expertise in linguistics, psychology, maths and philosophy), Chomsky has been a vocal critic of the powerful ruling classes in the US and elsewhere. Influenced by a range of political ideas including libertarian socialism and anarcho-syndicalism, Chomsky has tirelessly campaigned on numerous issues all over the world, including most recently the Occupy Movement. His classic text (with Edward S. Hermann) *Manufacturing Consent: The Political Economy of the Mass Media* (1988) demonstrates how the hegemony or domination is achieved by the powerful. The ownership and control of media organizations by multinational conglomerates such as News Corporation results in a distorted view of the world which suits the economically and politically powerful.

See: http://www.chomsky.info/

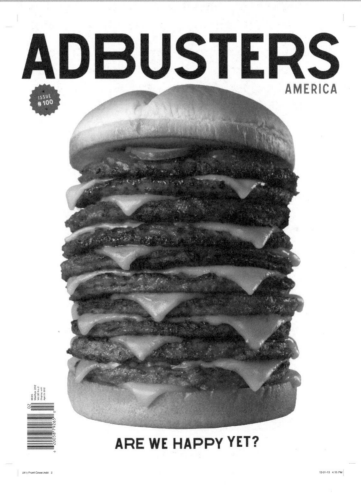

Plate 6.1 **Adbusters and counter-hegemony.** While hegemonic discourses prevail within the mainstream media it is also possible to find examples of powerful counter-hegemonic discourses many of which subvert hegemonic ideas. Image reproduced by kind permission of Adbusters.

Read on! 6.1   A propaganda model

E.S. Herman and N. Chomsky (1994) 'A Propaganda Model', *Manufacturing Consent: The Political Economy of the Mass Media*. London: Vintage, pp. 1–2.

The mass media serve as a system for communicating messages and symbols to the general populace. It is their function to amuse, entertain, and inform and to inculcate individuals with the values, beliefs, and codes of behavior that will integrate them into the institutional structures of the larger society. In a world of concentrated wealth and major conflicts of class interest, to fulfil this role requires systematic propaganda.

In countries where the levers of power are in the hands of a state bureaucracy, the monopolistic control over the media, often supplemented by official censorship, makes it clear that the media serve the ends of a dominant elite. It is much more difficult to see a propaganda system at work where the media are private and formal censorship is absent. This is especially true where the media actively compete, periodically attack and expose corporate and governmental malfeasance, and aggressively portray themselves as spokesmen for free speech and the general community interest. What is not evident (and remains undiscussed in the media) is the limited nature of such critiques, as well as the huge inequality in command of resources, and its effect both on access to a private media system and on its behavior and performance.

A propaganda model focuses on this inequality of wealth and power and its multilevel effects on mass-media interests and choices. It traces the routes for which money and power are able to filter out the news fit to print, marginalize dissent, and allow the government and dominant private interests to get their message across to the public. The essential ingredients of our propaganda model, or set of news 'filters,' fall under the following headings: (1) the size, concentrated ownership, owner wealth, and profit orientation of the dominant mass media firms; (2) advertising as the primary income source of the mass media; (3) the reliance of the media on information supplied by government, business and 'experts' funded and approved by these primary sources and agents of power; (4) 'flak' as a means of disciplining the media; and (5) 'anti-communism' as a national religion and control mechanism. ...

The elite domination of the media and marginalization of dissidents that results from the operation of these filters occurs so naturally that media news people, frequently operating with complete integrity and goodwill, are able to convince themselves that they interpret and choose the news 'objectively' and on the basis of professional news values. Within the limits of the filter constraints they often are objective; the constraints are so powerful, and are built into the system in such a fundamental way, that alternative bases of news choices are hardly imaginable.

? Stop and think 6.2

1. Think of at least three examples of where the mass media may be shown to disseminate propaganda.

2. What are the key arguments that you might make *against* Herman and Chomsky's propaganda model?

? Stop and think 6.3

Powerful texts and guerrilla readers

The debate about the contemporary media and their ideological effect (or not) may be caricatured as one in which there are, on the one hand, powerful media texts replete with dominant and other ideologies capable of shaping the thinking of audience members, and on the other hand audience members who are 'guerrilla readers', capable of either recognizing dominant and other ideologies for what they are or subverting the intended ideological meaning altogether. The challenge for the media student is to recognize exactly how and in what circumstances either the former or the latter takes place and to what extent. Media content shapes audience perceptions about the social world but the interpretative repertoires of audience members – their agency – allow audiences in certain circumstances to 'read against the grain' of the preferred reading of the text. In what circumstances do you think a critical reading of a media text is more likely to occur? In this context, does the medium or media genre matter?

(Continued)

Plate 6.2 Gramsci's writings on the concept of hegemony added significantly to how we understand the workings of ideology in society and in a media setting in particular. Photo of Antonio Gramsci reproduced courtesy of the International Gramsci Society.

A	Anarchism; Ageism; Anti-Globalism; Anarcho-Syndicalism
B	Bolshevism
C	Capitalism; Communism; Consumerism; Communitarianism; Colonialism
D	Dominionism
E	Ecological; Euro-communism; Egalitarianism
F	Feminism; Facism
G	Green; Globalism
H	Heterosexism; Humanism
I	Islamism; Islamaphobia
J	–
K	–
L	Liberalism; Libertarianism

M	Marxism; Monarchism
N	Nationalism; Neo-Nazism; Neo-Liberalism
O	Orientalism
P	Patriarchalism; Pacifism; Post-Colonialism
Q	Queer
R	Racism; Republican; Religious
S	Sexism; Secularism; Socialism; Social Democracy
T	Terrorism; Totalitarianism; Trotskyism
U	Utopianism
V	Vegetarianism; Veganism
W	White-centrism
X	Xenophobism
Y	–
Z	Zionism

Figure 6.2   **An A–Z of hegemonic and counter-hegemonic ideologies – but by no means an exhaustive list ...**

A CLOSER LOOK 6.2

A concept under attack?

In the last two decades of the twentieth century the continued use of the concept of ideology was called into question (see Corner, 1991). The attack happened on two key fronts. Within the field of social theory – and particularly in the context of the collapse of communism – it was argued by many that ideology was an ambiguous, outdated concept full of Marxist baggage that no longer had any use or relevance. Within cultural studies, and in media and communications studies in particular, the emergence of postmodernism as a dominant theoretical framework and the broad shift away from analyses of media effects and analyses of media content gave rise to a new emphasis on audience reception. Audiences were now conceptualized as being much more sophisticated in how they interpreted and engaged with media texts and thus the certainties of earlier ideological analysis were now in serious doubt (for further insights into the debate between those who favour and those who oppose the continued use of the concept, see e.g. Eagleton, 1991; Fiske, 1987; Frazer, 1992; Hawkes, 2003; van Dijk, 1998a).

Gramsci argued that the media managed to appear relatively autonomous in relation to the capitalist class and yet they were engaged in the production and reproduction of ideology that helped to maintain capitalism. (In reality, of course, the media can never ever be considered to be ideologically neutral.) The production and reproduction of ideology was not a static business, however. In Gramsci's estimation the capitalist class could not be certain of their hegemonic position, and therefore in order for hegemony to be achieved it had to be constantly negotiated and renegotiated. Gramsci saw the media as being a key source of hegemonic ideology. Gramsci's work has informed many of the attempts at undertaking media analysis from an ideological perspective. It has presented the production of ideology as an ongoing struggle between the dominant/hegemonic and the alternative/counter-hegemonic. His work has underpinned the approaches taken by feminist and Marxist media analysts in recent times.

 A CLOSER LOOK 6.3 ··

Radway and romance

Janice Radway's *Reading the Romance: Women, Patriarchy and Popular Literature* (1987) is a good example of ideological analysis that opts to combine an examination of the production, content and reception of media texts. The study focuses on the role of romantic novels in the lives of 42 women in a mid-western US city. It is deservedly heralded as a milestone in the field of feminist media and communications studies. Radway brings together interesting insights into the world of publishing and analysis of the narrative structure of romantic novels as well as a detailed account of the importance of these texts in the everyday lives of these female readers.

 A CLOSER LOOK 6.4 ··

Ideology and power in practice: neo-liberalism

There is a danger that when you hear about the term ideology that you think that it is just an abstraction which social theorists argue over. Let's look briefly at a real example of an ideology that has been directly responsible for radical changes in how economies and societies are organized in recent decades. The neo-liberal idea that it is best to organize the world according to market principles began to gain momentum in the 1970s. According to the neo-liberal standpoint, government or the state should either play a significantly reduced or non-existent role when it comes to the provision of goods and services in society. In addition, capital should be unfettered as far as possible and should be free from state interference. Neo-liberal marketization ideas have assumed a dominant or hegemonic position in the shaping of state policy in terms of how education, health and welfare are provided for its citizens. Citizens have within neo-liberal discourse been reconfigured as consumers. Some universities, for example, insist on referring to their students as 'customers'. Neo-liberal ideas underpin much of the deregulation of the media industry and have facilitated the rise to power of globally dominant multimedia conglomerates.

Purcell (2011: 43) reminds us that we should not fall into the trap of thinking of neo-liberalism merely as an economic policy agenda. He notes that:

> ... Harvey (2005) makes clear, the rise of neoliberalism constituted a successful ideological project to make competitive-market ideologies hegemonic. Wendy Larner (2000) and Henry Giroux (2004) have both emphasized the importance of understanding neoliberalism not just as a set of concrete policies, but as an ideology, a form of governmentality, and as Giroux terms it, a 'public pedagogy.' The hegemony of neoliberal ideas is important, because creating a dominant neoliberal 'common-sense' helps establish unquestioned assumptions that makes it very difficult to imagine, let alone achieve, alternative projects.

Critics of this now globally dominant ideology hold that it (neo-liberalism) serves the economic and political interests of the powerful global capitalist class whilst the poor and dependent at home and abroad are the ones who suffer most at its hands. As evidence of the more problematic aspects of neo-liberalism we can point to the global economic crisis resulting from deregulated financial markets, the continued exploitation of workers in cheap labour economies and the retreat of the welfare state in Europe and the USA. The deregulation of the media industry and its domination by a handful of multimedia conglomerates raises serious questions for contemporary society. Critics, rightly, point to the way in which commercial concerns override all others and they hold that it has resulted in the number and range of critical voices that we see or hear about in the mainstream media.

Stop and think 6.4

Find a recent example of media coverage of the provision of healthcare. Do neo-liberal ideas inform the basic assumptions of the report?

Ideology as dominant ideology

John B. Thompson's *Ideology and Modern Culture* (1990) has made a very significant contribution towards how we now understand ideology and the media's role in the production and reproduction of ideology. Prior to describing his suggested

Ideological analysis involves investigation into:		
The production and transmission or diffusion of symbolic forms	The construction of the media message – especially its discursive dimension	The reception and appropriation of media messages

Figure 6.3   **Three stages in ideological media analysis (Thompson, 1990).**

model of media analysis we briefly outline his attempts at rescuing the concept from a growing army of critics.

The importance of Thompson's work

Conceding that the concept has proved itself to be problematic in the past, Thompson argues that the concept should be used in its negative or critical sense. Significantly, he asserts that our thinking about ideology should be refocused on the interrelations of meaning and power, and more specifically on how meaning serves to maintain relations of domination (see Figure 6.3). In Thompson's words, the concept of ideology

> can be used to refer to the ways in which meaning serves, in particular circumstances, to establish and sustain relations of power which are systematically asymmetrical – what I shall call 'relations of domination'. Ideology, broadly speaking, is meaning in the service of power. Hence the study of ideology requires us to investigate the ways in which meaning is constructed and conveyed by symbolic forms of various kinds, from everyday linguistic utterances to complex images and texts; it requires us to investigate the social contexts within which symbolic forms are employed and deployed; it calls upon us to ask whether, and if so how, the meaning constructed and conveyed by symbolic forms serves, in specific contexts, to establish and sustain relations of domination. (1990: 6–7)

Thompson's (1990) emphasis on ideology as dominant ideology, used to perpetuate unequal power relations, carries with it a number of important implications. His approach underscores the fact that alternative or counter-hegemonic ideologies exist and that they may also circulate in a media setting. Not all media texts are ideological. They can be termed ideological only if they can be shown to help perpetuate unequal power relations. He also argues that it is not a prerequisite that ideology should necessarily be a form of false consciousness.

Thompson's (1990) work reasserts the importance of doing ideological analysis within media and communications studies. In repositioning the spotlight on ideology as dominant ideology he concedes that ideologies other than dominant ideologies exist and circulate within media texts. In his reformulation media texts that are ideological do not necessarily have to be false, erroneous or illusory, although they may be. By emphasizing, as he does, the hermeneutic dimension he privileges the role of the media audience in examining if and how an ideological effect takes place. Thompson's emphasis on the media audience mirrors the concentration on reception that had taken place in any event within media studies. The real value of his methodological framework is that he argues convincingly that we need to concentrate on all three key dimensions of the communication process – namely production, content and reception. His model of ideological media analysis is now outlined.

Ideological analysis: a tripartite approach

Thompson's (1990) tripartite model takes what he terms a 'depth herme-neutics approach' in examining the media's ideological role. An understanding of how media messages or texts help sustain or perpetuate relations of domination needs to place a firmer emphasis on the issues of meaning and interpretation.

A vast proportion of the media's activity is in the production of symbolic forms and our attempts at understanding the ideological effect – if any – of the media need to recognize the crucial importance of the interpretative work that takes place around and with media messages or texts. It is only through a detailed consideration of what Thompson (1990: 274) calls 'the everyday appropriation' of media messages or texts that questions surrounding their ideological effect can be addressed.

Although individual analyses of production, content and reception may go some distance in informing us about particular aspects of the ideological character of mass communication, a methodological framework using a combination of all three and with particular emphasis on the reception and appropriation of media messages or texts is potentially far more illuminating. According to Thompson:

> Rather than assuming that the ideological character of media messages can be read off the messages themselves (an assumption I have called the fallacy of internalism), we can draw upon the analysis of all three aspects of communication – production/transmission, construction, reception/appropriation – in order to interpret the ideological character of media messages. (1990: 306)

By engaging in what is admittedly a far more ambitious and demanding approach we can begin to address many of the weaknesses traditionally associated with ideological media analysis.

Thompson (1990) asserts that his tripartite model is well suited to ideological media analysis for a number of reasons. It is worthwhile quoting him at length to understand his position. He states:

> The analysis of production and transmission is essential to the interpretation of the ideological character of media messages because it sheds light on the institutions and social relations within which these messages are produced and diffused, as well as the aims and assumptions of the producers.

The study of the construction of the media messages is essential because it examines the structural features by virtue of which they are complex symbolic phenomena, capable of mobilizing meaning. Finally, the study of the reception and appropriation of media messages is essential because it considers both the social-historical conditions within which messages are received by individuals and the ways in which these individuals make sense of the messages and incorporate them into their lives. In drawing upon the analysis of these three aspects of mass communication, the process of interpretation may seek to explicate the connections between particular media messages, which are produced in certain circumstances and constructed in certain ways, and the social relations within which these messages are received and understood by individuals in the course of their everyday lives. In this way the process of interpretation can begin to explicate the ideological character of media messages, that is, the ways in which the meaning mobilized by particular messages may serve, in certain circumstances, to establish and sustain relations of domination. (1990: 306–7)

How ideology functions

Dominant ideology is fostered and maintained in a number of ways:

1. Legitimation

Unequal power relationships are created and maintained by being represented as legitimate and as being in 'everybody's' interest.

A key way in which legitimation works is through the process of universalization – that is, creating the sense in society that in spite of the existence of material differences between different social groups, the present economic or political system benefits all or has the potential to benefit all members of society. At election time, for example, political parties of all hues argue that sometime soon everybody will benefit from one or other policy.

2. Dissimulation

This occurs where relations of domination (such as gender inequality) are denied, hidden or obscured. Dissimulation can occur, for example, when unequal relationships of power are ignored altogether, glossed over or taken for granted. It is regularly in evidence in the tabloid print media in the (mis)representation of women, for example.

Dissimulation also occurs through the practice of omission, for example where alternative accounts of events are not included in a news report.

3. Unification

Hegemonic or dominant ideology unifies members of a society into a collective entity, usually in opposition to a real or imagined 'enemy'; for example, uniting (all) members of society against the 'threat of terrorism' or the assumed threat that immigration brings. This serves to further deflect attention away from the unequal power relationships between the rulers and the ruled.

In this context, particular use is often made in political or state discourse, for example, of unifying terms such as 'community', 'family', 'society' and 'we'. The use of othering discourses sets up clear distinctions between 'us' and 'them'.

4. Fragmentation

Hegemony is achieved and maintained through dividing or fragmenting the potential opposition and thus reducing or removing the perceived 'threat' they might otherwise pose. In short, the powerful adopt a 'divide and rule' approach.

A colonial power, for example, might foster divisions and enmity between different ethnic or class groups. A political party might encourage divisiveness between the underclass and immigrants around questions concerning work, social welfare or housing.

5. Reification

Unequal social structures are represented as being 'natural' and 'inevitable.' Relations of domination are represented as if they were divorced from history and were without specific economic and political contexts. See, for example, the belief that gender inequalities are based on 'natural' or biological differences between women and men, or Third World poverty or underdevelopment being discussed without reference to the exploitative contexts of colonialism or more recent global capitalism.

A CLOSER LOOK 6.5

How is ideological domination achieved? (see Thompson, 1990)

This tripartite model is strongly interpretative in orientation and draws upon a range of research methodologies to achieve the desired end. The production and transmission of media messages or texts may be best understood through the uses of social-historical analysis and ethnography. The structure of the media message is analysed through formal or discursive analysis. Audience reception and appropriation are explored through again using a combination of social-historical analysis and ethnography. We need therefore to combine these three aspects of media analysis in order to explore questions surrounding ideology. We need to understand the organizational circumstances in which specific media texts were produced, we need to closely examine the structure and content of these texts and we need to examine what happens with media texts when they are put into circulation.

Discourse and ideology

The second part of Thompson's tripartite model makes explicit reference to formal or discursive analysis of media texts. In this final section the importance of the discursive dimension of ideological analysis is examined. Within media and communications studies the concept of discourse can go a long way in better informing analyses of ideology (see e.g. van Dijk, 1998a). A growing amount of research work has recently emerged using this conceptual framework, and, to date, it has mainly examined media representations of unequal power relationships concerning race and class, for example, in a print media setting (see e.g. Bell, 1998; Fairclough, 2001; Fowler, 1991; van Dijk, 1991, 1998b).

Read on! 6.2   A social theory of mass communication

John B. Thompson (1990) 'A social theory of mass communication', in *Ideology and Modern Culture*. Cambridge: Polity Press, pp. 267–8.

This is a shortcoming because it cannot be assumed that the messages diffused by media institutions will have, by virtue of the organization of these institutions or the characteristics of the messages themselves, a given effect when the messages are received and appropriated by individuals in the course of their everyday lives. It cannot be assumed that the individuals who receive media messages will, by the very fact of receiving them, be impelled to act in an imitative and conforming way and thereby be bound to the social order which their actions, and the messages which allegedly impel them, serve to reproduce. The fact that the continuous and reverent portrayal of Ceauçescu and his entourage on Romanian state television did little to win them a secure place in the hearts and minds of the Romanian people is vivid testimony to the weakness of this assumption. Based on ... the fallacy of internalism, this whole approach to the ideological character of mass communication takes too much for granted and must be replaced by an approach which considers more carefully the specific contexts and processes in which the messages produced and diffused by media institutions are appropriated by the individuals who receive them.

We can begin to make this reorientation by situating the analysis of the ideological character of mass communication within the framework of ... technically mediated quasi-interaction. The structure and content of media messages must be analysed in relation to their production within the primary interactive framework and their reception within the primary reception region, as well as in relation to the quasi interaction sustained between communicators and recipients and the subsequent social interactions in which the content of media messages is incorporated and elaborated. Moreover, these interlocking frameworks of interaction are always embedded in broader sets of social relations and institutions which are structured in certain ways. It is only by analysing the structure and content of media messages in relation to these frameworks of interaction and encompassing sets of social relations that we can examine the ideological character of media products. For these products, like all symbolic forms, are not ideological in themselves; rather, they are ideological only in so far as, in particular sets of social-historical circumstances, they serve to establish and sustain relations of domination.

 ## Stop and think 6.5

1. What does Thompson mean by the term 'fallacy of internalism'?

2. Taking a media text of your choice, outline how you would apply Thompson's tripartite model of analysis.

A CLOSER LOOK 6.6

Dahlgren: television news and ideology

Dahlgren's study 'Viewers' plural sense-making of TV news' (1992), while supportive of the concept of ideology, argues that previous ideological analysis suffers from an overly simplistic interpretation in terms of how texts function ideologically. Dahlgren argues that the crux of this problem is one of reconciling the polysemic 'openness' of a media text with the narrow parameters that a preferred (dominant ideological) reading requires. Dahlgren (1992) argues that the very openness of the text can actually assist in the reproduction of ideology through dissimulation. His analysis of viewer discourses on television news suggests that the openness of the text, irrespective of whether it contains contradictions or not, helps in the obfuscation and the circulation of ideology. Television news, he argues, presents a range of possible meanings, none of which assists the viewer in locating herself politically or socially. In masking the social structure through the use of open texts, dominant ideologies are produced and reproduced.

Racial stereotyping

Paek and Shah's (2003) examination of how US magazine advertising represents Asian Americans demonstrates how racial ideologies are employed within the media industry. Using a combination of **quantitative content analysis** and textual analysis, the researchers examine how advertising contained within three mainstream publications (*Time, Newsweek* and *US News and World Report*) resort to using stereotypes of Asian Americans. In a white-centric society, media discourse typically constructs ethnic groups through the use of negative media constructions. Historically, Asian Americans were represented negatively. Paek and Shah's (2003) content and textual analysis shows, however, that their representation has now changed and the discourses used within advertising suggest that Asian Americans are a 'model minority' group. In the context of racist media representations of non-white groups, this might seem like a positive development. It is, however, problematic for a number of reasons. The homogenizing of Asian Americans ignores differences within the Asian American diaspora and it also implies the existence of a hierarchy in terms of the various ethnicities which make up US society, specifically in terms of those groups who are more like 'us' – that is, those who are enterprising, high-achievers and successful.

Hegemonic and counter-hegemonic accounts of racism

Fraley and Lester-Roushanzamir (2004) demonstrate how the print media engage in the dissemination of dominant ideology. By focusing on how race and class are portrayed, they compare media coverage of the shooting dead of Fred Hampton, the Chicago-based Black Panther leader in December 1969. Fraley and Lester-Roushanzamir (2004) show how the mainstream print media operated not as a public sphere but rather as a state ideological apparatus reproducing an ideology supportive of the (white) ruling class. The concepts of dominant ideology and moral panic are applied in order to reach a critical understanding of how the mainstream and Black press covered the killing of Fred Hampton and his colleague Mark Clark. The authors' textual analysis suggests that the *Chicago Tribune* clearly reproduced a dominant or hegemonic ideological position, whilst the *Chicago Daily Defender* countered this by offering an alternative account of the same set of events with particular reference to racism and unequal power relations. The hegemonic version relied heavily on police sources. This is an important example, they argue, of a 'discursive battle' (2004: 163) between mainstream/hegemonic and counter-hegemonic accounts of a single event. Fraley and Lester-Roushanzamir (2004) conclude that the mainstream print media fulfil an important ideological function for the powerful and that in the context of increased conglomeration it is becoming more difficult to identify a set of alternative discourses.

 Do it! 6.2

Go to the companion website and read the case study 'The Most Decisive Ideological Struggle of the Twenty-First Century'.

It's all in the discourse?

Like ideology, the concept of discourse is notoriously problematic. It suffers greatly from the often ambiguous ways in which it is used. There are tensions in the field between those who use both concepts in a complementary way and those who have abandoned the concept of ideology altogether in favour of discourse.

Postmodern and more traditional approaches to media analysis are sharply divided over whether ideologies can be shown to actually exist at all outside of media texts or representations. The postmodern focus on the connections between language and social structure draws heavily on Foucault's writings on discourse. Foucault was interested in examining how specific discourses or forms of knowledge exercise power over members of society. As Bilton et al. (2002) state:

> Foucault's perspective on social life is ... fundamentally concerned with power. Prevailing forms of knowledge or discourse exercise power over us because they provide us with the language we use to think about the world, and thereby 'know' about it. These discourses constitute us (make us what we are and what we think) because we have to use their vocabularies to make sense of events and phenomena. (2002: 235)

In Foucault's work a discourse or discursive formation 'is at once singularly authoritative and deployed in the interests of existing structures of authority and power' (Deacon et al., 1999b: 147). In attempting to understand the media many postmodernists argue that the only 'reality' – ideological or otherwise – that exists resides within the multitude of discursive formations which individual audience members encounter in the course of their media consumption, i.e. within media texts.

The postmodern perspective ignores the numerous attempts by elite groups to shape certain media agendas such as news programming in favour of their chosen ideological position. It also ignores the increasingly concentrated nature of media ownership by elite groups and the fact that the mainstream media do in actuality reflect the interests of these elite groups within much of their media content. A more traditional approach would hold that dominant ideologies such as racism or homophobia or capitalism, for that matter, do not merely reside within media texts. There are clear linkages between media representations of the social world and the existence and persistence of social inequalities.

⚡ Key thinker 6.5   Michel Foucault

Michel Foucault (1926–1984) was born into a middle-class family in Poitiers, France. A renowned and hugely influential philosopher, social theorist, historian of ideas and academic, he was heavily influenced by the German thinker Nietzsche. Rejecting many of the values and aspirations of his middle-class background, Foucault was a life-long activist and protested on behalf of marginalized groups such as prisoners, gays and those who were deemed mentally ill. The common thread in Foucault's work is his attempt to explain how power is wielded through knowledge and social control. This is achieved through discourse. Foucault wrote extensively about the history of madness and prisons. His multi-volume work on human sexuality was not completed owing to Foucault's premature death from an AIDS related illness in 1984. Foucault's (1994) comments on the extent of media saturation in French society are worth noting:

> What bothers me is the quality of French television. It's true! It is one of the best in the world unfortunately! ... What bothers and irritates me horribly in France, is that you are obliged to look at the program in advance to know what you can't miss, and you have to arrange your evening as a result. And then there is *Le Pain Noir* on Mondays. Result: every Monday is booked up ... It is this, which is the strength of television. People end up living according to its schedules. The news has been delayed by a quarter of an hour: well, you know that restaurants will see their diners arrive a quarter of an hour later. (1994: 705)

For more go to http://www.michel-foucault.com/

Marrying ideology and discourse

The concepts of ideology and discourse play complementary roles in furthering a critical understanding of the media's role in the reproduction of unequal power relationships in society. A critical discourse analysis has the potential to deepen our understanding of the media's ideological role. It can be used to examine how media texts are structured and how they may ultimately function at an ideological level. It can also be used to analyse the discourses employed by both media professionals and media audiences in the production and reception of media texts.

Discourse analysis is sometimes referred to as the analysis of text and talk (for an overview see van Dijk, 1998a). Deacon et al. (1999b) argue that, as a core part of a critical linguistics, discourse analysis has two main concerns. First, it is interested in examining the use of language in social life and, second, it is interested in investigating the relationships between language use and social structure. Deacon et al. (1999b) argue that discourse analysis:

> enables us to focus not only on the actual uses of language as a form of social interaction, in particular situations and contexts, but also on forms of representation [my emphasis] in which different social categories, different social practices and relations are constructed from and in the interests of a particular point of view, a particular conception of social reality. (1999b: 146)

It is this second strand of discourse analysis, with its emphasis on discourse within forms of representation and its focus on social structure/power relationships, that is of particular interest to us, given our interest in the mass media's ideological role.

Empirical research work using a discourse analysis approach has an interest in the ways in which text and talk represent **asymmetrical relationships of power**. Discourse analysis, with its detailed emphasis on the workings of language in respect of power relationships, has much to offer the media student. It can help us unpack the possible readings that may reside in a media text. For Deacon et al. (1999b: 150) the

> critical scope and potential of discourse analysis resides most of all in its examination of how relations and structures of power are embedded in everyday language use, and thus how language contributes to the legitimisation of existing social relations and hierarchies of authority and control.

Furthermore, they argue that discourse analysis is well suited to doing detailed investigative work into the ideological dimensions of talk and texts. They state:

> Discourse analysis can show these processes at work in the realm of natural language by pointing to attempts to close meaning down, to fix it in relation to a given position, to make certain conventions self-evidently correct, to do creative repair work when something becomes problematic, and to make the subject positions of discourse transparently obvious without any visible alternatives. (1999b: 154)

An understanding of the discursive dimension of media texts is a crucial aspect of doing ideological analysis. Discourses that are supportive of dominant ideology do so through legitimizing unequal relationships of power. Such relationships are reified and presented as natural and inevitable. By examining media texts at this micro-level in a detailed and systematic way we can begin to appreciate how texts are structured as discourses and ask whether or not these discourses support or challenge dominant ideologies. A critical understanding of media discourses is necessary if we want to ask about the production and reception of media texts that we consider to be ideological in orientation.

A CLOSER LOOK 6.9

Ideology and discourse

Van Dijk's study *Ideology: A Multidisciplinary Approach* (1998a) is an important account of how we should approach the analysis of dominant and other forms of ideology. Because of its very complexity, we need, he argues, to take a multi-faceted approach in order to understand more about how ideologies work. Van Dijk proposes that we concentrate on the conceptual and disciplinary triangle of cognition, society and discourse. If we want to move away from abstract and ambiguous notions of ideology towards seeing what ideologies 'actually look like' (1998a: 5) then we have to make use of the theoretical and methodological tools of analysis available to us from psychology, sociology and linguistics. In van Dijk's account, discourse plays a central (though not exclusive) role in the dissemination of ideology. He argues that:

> Discourse has a special function in the implementation and especially the reproduction of ideologies, since it is only through language use, discourse or communication (or other semiotic practices) that they can be explicitly formulated. This is essential in contexts of acquisition, argumentation, ideological conflict, persuasion and other processes in the formation and change of ideologies. (1998a: 316–17)

We need to examine, in detail, the discursive formations that occur in text, talk and other contexts if we wish to understand how ideologies are constructed, circulated and how they may change.

Van Dijk proposes a rigorous and detailed model of analysis in examining the discursive dimensions of ideology. As well as taking account of the type of com-municative genre and participants/participant roles involved, when we come to analyse communicative events in terms of their ideological aspect, our focus should not be restricted to their semantic properties. We should also consider, for example, their 'phonological, graphical, syntactic, lexical, stylistic, rhetorical, schematic (e.g. argumentative, narrative) pragmatic and conversational structures' (1998a: 317). The lexical dimension has received the bulk of attention from those interested in analysing the relationship between ideology and discourse. Here 'a negative concept of a group is represented in a model, and depending on context, the most "appropriate" word is selected, in such a way that an outgroup is referred to and at the same time an opinion about them' (1998a: 270). Thus we can read and hear about, for example, 'fundamentalists', 'welfare scroungers', 'bogus asylum seekers', 'the flood of refugees', 'foreign nationals', 'Refugee rapist on the rampage', 'the devil's poor', 'militant and terrorist groups' and 'striking workers'. When we come to undertake ideological analysis of this kind we are interested in examining how the lexical and the other aforementioned devices help to define 'us' and 'them'. How do they work to shape one group's thinking about another?

! Do it! 6.3

Go to the companion website and read Smith and Bell (2007) on the issues that arise in undertaking discourse analysis in a media context.

? Stop and think 6.6

Cinema and 'queer' discourses

Using elements of a traditional film genre (Cowboy/Western), *Brokeback Mountain* (2005) focused on the sexual and emotional relationship between two men. It reveals human sexuality to be multi-layered (both men subsequently marry female partners) and complex. The film is noted for not only dealing with bisexuality in a sensitive and non-sensationalist fashion but also for its critical and commercial success. Selecting a film of your choice that deals with being gay, lesbian or bisexual, try to identify the dominant and other discourses that reside within your chosen text. What are the key devices used by the filmmaker in constructing a particular discourse about being gay, lesbian or bisexual? How do these discourses relate to dominant hegemonic heterosexist ideologies? Is being gay pathologized or normalized? In examining queer discourses in a cinematic context, compare the film of your choice with the representation of gay men and women in mainstream television series such as *Queer as Folk*, *The L Word*, *Six Feet Under*, *Sex and the City*, *Queer Eye for the Straight Guy*, *Will and Grace*, *Ellen*, *Shameless*, *Family Guy* and *The Simpsons*.

For debate on current queer topics and the media see: http://www.afterellen.com/

Read on! 6.3   Popular culture and ideology

Nicholas Abercrombie (1990) 'Popular culture and ideological effects', in Nicholas Abercrombie, Stephen Hill and Bryan S. Turner (eds), *Dominant Ideologies*. London: Unwin Hyman, pp. 202–4.

What would be meant by saying that popular culture has ideological force? Provisionally the following four features are relevant.

1. Popular culture encapsulates a particular (hegemonic) view of the world, even if it has to accommodate other views.

2. This particular view of the world is widely available in society, perhaps the most widely available.

3. Popular culture conceals, misrepresents and secures an order of domination.

4. This concealment is in the interests of a particular (ruling) group, social formation or form of society.

What are the conditions for these propositions to be true? To illuminate this question it is useful, following Hall (1980) [,] to distinguish three moments – production, text and appropriation – when carrying out a sociological analysis of any cultural form. Generally speaking, any analysis of this kind is notoriously difficult and controversial. That reading, whether it is a television programme, film, book, or advertisement, establishes the dominant themes, codes, or discourses in the text. In so coding, a sociological problem is established, since the sociologist wants to know, on the one hand, why the text carries a particular discourse and, on the other hand, what an audience will do with the text. Therefore, a complete account has to start from the text but it has to move on from there to consider the means of production and appropriation. As Hall (1980) points out, it is not simply a matter of looking at the three moments independently; it is actually the way that they fit together that is of chief interest in considering the relationship between cultural form and ideology. ...

Before looking at the three moments of ideology in detail, a methodological problem needs to be mentioned. Can one say that there is ideology in a text independently of any audience reaction?

The proposal that ideology is really a particular effect of a discourse is seductive. If we are able to say that a discourse is ideological, to the extent that it affects an audience so that the existing relations of domination are secured, we would at least avoid traditional hermeneutic problems. Instead of arguing over rival interpretations of a text, we would only have to find out how audiences appropriate the text.

? Stop and think 6.7

What are the main theoretical and methodological problems that researchers must overcome if they wish to undertake an ideological analysis of a media text?

A CLOSER LOOK 6.10

Media discourses about gender and race/ethnicity

Walker's (2005) examination of the liberal Mexican newspaper *La Jornada* uses a critical discourse analysis approach in order to understand how unequal power relationships in terms of both gender and race/ethnicity are narrowly constructed within media discourse. Her research reminds us that borders are not merely geographical, political or economic constructs. They also operate at a symbolic level. As symbolic entities they are 'sexed' and 'raced'. In examining the discourses within three selected newspaper articles, Walker (2005) demonstrates that hegemonic rather than counter-hegemonic discourses are in evidence – despite *La Jornada*'s liberal reputation. Using a qualitative content analysis approach and a close critical reading of the newspaper articles, Walker (2005) shows how '... discursive violence, "narratives of eviction" and silences are implicated in the construction of women as weak, sexualized objects, and Mexicans as raced, backward "others"' (2005: 95). By focusing on the discourses employed within media content, Walker (2005) interrogates many of the assumptions contained within media discourse. A basic assumption is that underdeveloped Mexico can and should move along the same path of economic development as its neighbour the United States. The exploitation of women (in a variety of ways) is assumed to be a mere symptom of the globalization process. Walker (2005: 95–6) identifies four discursive moments in terms of the representation of women. These are discourses which construct women as: (1) anonymous replaceable bodies; (2) victims of the border city; (3) dependent appendages; and (4) 'Guada-Narco-Lupe' (combining images of virginity and criminality, especially in relation to drug-trafficking). Mexicans, as a whole, are constituted as a racialized 'other' to the inhabitants of the USA. She notes that within media discourses about Mexicans the words '"poverty"', "lack", "marginalization" and "empty communities" appear repeatedly' (2005: 106). Walker (2005) situates the examination of discourse within a media setting in a much larger ideological context. Her critical reading of these three newspaper articles is grounded in the wider ideological context of US–Mexican political and economic relationships. The 'scripting' of women and Mexicans by hegemonic media discourse has to be read in terms of dominant patriarchal and racist ideologies in existence outside of the media texts examined.

Conclusion

The postmodern world is often characterized as being fragmented. It is clearly a divided and unequal world. The collapse of communism and the decline in structuralist sociology in the 1990s had significant implications for the concept of ideology. At the beginning of this chapter we noted that at a time when the Right is in resurgence, when the social world is being increasingly privatized, when **citizenship** is being downplayed in the context of the new-found emphasis on the market and consumption, and when fundamentalism – both Christian and Islamic – is re-emergent, the death knell of the concept of ideology is being prematurely heralded by many. This chapter has attempted to restate the significance of ideology as a concept within social theory. In this chapter we have warned against a metaphorical 'throwing out of the baby with the bath water'. Ideological analysis of the media is clearly a contentious zone within media studies. Such analysis of the media – if undertaken properly – should be retained as a critical component in terms of how we understand the media. We need, however, to proceed with some caution.

One way of overcoming the kinds of pitfalls traditionally associated with doing ideological analysis is to combine analyses of production, content and reception. By emphasizing the hermeneutic dimension we can begin to examine how certain kinds of media content reinforce or challenge existing public discourses by reference to what audiences ultimately believe.

The concentration in this chapter on ideology as dominant ideology means that, by definition, a wider range of ideologies potentially exists within media content. A sophisticated ideological analysis of the media should pay particular attention to the potential range of ideological positions among the media professionals involved, the kinds of discourses (dominant and otherwise) used in the text and the range of possible readings that audiences may place upon the text. The ideological import, however, of media content is not of itself obviated by alternative audience readings of a text.

Added to this should be a realization that certain kinds of media genres such as television news, tabloid newspapers and magazines are more amenable than others to the reproduction of ideologies that sustain unequal relations of power. A balance needs to be struck between the capacity of audience members to reject or reconstruct dominant ideology and the fact that media organizations and media content have been shown to possess significant power in constructing and shaping the ideological effect in the short, medium and long term.

Chapter summary

1. This chapter makes a strong case for why the concepts of ideology and dominant ideology remain relevant for media analysis.

2. The concept of ideology and its application within a media studies setting was shown to have shifted from the use of closed/materialist definitions to more open/relaxed definitions.

3. A number of key figures (e.g. Marx, Althusser and most noticeably Gramsci) have contributed much towards our understanding of how the concepts of ideology and hegemony can be usefully applied in a media setting.

4. Thompson's (1990) tripartite model, which places an equal emphasis on focusing on the production, content and reception of media texts in undertaking ideological analysis, was shown to be of major importance.

5. The chapter also explained the emergence and application of the concept of discourse. A critical understanding of the concept of discourse is central to understanding how ideological domination is achieved by the powerful.

6. The concept of ideology should not be restricted to understanding unequal power relationships in the strict Marxist sense (i.e. solely focused on class inequalities), but rather it can be usefully applied to a much wider range of contexts involving unequal power relations.

(Continued)

7. While postmodernism would cynically reject the concept of ideology, this chapter argues that now, more than ever, media analysis which is focused on unequal power relationships is essential. This need to undertake such analysis has been exacerbated by the rise of neo-liberal understandings of the economy and society.

Further reading

Bell, A. and P. Garrett (eds) (1998) *Approaches to Media Discourse*. Oxford: Blackwell. Nine essays by some of the world's key thinkers on discourse, including van Dijk, Bell, Fairclough.

Byerly, C. and K. Ross (2006) *Women and Media: Critical Issues*. Oxford: Blackwell. A critical account of how media reproduce gendered and other exclusionary discourse. See also Ross, K. *Gendered Media: Women, Men and Identity Politics*. Lanham MD: Rowman and Littlefield Publishers.

Gitlin, T. (2003) *The Whole World is Watching*. Berkeley, CA: University of California Press. This new edition of Gitlin's (1980) text contains an updated preface by the author. The text is an essential read for media students.

Hawkes, D. (2003) *Ideology*, 2nd edn. London: Routledge. The second edition of Hawkes's book examines the continued importance of ideology in a post 9/11 world. See Chapter 4 on Marxism in particular.

O'Keefe, A. (2006) *Investigating Media Discourse*. London: Routledge. O'Keefe's book is focused on how we analyse the spoken word in a media setting. Her text includes analysis of interviews with George Bush and Tony Blair.

Van Zoonen, L. (1994) *Feminist Media Studies*. London: Sage. Van Zoonen's now classic text convincingly demonstrates how the media are centrally involved in the production and circulation of patriarchal ideologies.

Online reading

Go to the companion website and read the following:

- Philo, G. (2007) 'News content studies, media group methods and discourse analysis: a comparison of approaches', in E. Devereux (ed.), *Media Studies: Key Issues and Debates*. London: Sage.

- Smith, P. and A. Bell (2007) 'Unravelling the web of discourse analysis', in E. Devereux (ed.), *Media Studies: Key Issues and Debates*. London: Sage.

CHAPTER  7

Media 'Re-presentations' in an Unequal World

Chapter overview

This chapter introduces you to the following:

- The main issues surrounding the analysis of media content
- Quantitative and qualitative content analysis
- Media representations of poverty in the developed world and the Third World
- Media representations of class, ethnicity, gender and sexuality
- Media representations of the places in which the poor and excluded live.

Key concepts

- Media content
- Representation/'re-presentation'
- Quantitative content analysis
- Qualitative content analysis
- Semiotic, discourse, frame and narrative analysis
- Social structure
- Stigmatization
- Class, ethnicity, gender and sexuality
- The 'deserving' and the 'undeserving' poor

Introduction

In this chapter the main issues involved in approaching the analysis of media content are discussed. In an attempt to further our discussion of ideology and discourse, an emphasis is placed upon examining how media content represents unequal power relationships in the social world. Media content is socially constructed. It is not fixed but rather changes over time. At any one time, it contains many clues as to the make-up of the social structure that determines so much about all of our lives. Media content matters because it is within media content that the shaping and framing of our understanding and perceptions of the social world takes place. Media content provides us with the many 'scripts' necessary for us to negotiate and make sense of the everyday social contexts in which we find ourselves. Media content informs us about the personal and the political. Understanding media content is crucial in terms of reaching a more informed understanding of how we form views, opinions and attitudes about groups who are considered 'other'. The 'other' may comprise of a range of 'out' groups in any society. They may be the poor, the homeless, members of the LGBT community, the colonized, the underclass, residents of stigmatized neighbourhoods, ex-prisoners, the mentally ill and immigrants, for example. Those who are othered are regularly constructed as a threat to the moral and social order. Media content not only shapes our understanding of the social world but may also influence our actions (or inaction) about issues concerning fairness, justice and equality.

Content analysis of both quantitative and qualitative persuasions is outlined. Generally speaking, two competing approaches to analysing media content exist. The first is enumerative, usually involving the analysis of specific aspects of a large volume of media texts. Quantitative content analysis has been extensively used in the analysis of the traditional print and broadcast media. The second form of content analysis is strongly interpretative in orientation. Selected media texts are analysed in terms of both their manifest (obvious) and latent (hidden) meanings. Qualitative content analysis has been employed to examine a wider range of media than its quantitative counterpart. It has been successfully used in conjunction with analyses of audience reception and ethnographic accounts of media production (see Devereux, 1998). While quantitative content analysis remains in use, the paradigm shift within media and cultural studies towards a focus on *discourse* means that qualitative content analysis (in its various guises) has to come to predominate.

Given the overt emphasis in this textbook on unequal power relations and the particular focus in this chapter on the 'divided world', we discuss a number of examples of how qualitative content analysis has been applied in furthering our understanding of media representations of poverty, inequality and exclusion in the developed world and the Third World. The chapter proceeds to examine media representations of class, ethnicity, gender and sexuality. These aspects of social structure are discussed by drawing upon a range of qualitative methodological approaches applied to a range of media.

? ## Stop and think 7.1

How do we know what we know?

When sociologists and others ask about knowledge and understanding they are said to be asking **epistemological** questions. Given the centrality of media content in explaining the complexities of the social world, then, the need to critically evaluate and understand the make-up of media content is of crucial importance. Can you think of three examples where media content does matter in terms of our understandings of the social world?

Representation/re-presentation and 'reality'

An appreciation of how and why we should analyse media content is critically important for a number of reasons. First, media content is obviously a powerful source of meaning about the social world (see e.g. Breen, 2000; Dahlgren, 1981; Iyengar and Kinder, 1987). Take, for example, how ethnic minorities are represented in a media setting. That media coverage tends to problematize minorities is confirmed by a large number of studies. Gomes and Williams (1991), for example, examine how the media construct a connection between race and crime. Soubiran-Paillet (1987) investigates the representation of minorities in crime reports in the French and Swiss press (see also Winkel, 1990). Importantly, this kind of media coverage has been found to be of significance in the shaping of public attitudes towards minority groups such as refugees or asylum seekers (see e.g. Haynes et al. (2005, 2006) and the discussion of van Dijk's (1991) work, later in this chapter).

Second, while media content does not equate with social reality, it is essential that we critically examine how media content represents, or more accurately, as Hall (1974) notes, 're-presents', the realities (and inequalities) involved in social, economic and political relationships. Given the apparent shrinkage of media content of a more critical nature – owing in no small part to growing concentration and conglomeration – this issue is particularly germane. Whose version of 'reality' do we mainly see or hear about in a media setting? Does the predominance of a hegemonic discourse about class, ethnicity, gender or sexuality have a bearing on what audiences believe about the social world?

In this regard it is essential that a critical media studies continues to ask questions such as:

1. What does media content tell us about unequal relationships of power?
2. Whose interests are served by misrepresentation (or under-representation) within media content?

3. What discourses and/or ideologies are employed in order to tell stories about the social world?

4. What aspects do they highlight?

5. What aspects do they ignore?

6. How do particular forms of media content shape public opinion and public policy?

7. Do hegemonic representations result in state action or inaction as evidenced in how social or public policy is created and applied (e.g. policies concerning the poor or marginalized)?

8. Do hegemonic representations determine audience action or inaction in the face of inequalities or injustices?

9. How and why do particular forms of media representation about class, ethnicity, gender or sexuality change over time?

 A CLOSER LOOK 7.1

Arguments for content analysis

Analysing media content is a contentious business. If audiences are active agents in the construction of meaning why should we bother to analyse content at all? A critical understanding of media content is essential in that it is an important part of understanding where power resides in creating meaning for audiences. In a strong defence of why we should continue to have an interest in the effects of media content Kitzinger argues convincingly that: 'We cannot afford to dismiss inquiry into media influence as "old-fashioned" or doomed to failure as it confronts the complexity of text–audience relations. Cultural representations and media power matter' (1999: 15).

Media representations matter because they shape public beliefs and behaviour, a fact that is not lost on the economically or politically powerful. A balance needs to be struck, therefore, between the power of media audiences to deconstruct and resist media content and the power of media content to shape public perceptions about the world. Many postmodernists would contest the very idea that we examine the relationship between media content and 'social reality'. From their perspective, media content constitutes a 'hyper-reality' for media audiences. An analysis of the relationship between media content and social structure would in this version of media studies appear to be redundant. Much of the empirical research work that has stemmed from the postmodern perspective has tended, however, to overstate the phenomenon of audience resistance. In examining some of the difficulties inherent in the postmodern perspective, Fenton notes that:

To claim that the media are our reality is further criticized by those who wish to point to the oppression of women as real. In this retort, reality is recognized as disorderly and fragmented but as also showing patterns of inequality. If the media are our reality it is argued that we effectively deny the existence of material inequalities unless they occur in representation. (2000: 729)

Quoting Kitzinger and Kitzinger, Fenton underlines the difficulties that postmodernism presents for a critical media studies:

Feminists struggled for decades to name 'sexism' and 'anti-lesbianism'. We said that particular images of women – bound and gagged in pornography magazines, draped over cars in advertisements, caricatured as mothers-in-law or nagging wives in sitcoms – were oppressive and downgrading. The deconstructionist insistence that texts have no inherent meanings, leaves us unable to make such claims. This denial of oppressive meanings is, in effect, a refusal to engage with the conditions under which texts are produced, and the uses to which they are put in the dominant culture (Kitzinger and Kitzinger, 1993, 15). (Fenton, 2000: 729).

What is content analysis?

Content analysis is typically used to identify the intentions and other characteristics of communicators, detect the existence of latent propaganda or ideology, reflect cultural patterns of groups, reveal the foci of organizations and describe trends in communication content. It is often used as a way of comparing media content with the 'realities' of the social world. Researchers compare media representations about gender, ethnicity or class, for example, with social reality, as they interpret or experience it. Analyses of media content on asylum seekers or refugees for example might be examined in the light of other empirical (and reliable) data on inward migration.

Two main types of content analysis – quantitative and qualitative – are used within media research. Both have proved themselves to be popular if sometimes contentious research methods. Quantitative content analysis has its roots in the positivist social science tradition, while the qualitative content analysis approach has been influenced by developments within both structuralism and postmodernism. Qualitative content analysis is in fact a broad amalgamation of approaches, with different camps stressing the importance of examining, for example, the semiotic, framing, discursive or narrative dimensions of media texts. Many researchers use these approaches either singly or in combination, and, given the positivist associations of the original term, many would not describe their work as being a form of content analysis at all.

Content analysis (whether quantitative or qualitative) is best employed as a research method in conjunction with other methodologies that focus on media producers who create the content in the first place and/or on media audiences who receive the media texts in question. A small number of researchers have combined quantitative and qualitative content analysis approaches to good effect. The obvious danger in relying solely on content analysis is that meaning cannot simply be 'read off' a selected text, either through atomizing individual parts of a media text (such as a newspaper headline or the cover photograph of a magazine) within the quantitative paradigm or as in a 'close reading' of a media text within the qualitative model. One obvious use (and genuine strength) of content analysis is that it can be utilized as part of a larger research process called **triangulation**. Findings (on dominant themes, frames, discourses, source bias, etc.) can be set against the perspectives of the creators of media content or audience readings of the texts in question.

A CLOSER LOOK 7.2

Content analysis research in practice

In *Bad News* (1976) the Glasgow University Media Group adopt what McQuail (1983) refers to as a 'hybrid' methodological approach in undertaking a content analysis of British television news. They combine traditional quantitative content analysis with a structuralist approach in an attempt to unpack the coding of television news about industrial relations issues. Their focus is not only on the various elements that make up news content about industrial relations issues, but also on the cultural codes that predominate within the media organizations that produce the media texts in question. The Glasgow University Media Group's research is located between quantitative and qualitative poles. In undertaking this path-breaking research their task was not simply a counting of industrial relations news items; but rather; it was an attempt to interpret the meaning of those messages by searching beneath the manifest text to reveal the latent assumptions about social class. It is worth noting that, in more recent times, the research group has developed the News Game exercise in order to examine how audiences interpret media texts. This exercise and other qualitative methods have been used in combination with content analysis of media texts and is discussed in more detail in Chapter 8.

Quantitative content analysis

The technique of traditional quantitative content analysis developed primarily by Berelson (1952) is based on the counting of phenomena. Berger (1982) defines this form of content analysis to be:

> [a] research technique based upon measuring (counting) the amount of something (violence, percentages of Blacks, women, professional types or whatever) in a sampling of some form of communication (such as comics,

sitcoms, soap operas, news shows). The basic assumption implicit in content analysis is that an investigation of messages and communication gives insights into the people who receive these messages. (1982: 107)

Quantitative content analysis, if designed properly, can be a useful research tool. It allows us to compare selected aspects of large amounts of media content over time or between media organizations, for example. One obvious problem with traditional content analysis is its assumption that specific forms of media content will have an effect (usually a negative one) on audiences. Traditional content analysis does not engage in any meaningful way with the multiple meanings that media texts might possibly have for audiences.

Stop and think 7.2

What types of media genres would you think best suit a quantitative form of content analysis?

Qualitative content analysis

Despite the continued use of quantitative content analysis by some researchers (see e.g. Evans et al., 1991), the quantitative approach came in for a great deal of criticism in the last quarter of the twentieth century and was eventually supplemented by a form of qualitative content analysis that emphasized the notion of discourse (Woolacott, 1982). The move within media analysis from quantitative to qualitative content analysis is best summarized as a shift from empiricism to discourse. Van Der Berg and van Der Veer (1989) trace the move away from enumerative content analysis to an approach of a more qualitative kind. Because of its tendency to isolate specific elements of a media text, quantitative content analysis, they argue, 'is not capable of analysing communications as *discourses*' (1989: 161, emphasis added).

The newly found focus on media texts as a whole, rather than just specific parts of media messages (for example, instances of particular kinds of representation, such as the age, class, colour, ethnicity or shape of women in television advertising), meant that traditional quantitative content analysis came to be displaced.

The qualitative turn

The emerging, and ultimately more sophisticated, qualitative content analysis approach within media research was influenced, in turn, by important developments within semiotic, discourse, frame and **narrative analysis**. Readings of media texts as a whole, examining the latent as well as the manifest elements of content, relating specific media discourses to other discourses, became more of the norm within media research. Qualitative content analysis focusing on the symbolic, discursive, framing or narrative dimensions of media texts has worked in tandem with the reception analysis model of audience-based research.

Stop and think 7.3

What types of media genres would you think best suit a qualitative form of content analysis?

Content analysis: where to start?

Many students are very apprehensive about undertaking a content analysis. The following books contain accounts of content analysis that are accessible and easy to understand.

For qualitative content analysis techniques consult: K. Bruhn Jensen and N.W. Jankowski (eds) (1991) *A Handbook of Qualitative Methodologies for Mass Communication Research*. London: Routledge; and D.L. Altheide (1996) *Qualitative Media Analysis*. London: Sage.

For quantitative content analysis see the following texts: A.A. Berger (1998) *Media Research Techniques*, 2nd edn. London: Sage; A. Hansen, S. Cottle, R. Negrine and C. Newbold (1998) *Mass Communication Research Methods*. London: Macmillan; K. Krippendorf (2012) *Content Analysis: An Introduction to its Methodology*, 3rd edn. Thousand Oaks, CA: Sage; and K. Krippendorf and A. Bock (eds) (2008) *The Content Analysis Reader*. Thousand Oaks, CA: Sage.

Do it! 7.1 Comic books, gender roles and content analysis

Select two stories from a comic book and carry out a simple quantitative and a qualitative content analysis of the representation of gender roles. In the case of the quantitative content analysis itemize the variables that you intend to count. In doing the qualitative analysis clearly identify the themes that you propose to analyse. Having undertaken this research exercise, what do you think are the implications of choosing either a quantitative or a qualitative research approach in the analysis of content? Are you convinced of its usefulness in doing media research?

Media re-presentations in a divided world: four approaches outlined

Four examples of qualitative content analysis (semiotic, frame, discourse and narrative analysis) are now briefly examined (see Figure 7.1 for an elaboration). All examples are concerned with examining how mainstream media content represents poverty and inequality.

Sebeok defines semiotics as: 'the study of the exchange of any messages whatever and of the systems of signs which underlie them, the key concept of semiotics remaining always the sign' (1974: 108). Discourse analysis, as we have seen in Chapter 6, refers to the analysis of text and talk in terms of how unequal power relationships are reproduced. **Frame analysis** is concerned with the interpretative frameworks used by media professionals in telling stories to media audiences (see Caragee and Roefs, 2004; Kitzinger, 2000). Framing theory evolved from earlier concerns about the media's capacity to shape and determine public discourse. The decision to focus on specific issues and the selection of frames for thinking about these objects sees the media play a powerful agenda-setting role. McCombs and Shaw (1972) stress the need to think critically about the discursive cues or frames (both conscious and unconscious) that media

---

Semiotic analysis: The content of media texts function at a symbolic level. Meaning is conveyed through the use of signs or symbols, e.g. The Eiffel Tower signifies Paris. Paris, in turn, may signify romance and its Left-Bank bohemianism.
Discourse analysis: Media content makes use of hegemonic and other forms of knowledge to make sense of the world. Critical discourse analysis is concerned with identifying and explaining how particular discourses work to perpetuate unequal power relations, e.g. anti-immigrant discourses, discourses which are pro-employer, or discourses which foreground the interests of multinational corporations.
Framing analysis: Media content and its meaning for audiences is structured by the use of interpretative frames or templates, e.g. Climate change; eco-friendly; the obesity 'epidemic'; the African AIDS/HIV 'time-bomb'; the 'fiscal cliff'.
Narrative analysis: Media (and other) texts conform to a set of norms or unwritten rules. In a soap opera 'good' will always triumph over 'evil'; a James Bond movie follows a set narrative structure in which the white Western hero always ultimately prevails. (The ideological context in an individual Bond movie may vary according to the prevailing geo-political climate.)

Figure 7.1 **Four types of content analysis at a glance.**

professionals employ in communicating about particular phenomena. As Entman (1993: 52) tells us: 'To frame is to select some aspects of perceived reality and make them more salient in a communicating text, in such a way as to promote a particular problem definition, causal interpretation, moral evaluation, and/or treatment recommendation'. The focus of narrative analysis is on the narrative structure of individual media texts. Many researchers use these approaches in one or other combination, with discourse analysis being the most popular choice in recent times.

Semiotic analysis

Taking a semiotic approach, Benthall's *Disasters, Relief and the Media* (1993) examines media images of disaster and disaster relief. Relief agencies and the media are critically examined in terms of how they use (and abuse) children as potent sources of imagery in the construction of media texts about the Third World.

Benthall divides his analysis of the semiotics of disaster relief into two periods, namely the pre- and post-1980s. He argues that in the pre-1980 period the imagery tends to be of a patronizing sort: 'Virtually all appeals for charity until the 1980s tended to picture helpless passive victims and heroic saviours' (1993: 177). These campaigns involve using both realistic photographic styles and the flagrant abuse of starving children. In the post-1980s period, Benthall states, his semiotic reading of the dominant imagery reveals that, in the West, 'we' portray colonized peoples in the same way as men portray women. This portrayal, he argues, exhibits anxiety about our expendability and the fear of forces that are beyond our control. Thus the West views Third World poverty as a threat because of the perceived implications it may have for Western society in terms of mass migration.

Benthall's semiotic analysis also suggests that in the West we both exaggerate and misunderstand Third World poverty. He argues that essential questions in the overall equation, such as colonialism and global capitalism, are absent in terms of how we explain the Third World at a visual and a symbolic level.

Benthall's fascinating study draws upon the work of the Russian formalist Vladimir Propp (1928). In doing so he suggests that we should examine media images of the Third World as a form of folk narrative. Just as the folk tale follows a set of narrative conventions (having villains and heroes, etc.) so do images and stories about the Third World. They have heroes (from the West, usually white and middle-class, often well known in another role as actress, politician or pop star); villains (often portrayed as greedy dictators or tyrannical Marxists); donors (who are given magical powers) and false heroes (such as fund raisers who make off with the proceeds of a collection for the poor and starving).

Discourse analysis

In 'Mass media and discourse on famine in the Horn of Africa' Sorenson (1991) uses a discourse analysis approach in order to examine the activities of media organizations and the stories that they produce about the Third World. The media content that Sorenson analyses draws upon a number of discourses. These discourses emphasize famine as crisis – Ethiopian rather than African famine – and that famine is the result of either natural causes or native culpability. These media discourses, he concludes, may be read as ideological texts. They are ideological because they do not challenge or question the existing power relationships between Africa and the West.

Sorenson's work (1991) confirms the general invisibility of Third World issues in a media setting (see e.g. Nohrstedt, 1986). He notes that, despite the availability of film footage and information about African famine in the early 1980s, the mass media in the West were reluctant to cover the story. He cites an unnamed journalist as saying: 'the Third World isn't news and starving Africans in particular are not news' (1991: 224). Sorenson argues that during the 1980s the African famine story was largely absent from the Western media's agenda because it had, in media terms, 'a low entertainment value'. Coverage only occurred when a crisis point was reached in the famine.

A key feature, Sorenson stresses, 'in the discursive construction of famine in the Horn [of Africa] is that of aestheticisation, the packaging of famine as a shocking and dramatic crisis' (1991: 225). Thus famine, itself a common feature of many African countries, is not in itself deemed to be 'newsworthy', and is only given coverage through a discourse of impending or actual crisis. A further key element in the 1980s media's discourse on African famine is the emphasis on Ethiopia as opposed to other stricken areas (presumably because of the presence of the Western media – albeit belatedly – in Ethiopia in 1984; for a critical account see Philo (1993a)). The 'naturalization' dimension of the coverage is also stressed – coverage tends to emphasize the notion that famine occurs as a result of natural causes (such as climate or crop failure) as opposed to man-made ones.

Sorenson's main assertion is that media coverage of famine represents an ideological parable:

> Analysis reveals imposition of a narrative structure through the use of standard rhetorical techniques to construct famine as an ideological parable. This parable demonstrates the abuse of Western charity by treacherous Third World regimes allied with the Soviet Union. Media reports are related to other discursive constructions of Africa which offer a similar narrative structure. (1991: 223)

Sorenson uses an analysis of *Newsweek* magazine (26 November 1984) to illustrate this argument. He concludes that the discourse of this edition 'reveals a mythologizing of famine and the imposition of a narrative structure which serves to emphasize the culpability of Africans' (1991: 227). Africans are represented as being either incompetent or greedy, while the West is represented as a kind and generous benefactor.

Drawing on the approach taken by French theorist Roland Barthes in his book *Mythologies* (1973) Sorenson concludes that this type of media activity is in fact a form of inoculation. In engaging in this kind of practice the media admit to the occurrence of 'accidental evil' (poverty and famine) and yet function to conceal the wider structural inequalities that cause Third World poverty and famine. Within this media discourse the locus of blame rests with Africans, especially the peasant farmers, who are portrayed as being backward and incompetent. Media coverage of this kind is loaded with assumptions about the 'primitivism' of our African opposites or cultural others (see also Dahlgren and Chakrapani, 1982).

Frame analysis

In a media setting it is commonplace to narrate stories about poverty in individual/biographical rather than structural terms (Devereux, 1998). One of the net results of individualizing stories about the poor is that it reduces the likelihood of threatening the status quo. This aspect of media coverage of poverty is not restricted to Third World poverty. In recognizing this, Iyengar's study 'Is anyone responsible? How television frames political issues' (1991) subjects US media coverage of poverty to a frame analysis (see also Gamson, 1989; Gamson and Modigliani, 1987). The study examines how network television frames issues about poverty, unemployment and racial inequality. Iyengar's results demonstrate how framing takes place in terms of attributions of responsibility for poverty and inequality.

Network news is analysed in order to see if it does frame poverty, unemployment or racial inequality in terms of either 'thematic' or 'episodic' frames. Iyengar (1991) defines episodic news frames as those which 'take the form of a case-study or event-oriented report and depict public issues in terms of concrete instances (for example, the plight of a homeless person or a teenage drug user, the bombing of an airliner or an attempted murder)' (1991: 14). Thematic news frames, on the other hand:

> … place public issues in some more general or abstract context and take the form of a 'takeout' or 'backgrounder', report directed at general outcomes or conditions. Examples of thematic coverage include reports on changes in government welfare expenditures, congressional debates over the funding of employment training programs, the social or political grievance of groups undertaking terrorist activity, and the backlog in the criminal justice process. (1991: 14)

Iyengar concludes that, in general, US network news is not overly concerned about poverty or racial inequality as news stories. In the coverage that did take place 66% of stories were found to be episodic. Iyengar suggests that audiences are twice as likely to encounter a story that was episodic as they were to encounter one that was thematic. Unemployment coverage, by contrast, was mainly thematic. This is explained by the fact that while unemployment is recorded on a monthly basis and regularly the subject of government announcements, poverty receives much less attention because governments measure and report on it less frequently.

As part of the research project Iyengar (1991) carried out a number of experiments using five news reports that were classified as having either thematic or episodic frames. After viewing the news reports in question his study groups were asked to discuss whether poverty or racial inequality resulted from societal or individual inaction. His analysis suggests that news stories from network television were significant in shaping people's beliefs about the responsibility for poverty or racial inequality. Framing that was deemed to be episodic was found to increase the chances of audiences placing responsibility in the hands of the individual, while framing that was deemed to be thematic was found to increase the likelihood of audiences viewing the responsibility for the problem in structural or societal terms.

Narrative analysis

Campbell and Reeves's study 'Covering the homeless: the Joyce Brown story' (1989) also makes reference to how media coverage of poverty relies upon individual rather than structural explanations. Their work analyses the narratives of news reporting on Joyce Brown, a New York 'bag lady' (who was allegedly schizophrenic). She refused the attentions and offers of help from social workers. They argue that network television framed and narrated the question of homelessness through four distinct stages of the routine news package. They suggest that: 'the major socio-economic problem of homelessness which requires collective participation for resolution often plays out in the news as an isolated personal problem demanding individual attention' (1989: 23).

Stop and think 7.4

How do the analyses by Benthall and Sorenson of media representations of the Third World compare with the findings of the case study on Third World news discussed in Chapter 3 online in the companion website?

Do it! 7.2   Analysing television news content

Select a television news report on homelessness or unemployment. Apply each of the approaches outlined above (semiotic, discourse, frame and narrative) to the report. What are the individual strengths of each method? What insights (if any) did each method give you in terms of deepening your understanding of the report's content?

Media re-presentations of social class

Media representation of social class has received less attention from mass-media researchers. This may be, in part, due to the fact that many issues that are in fact class based are not framed as such within media content. Media content, can, as we have already noted in Chapter 6, obfuscate the very existence of structural inequalities whether they are based upon class, ethnicity or gender (or a combination of all three). Of the limited research work that exists, two important trends are worth commenting upon. There has been a particular focus on media representation of the **working class** and those who are dependent on state welfare. Two competing discourses emerge from this analysis. The working class are, in many instances, portrayed as the 'happy' or **'deserving' poor** while those who are on welfare are regularly represented within media content in a negative light. Specific sub-groups within the working and underclass are the targets of media driven moral panics. Many of these moral panics have a marked gendered dimension. Female lone mothers, Roma Gypsies, immigrants, Irish Travellers and 'Chavs' in the UK, 'Welfare Queens' and 'Trailer Trash' in North America have been the subject of significant levels of negative media representation.

Read on! 7.1   Luxurious lifestyles

Peter Golding and Sue Middleton (1982) 'Luxurious lifestyles', from *Images of Welfare: Press and Public Attitudes to Poverty*. Oxford: Blackwell, pp. 62–3.

Every story made sure to mention cigars, suits and indolent comfort. For some time this was paramount. The *Daily Telegraph*, which had two separate stories the same day, headlined one '£10,000-a-year Lifestyle for Dole Fiddler', opening its coverage by noting Deevy's life of splendour. The *Sun* front-page headline '£36,000 Scrounger' was followed by an underlined sub-headline, 'Six Years for Dole Cheat who Spent £25 a week on the Best Cigars'. The *Daily Express* coined the epithet King Con, and above their front-page headline 'Incredible Reign of King Con' was a strap '£200-a-week tycoon on social security'. The story gave great prominence to the Judge's remarks about people asking 'What's the good of working?' The *Daily Mail* front-page story 'Biggest Scrounger of the Lot' also drew attention to Deevy's Corona cigars and expensive suits. The *Daily Mirror* lead story 'King of the Dole Queue Scroungers' (a phrase clearly implying a host of like followers) began 'Nothing was too good for Derek Deevy. His weekly cigar bill came to £25 and he regularly bought expensive suits. The fact that he was out of work didn't spoil his life at the top.' ... Deevy was immediately enthroned as King of a teeming population of scroungers and spongers. ... The question 'How many others?' seemed always to be rhetorical, inviting the reader to nod knowingly in affirmation of the suspicion that prompted the question.

The *Daily Express* (14 July) carried a centre-page feature by Iain Sproat headed 'I believe we have seen only the tip of the iceberg,' which recounted the by now familiar tales from Mr Sproat's postbag to illustrate his point that the Deevy case exploded 'the myth that abuse of the welfare system is some minimal problem'. The *Daily Mirror* began to gather in the evidence in a story (15 July) headed 'Doing the Scrounge Rounds'. This featured four cases (three in Manchester) of people 'on the scrounge'. Given this massive evidence it was no surprise to learn in the first line of the story that 'Britain's army of dole-queue swindlers were on the run last night as a Government Minister warned he was going gunning for them'.

 ## Stop and think 7.5

1. How, in your opinion, does media coverage of the crimes of the relatively powerless compare with coverage of the crimes of the powerful?

2. Re-read this extract and highlight how lexicalization is used to define and express an opinion about those who engage in welfare fraud.

A CLOSER LOOK 7.4

'Chavs' and media visibility of the underclass

The mainstream media have proven themselves to be reluctant to frame social issues as being class based. The world of the working or blue-collar class is disproportionately underrepresented within media content. There have, however, been occasional moral panics engaged in by the print and broadcast media in Europe and the USA, for example, on the 'problem' of the underclass, with the 'problem' being defined mainly in terms of the cost of social welfare provision and portraying the underclass as living – in labour market terms – unproductive lives. These moral panics have become increasingly gendered, with a growing focus on female lone mothers.

In the early years of the twenty-first century the British print and broadcast media began to focus more and more on the emergence, as they termed it, of 'Chav' culture. Skeggs notes the media's obsession '… with "chavs" (white working-class men and women depicted as tasteless, excessive, ungovernable and atavistic)' (2005: 966).

The term 'Chav' – based upon an old Romany/Gypsy word for a child – came to signify membership of the white (usually unemployed) underclass. Unlike older examples of the 'dishonest' or **'undeserving poor'**, Chavs were defined in terms of their excessive (but tasteless) consumption (Hayward and Yar, 2006). Clothing brands – such as Burberry – which were once seen as the preserve of the middle and upper classes, were appropriated to become a signifier of Chav identity. The conspicuous wearing of 'bling' jewellery such as gold chains or sovereign rings by both male and female Chavs was also criticized within media content. Within this media discourse Chavs lead excessive and feckless lives. An interesting twist within this media coverage was the focus on the 'celebrity Chavs' who were in evidence on reality television programmes and in tabloid newspapers and magazines (Hayward and Yar, 2006).

The pathologizing of the Chav represents an interesting example of how the mainstream media are directly involved in the forging and re-casting of class identities. As an 'other', Chavs came to represent, in a very powerful way, a key component of the immoral poor. In spite of the dominant state discourse of social inclusion, which was a key aspect of New Labour ideology, Chavs exist beyond the pale. They are 'other' to the 'respectable' working class and expanding middle classes. The media's obsession with Chavs happened in a very particular ideological context. It is no accident that such representations arose when neo-liberal ideologies had come to predominate in political and media discourse. Neo-liberal ideology places a firm focus on personal and individual responsibility and has not been slow to blame the poor and others for the situation they find themselves in (see Tyler, 2008).

See: http://www.chavtowns.co.uk/

Read on! 7.2   Film producer B

Eoin Devereux (1998) 'Film producer B', from *Devils and Angels: Television, Ideology and the Coverage of Poverty*. Luton: University of Luton Press, pp. 34–5.

This producer opted for a docu-drama approach in making his appeal segments. His belief was that he should keep these ninety-second films documentary in style, but also incorporate elements of drama as well. True to his realism, he felt that there were certain things which needed to be shown, and in the case of the Cork homeless boys piece, there was a necessity to act out certain otherwise unseen activities. In filming in Cork he spoke to the centre's founder about what he wanted to do. He maintained that the centre's founder realised that if he wanted to find young boys glue-sniffing or drinking spirits he could easily do so out on the streets, so instead he filmed some boys from the centre in a reconstruction of these activities. He maintained that it was essential for the audience to fully understand the implications for these young boys of allowing such a lifestyle to persist. He shot the piece of film in the backyard of the centre, using some of its clients – all of whom agreed to appear in the piece.

In describing the film segment he said:

> I did it as a straight documentary, but dramatising one element. Why? Because I could talk about it … they sniff … and people would say we don't really believe that. So you show it. Then I had to make up my mind about creating it … If I had to go out and find it, it might take me a week. … So I created it. I didn't put up a caption saying 'This is a reconstruction' because that again enters into the realm of disbelief on the part of the viewer.

In the context of … the unease … about this reconstruction, Producer B asserted his 'moral right' not to explain his filmmaking processes to the others in the production team, as he claimed the reconstruction was simply a creation in documentary form. His intention in making the piece of film was to create a connection between the message at the end of the film 'Our young people must not be allowed to die from drugs' and the images of solvent and alcohol abuse contained within the mini-dramatisation at the beginning. He maintained that what the audience was therefore being given was a certain degree of drama in two forms incorporating both the fictional and the factual documentary styles.

? Stop and think 7.6

1. Why is it useful to take account of the media professional's perspective in undertaking an analysis of media content?

2. How does the film director in question view his potential audience?

An example of print media representations of the poor

'It's Shabby Values, Not Class, That are to Blame for Society's Ills' by Amanda Platell, *The Daily Mail*, 30 January 2010. Reproduced by permission of *The Daily Mail* © 2010.

Harriet Harman's 'equality bible' was published this week – 450 pages of dripping, liberal invective that lays all the blame for society's ills on the class system. According to this queen of social engineering, people's 'life chances, from cradle to grave, are shaped' by their class origins. Yet when it comes to looking for the real cause why so many of the working class do worse at school, earn less and die younger, the blame must be placed elsewhere – on the countless numbers of feckless parents. Ms Harman would be wise to dump her obsessive equality agenda and learn from the shocking insight into Britain's underclass that was provided this week when a Tesco store banned customers from shopping in pyjamas. Welcome to the world of Britain's slum mums, where women without an ounce of self-respect go shopping dressed like slobs in elasticated-waist nightwear and fluffy slippers. One of those banned from the store (in a rundown inner-city area once controversially branded 'the estate of missing fathers') whinged: 'Do they have any idea how difficult it is to get three kids off to school when you are a single parent? We haven't got time to get all dolled up.'

The working class of the past had enormous self-respect. Men, however poor, wore suits and ties. Women scrubbed front steps. Mothers wouldn't have been seen dead wearing pyjamas in their own kitchen, let alone in public. The tragedy is that the shabby values of these slum mums are passed on to their children. Until this sloth changes, no amount of social engineering will have any effect.

The truth is that it's not being born working class that destroys children's chances in life, but the way they are brought up in broken homes by parents married to a welfare culture that leeches away any sense of self-respect or ambition. If your only role model is a slob of a mother who doesn't work, can't bother to get dressed in the morning, lazes around smoking, eating junk food and watching Jeremy Kyle-style TV shows all day, what chance is there for you? The solution is not more of Labour's failed social engineering, but a government that has the willpower to dismantle Britain's ruinous benefits system that keeps rewarding slum mums for bringing up generations of children destined for illiteracy, worklessness and premature death.

Stop and think 7.7

1. How does Platell's article explain the persistence of social inequality in the UK?

2. How does the article represent lone mothers? What sort of language is used to describe lone mothers?

3. Having read the previous chapter on ideology and discourse is it possible to identify a dominant ideology in this piece?

Stop and think 7.8

'It's the poor wot gets the blame ...'

1. In addition to 'Chavs', what other social groups are demonized in a media setting?

2. If you live outside of the UK consider how the mass media represent members of the underclass in your country.

3. How do ethnicity and gender intersect with representations focused upon social class in a media setting?

4. The media's treatment of rich people and poor people is radically different. Why do you think this is the case? Whose interests are served by demonizing or blaming the poor for their poverty?

Media coverage of the underclass: stories about welfare

Dedinsky (1977) stresses how media coverage of welfare and poverty in the United States tends to be sensationalist, short-lived and with very little in-depth analysis of the many complex issues at stake. She argues that the media have successfully convinced the public that the welfare system is a 'mess', but have not adequately explained why this might be. Barkin and Gurevitch's (1987) study 'Out of work and on the air: television news of unemployment' examines news coverage of unemployment in the United Kingdom in the 1980s. The authors focus on the thematic structure of news and the explanations given for unemployment. As such, few explanations for unemployment are offered by television news, and they argue that the very diversity of thematic structures reveals the societal frameworks within which television journalists construct stories about this issue.

Deacon (1978) examines the 'facts' behind scrounging or welfare fraud in the media. He investigates the reality of welfare abuse – which is in fact quite low – and the amount of undue attention given at times to this issue in the print and broadcast media. Golding and Middleton, similarly, in their studies 'Making claims: news media and the welfare state' (1979) and *Images of Welfare* (1982) examine media-generated moral panics about alleged welfare abuse. During their six-month content analysis-based study, Golding and Middleton (1979) found that welfare issues, as such, did not make the news. Significantly, welfare was considered worthy of coverage only when it was connected with other issues such as crime, fraud or sex. A key theme uncovered in their analysis – and developed further in their 1982 study – was that the poor are constructed in a media context as either deserving or undeserving. Media demonization of certain sections of the underclass has contributed in no small way to legitimizing both welfare cutbacks by the state and the furtherance of hegemonic ideologies about the poor and the underclass.

The happy poor: representations in fictional media content

A number of critical studies have examined how the media represent social class within fictional genres. Thomas and Callanan's (1982) study 'Allocating happiness: TV families and social class' is critical of fictional television for disseminating the myth of the 'happy poor'. By analysing prime-time television series on the US networks ABC, NBC and CBS, they conclude that fictional programmes such as *The Waltons* and *Little House on the Prairie* propagate a world-view that suggests that 'money clearly does not buy happiness ... in fact relative poverty does' (1982: 16). Thomas and Callanan argue that the poorer characters in these programmes were more likely to be portrayed as 'good' or 'straight' characters and they were more likely to see their problems resolved and to find happiness at the conclusion of a programme.

Gould et al. in 'Television's distorted vision of poverty' (1981) also explore how prime-time US television portrays blue-collar or working-class life. They argue that:

> [in] the depiction of poverty during prime-time broadcasts, television networks present a sentimentalised vision of economic deprivation that omits or minimises hardship while idealising the supposed benefits of a spartan way of life. Much happier than harried members of the middle and

upper-income groups, poor and working people on television seldom strive against their economic fates or against the system. (1981: 309)

In *Upscaling Downtown: Stalled Gentrification in Washington DC*, Williams (1988) explores the hermeneutics of television serials from a social-anthropological perspective. He explores the 'prime-time divide' whereby programmes that are aimed at specific social classes often portray members of one social class to another. The poor, he argues, watch television programmes about the wealthy, while the middle classes are drawn to programmes that feature the inner city and the down-and-out. In the middle-class Elm Valley viewers witness 'an uneasy and uncomfortable city, many crazed and violent people, but very few supportive creative people in charge of their own lives. Thus they may get from television an important sense of how poverty batters and victimizes people' (Williams, 1988: 112). Programmes such as *Hill Street Blues* offer 'powerfully negative views of the poor in the city as exotic, often repellent "others", and these views are filtered through the eyes of the police' (1988: 113).

A CLOSER LOOK 7.6

Shameless

'It's not *My Name Is Earl* or *Roseanne*. It's got a much graver level of poverty attached to it. It's not blue collar; it's no collar' – Paul Abbott, Creator of *Shameless* (Rochlin, 2010).

Channel 4's (UK) BAFTA award winning series *Shameless* portrays the lives of the underclass on Manchester's fictional Chatsworth 'sink' estate. (It has also been remade as *Shameless USA* and located in the suburbs of Chicago.) Devised by Paul Abbott, the series examines the many trials and tribulations of the Gallagher family. Combining humour and social realism, the programme brings us into the lives of people who have been described (and dismissed) in other sections of the media as being 'Chavs'. Above all else, *Shameless* is a story of survival. Surrounded by dysfunction, the Gallaghers have been abandoned by their mother (who has run off with her lesbian lover), and their father Frank is unemployed, an occasional soft-drug user and a chronic alcoholic. Unlike the dominant view of the underclass as being lazy and unresourceful, *Shameless* demonstrates how the underclass manages to survive. Family and community ties are shown to be strongest in the face of adversity. The programme's main female characters are especially resilient. When 'establishment' or 'official' Britain – in the shape of the police, social welfare officials or social workers – intervenes in the lives of the Gallaghers, the family always wins the day by drawing upon their own resources or the help of their immediate neighbours. The 'excesses' associated with the underclass are very much in evidence in the series, with soft-drug use, drunkenness and violence being common. *Shameless* has not been afraid of examining a range of social and personal issues, such as 'coming out', inter-racial sexual relationships, welfare fraud, the black or informal economy and petty crime. It is somewhat ironic that Frank Gallagher's mother was once an (old) Labour Party representative. Although Frank makes reference to the rights of the 'working man' he has nearly always been unemployed. *Shameless* represents a metaphorical 'two-fingers' to the Britain of New Labour with its new-found emphasis on 'social inclusion'.

Do it! 7.3

Watch an episode of either *Shameless* or *Shameless USA*. Do you think that the series challenges hegemonic assumptions about the poor or does it lend itself to a voyeurism on the part of middle-class audiences?

 A CLOSER LOOK 7.7

Media stigmatization of poor neighbourhoods

Analyses of how the poor and socially excluded are represented by the media have consistently demonstrated that discrete categories of the poor and underclass are constructed as 'Devils' or the 'undeserving poor.' In addition to the stigmatizing and 'othering' of members of the underclass or poor, a growing number of researchers have sought to understand how the places in which these groups live also come to be stigmatized (see e.g. Blokland, 2008; Devereux et al., 2011b; Greer and Jewkes, 2005; Hastings, 2004). Influenced largely by Erving Goffman's (1963) classic sociological treatise, which understood stigma as 'spoiled identity', this research has examined how media and other social forces contribute to the creation of negative stereotypes, which damage the reputations of the places in which the underclass or poor reside. The research convincingly demonstrates how the negative reputations of such places can, in themselves, have a profound effect upon the life chances, experiences and self-image of those who live in neighbourhoods which carry a stigma (Permentier et al., 2009). **Stigmatization** processes are complex and affect the perspectives of both those inside and outside such places.

Negative and sensationalist media coverage of poor neighbourhoods is consistently referred to in studies which attempt to explain how neighbourhoods come to suffer from endogenous stigmatization. Oresjo et al. (2004) illustrate how the media play a key role in constructing and disseminating fear about specific neighbourhoods in Sweden. Palmer et al. (2004: 411) argue that these spaces are constructed in a media setting (and in many people's minds) as 'problem places' for 'problem people.' In examining the Australian experience, for example, Palmer et al. (2004: 411) contend that:

> The media, in particular, but by no means exclusively, contributes to the stigmatisation of certain suburbs and those who live in them, by promoting images and reputations of suburbs overrun by drugs, crime, mental health issues, youth disorder and the perennial favourite – 'single mothers'.

Media (and other) discourses about the places in which the poor live can be classified as either normalizing or pathologizing (Hastings, 2004). Normalizing discourses are critical, even dismissive, of an estate's stigmatized image. They reject the idea that the behaviour of residents as a group exceeds the limits of expected deviance or differentiates them from residents of other estates. They depict anti-social behaviour as the actions of a small minority. They explain an estate's stigmatization and problems in terms of structural causes. A neighbourhood's pathologized identity can negatively impact on residents' self-image and life-chances, health, employment opportunities (so-called 'red-lining') and access to service provision.

Media representations of ethnicity: a discourse analysis approach

In Chapter 5 we referred to van Dijk's (1998a) work on ideology and discourse. Adopting a critical anti-racist perspective, van Dijk has undertaken detailed discourse analyses of the print media's role in reproducing racist ideologies in the Dutch and British press (van Dijk, 1988, 1991, 1998a, 1998b). In addition, in his text *Ideology: A Multidisciplinary Approach* (1998a) he subjects Dinesh D'Souza's (1995) book *The End of Racism: Principles for a Multiracial Society* to a detailed critical analysis in terms of how it understands race and ethnicity in the United States. Here, we will briefly examine his text *Racism and the Press* (1991), and focus, for reasons of space, on the semantic aspects of one selected example of media content about ethnic issues.

Van Dijk's (1991) study is a hugely detailed multidisciplinary investigation into the British print media. In excess of 2,700 newspaper articles on ethnic issues were analysed for the period 1 August 1985 to 31 January 1986. In terms of an overall methodological approach, the researcher tells us that, in this study, when media discourses about ethnic issues are analysed:

> it is first established what is being said or written about ethnic minority groups or ethnic relations in general. This analysis yields an account of the contents of the discourse, namely in terms of global topics and local meanings. However, textual analysis pays special attention to how such contents are formulated, that is to style, rhetoric, argumentative or narrative structures or conversational strategies. (1991: 6)

Van Dijk's approach recognizes the importance of examining the connections between unequal power relations in society (in this instance in terms of ethnicity), media content and public or audience attitudes and beliefs. Thus the findings emanating from his discourse analysis of media texts are related to measured public attitudes and beliefs about ethnicity. The study seeks to explain how 'white in-group members tend to express and communicate their ethnic attitudes to other members of the group and how such attitudes are spread and shared in society' (1991: 6). Van Dijk's research is based upon detailed and systematic analysis of the print media's role in the reproduction and circulation of dominant ideological interpretations of race and ethnicity.

In the latter part of *Racism and the Press* (1991) van Dijk examines news discourse about ethnicity at the micro or local level. This is defined as: 'the meaning, style and rhetoric of its actual words and sentences' (1991: 176). In Chapter 7, for example, he presents us with a powerful example of how we might examine the ideological aspect of media discourse. He reproduces an extract from an editorial on immigration published in the *Mail* newspaper on 28 November 1985. It states:

> That is why we have to be more brisk in saying no, and showing the door to those who are not British citizens and would abuse our hospitality and tolerance. To do that is not to give way to prejudice, but to lessen the provocation on which it feeds. (1991: 177)

This editorial conforms to a wider conservative or right-wing discourse about ethnic issues. Van Dijk identifies five meaning structures and strategies in this brief extract. These are as follows:

1. The editorial 'presupposes' that 'we [British] are hospitable and tolerant' (1991: 176).

2. It rejects the notion that 'showing the door to those who are not British' might be construed as being prejudiced (1991: 176).

3. The editorial represents immigrants 'in a negative way by the use of the verb "to abuse", which also presupposes that immigrants do indeed abuse British tolerance. At the same time, this use of "abuse" establishes a contrast between the negative properties of the abuser and the good ones of the "tolerant" British' (1991: 177).

4. The use of the phrase 'those who are not British citizens' (1991: 177) would, on the face of it, seem to suggest that the editorial is critical of those who do not hold British passports. Van Dijk contrasts this with the newspaper's more general coverage of immigration issues and concludes that it really means non-white immigrants.

5. The editorial employs a number of euphemisms when applied to how 'we' should deal with immigrants. We (or us), the tolerant and hospitable British, must be 'brisk', 'in saying no', 'in showing the door' to them (immigrants).

A CLOSER LOOK 7.8

Media framing of asylum seekers and refugees

Writing in an Irish context, Haynes et al. (2006) undertook a content analysis of 188 broadsheet and tabloid newspapers to ascertain what kinds of frames were used in a media setting to explain the phenomenon of inward migration to Ireland. They discovered that eight key frames were in use – five of which the authors argue work to 'other' asylum seekers and refugees. The remaining three (and numerically in the minority) frames were classified as Human Interest, Positive and Supportive Coverage Frames. Through their detailed frame analysis the authors conclude that the majority of media coverage of asylum seekers is negative and conveys an overwhelming sense of threat to Irish society (see Figure 7.2).

Othering Frames	The illegitimacy of asylum seekers and asylum seeking e.g. 'ASYLUM UTD – REFUGEE SCAM NIGERIANS TELL IRISH CLUBS: "WE CAN GET YOU A FIGO, RONALDO OR BECKS"'
	Asylum seeking and asylum seekers as a threat to local and national integrity e.g. 'REFUGEE SHAMBLES; EXCLUSIVE: THREE COUNTIES SWAMPED BY LION'S SHARE OF ASYLUM-SEEKERS'
	The 'other' as a contaminant e.g. 'AIDS TEST REFUGEES EVERY FRIDAY; FURY AS NOONAN PLEDGES TO SCREEN "ILLEGALS"'
	Asylum seekers as a criminal element e.g. 'GARDAI HUNT SUSPECT REFUGEE KNIFE KILLER; ALGERIAN WANTED FOR MURDER AND BENEFITS RIP-OFF'
	Asylum seekers as an economic threat e.g. 'MATERNITY HOSPITAL HIT BY REFUGEE BABY BOOM; TOP DOC PREDICTS "DOOMSDAY" CRISIS'

Figure 7.2 **Haynes et al. (2006) demonstrate how media frames serve to 'other' immigrants. (Source: Haynes et al., 2006).**

A CLOSER LOOK 7.9

Print media representations of Muslim and Arab Australians

Foster et al. (2011) demonstrate how the Australian print media continue to problematize Muslim and Arab Australians. In spite of Australia's secularism and its aspirations to being an inclusive multicultural society, this important research demonstrates how Arab and Muslim Australians are negatively constructed in a media setting. Although there has been a long history of migration to Australia and significant numbers of Arabs and Muslims have in fact been born in Australia, Foster et al. (2011) evidence how there has been a hardening of attitudes. The researchers note that previous studies show how Arabs and Muslims are represented as 'enemies' and 'other' and how such groups are conflated with terrorist events such as 9/11, the Bali bombings and the 7/7 London bombings. The researchers undertook a detailed content analysis of a sample of daily and weekend broadsheet and tabloid newspapers published in Australia's capital cities. A total of 3,613 articles were included in the sample (they compared content from August 2001, August 2004 and August 2007) which allowed the researchers to compare coverage before and after 9/11. The researchers examined the selected content to see what kinds of discourses were in use. Their findings show how media discourses may be seen to be on a continuum ranging from those which emphasize the otherness of Arabs and Muslims to ones which stress the degree to which many Arabs and Muslims have integrated into Australian society and culture. Foster et al. (2011) provide clear evidence of the continued presence of negative, stereotypical, simplistic, essentialist, racist and othering discourses within some media content which serves to militate against the stated Australian project of multiculturalism.

Media representations of gender and sexuality

Within media content and across a variety of media genres we are presented with a range of representations about gender. Media content plays a hugely significant role in shaping our perceptions of what it is to be 'male' or 'female'. It also carries a set of hegemonic assumptions about human sexuality. Research on media representations of gender has focused on how women are objectified and exploited in a media context (especially in advertising and in pornography) and on the gap between social reality and media constructions of femininity and masculinity.

The feminist perspective has been to the fore in critiquing mainstream media content in terms of how it misrepresents and under represents women (Rakow, 1990). Media representations pertaining to being 'a man' or being 'a woman' are not fixed entities and they, demonstrably, change over time. If you were to undertake even a brief content analysis of the representations of roles ascribed to women and men in contemporary television advertising, for example, and compare it with representations in the 1960s or 1970s you would undoubtedly see differences in the discourses employed. One obvious difference might be the shift from firmly locating women in the domestic sphere to one that now emphasizes an independent career in the world of paid employment – although even now some advertisers continue to stress both the domestic and the external world of work responsibilities for women!

Media content reflects changing dominant discourses about femininity and masculinity. That is not to say that media content is a mirror image of the realities of gender identities in the social world. The gulf between representations and reality has been much commented upon. Van Zoonen and Costera Meijer, for example, argue that:

It is indeed easy to see that real women are much more different and more diverse than their representations in the media would seem to suggest. If media images were indeed a reflection of reality, 'real' women would be relatively rare in most parts of the real world, and Black, older, disabled, lesbian, fat, poor, or Third World women would be virtually nonexistent. (1998: 298)

We could equally create a list of men who do not conform to the dominant discourses surrounding masculinity and who are largely invisible within mainstream media content. This is particularly true in terms of men who are gay or bisexual.

In *Media, Gender and Identity* (2002) Gauntlett examines the invisibility of bisexuals, gay men and lesbians on television (see also Dow, 2001). He traces how mainstream television in both the United Kingdom and the United States is (slowly) beginning to examine the lives of bisexuals, gay men and lesbians in a fictional setting. Such coverage is not without its constraints, however. He notes that:

As recently as 1990, even the sight of two men sitting in bed together talking, with no physical contact – in the US drama series *Thirtysomething* – prompted half the advertisers to side with homophobic campaigners and withdraw their support, reportedly losing the ABC network over a million dollars ... Even in 1997–1998, Ellen DeGeneres's coming out as a lesbian in her sitcom *Ellen* (as well as in real life) caused an even bigger controversy with advertisers fleeing, and ABC/Disney dropping the popular show after one 'lesbian' season. (Gauntlett, 2002: 82)

While changes are gradually occurring in terms of covering storylines concerning alternative sexualities they are still novel.

Read on! 7.3   Villains or victims?

Helene A. Shugart (2003) 'Villians or victims: media representations of gay men and lesbians', from 'Reinventing privilege: the new (gay) man in contemporary popular media', *Critical Studies in Media Communication*, 20(1): 67–91, pp. 68–9.

Historically, representations of gay men and lesbians in the mainstream US media have been sparse and selective. ... Although 'homoerotic images and behavior were used as comic devices' (Fejes & Petrich, 1993, p. 397) such as cross dressing and role reversals, 'as expressed onscreen, America was a dream that had no room for the existence of homosexuals ... And when the fact of our existence became unavoidable, we were reflected, onscreen and off, as dirty secrets' (Russo [1981], p. xii). When presented in mainstream film or

▶

television until quite recently, gay characters were almost exclusively portrayed negatively, as either villains or victims (Gross, 1994). In both capacities, they were rendered as problems to be solved and almost always reflected gendered stereotypes that characterize gay men as effeminate and lesbians as masculine.

Attendant to the emergent gay rights movement in the 1970s, although standard negative tropes did not disappear, mainstream film and television began to feature more positive portrayals of gay characters. ... By the 1990s, the representation of gay men and lesbians in the popular mainstream media became *de riguer* for film and even obligatory for television fare. Major box-office hits like *Philadelphia*, *The Birdcage*, *To Wong Foo, Thanks for Everything! Julie Newmar*, and *In & Out* featured sympathetic gay protagonists, and the secondary-but-permanent character became a staple of the majority of mainstream television dramas and situation comedies, including, for example, *NYPD Blue*, *Chicago Hope*, *ER*, *Mad About You*, *Roseanne*, *Spin City*, and *Friends*. This television trend ultimately culminated in prime-time shows that featured lead gay protagonists in dramas like *Melrose Place* and *Dawson's Creek* and, more prominently, in the situation comedies *Ellen* and *Will & Grace*.

As many critics have argued, however, the 'chic' visibility of gay men and lesbians in the mainstream media is not unproblematic. ... Nearly all of these portrayals skirt the realities and implications of homosexuality by desexualizing the characters – i.e. by almost never depicting them in romantic or sexual situations. ... Some of these representations, as in *Personal Best*, depict homosexuality 'as a temporary interruption in the flow of heterosexual life' (Gross, 2001, p. 74). More common themes are that, first, gay characters are presented as devoid of gay social and political contexts ... thus capable of being grafted onto established heterosexual communities and contexts; and second, that their presence is used as a catalyst for heterosexual characters' growth and understanding. ...

 ## Stop and think 7.9

1. Why do you think media representations of gay men and lesbians have become (relatively) more common within mainstream media texts?

2. Critically evaluate the ways in which *Will & Grace* represents gay men. What are the main limitations evident within its portrayals?

Conclusion

Formal analysis of media content remains important. This chapter has outlined the main models of content analysis. Your choice of opting for a quantitative, qualitative or mixed model of content analysis depends on your research question and the type of media genre you wish to study. Media globalization has resulted in the wider circulation of many media texts. Concentration and conglomeration have altered the scope of media content. These structural changes add weight to the argument for a formal (and comparative) analysis of media content. A sophisticated content analysis of media texts drawing upon discourse, semiotic or framing analysis, for example, can assist us greatly in understanding more about the reception of media texts, a theme to which we now turn in Chapter 8. An appreciation of the intricacies of much media content can also deepen our understanding of how media content works to secure hegemonic definitions or understandings of social reality. All of the evidence presented in this chapter has raised a fundamental (and thorny) issue. In spite of many claims to the contrary, media representations of the social world reproduce hegemonic understandings of how the social world should be organized. This chapter has presented you with compelling evidence demonstrating that media discourses reproduce dominant perspectives about class, gender, ethnicity and sexuality which are far from being impartial. This raises fundamental questions about the power of the media to inform and misinform audiences about the complexities of the social world. In an age of media saturation, globalization and neo-liberalism, we are in fact witnessing a narrowing in the range of perspectives, opinions and explanations about the make-up of the social world. Even in many new media settings we can witness the recycling of half-baked truths and assumptions about the most vulnerable in society.

Chapter summary

This chapter has emphasized the following:

1. Content analysis (whether qualitative or quantitative) remains a crucial part of understanding media discourses and media power.
2. Quantitative and qualitative content analysis were each shown to have distinguishing features and to have distinct advantages and disadvantages in terms of trying to reach a more critical understanding of the media.
3. Semiotic, discourse, framing and narrative analysis each focus on specific elements of a media text.

(Continued)

4. Media coverage of the poor and underclass and the places in which they live is negative, biased and reflects dominant class interests.
5. In order to fully understand media influence and power we need to engage critically with media content.

Further reading

Breen, M., A. Haynes and E. Devereux (2006) 'Citizens, "loopholes" and maternity tourists: media framing of the 2004 Citizenship Referendum', in M. Corcoran and M. Peillon (eds), *Uncertain Ireland*. Dublin: IPA. This essay is an example of how framing theory may be applied to reach a better understanding of media discourse about a contentious social issue.

Chandler, D. (2007) *Semiotics: The Basics*, 2nd edn. London: Routledge. This text introduces you to the key aspects of semiotics and their application in a research setting.

Class Dismissed (2007) is available on DVD. Introduced by Pepi Leistyna and directed by Loretta Alper, *Class Dismissed* examines the invisibility and misrepresentation of the working or blue-collar class on mainstream American television. Using a wide range of historical and contemporary examples, the film shows how inequalities based upon ethnicity, gender and sexuality all intersect with social class in the make-up of how television represents social class. The DVD is accompanied by a useful study guide for teachers and students. For further details see http://www.mediaed.org/.

Kendall, D. (2005) *Framing Class: Media Representations of Wealth and Poverty in America*. Lanham: Rowman and Littlefield Publishers. Kendall uses a content analysis of newspaper and television to examine the underlying assumptions contained within US media content about social class.

Online reading

Go to the companion website and read the following:

- Haynes, A. (2007) 'Mass media representations of the social world: ethnicity and "race"', in E. Devereux (ed.), *Media Studies: Key Issues and Debates*. London: Sage.

- Kitzinger, J. (2007) 'Framing and frame analysis', in E. Devereux (ed.), *Media Studies: Key Issues and Debates*. London: Sage.

CHAPTER  8

Media Audiences and Reception

Chapter overview

This chapter examines the third, and arguably, the most intricate, part of the 'trinity' of production, content and reception described earlier. It aims to explain the complexities of media audiences by highlighting the following:

- The main paradigms or models which have been used in order to try to understand media audiences
- The main quantitative and qualitative methodological approaches to media audience analysis
- The continuing significance of reception analysis based upon a model that stresses the notion of discourse
- The 'ethnographic turn' within audience research
- The ongoing debate over the extent to which audiences have agency
- The usefulness of understanding audiences as fans
- The continued importance of marrying the understandings we may get from a reception-based model of media analysis with those obtained from a content- or production-based approach.

Key concepts

- Reception analysis
- Media discourse
- Effects
- Uses and gratifications
- Constructionist
- Active audiences

(Continued)

- Open and closed texts
- Audience resistance
- Fans and fandom
- Resistance
- Public knowledge
- Prosumers/produsers
- Popular culture
- Performative
- Participatory cultures

Introduction

Fears and concerns about the relationship between media and audiences have been a consistent feature of media history. From worries about the supposed effects of comic books on the minds and behaviour of children in the 1930s, to anxieties about the apparent overuse and misuse (e.g. cyber-bullying on Facebook and Ask FM) of social media in the twenty-first century, it is clear that the notion of it being problematic relationship is a recurring theme. This chapter does not sub-scribe to such a simplistic understanding of audiences or media power. While the power of audiences is recognized (and celebrated), this book does not subscribe to the postmodern viewpoint in which audiences exist in some kind of interpretative free-for-all. The power of media content to shape and frame our understanding and experience of the social world is firmly recognized. In doing so, however, the capacity that audiences have to critique, contest and resist dominant discourses is also acknowledged. It is these tensions which make the study of audiences a fasci-nating experience for all of us, as citizens and as students of the media.

In discussing audiences in this fashion, the complexities involved in the reception of media texts are acknowledged from the very outset. Such com-plexities have been accentuated in our radically altered mediascape resulting from globalization and technological change. Indeed, some commentators have questioned whether we can usefully talk about a media audience anymore (see, in particular, Livingstone, 2004; Stevenson, 2002), and some have gone as far as writing its obituary. While the audience is not dead, its disaggregation and reconfiguration do need to be engaged with if a critical understanding of what audiences are all about is to be arrived at.

With this in mind, this chapter does not rehearse, at any great length, the histories of the various traditional approaches to media audiences (effects and uses and gratifications, etc. that have come to typify many introductory text-books (see Ruddock, 2000, for a comprehensive overview)). Rather, it specifically examines the question of *reception* in some detail. The chapter emphasizes the *hermeneutic* or interpretative dimension of the relationship between media texts and media audiences, questions which have already been explored here in the context of our investigations into the workings of ideology, dominant ideology and discourse in Chapter 5 and in terms of diasporic and other audiences, media globalization and glocalization in Chapter 3.

This chapter begins with an overview of the key paradigms within reception analysis. It outlines the main quantitative and qualitative methodological approaches to media audiences. The 'ethnographic turn' is examined in detail. Three examples of reception analysis research are then discussed. Chapter 9 on new media and social media includes a consideration of audiences in terms of debates about concerning participatory and prosumer/produser cultures. This chapter also discusses these important themes by means of an extended case study on the Latino/Chicano fan cultures associated with the second-generation Irish singer Morrissey as well as a discussion on audiences as producers/produsers.

 Stop and think 8.1

Being an audience member

Before you read in more detail about how audiences, and the concept of reception in particular, have been understood by media theorists and empirical researchers, reflect for a while on your own experiences as an audience member. Compile a list of the variety of situations in any one day in which you may be a member of a media audience and consider the following issues:

1. How many media audiences do you actually belong to?

2. What sorts of media genres are you predominantly interested in?

3. In what social situations are you mainly an audience member?

4. Do these social contexts have a bearing on how you interpret the multiplicity of media messages that you encounter?

5. How active or reflexive are you as an audience member?

6. Where might you see agency or reflexivity in your everyday media experience?

7. Which paradigms (effects, uses and gratifications, reception, produser/ prosumer) best fit with your personal experiences of being an audience member?

Themes and tensions: competing theoretical and methodological approaches in audience research

As was discussed in Chapter 2, early behaviourist media research (effects and uses and gratifications) was quite problematic in the ways in which audiences were conceptualized. Within this body of research audiences were understood as either responding slavishly to media messages or simply using and responding to media messages in order to gratify their needs. There was little or no focus on the complexities of media content or how it might be variously understood by different audiences in different social contexts. With this in mind, this chapter takes that most important juncture in the overall development of media and audience research – reception analysis – as its key starting point and considers reception analysis and the subsequent paradigms of audience research in more detail.

The methodological fractures and factions evident within the larger project of media analysis – and within the social sciences more generally – come into clearer focus when we examine how empirical research is undertaken on media audiences. Two competing methodological paradigms – the quantitative and the qualitative – have traditionally been used within audience-based research. Despite the calls in recent times by some researchers for a more integrated methodological approach, the marked 'stand-off' between the quantitative and qualitative camps remains (Schroder, 1999). Crucial epistemological, theoretical and methodological differences exist between these two contrasting approaches (see Figures 8.1 and 8.2). The degree to which audiences are conceptualized as either active or passive in their encounters with media texts and technologies is a key debating point. These two paradigms are divided over the relative amount of power attributed to either the media text or the media audience.

Paradigm	The degree to which audiences are assumed to be passive or active
Effects	**Passive**
Uses and gratifications	**Active:** *some* human agency is acknowledged in how audiences satisfy social and psychological needs through their media use
Reception	**Active:** the prospect of audiences exercising agency is assumed, e.g. Hall's encoding/decoding model
Constructionist	**Highly active:** the capacity of audiences to subvert dominant media discourses is celebrated. Audiences possess the power to resist and as such are seen as being strongly agentic
Produser/prosumer	**Highly Active:** The traditional boundaries between the media and audiences are understood to have much less relevance than previously assumed

Figure 8.1   **How are audiences understood?**

Main methods used in audience research	
Quantitative paradigm	**Qualitative paradigm**
Research methods: • Experiments • Surveys • Questionnaires • Other, e.g. Nielson ratings	Research methods: • Interviews (structured, semi-structured, unstructured) • Focus groups • Participant observation • Observation • Journal/diary keeping • The News Game • Online or virtual ethnography
Paradigms Effects Uses and gratifications	**Paradigms** Encoding/decoding Ethnographic Constructivist Produser/prosumer

Figure 8.2   **Main methods used in audience research.**

The quantitative approach makes use of experiments and surveys in order to measure both media power and audience behaviour. Those following an effects or uses and gratifications model of media analysis have typically examined large numbers of audience members in an attempt to examine the power of specific media texts or messages. The media industry – and the advertising and marketing sectors in particular – continue to draw upon a quantitative approach in their analysis of audience behaviour and preferences. Ratings data on audience response to television programmes or radio stations, for example, are used to sell air time to the advertising industry. **Quantitative research** can provide useful information to those in the commercial sector who wish to target a specific demographic group in society. More recently, conglomerates such as Facebook have engaged in data mining of usage patterns in order to sell tailored advertising to particular groups of users based on their age, gender, ethnicity and location, for example.

The qualitative approach uses interviews, focus group interviews and participant observation as the main methodological tools in examining media audiences. Here there is an emphasis on how meaning is created by media audiences. Media discourses are examined in the context of the workings of other – and sometimes more powerful – discourses that may prevail on questions of gender, ethnicity or class in the day-to-day lives of audience members. The qualitative paradigm examines the reception of media texts in a wider social context than its quantitative counterpart. While the reception and ethnographic approaches are generally accepted to be 'rich' in terms of the data yielded, many of these studies are based upon relatively small sample sizes and are genre specific, raising questions as to the extent of their representativeness and the extent to which we can generalize about the wider process of media effects. Qualitative methodologies are also used by the media industries. It is common, for example, for the movie industry to pre-test audience response to a series of alternative endings for films that are intended for mainstream consumption and distribution through the use of focus groups. Online ethnographies use participant observation, observation and other forms of discursive analysis in examining audience use of virtual media spaces such as discussion fora, blogs and other forms of social media.

Power to the people? Three phases in reception research

Reception analysis is now considered in closer detail. In contrast to effects and uses and gratifications research, reception analysis is marked by a growing emphasis on the degree to which audiences are agentic in their encounters with the media. Alasuutari (1999) refers to the existence of three 'phases' or 'generations' of reception research. These are the encoding/decoding paradigm, the audience ethnography paradigm and the **constructionist** or discursive paradigm. While these developments within reception research have been neither smooth nor linear, the last three decades or so have witnessed a series of significant theoretical and methodological ruptures in terms of how audiences are conceptualized and researched. These developments mark a radical break with the behaviourist/effects understanding of the media audience because they stress the potential power of audiences to reshape and resist the contents of media texts. They also underscore significant changes in the kinds of media genres analysed, the methodologies used and the nature of the questions raised within empirical audience research. Reception analysis has focused predominantly on television, although this has recently given way to a new set of concerns about the role of new media technologies in the home and the emergence of postmodern mediascapes.

Encoding/decoding

In Chapter 5 Hall's (1974) encoding/decoding model was discussed in some detail. The encoding/decoding paradigm was highly significant in the initial development of reception research. Heavily influenced by semiotics, Hall (1974) concentrates on two important 'moments' in the communicative exchange, namely the encoding undertaken by media professionals in the making of media messages, and the decoding that takes place among audience members once the message has been received. Typically, audience members can make use of four codes in the process of interpreting a media message. These are the dominant code, the professional code, the negotiated code and the oppositional code.

The encoding/decoding paradigm allows for audience agency in that individual audience members can reconstruct or resist the media message. Hall's (1974) model gave rise to a growing amount of empirical research on how audiences variously decode media messages, the most famous of which is Morley's (1980) *Nationwide* study, which is discussed later in this chapter. The period that followed Morley's (1980) application of Hall's encoding/decoding model saw the beginnings of a move towards analysing the content and reception of fictional television genres. Focus group interviews and in-depth interviews with individual audience members were used to explore the readings that were made of specific media texts. This shift in emphasis gave rise to a new phase of qualitative audience research that engaged with questions about the gendered realities of media use and consumption.

Audience ethnography

The second phase or generation of reception research usually describes itself as ethnographic. In describing its emergence Alasuutari (1999) argues that three key features characterize the new audience ethnography. First, it was strongly influenced by the feminist perspective. Alasuutari states that:

> This can be seen ... in the fact that a slackening of interest in the reception of public affairs programmes was balanced out by a growing interest in fictional programmes, particularly romantic serials. These studies concentrated on the politics of gender, on the discourses within which gender is dealt with in the programmes, and how women viewers interpret and make use of the offered readings against the background of everyday life and experiences. (1999: 5)

Second, the earlier concentration on the content and reception of media texts as evidenced in the encoding/decoding model gave way to a much broader interest in the functions of specific kinds of media in people's day-to-day lives. Researchers examined the uses of new media technologies in a domestic setting: the 'television talk' of everyday life as well as the ways in which gender discourses shape the uses of television in the home (see Lull, 1980; Morley, 1986; Silverstone et al., 1991). Third, the audience ethnography phase of reception research placed a new emphasis upon understanding reception in the context of people's daily lives.

The constructionist approach

The third phase of reception research is referred to as the constructionist or discursive approach. The certainties that once characterized the encoding/decoding and ethnographic approaches have been replaced with a new set of concerns (and doubts) within audience research. Under the influence of postmodern theory the youngest of the three generations of reception research seeks to understand more about the mediascapes that define the postmodern experience. In explaining this approach Alasuutari (1999) argues that:

> The third generation entails a broadened frame within which one conceives of the media and media use. One does not necessarily abandon ethnographic case studies of audiences or analyses of individual programmes, but the main focus is not restricted to finding out about the reception or 'reading'

of a programme by a particular audience. Rather, the objective is to get a grasp of our contemporary 'media culture', particularly as it can be seen in the role of the media in everyday life, both as a topic and as an activity structured by and structuring the discourses within which it is discussed. One is interested in the discourses within which we conceive of our roles as the public and the audience, and how notions of programmes-with-an-audience or messages-with-an-audience are inscribed as media messages and assessments about news events and about what is going on in the 'world'. The third generation resumes an interest in programmes and programming, but not as texts studied in isolation from their usage as an element of everyday life. Furthermore, it adds a neglected layer of reflexivity to the research on the 'reception' of media messages by addressing the audience's notions of themselves as the 'audience'. (1999: 6–7)

In the newly emerging constructionist understanding of media audiences there is an emphasis on *discourse* and audience reflexivity that was previously absent in the encoding/decoding and audience ethnography paradigms. Alasuutari (1999) argues that there has been a shift from an emphasis on audience psychology to audience sociology. In this account, the encoding/decoding model of audience reception is decidedly cognitive in its orientation. In the face of a media text with a preferred dominant ideological encoding on patriarchy, homophobia or 'terrorism', does an audience member accept, reconstruct or reject the encoding? The constructionist version of audience reception is more concerned with the broader social and discursive context in which reception takes place. As Alasuutari notes:

From this perspective, the 'reception' of a programme or genre can be given a more sociological meaning. We are interested in it as a topic in a given society. What are the embedded problems and concerns that evoke it as a topic? What are the viewpoints and subject positions taken in the discourse? How, and by whom, is it discussed in public and how do people in everyday-life conversations refer to or comment on the public discussions about it? (1999: 16)

? Stop and think 8.2

Talking about media texts

List three examples of where and when you might talk (either face to face or virtually) about media content with friends or family in your daily life. How, in your opinion, does talking about media texts possibly affect their influence on you and others? Consider how your interpretation of media texts might be influenced by the ways in which elite figures such as rock stars or politicians may have spoken about the texts in question. The so-called 'Two-Step Flow' theory, which emerged in the second wave of effects research in the 1940s, stressed the role played by elite figures in shaping wider public understandings of events.

Read on! 8.1   Reading and reception

Jenny Kitzinger (1999) 'A sociology of media power: key issues in audience reception research', in Greg Philo (ed.), *Message Received*. Harlow: Addison Wesley Longman, pp. 15–18.

... Cultural debate and intervention must include engaging with the production, content and reception of such messages. In this sense, mass communication is too important to leave to the mass communication experts ... It would be a sad irony if communication studies researchers only communicated with each other, and if communication itself failed to lead to productive dialogue.

First ... the ability to deconstruct media messages and develop a critical reading in a research setting is not necessarily the same as being able to reject the message conveyed via the media on a day-to-day level. It was sometimes only when invited to do so, within the research setting, that people challenged attitudes or facts conveyed by the media which they had previously accepted without question. Evidence of critical readings from organised research sessions should not be unproblematically extrapolated to routine media–audience encounters.

Second ... the term 'reading' itself needs to be unpacked. ... sometimes people do not just 'read' a report 'differently' but simply refuse to believe the facts conveyed, or blatantly disagree with the media's interpretation. An intertwined issue is that the polysemy of texts has been exaggerated. ...

Third, it is important to recognise that 'deviant readings' may be as much influenced by other media messages as by some kind of counter-cultural reservoir of alternative perspectives. Observing that people 'resist', or read against the grain of any individual media product, does not mean that the media lack power. In any case, it is misleading to play off textual power against reader 'freedom' as if the reader came to the text with an independent view. ...

This leads to the fourth point ... the 'active' audience is not immune from influence. Indeed, the way in which people use the media (and incorporate soap opera plots, media stories or slogans from advertisements into their everyday lives) can strengthen, rather than weaken, media effects. The way people re-read individual texts or take unexpected pleasures can actually reinforce, rather than undermine, broad media influence over public understandings.

The fifth ... point ... is that 'resistance' becomes a problematic concept, once applied empirically to substantive topics. ... Should 'audience resistance' be celebrated if people reject the primary message of a mass media campaign to encourage safer sex or discourage violence against women? ... Clearly audiences do not always accept the dominant message, but I would argue that the normative implications of a word such as 'resistance' should be questioned.

? Stop and think 8.3

1. Why in Kitzinger's view is the question of media effects still important?

2. What are, according to this extract, the potential problems with the terms 'audience reading' and 'audience resistance'?

 A CLOSER LOOK 8.1

What is ethnography? What is media ethnography?

In its most basic sense ethnography refers to writings or drawings about people or folk in a traditional cultural setting. The ethnographic method pre-dates contemporary media analysis. Its origins lie in social anthropology and sociology, which is sometimes also referred to as micro-sociology. Ethnography first came to prominence in the late nineteenth century as European colonial powers attempted to understand more about so-called 'primitive' cultures. Social anthropologists would spend long periods of time (two or three years would not be unusual) doing fieldwork, immersing themselves in the minutiae of local societies and cultures. Ethnographic work of this kind is highly detailed and potentially a very rich source of data. Its distinct advantage is that it allows for the checking and re-checking of data. As Fetterman notes:

> The ethnographic study allows multiple interpretations of reality and alternative interpretations of data throughout the study. The ethnographer is interested in describing a social and cultural scene from the *emic*, or insider's perspective. The ethnographer is both story-teller and scientist; the closer the reader of an ethnography comes to understanding the native's point of view, the better the story and the better the science. (1993: 12)

Unlike quantitative methods such as the survey or experiment which captures a 'snapshot' of social reality, the ethnographic approach allows for a far deeper understanding of the social world. Proponents of media ethnography see similar advantages. According to Lull (1980) media ethnography is:

> An integrated means for understanding the everyday world of social groups, their patterns of communication, and their uses of the mass media. The intent of the ethnography of mass communication is to allow the researcher to grasp as completely as possible with minimal disturbance the 'native's perspective' on relevant communicative and socio-cultural matters indigenous to him. (Lull, 1980: 199)

While some researchers see media ethnography as being synonymous with reception analysis, others see a clear distinction between them. Schroder et al. (2003) understand ethnography to be a research approach that is concerned with media use as part of people's everyday lives, while reception analysis is focused on the narrower interpretation of specific media texts. Using informal interactions with and observations of audiences, the ethnographic approach can help us to begin to make sense of the complex processes arising from media saturation.

Reception analysis and the 'ethnographic turn'

Critical ethnography has dominated qualitative audience analysis in recent times. Championed by feminist and postmodern researchers alike, the so-called 'ethnographic turn' within audience research constructs audience members as active agents, capable of resisting and reconstructing media texts. Lull (1991), for example, used the ethnographic approach to examine how Chinese television viewers engaged in resistive practices. Radway (1987) similarly, explored female readers' resistance in her celebrated study of romantic fiction (see Chapter 5). In this research approach, audiences are celebrated as being active and resistant in their everyday encounters with media texts. Far from being the slaves of hegemonic ideology, audience members have, it is argued, the capacity to resist, to *read against the grain* of dominant and other ideologies. In the postmodern account, audiences are characterized as being more sophisticated in their encounters with media discourses. They possess the power to play with and subvert media texts. Some proponents of the ethnographic approach like to stress their empathy with those who have less power in society, and this is reflected in many of the research themes that have been chosen for investigation (Gray, 1999; Ruddock, 2000).

The rise of the ethnographic approach marks a new emphasis on audience reception in its own right and not merely as one constituent part of the longer communicative chain of production, content and reception. From the ethnographic perspective, media discourses may be understood only in what Ruddock (2000) terms the 'total context of reception'. The rationale for the ethnographic turn within reception analysis is given by Moores as follows:

> In attending to the meanings produced by social subjects and to the daily activities they perform, qualitative audience researchers have frequently sought to explain those significances and practices by locating them in relation to broader frameworks of interpretation and to structures of power and inequality. This is the mark of ... a 'critical' ethnography. It is an approach which takes seriously the interpretations of the media constructed by consumers in their everyday routines. At the same time, it is not afraid to interrogate and situate their spoken accounts. (1993: 4–5)

Ethnographers use a range of interviewing styles (in-depth interviews, structured and semi-structured interviews, focus group interviews) as well as observation and participant observation in order to understand how audience members construct meaning. The reception of fictional genres such as romantic novels, women's magazines, serialized television dramas and soap operas has been a major focus of this research approach.

Unlike more traditional ethnographic research, where the researcher spends a long period of time observing and interviewing in the 'field', audience ethnographers typically have to rely upon far more restricted contact with their subjects (for an exception to this rule see Miller and Slater's (2000) detailed ethnography of internet culture and consumption in Trinidad). The taped in-depth interviews are often no more than one hour in length. Prolonged access to informants or interviewees in their private domestic settings may also prove problematic. Observation of media consumption in the private sphere raises many ethical questions. For practical as well as budgetary reasons, sample sizes are usually small, leading some to question just how representative individual studies are. Nevertheless, as Gray points out:

> We can learn a great deal more from these audience reception studies which are not necessarily very much to do with audiences themselves but rather the processes by which media forms and technologies take their place in

everyday settings. Furthermore, critical and analytical empirical work can enter into a productive dialogue with our theorization of audiences and consumption practices. (1999: 32)

According to Moores (1993: 5) the ethnographic turn has made a worthwhile contribution that has deepened our understanding of media audiences. It has contributed much to the debate over the power (or not) of media texts to shape audience readings and interpretations. It has helped explain the variations in audience tastes for different media genres (see e.g. Lull, 1980). Audience ethnographies have focused on the politics of the private domestic sphere in order to understand more about the gendered realities of media consumption and interpretation (see e.g. Radway, 1987). A growing amount of ethnographic work is focused on the uses of new ICTs as well as older media technologies in the home (see e.g. Livingstone, 1998; Silverstone et al., 1991).

Read on! 8.2   Living room wars

Ien Ang (1996) 'Politics of empirical audience research', in *Living Room Wars: Rethinking Media Audiences for a Postmodern World*. London: Routledge, pp. 50–2.

What clearly emerges here is the beginning of an interpretative framework in which differences in television-viewing practices are not just seen as expressions of different needs, uses or readings, but are connected with the way in which particular social subjects are structurally positioned in relation to each other. In the context of the nuclear family home, women's viewing patterns can only be understood in relation to men's patterns; the two are in a sense constitutive of each other. Thus, if watching television is a social and even a collective practice, it is not a harmonious practice. Because subjects are positioned in different ways towards the set, they engage in a continuing struggle over programme choice and programme interpretation, styles of viewing and textual pleasure. ...

Television consumption ... contributes to the everyday construction of male and female subjectivities through the relations of power, contradiction and struggle that men and women enter into in their daily engagements with the television sets in their homes. At this point, we can also see how [David] Morley's research enables us to begin to conceive of 'the ideological operations of television' in a much more radical way than has hitherto been done. The relation between television and audiences is not just a matter of discrete 'negotiations' between texts and viewers. In a much more profound sense the process of television consumption ... has created new areas of constraints and possibilities for structuring social relationships, identities and desires. If television is an 'ideological apparatus', to use that old-fashioned-sounding term, then it is not so much because its texts transmit certain 'messages', but because it is a cultural form through which those constraints are negotiated and those possibilities take shape. ...

[D]o we need empirical research, or more specifically, ethnographic audience research, to arrive at such theoretical understandings? Why examine audiences empirically at all? After all, some critical scholars still dismiss the idea of doing empirical research altogether, because, so they argue, it would necessarily implicate the researcher with the strategies and aims of the capitalist culture industry. ...

Ethnographic work, in the sense of drawing on what we can perceive and experience in everyday settings, acquires its critical edge when it functions as a reminder that reality is always more complicated and diversified than our theories can represent, and that there is no such thing as 'audience' whose characteristics can be set once and for all.

 ## Stop and think 8.4

1. Why do you think gender is of importance in reaching a critical understanding of your television viewing?

2. How do you think Ang's research differs from one taking a uses and gratifications approach?

 A CLOSER LOOK 8.2 ....

Alternative styles of reception analysis: the 'News Game'

As part of its ongoing research into media effects and audience beliefs, the Glasgow University Media Group make use of an innovative research technique known as the 'News Game' (see Kitzinger, 1990, 1993; Philo, 1990, 1993b, 1999).

The method has been used to examine media effects and audience beliefs about a wide range of 'public knowledge' issues, including media coverage of strikes, AIDS, mental health, the war in Northern Ireland and, most recently, the Israeli–Palestinian conflict (see Philo, 2002). The News Game has been a central part of the group's attempts at investigating the workings of dominant and other ideologies in a media setting. The News Game was devised initially as a teaching aid. It was intended as a means of generating debate among students on how the media engage in the social construction of reality. In this research model audience groups are given a set of photographs from actual media coverage of a specific theme. The members of each audience group are then asked to pretend that they are journalists and are requested to write a story or a report to accompany the photographic images that they have selected. Greg Philo first used the News Game in audience-based research when he examined audience understandings of the 1984–85 miners' strike in the United Kingdom. In addition to the research group's dissatisfaction with the behaviourist model of effects research, a primary motivation behind using the News Game was to establish what attitudes and beliefs existed among audiences before the research exercise was undertaken. In Philo's words:

> It seemed clear that much of the process of attitude and belief formation would have taken place before such an experiment could be conducted. In a sense we needed to establish what people already 'knew' and to show the processes by which they had arrived at their beliefs. We devised a new method which involved asking audience groups to write their own news programmes. This would show what they thought the content of news to be on a given issue. It would then be possible to compare this with what group members actually believed to be true and to examine why they either accepted or rejected the media account. ... This approach has enabled us to look at long-term processes of belief, understanding and memory. (1993b: 258)

In the miners' strike study (Philo, 1990), for example, 16 'naturally occurring' audience groups, with a total of 169 participants, were interviewed on their beliefs about and memories of the strike. Working in groups of three or four, they also took part in the News Game. Their 'journalistic' accounts of the strike were then compared with actual coverage on the BBC and ITN. Philo (1990) found a remarkable similarity between the participants' and the television news's versions of the strike. The third and final part of the study involved asking the participants about their beliefs on what had taken actually taken place. The research found that significant numbers of audience members believed the accounts given to them by television and the press. Dominant ideological constructions of the strike – such as the notion that the strike was a violent one – were not only reproduced in the News Game exercise, but also surfaced in the interviews and discussions held with the study's audience groups. The Glasgow University Media Group have continued to use this innovative and revealing research strategy, focusing more recently on themes including the national debt and inward migration to the UK. In addition to using pre-existing media content they have also experimented with creating media content about future scenarios in British society concerning the economy, society and politics.

For more see: http://www.glasgowmediagroup.org/

Qualitative audience research: three examples

We turn now to examine three examples of qualitative research on media audiences. These studies focus on factional and fictional media genres from the print and broadcast media. A variety of research methodologies are used (interviews, focus group interviews, observation, as well as narrative analysis) in order to examine audiences. The studies vary in terms of whether they examine audience members in a 'natural setting', that is, in the home, or whether 'naturally occurring' groups (based on occupation, gender or ethnicity) were convened for the purposes of the study. In all three examples, audiences are constructed as being active and reflexive in their encounters with media texts.

The 'Nationwide' audience by David Morley

Morley's (1980) analysis of the popular BBC current affairs programme *Nationwide* is justifiably hailed as a classic within the field of empirical audience research. Reflecting a seismic shift in emphasis from textual to reception analysis, it sought to examine the complexity of audience response to current affairs television using Hall's encoding/decoding model of media analysis. (See Chapter 4 for an elaboration of the encoding/decoding model.) Using a semiotic approach, Brunsdon and Morley (1978) had previously examined the *Nationwide* programme in terms of its mode of address and its ideological make-up. Following on from this, Morley's (1980) study set out to examine audience interpretations of *Nationwide* using Hall's dominant, negotiated and oppositional readings as his key. However, as Abercrombie and Longhurst (1998) point out, Morley 'assumed that there would be also differences within them [dominant, negotiated and oppositional readings] and his research design aimed to tap those internal differences in interpretation' (1998: 16). Morley was interested in investigating whether there was a demonstrable link between the readings produced by audience members and their socio-economic status. He was also interested in investigating how media consumption practices were shaped by factors such as class, gender and race. Twenty-nine audience groups made up of apprentices, managers, trade unionists or students were shown one of two selected recordings of *Nationwide*. These groups were already involved in education or training. They were convened for the purposes of the research project outside their usual domestic viewing contexts. Using the group interview method, their responses to the style and ideological orientation of specific episodes were tape-recorded and analysed in order to ascertain whether they engaged in dominant, negotiated or oppositional reading of the texts in question. The analysis of audience response was related to the ideological structure, mode of address and style employed in the selected texts.

In summarizing the main findings of the *Nationwide* study Taylor and Willis (1999) argue that:

> the most important aspect of Morley's findings was the discovery that the socioeconomic background of the respondents did not necessarily determine their readings. In fact, respondents who shared similar backgrounds sometimes produced different responses. He also found that other cultural frameworks and institutions, for example, affiliation to institutions such as trade unions as well as the impact of informational sources such as the press, worked to shape audience responses to the text. For example, he found that the three reading positions simply could not accommodate the black students he interviewed. These students found very little in *Nationwide* to engage with; in fact, they declined to respond at all to the text and as a result their responses fell outside the three dominant positions. But it was not the only limitation Morley found in the reading positions laid out in the encoding/decoding model. He also found that while the managers broadly affirmed the ideological sentiments of *Nationwide*, they were disparaging about the populist presentational style of the programme. The shop stewards he interviewed, however, were comfortable with the programme's populist production values, but voiced dissatisfaction with what they saw as its favourable treatment of management. As Shaun Moores argues, this type of difference between cultural ideas about taste could not be accounted for within the confines of Hall's model. Yet the findings do reveal important information about the relationship between audience decoding and class habitus. (1999: 173–4)

Morley's analysis then pointed to significant differences of interpretation between and among the four main audience groupings. His findings emphasized the complexities involved in audience interpretation of media texts and to the limitations of the encoding/decoding model. Morley's study found that one's class position did not necessarily determine the way in which one read or decoded a media text. Rather it pointed to a wider range of contexts that were influential in shaping the meanings derived from a media text. Proponents of reception-based research deservedly celebrate the *Nationwide* study. As Gray (1999) states, its significance rests upon the fact that:

> [it] sought to combine textual construction and interpretation, it granted viewers interpretative status (but always within shaping structural determinations) and developed ways of conceiving of the audience as socially structured, suggesting that decoding is not homogeneous. Thus the text and audience are conceptualized within and as part of the social structure organized in and across power relations of dominant and subordinate

groups, of which the media were seen to be occupying a crucial position and role. Although the viewer was considered to be interpreting specific programmes in different ways, these were not entirely and absolutely open to the viewer; she or he was limited, shaped by her or his own social positioning as well as the limitations and closures of the text itself. (1999: 27–8)

'Discursive texts, reflexive audiences: global trends in television news texts and audience reception' by Andy Kavoori

Using a combination of narrative and reception analysis, Kavoori (1999) examines news texts about 'political conflict' and their reception by audience members in an age of media globalization. This detailed qualitative study is based upon comparative research carried out in Britain, France, Germany and the United States. The research analyses the narrative structure and audience interpretation of news texts concerning political conflict broadcast by the BBC and ITN, A2N, ZDF and ABC television channels.

The stories in question reported on rioting by students in South Korea and a politically inspired slaughter of train passengers in South Africa. Kavoori's work is informed by two key research questions. In terms of news content he asks, 'How does television news portray foreign news events? (What is its narrative construction of the outside world?) Specific to stories on "political conflict", what vision of cultural "others" becomes narrative?' (1999: 387). With respect to audience interpretation he asks, 'How do audiences make sense of foreign news on television? What patterns of mediation of the narratives on political conflict emerge as constructed by television news?' (1999: 387).

The first stage of the study involved recording television news programmes in 1987 and 1990 in Britain, Germany, France and the United States. The contents of individual news programmes were subjected to a narrative analysis and subsequently compared. The second stage of the study examined audience reception of the stories concerning the Korean unrest and the South African train violence. Six focus groups comprising between nine and 12 members per group were convened in each of the four countries. Kavoori's study did not segment the focus groups according to age, race or gender. Instead, there was an attempt to involve a wide range of socio-economic groups. The audience groups were constructed on the basis of income and were recruited by academic institutions in each of the respective countries. Kavoori (1999) describes how the reception analysis was undertaken:

Focus group transcripts were analysed for issues of variation across countries and power (the extent to which the audience reiterated the discursive features of the text). Each question by the moderator was followed by discussion. Transcripts were divided into discussion segments. Summary statements were written for each discussion segment. These statements were used as the basis for identifying modes of interpretation comprising audience mediation.

> Each focus group began with viewing of the news story aired in that country. The audience was asked to retell the story in their own words. This was followed by questions about media coverage and content, including the dominant themes identified by the researchers. (1999: 388)

Kavoori argues that, in terms of its narrative dimension, television news represents the 'other' world as 'a violent, unstable world' (1999: 395). He finds striking similarities across the four countries in how stories about 'violence' and 'democracy' are framed. He suggests that:

> The effect of television news discourse ... is discursive, i.e. the news the narrative constructs in each country draws upon frameworks common in each country. But the news also displays cross-cultural, global trends. These cross-cultural trends provide a narrow and negative construction of the 'other'. (1999: 396)

In its television news coverage the global media industry continues to construct the world in terms of the West and the (uncivilized) rest.

Kavoori's (1999) reception analysis found a significant amount of reflexivity among audiences in their encounters with foreign news on television. The findings of his study would suggest that audiences are increasingly critical in their engagement with news texts. Kavoori (1999) argues that 'Part of political work that television news audiences perform is reflexive, re-articulating the terms of the news texts through a specific set of analytical practices' (1999: 396). His research suggests that we are now witnessing the arrival of a 'global culture of critical media consumption' (1999: 396). Audiences are increasingly critical because of 'a familiarity with the narrative conventions of the genre; an awareness of the institutional imperatives of the media industries and, more generally, the cultural, political and ideological contexts of media coverage' (1999: 396).

Reading women's magazines by Joke Hermes

Hermes (1995) used a postmodern feminist perspective to analyse the everyday use of women's magazines. Starting from a position of 'respect' rather than 'concern' for her research subjects, her work is an exemplary qualitative study. With the exception of Winship's (1987) celebrated work *Inside Women's Magazines*, Hermes expresses her disillusionment with the ways in which this popular media genre has been traditionally approached by researchers. Using analytical techniques associated with socio-linguistics and discourse analysis, she draws upon detailed interview data based upon 80 conversational interviews with 15 men and 65 women. Unlike many other 'ethnographic' studies of popular media genres where sample sizes are notoriously small, Hermes's sample is sufficiently large for her to draw sound conclusions from the findings.

The study focuses on the everyday uses of Dutch and British magazines. Hermes's work is written in an accessible style and is strongly reflexive, particularly in terms of her chosen methodological approach. Her specific focus is on meaning, and therefore she is steering a middle-ground position between audience research that has either combined textual and reception analysis with a clear focus on texts or genres (e.g. Ang, 1996; Radway, 1987) and audience research that has focused on the uses of media technology and form in the context of power relationships in everyday (domestic) life (e.g. Gray, 1999; Morley, 1986).

Hermes's ambitious task was 'to find out how women's magazines become meaningful in everyday life and what "meaning" can be taken to be in everyday contexts' (1995: 11).

What sorts of 'interpretative repertoires' do ordinary readers bring to women's magazines? Hermes (1995) tells us that she:

> wanted to know how women's magazines became meaningful for readers and readers told me that women's magazines have hardly any meaning at all. They are convenient, my informants said, easy to put down when other things need to be done, but of little cultural value and therefore not very meaningful. They would also point out that while women's magazines have little cultural value, they do have practical value: all those tips, recipes and dress patterns. What more meaning would a medium need than to be of such a practical use? Although reading women's magazines is a complex activity that certainly has more than one side to it, readers would mainly speak of its cultural insignificance. (1995: 143)

Hermes (1995) uses an interview-based ethnographic approach. With an average length of one and a half hours, the interviews were recorded and transcribed, giving the author a large volume of research data. She stresses the 'inherently unequal positions of interviewer and interviewed [.] I cannot claim this text is a series of dialogues or a polylogue – a goal interpretative ethnography should aim for according to some of its practitioners' (1995: 11).

The text provides an insightful account of both the female and the male readers of women's magazines. We are given detailed portraits of two readers based upon interviews with the author's mother and one of her informants – Joan Becker. Both interviews provide us with important contextual information on the everyday use of women's magazines, and the author's interview with her mother is particularly moving. While even the most cursory glance at a magazine shelf in a newsagent's would suggest that the publishing industry segments its readership base according to age and interests (gossip, clothes, celebrity, lifestyles, domestic know-how, etc.), Hermes found that 'readers read unpredictable and changing combinations of magazines' (1995: 155).

Hermes concludes that:

> the most important aspect of women's magazines for readers was not that they are so full of practical information, even if that is a common justification for spending money and time on them, but that they blend easily with other

obligations, other duties and activities. Women's magazines as a text are not highly significant, but as an everyday medium they are a means of filling a small break and of relaxing that does not interrupt one's schedule, because they are easy to put down. (1995: 144)

Furthermore, she argues that:

A second, less manifest aspect of reading them is that women's magazines offer material that may help you imagine a sense of control over your life by feeling prepared for tragedy, or a more perfect version of yourself by supposing that you would be able to answer any questions regarding the difficult choices in life someone else might ask. (1995: 144)

···· **A CLOSER LOOK 8.3** ·· 👁

Sex differences in video game play

At the outset of this chapter it was noted that media audiences are becoming disaggregated. A particular focus in recent years has been on the adoption and use of newer forms of media technology in the home, with a particular concentration on the gendered realities behind these developments. Lucas and Sherry (2004), for example, examined gender differences in video game playing. Drawing upon the results of a large-scale survey of 593 college students who were aged between 18 and 24 years, they found significant differences between female and male respondents. Females played video games less frequently and were not as motivated to play video games in social situations. Unlike their male counterparts, female respondents were less interested in games which were competitive in orientation.

See also Kerr (2006) for an excellent introduction to games and gaming.

Audiences, fans and participatory cultures

Although fans and **fandom** are often maligned within public and media-based discourse, analyses of fans and the phenomenon of fandom represent a further important trend within audience research (see Jenson, 1992). Typically focused on popular forms of media, this work attempts to understand more about the significance of media content and their related activities in people's everyday (media) lives. This recent development mirrors a more general concern within sociology and cultural studies which has tried to make sense of the complexities of identity formation and sub-cultural affiliation – particularly in terms of sport (soccer) and music (punk rock, Goth), for example (see Bennett, 2006; Hodkinson, 2002). Conceptualized as fans, audience members are viewed as possessing considerable agency. They have the power to subvert intended meanings and to produce and circulate new media texts, either replacing the original text altogether or creating new texts which in turn may influence how the original text is understood. Researchers have used interviews, focus groups, observation/participant observation and discourse analysis in order to understand audience members as fans. As will shortly be seen in the extended case study of the singer Morrissey, there is a strong emphasis on the question of identity formation within fan studies as well as its performative and affective or emotional dimensions.

In its popular usage, being a fan often implies an obsessive or unhealthy interest in a star, a football team or a particular media genre. Defining fandom in this pejorative or negative way is highly problematic in that nearly all of us who live in a media saturated world are fans or followers of one or more kinds of media genre. Fandom is not monolithic. It has to be understood as a continuum. One fan of David Bowie may buy all of his recordings and listen to his music regularly. Another fan may also buy the same set of recordings but also be an active member of the subscription-based service Bowie.net. She may trade bootleg recordings and other items of interest such as posters or badges with other collector fans. She may also contribute regularly to a range of fora discussing Bowie's latest touring or recording plans with people she has never met. Similarly, one fan of *Sex and the City* may watch the programme when she has the time, whereas another may watch all episodes when they are broadcast, purchase all of the series on DVD and discuss the programme's characters and storylines with other fans in either a real or virtual setting. The fans of David Bowie and *Sex and the City* may also be fans of other types of media genres. In this regard Abercrombie and Longhurst (1998) suggest that we need to differentiate between *fans, cultists* and *enthusiasts* in terms of reaching a more critical understanding of audiences as fandom.

Fan studies have been strongly influenced by postmodern theory, cultural studies and feminist approaches to media. It is hardly surprising then that fans have been examined in terms of their attachment to specific popular media genres (e.g. soap operas, romantic novels, women's magazines, 'reality' television shows and science fiction series such as *Star Trek* (Jenkins, 1992) and Hollywood blockbusters) and/or attachment to particular 'stars' or 'celebrities' such as Justin Bieber, Kylie or Beyoncé.

Fandom is now usually understood in terms of its affective dimension in that researchers have examined the role that being a fan plays in people's everyday emotional lives. They ask: What sorts of connections occur between the content of the chosen media text(s) and the everyday emotional experiences of fans? How are these connections cemented? Vroomen (2004), for example, has examined the listening practices of older fans of Kate Bush who consume her music in a private setting. Does being a fan of a particular media genre alter in any way the meanings and pleasures derived from the text? Does a committed fan of say *Queer as Folk* or *Modern Family* interpret an episode differently than a less regular viewer?

Fandom is increasingly participatory. The merging of old and new media technologies allows for greater audience participation through voting, texting or email. Fans, as Jenkins (1992) has argued, may be textual poachers as well as cultural nomads. They are not necessarily restricted to one medium and migrate across media in search of texts concerning the object of their interest. Livingstone notes that:

> Fandom is increasingly important as audiences fragment and diversify. And as media become interconnected, increasingly intertextual, it is content irrespective of medium that matters to people *qua* fans, for they follow it across media, weaving it seamlessly also into their face-to-face communications. (2004: 81)

As we pointed out at the start of this textbook fandom can also be about audience members becoming producers – albeit in a basic sense. Fans produce publications such as fanzines and e-zines. Some of the fans of *Buffy The Vampire Slayer* who were disappointed at Fox's decision to axe the programme after its seventh series wrote their own follow-up series. Fans are active in the blogosphere, sharing ideas and thoughts with fellow fans about their mutual interest. Increasingly, being a fan is about being a member of an imagined community which exists only in cyberspace. Fans of *Arcade Fire* (http://forums.arcadefire.net/), for example, converse with one another, sharing their thoughts and ideas about the Canadian band. Membership of an imagined transnational community allows individual fans to take on assumed identities.

At its core, fandom is about identity formation. It is at once both public and private. It is about saying to the world (or at the very least to your family, friends, neighbours and work/study colleagues) that 'I am a fan of X, Y or Z'. It involves laying down all sorts of semiotic markers as to who you think you are. It is not just about media consumption *per se*, but may involve shaping how you present yourself to the world in terms of your overall style/dress code or involvement in related leisure activities such as attending a concert or a fan event such as a *Star Trek* or Elvis convention. Being a fan is also a private act in that the relationships that fans have with media texts or genres can come about as a result of subjective or personal experiences. Such experiences are of course determined in turn by one's relative amount of power in terms of one's class/ethnicity/gender.

Political economists might argue that there has been too strong an emphasis on examining popular culture within everyday life to the detriment of a focus on more important economic and political questions. Furthermore, fandom – in its more extreme guises – can be seen as the manifestation of conspicuous consumption, much favoured by the global capitalist class. Whatever their shortcomings, studies of fandom have important things to say about audience members in terms of consumption, meaning and identity formation.

Buffy The Vampire Slayer

Joss Whedon's *Buffy The Vampire Slayer* began life as a movie in 1992. This was followed by a seven-year run as a television series – initially on Warner Brothers and then on the United Paramount Network (UPN) in the USA. The seven seasons of *Buffy*, chronicling the life of its heroine Buffy Summers, between the ages of 16 and 22, had immense appeal to teenage female audiences across the globe. The recurring theme of adolescent angst was of major importance in helping to create the connection that teenage fans felt with the series.

Plate 8.1 **An iconic figure, Morrissey attracts a fandom that is sometimes seen as fanatical. Photograph reproduced by kind permission of Sanctuary Music (London) © 2005.**

Whedon's creation inverts the usual ingredients of the horror genre which typically portray female characters as being helpless. As a media text which uses the key elements of a number of genres such as horror and comedy as well as some aspects of intertextuality, *Buffy* is seen by many critics as being representative of so-called 'girl-power', where young women are portrayed in heroic roles. Of significant commercial importance to both Warner Brothers and UPN, the programme gave rise to a range of spin-offs, such as the television series *Angel* and *Buffy* comic books and novels, as well as official and unofficial websites and discussion forums. Many of *Buffy*'s fans continue to communicate with each other on the web. Following the series discontinuation in 2003 some fans went so far as to write their own eighth series of the programme. The programme has also attracted a considerable amount of interest from academics within the field of media and cultural studies. For example, Labre and Duke (2004) examine the construction of *Buffy* in a video game based on the television series, while Bloustien (2002) explores the relationship between female adolescent fans of *Buffy* in an Australian context. Bloustien uses an ethnographic approach in attempting to understand more about the significance of globalized texts such as *Buffy* in the everyday lives of younger female fans. The academic interest in *Buffy* has even given rise to a peer-reviewed journal called *Slayage*. For more details see: http://slayageonline.com/.

Case study 8.1 From Manchester to 'Moz Angeles': Morrissey, identity and fandom

'His music is the soundtrack of my life, he reaches my innermost thoughts and fears and aspirations and longing. For a long time, I felt isolated and alone. Only Morrissey comforted me' – Female Latino fan, *Passions Just Like Mine* (Koch, 2010)

'What appeals to me most about Morrissey is his look on life ... how there can be a depressing side but still find hope and live life to the fullest I guess' – Male Latino fan, *Passions Just Like Mine* (Koch, 2010)

As leader of the seminal post-punk group The Smiths and as a solo recording artist since 1987, the singer Morrissey has attracted a fandom that is sometimes seen as fanatical. His fans have been described, somewhat unfairly, as being 'High-IQ misfits and fervent introverts' (Evans, 1996). Morrissey concerts are the site of quasi-religious fervour with (typically male) fans competing to touch his hand or hug this reluctant icon (Devereux, 2010). Even a cursory scan of the many fan websites and fanzines dedicated to Morrissey indicates the centrality of the star in the very meaning that fans make of their own lives (see e.g. http://www.morrissey-solo.com/). Morrissey's fandom is marked on- and offline by its participatory, performative and glocalizing aspects. His fandom is explored in

(Continued)

this case study with particular reference to the emergence of the Chicano/Latino fan subculture in the United States and Latin America.

Morrissey occupies a contradictory space. Famously shy and reclusive, he is a narcissistic star. He is heralded as a gay icon but he appeals to 'straight' men. His previous band The Smiths are sometimes (somewhat problematically) seen as being the quintessentially 'English' band of the 1980s, yet all four members were the children of Irish immigrants. The songs of The Smiths and Morrissey are just one example of a larger shift within British popular culture, which has fetishized and commodified a particular version of (white) Northern English working-class life – a theme which is also very much in evidence in the later so-called 'Britpop' phenomenon of the early 1990s (see e.g. Bracewell, 2009; Campbell and Coulter 2010; Devereux et al., 2011a; Hopps, 2009; Martino, 2007; Stringer, 1992; Zuberi, 2001a). In addition to provoking us to question received notions concerning gender and sexuality (Hawkins, 2009; Hubbs, 1996), Morrissey has consistently put the issue of class and its representation at the very heart of his artistic oeuvre. A champion of the 'other', in a variety of guises (such as the disabled, skinhead gangs and Latino/Chicano immigrants for example), Morrissey is consistently revealed as a 'raconteur of the marginalized' working class (see Manco, 2011; Power 2011). Devereux et al. (2012) have shown how Morrissey has articulated a counter-hegemonic version of class and power relations by concerning himself with the lives and experiences of the welfare class.

Fan activity

Many Morrissey fans are active members of virtual communities. On a daily basis they dissect the latest piece of news about their anti-hero and communicate with one another via bulletin boards, texting, Twitter and Facebook about concerts, recordings or rumours (for a critical account of some of the more fanatical aspects of Morrissey's fandom concerning debates about race and immigration, see Snowsell, 2011). Fans have published online essays on the significance that Morrissey has for them in their personal lives (see e.g. Nylén, 2004; Taylor, 2006). Fans will typically narrate a personal version of how Morrissey's lyrics and music has helped them through a difficult phase in their own lives. Many have gone on 'pilgrimages' to the Salford Lads Club in the UK and other locations associated with Morrissey, such as Chelsea or Sloan Square in London (UK) or Fairmount Indiana (USA) in attempt to capture an 'authentic' fan experience through recreating a moment from the Smiths/Morrissey canon (see Hazard, 2011).

While Morrissey's fans are predominantly male and aged 35 and older, his fan base is quite heterogeneous. Viitamäki (1997, 40) suggests, for example, that Morrissey's American fans include '… androgenic teenagers, Latino gangsters, skinheads, well-dressed 30 year olds, gays and some older fans'. Morrissey's songs speak to an audience that may be gay, straight, bisexual, celibate or transgendered. Queer discourses are strongly in evidence in

Plate 8.2 Image of fan petitions from The Smiths Room, Salford Lads Club, Salford, UK. Photo by Martin Power. Reproduced by kind permission © 2013.

much of the iconography (record covers, posters, stage backdrops, t-shirts, etc.) associated with both The Smiths and Morrissey.

Fandom is graduated however. Amongst Morrissey's fans are those who are effectively 'full-time' in their fandom – whom Morrissey himself has termed the 'regular irregulars'. Cheaper air travel has resulted in a core group of fans following entire concert tours. Information on tickets, travel and cheap places to stay is exchanged on fan websites. Full-time Morrissey fans have been known to drop out of school, college or paid employment in order to follow their idol's concerts. Some fans collect a wide range of artefacts associated with the singer. Ticket stubs, autographs, photographs and bootleg recordings are regularly traded on eBay.

(Continued)

At Morrissey concerts and other Morrissey/Smiths related events many fans mimic their idol in terms of their personal appearance. In an ethnographic account of one Morrissey concert, Devereux notes that:

A specific hairstyle and style of dress mark out the (male) Morrissey fan. The dress code involves wearing either a Morrissey t-shirt usually emblazoned with Morrissey's face … Many of the t-shirts make use of gay iconography. Additional items of clothing include the wearing of a Harrington-style jacket and Dr. Martens shoes or boots. The James Dean/Elvis-style quiff is the most common hairstyle. Some fans have the nickname 'Moz' shaved into the back of their heads. Tattoos, of either Morrissey's image or selected quotes from his songs, are also used as signifiers of fandom. Other fans wear t-shirts quoting lyrics from his songs. (2006: 239–40)

Fan practices include the formation of Morrissey/Smiths tribute bands. Perhaps the most notable example are These Charming Men (from Dublin, Ireland) [,] who in addition to playing at The Smiths Convention in Los Angeles had to deputize for Morrissey himself at a Japanese rock music festival. This phenomenon of tribute bands is replicated elsewhere, most notably in the USA, New Zealand, Italy, Finland and the UK. Concerts by tribute bands allow fans to recreate their experiences of attending 'real' Morrissey/Smiths concerts.

Participation in Karaoke-style events takes this one step further in that fans can 'become' their hero for four minutes or longer. Using musicians from Bogotá, Columbia, the video artist Phil Collins has recorded a Karaoke soundtrack of a Smiths' compilation called *The Songs That Saved Your Life*. This has been used as the basis of a series of videos recorded in many locations including Ireland, Turkey and Greece, involving fans (both male and female) who 'become' Morrissey during their performance.

Morrissey's appeal is often explained by reference to the themes of his songs. His lyrics are abundant with sadness, humour and irony. Morrissey sings, typically in the first person, about depression, suicide, failed relationships and relationships that will never happen. He sings about the dispossessed, the long-term unemployed, the disabled and the lonely. The displacement experienced by immigrants has also been explored. There has been a recurring focus on themes associated with gay sub-culture. He has written about boxers, football hooligans and skinheads. Songs are written invariably from the point of view of the outsider. Renyolds (1995, 332) asserts that '… Morrissey exposed the hidden truths of adolescence: awkwardness, sexual incapacity, neurasthenia, emasculation'. Fans repeatedly refer to the personal connection they feel with Morrissey's lyrics and relate them to their own emotional experiences, thus agreeing with Wells's (1990) research into the affective aspects of fandom.

Identity politics are central to understanding Morrissey's fandom. In combining social realism and ambiguity about sexuality and gender (often in a wry and humorous fashion), Morrissey provokes strong feelings of empathy from his fans. His attraction may be explained by reference to his ability to write well-crafted songs which draw upon a bricolage of images associated with white Northern English working-class life, and which manage to present a sense of authenticity and 'realness' to his fans. He taps into a nostalgia for a particular version of working-class life whose key elements are now disappearing or have gone altogether. At a more general level, he expresses feelings of loss, alienation and *anomie*, which may help explain his transnational appeal. As the perennial outsider Morrissey's songs speak directly to the disenfranchised and the disenchanted.

Side by side with this, is a consistent gay and camp discourse. Hawkins notes that the ambiguity in evidence in his songs and associated imagery means that both gay and heterosexual fans are allowed to 'address the complexity of their own sexualities and desires' (2002: 75). Morrissey manages to sing from a range of viewpoints that address both male and female subjects. Sometimes it is not altogether clear whom exactly he is addressing. In recognizing this ambiguity, Hubbs (1996) stresses the variety of ways in which Morrissey's audience can read his songs and points out that whilst gay fans have no difficulty in decoding the gay discourse inscribed in Morrissey's work, many heterosexual fans do not adopt a so-called 'queer' reading of his texts.

Morrissey once described his music as being for 'the fourth gender' (Hubbs, 1996). Apart from his obvious ability as a songwriter, Morrissey's appeal may be explained in terms of how he manages to combine both ambiguity and authenticity all at once.

His refusal to be classified in terms of one specific sexuality and his ability to sing from a range of gender perspectives (male to male; male to female; female to male; female to female) serve to create an ambiguity and fluidity in which a wide range of fans can see themselves. In doing so, Morrissey's creative output and his concerts deviate significantly from the usual patriarchal – or so-called 'cock rock' – aspects of rock 'n' roll culture. Morrissey's concerts are places where many male fans can express the complexities which have come to typify masculinity in the early twenty-first century.

Morrissey's songs have crossed many geographical and cultural boundaries in terms of their meaning and their appeal. Morrissey has attracted a following in places like Bogotá, Columbia, as well as, most notably, amongst Chicano/Latino immigrants in the United States.

In the early 1990s a fan subculture focused on Morrissey emerged in the eastern suburbs of Los Angeles. Undoubtedly inspired by Morrissey's own relocation to Los Angeles, the Chicano/Latino fan subculture played a significant role in reviving his career in commercial terms. Chicano/Latino fans rehearse the same fan discourses which may be found elsewhere amongst Morrissey's fans. Fans localize certain aspects of fan culture associated more generally with Morrissey. This is in evidence in dress code, for example mimicking Morrissey's earlier Rockabilly style, or in tattoo artwork or in wearing t-shirts

(Continued)

with slogans like 'Mexican Blood/American Heart' and 'Moz Krew: LA from Westside to the South Bay'. A group of Mexican immigrants play in a Smiths/Morrissey tribute band called 'Sweet and Tender Hooligans'. As a tribute to their (anti)hero, Morrissey's Chicano/Latino fans have renamed their adopted hometown as 'Moz Angeles'. Many of his Chicano/Latino fans refer to how his songs have strong redemptive qualities, often describing their icon in quasi-religious terms. Morrissey's authenticity and ambiguity allow for a wide range of fan readings of his work. The Chicano/Latino subculture is an obvious example of the glocalizing tendencies of popular culture. Morrissey's own status as the outsider's outsider and, particularly, his second generation and lapsed Catholic status are obvious points of connection between him and his Chicano/Latino fans. His singing style has been compared to the Mexican 'Ranchera' genre and he has engaged directly with Chicano/Latino experience in songs like 'The First of the Gang to Die' and 'Mexico'. The Chicano/Latino fan subculture has attracted widespread media interest. Media discourse, perhaps predictably, tends to focus on what it perceives as its cult-like, fanatical and obsessive aspects rather than seeing it as an interesting example of fan creativity.

 ## Stop and think 8.5

1. Having read about this example of fandom can you identify its participatory and performative aspects?

2. This case study suggests that glocalization is an important facet of fandom. How does the Chicano/Latino fan subculture evidence glocalization?

3. Morrissey seems to appeal to a very wide range of fans (in terms of gender/sexual orientation, ethnicity, location). How is this achieved?

4. Can Morrissey's fans be described as prosumers/produsers?

Read on! 8.3   Fans, poachers and cultural nomads

A. Gray (2003) 'Fans: poachers and cultural nomads', from *Research Practice for Cultural Studies*. London: Sage, pp. 47–8.

… Jenkins has carried out some work to identify fan groups (for a particular programme, performer, musical style, film genre) who inhabit an imagined community which is likely to be dispersed and connected, not within locatable or bounded space or community, but through a variety and number of mediated practices: media text, fanzines and websites. Jenkins argues that in order to understand the 'fan' we must:

> focus on media fandom as a discursive logic that knits together interests across textual and generic boundaries. While some fans remain exclusively committed to a single show or star, many others use individual series as points of entry into a broader fan community, linking to an intertextual network composed of many programmes, films, books, comics and other popular materials. (1992: 40)

'To focus on any one media product – be it *Star Trek* or "Material Girl" is to miss the larger cultural context within which that material gets embedded as it is integrated back into the life of the individual fan' (ibid.: 41). Thus, the studies of investments which fans make in a popular culture takes us back to the importance of how these practices relate more broadly to the cultures of everyday life.

As Jenkins suggests, many of the traditionally assumed boundaries, such as that between the producer and consumer and between commercial and creative products are broken down. 'Fandom here becomes a participatory culture which transforms the experience of media consumption into the production of new texts, indeed of a new culture and a new community' (ibid.: 46). And, we might add, the boundaries of researcher and researched as they share their pleasures in the consumption of popular texts.

Those scholars who have studied fans and fan cultures have looked at the appeal of specific genres or texts for individuals. To be a 'fan' is to have extraordinary recognitions and identifications with aspects of popular culture. The insights gained here, especially into the construction of subjectivities are very interesting indeed and reveal the complex processes of such identifications. They take us into the realm of fantasy, desire and give us some understanding of the role of the popular in giving us a sense of who we are, or who we might be.

Stop and think 8.6

Apply Gray's ideas to the case study of Morrissey's fans.

1. Do you think Morrissey's fans inhabit an imagined community?

2. How is it possible that a wide variety of fans (male/female; gay/straight/transgendered) can strongly identify with the same performer?

Conclusion

While quantitative audience research has its place within the broad church of media studies, a qualitative approach is potentially the most fruitful in assisting us in our efforts to better understand media audiences. As an antidote to the crude determinism evident in the behaviourist/effects model of audience research and as a bulwark to the often simplistic assumptions made about media effects within public (and media) discourse, the qualitative approach recognizes the dynamic and often complex nature of the relationship between media audiences and media texts.

While we accept that media texts have the power to shape and frame audience interpretations, we can never be fully sure about how audiences will interpret media content. The research methodologies used by those following a reception or ethnographic research approach offer us the best chance of understanding more about these processes. Interpretative activity has to be examined in terms of where audience members are socially situated and in terms of the relative amount of power they possess. Ideally, analyses of reception should be undertaken not in isolation but rather as part of a research framework that gives adequate attention to questions concerning production and content. Reception analysis need not be confined to analysing fictional genres. It is applicable to both factual and fictional media genres. The ethnographic approach has produced valuable insights into the processes associated with media globalization and on the gendered dimensions of new media technologies. It has been particularly insightful in terms of understanding the world of the fan and fans of popular cultural forms in particular.

Chapter summary

1. Given the complex characteristics of the contemporary mediascape it is essential that the tools (both methodological and theoretical) we use to understand audiences allow us to engage fully with such complexities.
2. Behaviorist/positivist approaches to understanding audiences are at best limited in what they can reveal.
3. Reception analysis focused on the extent of audience power and agency offers us the possibility of understanding audiences more critically. This chapter identified three key phases in reception analysis as well as an alternative approach in the form of the News Game.
4. Some caution needs to be taken with audience research which styles itself as ethnographic. Specifically, we need to be concerned with the degree to which research findings are generated from (usually) small samples of research participants.
5. Rejecting pathologizing accounts of fandom, this chapter suggests that we can learn a great deal about how audiences as fans best exemplify the participatory and performative aspects of media cultures.

Further reading

Abercrombie N. and B. Longhurst (1998) *Audiences*. London. Sage. This engaging text is a critique of the dominant paradigms within audience research. See in particular Chapter 5, 'Fans and enthusiasts', for the authors' differentiation of fans, cultists and enthusiasts.

Brooker, W. and D. Jermyn (2003) *The Audience Studies Reader*. London: Routledge. Contains essays by a wide range of well-known audience theorists including Ang, Gillespie, McRobbie, Schlesinger and Radway.

(Continued)

Gillespie, M. (2005) (ed.) *Media Audiences*. Maidenhead: Open University Press. This is an excellent introduction to the study of media audiences. It has a strong focus on audiences in the contexts of technological change and debates about citizenship. See in particular Chapter 1 by Livingstone and Chapter 4 by Gillespie.

Gray, A. (2003) *Research Practice for Cultural Studies*. London: Sage. Gray's text is invaluable for students of media and cultural studies. She offers a critical account of ethnographic research as well as practical advice on how to undertake research of this kind.

Kim, S. (2004) 'Re-reading David Morley's The "*Nationwide*" Audience', *Cultural Studies*, 18(1): 84–108. An important and detailed reassessment of Morley's study.

Morley, D. (2006) 'Unanswered questions in audience research', *The Communication Review*, 9(2): 101–21. A wide-ranging critical essay on the persistent challenges faced in audience research, including an updated reflection on the *Nationwide* study.

Ross, K. and V. Nightingale (2003) *Media and Audiences*. Maidenhead: Open University Press. A well-written and highly accessible text. See, in particular, Chapters 5, 6 and 7, which deal with audiences, in turn, as citizens, fans and as consumers of new media.

Ruddock, A. (2008) 'Media studies 2.0? Binge drinking and why audiences still matter', *Sociology Compass*, 2(1): 1–15.

Schroder, K., K. Drotner, S. Kline and C. Murray (2003) *Researching Audiences*. London: Arnold. This practical text is a must for students intent on undertaking reception analysis. See, in particular, Chapters 7, 8 and 9 on the realities of doing reception-based research.

Online reading

Go to the companion website and read the following:

- Bennett, A. (2006) 'Punk's not dead: the continuing significance of punk rock for an older generation of fans', *Sociology*, 40(2): 219–35.

- De Kloet, J. and L. van Zoonen (2007) 'Fan culture – performing difference', in E. Devereux (ed.), *Media Studies: Key Issues and Debates*. London: Sage Publications.

- Stevenson, N. (2009) 'Talking to Bowie fans: Masculinity, ambivalence and cultural citizenship', *European Journal of Cultural Studies*, 12(1): 79–98.

CHAPTER 9

New Media, Social Media

Chapter overview

Building on core themes previously discussed (such as the power of multimedia conglomerates, the relative degree of agency possessed by audiences and the changing nature of the media industries themselves), this chapter presents a critical account of new media and social media. Drawing from the political economy perspective, it explains how:

- Unequal power relationships and the hegemony of multimedia conglomerates in particular continue to shape and determine the uses of both new media and social media
- It is problematic to assume (as some utopian commentators do) that new media and social media offer audiences unlimited possibilities in terms of creativity or agency. In fact, the growth in audience participation in a new media setting can be seen as a source of free labour for multimedia conglomerates
- Notwithstanding the positive developments that have taken place in terms of citizen journalism, new media and social media have also had negative impacts for the production of news and some sections of the media industries. This is of particular importance when we focus on issues concerning the extent to which new media have facilitated active citizenship in a media setting.

Key concepts

- Social media
- New media
- Convergence
- Public sphere

(Continued)

- Citizenship
- Netizens
- Networked individuals
- Political economy
- Democratization
- Produsers/prosumers
- Blogging
- Citizen journalism

Introduction: New media and social media – empowering audiences, but who is holding the tiger's tail?

Developments in new media and the emergence of social media networks have radically altered how we now understand the media. Technological innovations in terms of the media devices, software and apps we use have resulted in new ways of experiencing and using the media. Although many early new media theorists heralded the advent and spread of the internet as being a great leveller – a force for democracy, innovation and sharing of information and knowledge amongst the world's citizens – the reality is somewhat different. While free content (e.g. Wikipedia), free software and other applications (e.g. Open Source) are available, the majority of new media usage takes place using technologies produced, distributed and controlled by global multimedia conglomerates (e.g. YouTube). The internet is still more likely to be used to source pornography, to check out the vital statistics of the latest model of car or to catch up with the latest celebrity gossip than it is to be a public sphere facilitating informed debate and argument about how society might be best organized. As will be clear from this chapter, the availability of new media and the spread of social media networks are of major importance where both media organizations and media audiences are concerned. New media present both opportunities and challenges for multimedia conglomerates. As was previously pointed out in Chapter 3, new media technologies allow not only for **convergences** between old and new media but also the possibility of generating further profit through the development of new media technologies and the re-selling of existing media content in new formats.

New media also present challenges to the hegemonic position of multimedia conglomerates. Many of the technologies which the media companies produce and sell in the first instance allow for audiences to freely share media content.

The most obvious evidence of this is in the form of the online file-sharing of music, games, films and books. Social media sites owned and controlled by the multimedia conglomerates facilitate 'piracy' and breaches of copyright. The owners of newspapers and other forms of print media are under severe financial pressure as many readers have migrated to online versions of content and are highly resistant to the prospect of a pay-wall. The arrival of social media networks such as Facebook and Twitter, and a variety of freeware allowing for the creation of blogs, has also fuelled the development of what is most commonly referred to as citizen journalism (see this chapter's later discussion on blogs and blogging). Arguably the most interesting aspects of both new media and social media are the implications for media audiences and how media audiences are understood. As we saw in Chapter 8, audiences are now more likely to be involved in participatory cultures (especially in terms of fan subcultures and practices), leading some theorists to suggest that audiences have been, in fact, reconstituted as produsers or prosumers who can either create or appropriate media content for dissemination.

This chapter proposes that we need to cast a critical eye over such claims. It begins by examining two recent and well-known examples of citizen activism – the Arab Spring and the Occupy Movement. The political and other possibilities afforded by the internet are then investigated. The re-casting of audiences as produsers is then discussed, with a particular focus on a critical understanding of blogging. The chapter concludes by considering the implications which new media and social media have for the production of news.

Given the scale of media saturation and intrusiveness in our everyday lives as a result of developments in new media and social media, it is crucial that we do not forget that powerful economic (and political) interests still retain significant levels of control over these technologies and networks. That said, it is an interesting contradiction that those interests who have actively promoted globalization and neo-liberal understandings of the world have also, to a large degree, facilitated the dissemination of a robust critique of the establishment. The tiger may have been unleashed, but who exactly is holding on to its tail?

Will the revolution be digitalized?

In the final weeks of December 2010, the martyrdom of a young Tunisian fruit vendor named Mohamed Bouazizi rapidly gave rise to a series of events in North Africa and the Middle East which are now referred to as the Arab Spring. The Arab Spring witnessed protests, uprisings and ultimately the replacement of a number of oppressive political dictatorships (in Tunisia, Egypt, Yemen and Libya). Citizen journalism and the use of new media and social media networks, in particular, have all been heralded within many mainstream media narratives as playing a key role in the push towards democracy. Although, as you will see later in this chapter, the actual degree to which new media and social media instigated these various forms of political activism has come to be hotly debated.

Nine months later, on 17 September 2011, in the heart of global capitalism, a group of protestors occupied Zuccotti Park at Wall Street in New York City. The activists were inspired by the Arab Spring and the radical Canadian publication *Adbusters*; the Occupy Movement spread quickly to over 1,000 cities and towns throughout the world. Activists were protesting about the poverty and inequality resulting from corporate greed. They were also giving voice to concerns about the implications for democracy given the hegemonic or dominant position held by banks and other transnational corporations (including multimedia conglomerates).

The role played by social media in attempting to generate counter-hegemonic resistance was heavily stressed within much media commentary. However, the Occupy Movement's media practices and cultures were, in fact, quite complex. Costanza-Chock shows how the caricature of the digital savvy protestor, 'They all have Apple Computers and i-Phones' (2012: 4), is inaccurate. In reality, a mixture of low- (e.g. posters, flyers) and high-tech forms of media were utilized, relying upon what Costanza-Chock refers to as 'transmedia mobilization' in getting their message ('We Are The 99%') into circulation. Facebook and face-to-face communication predominated in terms of spreading the movement's key messages. A smaller cohort of activists resorted to more time- and labour-intensive forms of communication – e.g. blogging, video-production, live-streaming and newspaper production. Many of the these activists brought a wealth of media expertise from their experiences in earlier protest movements.

As the Occupy Movement gained momentum (and mainstream media coverage), there were external and internal pressures for it to provide designated spokespersons. As a deliberately 'leaderful' rather than 'leaderless' open and participatory movement these demands were resisted. Participation in social movements, however, is shaped by structural inequalities along race, class and gender lines. In the case of the Occupy Movement, Costanza-Chock (2012) found that it consciously made an effort to be inclusive of women, people of colour and the LGBT community in its communications processes. The Occupy Movement represents a concrete example of how hegemonic ideologies can be resisted through the media – many of which are owned and controlled by transnational corporations which the movement was critical of (for more details see: http://occupywallst.org/).

 Stop and think 9.1

Ideology, hegemony and social media

In recent years the use of social media such as Twitter, Facebook and YouTube have been celebrated as the means by which ordinary citizens can challenge the status quo. The Occupy Movement, the Arab Spring, and the 2013 upheavals in Syria and Turkey are amongst the better known examples. In your opinion, is the role of social media in helping to overthrow or resist oppressive regimes real or overstated? Do you think audiences are more likely to trust content disseminated via social media or by the more established media organizations?

Read on! 9.1   Political economy, power and new media

Robin Mansell (2004) 'Political economy, power and new media', *New Media & Society*, 6(1): 96–105, pp. 97–8.

There is a very substantial tendency in studies of new media to emphasize the abundance and variety of new media products and services, and to concentrate on promoting access with little regard for the associated structures and processes of power that are embedded within them. There are undeniably major changes in the scope and scale of new media supply and in the ways that our lives are mediated by digital technologies and services. However, there is continuing evidence of scarcity in relation to new media production and consumption. This condition of scarcity is being reproduced as a result of various articulations of power. These are not inconsequential. They are contributing to the maintenance of deeply-rooted inequalities in today's so-called 'information' or 'knowledge' societies (Mansell, 1999, 2003).

A synthesis of past and current contributions to the political economy of media and communications could encompass the works of many authors. Depending on the selection criteria, different themes would be accentuated. However, at the core there would be an interest in the analysis of the specific historical circumstances under which new media and communications products and services are produced under capitalism, and with the influence of these circumstances over their consumption. Dallas Smythe, who was a major contributor to early studies in this tradition, emphasized research on all aspects of 'the power processes within society' (Smythe, 1960: 463). He focused on production, quality and allocation, and on the role of capital, organization and control in the media and communications industries. Although studies in this tradition are often criticized for being overly concerned with the structure of

▶

production rather than with content, meaning and the symbolic, Smythe's (1981) work did not neglect the possibility of resistance to dominant trends in media and communications production through alternative consumption strategies. Another central figure in the political economy of media and communications tradition, Nicholas Garnham (1990, 2000), focuses on both the structure of production of services and technologies and on the consumption of their symbolic content. Garnham's interest in the 'old' and the 'new' media has been in developing explanations for emerging social structures, hierarchies of power and their legitimation. Following in these traditions, any political economy of new media must be as concerned with symbolic form, meaning and action as it is with structures of power and institutions. If resources are scarce, and if power is unequally distributed in society, then the key issue is how these scarce resources are allocated and controlled, and with what consequences for human action. Distinctions between the older and newer media relate to how and why scarcity conditions emerge and the extent to which they contribute to the reproduction of unequal social conditions. Without research that gives a central place to power as a 'headline' issue in new media studies, we can only speculate about how inequality may be reproduced and then seen as the 'natural' outcome of innovations in new media technologies.

 ## Stop and think 9.2

1. What according to Mansell (2004) are the gaps in research on new media?

2. Does the reading express an optimistic or pessimistic view on new media?

3. What, according to this extract, are the core concerns expressed by Dallas Smythe and Nicholas Garnham concerning the media and power?

The promise and reality of the internet

The internet has been heralded by many as having major potential as a media-based public sphere (see Chapter 4 for an elaboration of the concept of the public sphere). One can search for information on everything from bomb-making to basket-weaving, or engage in online discussions about a seemingly endless list of topics, many of which are critical of the status quo. Online discussion fora, blogs and other forms of social media are regularly cited as examples of where democratic dialogue and debate can take place. The internet has been celebrated by many for flattening all of the traditional structures around media ownership; bringing about economic transformation; allowing just about anyone to be a media producer; and having huge significance in terms of democratic dialogue and political actions. On the face of it, the internet seems to offer almost utopian possibilities.

However, in a powerful set of arguments Curran et al. (2012) remind us of the widening gap between the internet's promise and its reality. The internet continues to be dominated by Goliath multimedia conglomerates. Earlier in the book we referred to how even hyper-capitalist organizations such as News Corporation and Google reached agreement with state communist political systems to facilitate censorship (see Chapter 4 for more on the power and scale of multimedia conglomerates). The colonization and commercialization of internet space is evident every time you log on to the internet via one of the major Internet Service Providers (ISPs), with these being owned and controlled by a tiny number of multimedia conglomerates. The hegemonic position of capital is witnessed in the preponderance of banner adverts, in the practices of data harvesting and surveillance and in the dominant positions assumed by Microsoft, Google and Apple, who structure and determine the majority of web usage (Curran, 2012a). The conglomerates loom large in the realms of music downloading, social networking sites and access to news and current affairs (Freedman, 2012).

Access to this potential public sphere is not equal. The English language has assumed a hegemonic position and the internet remains a place of hate content. Users of the internet are more likely to be searching for pornography than for matters of public concern. While social media have been celebrated as forming the sites of counter-hegemonic resistance, to what extent does this happen in reality? In critiquing the political economy of social media, the media sociologist Natalie Fenton (2012) notes how platforms such as Twitter can function to embed individualism (a sort of narcissistic 'daily me') rather than a sense of the collective (see Figure 9.1).

Many political dictatorships have managed to successfully control access to the internet.

The internet retains the potential to operate as a public sphere. It has not, as yet, realized that role. As Breen (2007), McChesney (1999) and Patelis (2000) stress, we must be very cautious about the idea that the internet represents an unproblematic public sphere.

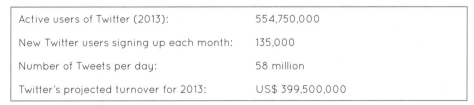

Active users of Twitter (2013):	554,750,000
New Twitter users signing up each month:	135,000
Number of Tweets per day:	58 million
Twitter's projected turnover for 2013:	US$ 399,500,000

Figure 9.1 **Twitter at a glance (data source: Twitter.com).**

A CLOSER LOOK 9.1

Audiences as 'netizens'

In 2009 the Chinese state-controlled CCTV television station broadcast a report which was highly critical of Google. The station interviewed a young university student – Gao Ye – who claimed that the internet (owing to the preponderance of pornography) had made him feel 'restless'. It was soon discovered, however, that, in fact, Ye was employed at the station as an intern and that the report on Google was merely a ploy by the Chinese authorities to deflect attention away from their efforts to introduce filtering software (referred to as the 'Green Dam') on all new PCs being sold in China. This discovery led to high levels of online criticism of both Ye and of the TV station CCTV. In an optimistic account of this and two other 'internet incidents', Tang and Sampson (2012) argue that audiences can resist hegemony and influence mainstream news agendas. Such resistance takes place in the context of state censorship and control. They discuss how *some* audience members (**netizens** – i.e citizens who use the net) manage to overcome state censorship and internet monitoring. Citing Castell's (2007, 239) notion of audience 'counter-power' – defined as 'the capacity of a social actor to resist and challenge power relations that are institutionalised' – Tang and Sampson (2012: 469) demonstrate how online netizen activity results in state hegemony being resisted and challenged (read their article in full on the companion website).

Do it! 9.1   Facing up to Facebook

The social network site (SNS) Facebook has been understood by some researchers as being a virtual or imagined community where members present an idealized version of themselves to their Facebook friends (Acquisti and Gross, 2006; Taraszow et al., 2010). In the context of the EU, the Kids Online research project examined how a sample of Cypriot youths used Facebook. Their work found low levels of awareness concerning privacy matters amongst 18–22-year-olds in particular. They also discovered significant gender differences in terms of disclosure. Males were more likely than females to provide details of their instant messaging names, their home addresses and mobile or cell phone numbers.

Think about the following:

1. What is the extent of your use of Facebook on a daily basis? How does this compare with your use of traditional media?

2. Is your personal experience of Facebook in agreement with the work of Acquisti and Gross (2006) and Taraszow et al. (2010)?

3. As a Facebook user do you have any concerns about either privacy or how data pertaining to your online life may be used?

Read on! 9.2   Arab Spring and digital media

Philip N. Howard and Muzammil M. Hussein (2011) 'The role of digital media', *Journal of Democracy*, 22(3): 35–48.

On 17 December 2010, Mohamed Bouazizi set himself on fire. The young street vendor in the small Tunisian city of Sidi Bouzid had tried in vain to fight an inspector's small fine, appealing first to the police, then to town officials, and then to the regional governor. Each time he dared to press his case, security officials beat him. Bruised, humiliated, and frustrated by this cruel treatment, Bouazizi set himself alight in front of the governor's office. By the time he died in a hospital on January 4, his plight had sparked nationwide protests. The news had traveled fast, even though the state-run media had ignored the tragedy and the seething discontent in Sidi Bouzid. During the angry second half of December, it was through blogs and text messages that Tunisians experienced what the sociologist Doug McAdam calls 'cognitive liberation.' In their shared sympathy for the dying man, networks of family and friends came to realize that they shared common grievances too. The realization hit home as people watched YouTube videos about the abusive state, read foreign news coverage of political corruption online, and shared jokes about their aging dictator over SMS. Communicating in ways that the state could not control, people also used digital media to arrive at strategies for action and a collective goal: the deposition of a despot. For years, the most direct accusations of political corruption had come from the blogosphere. Investigative journalism was almost solely the work of average citizens using the Internet in creative ways. Most famous is the YouTube video showing Tunisia's presidential jet on runways near exclusive European shopping destinations, with onscreen graphics specifying dates and places and asking who was using the aircraft (the suggestion being that it was Ben Ali's high-living wife). Once this video appeared online, the regime cracked down on YouTube, Facebook, and other applications. But bloggers and activists pushed on, producing alternative online newscasts, creating virtual spaces for anonymous political discussions, and commiserating with fellow citizens about state persecution. With Bouazizi's death, Ben Ali's critics moved from virtual to actual public spaces. Shamseddine Abidi, a 29-year-old interior designer, posted regular videos and updates to Facebook. Al Jazeera used the content to carry news of the events to the world. Images of a hospitalized Bouazizi spread via networks of family and friends. An online campaign called on citizens and unions to support the uprising in Sidi Bouzid. Lawyers and students were among the first to take to the streets in an organized way. The government tried to ban Facebook, Twitter, and video sites such as DailyMotion and YouTube. Within a few days, however, people found a workaround as SMS networks became the organizing tool of choice. Less than 20 percent of the population actively used social media, but almost everyone had access to a mobile phone. Outside the country, the hacker communities of Anonymous and Telecomix helped to cripple the government by carrying out denial-of-service attacks and by building new software to help activists get around state firewalls.

 ## Stop and think 9.3

1. Could the Tunisian uprising and the subsequent Arab Spring (2011) have occurred without social media?

2. The extract suggests that in addition to social media, more conventional media (from abroad) also played a role in spreading counter-hegemonic ideas. Do you agree?

3. In the face of state censorship what sorts of media tactics did the Tunisian citizen activists resort to? What does this tell you about the potential for audience agency in the face of attempted state control and censorship?

4. The authors note that the level of internet access in Tunisia in 2010 was relatively low at 20%. Many journalistic accounts of the Arab Spring initially stressed the role played by social media in encouraging oppressed people to revolt. Do you think that the role of social media activism was overstated?

We are all 'produsers' now, are we? Audiences and new media

In some quarters it has become commonplace to argue that the traditional boundaries between producers and consumers of media texts have become either blurred or have disintegrated altogether. Ritzer et al. (2012) show how many theorists have come to reconfigure consumers (audiences) as either 'prosumers' or 'produsers'. Such thinking has its roots in the work of futurist writer and thinker Alvin Toffler (1980). Much postmodern theory downplays the role of the cultural industries (as institutions or organizations) and, instead, focuses on user-generated content in the Web 2.0 era. In this version of media production, audiences create, recreate and recycle media content through their use of blogs, Facebook, Tumblr, Twitter, Wikipedia and YouTube. So, as well as consuming media texts, audience members have the capacity or potential to produce and circulate media texts.

CHAPTER LINKS

More traditional understandings of media production are discussed in Chapter 5.

While not wishing to deflate such arguments (and in particular in terms of the *potential* that audiences as produsers might have in terms of circulating ideas that are critical of the *status quo*) it is important that such arguments are treated with caution. In our earlier discussion of media globalization (see Chapter 3) it was noted that many constraints persist in terms of equal access to the media and new media in particular. It is also the case that the production and circulation of the overwhelming majority of media texts which are consumed by audiences remains in the hands of powerful multimedia conglomerates.

Prosumption often involves the recasting or recirculation of content which, in the first instance, was created by one of these conglomerates. Perhaps more importantly, audience activity of this kind serves as a form of profit and unpaid labour for some conglomerates (see Bruns, 2008). While Twitter and Facebook could not exist without produser activity, the net result of such activity is significant levels of profit and wealth for the conglomerates in question. The true economic value of Facebook rests on its ability to harvest vast amounts of data about its produsers. Using a critical political economy approach, Fisher (2012) shows how social networking sites such as Facebook rely upon free audience labour. This activity may be understood to be exploitative in the traditional Marxist use of the term; however, social network sites also allow for the reduction of possible alienation in that they facilitate communication and leisure activities.

New media and citizen journalism: blogging

Since 1997 'weblogs' or 'blogs' as they are more commonly known have emerged as a significant feature of daily internet activity. 'Blogs' and the practice of 'blogging' are of interest because they allow 'ordinary' people to become media producers in their own right (see Tremayne, 2007). At the most basic level we can see the production of content for consumption by others who may be known or unknown to the producer. The technology is free (or cheap) and is easy to use. Blogs allow for the creation of new content, for commentary or reactions to previous entries and for links to other blogs or websites. Blogs are concerned with an ever-widening range of topics and are governed by a blog etiquette. Matheson (2005: 171–4) shows how the freelance journalist Christopher Allbritton's blog *Back to Iraq* offered his readers a detailed understanding of the conflict during 2003. His success in developing a relationship with his online readers resulted in 320 of them sending him money in order for him to return to Iraq. Matheson (2005) argues that over time the content of the blog is shaped by the reactions of its readers.

addition to reflecting the views and concerns of ordinary citizens, blogs are singly being used by powerful interest groups in society such as politicians litical parties as well as appearing as an adjunct to existing mainstream uch as newspapers and television news programmes. Alongside podcasts, ogs are an interesting example of where audience members can exercise their agency and express their points of view to the wider public.

Blogs are often mistakenly characterized as being the online equivalent of a personal diary, replete with confessions of a personal nature for all to see. Nardi et al. (2004), however, in an ethnographic study of North American bloggers, point to the numerous variations involved in this kind of media activity. Blog content as well as levels of access to blogs varied. Nardi et al. focused on blogging as a social activity, noting how blog content could change as a result of reader/audience reactions. An on-line etiquette is observed by most bloggers. Nardi et al. (2004) also found that the exchanges between bloggers carried over into other forms of media such as email and text messaging. Bloggers communicate with people they know and to a wider public they will never encounter in their daily lives, referred to as the 'blogosphere'. Nardi et al. (2004) differentiate between bloggers who create content for people they know, such as family and friends, and for those who generate content in order to influence public opinion about a political or human rights issue, for example. Far from being a confessional diary-like space, blogging is, they argue, a social activity and needs to be understood as such.

New media, news and the media industries

Fenton (2011) takes the crisis evident with news media much further by examining the debasement and decline of news within a political economy framework. Her evidence is based upon a two-and-a-half-year study on news and the new media in the UK, as well as an investigation into news needs of local communities. The predominance of neo-liberalism both as an ideology and as a business model in advanced capitalist societies is shown to lie at the heart of the crisis. The adoption of new media technologies and the rationalization of journalism as a profession are shown to have had a profoundly negative impact on news and news makers. Conglomeration has resulted in an insatiable search for profit, a reduction in the number of news outlets such as local and regional newspapers, cuts in the number of journalists employed, and greater pressures to generate content across media platforms. A growing number of journalists are desk-bound and spend their time 'mouse-chasing' or, in Fenton's words, 'Speeding it up and spreading it thin' (2011, 65). The marketization of news and the economies being imposed by media conglomerates means fewer resources for a critical journalism. Democratic dialogue and debate is the main casualty in the crises affecting news journalism. The decline of local media and its watchdog role in particular was noted by many of the interviewees in the local news needs study. While Fenton acknowledges the possibilities afforded by new media technologies in terms of the generation and distribution of news, she cautions against a utopian view of new media as a panacea to the news needs of citizens. It has not brought about a renaissance in journalism. Curran (2012a) shows how television news remains the most important source of trustworthy and credible news for audiences. If anything, the advent of the internet has had negative implications for print journalism. Curran (2012a) notes how the migration of advertising revenues from print to online platforms has created serious challenges for more traditional forms of journalism.

Read on! 9.3   Social media, newsrooms and journalism

From John V. Pavlik (2013) 'Trends in new media research: a critical review of recent scholarship', *Sociology Compass*, 7(1): 1–12, pp. 2–3.

Research suggests social media also can exert an influence on the practices and journalism routines in newsrooms (Shim et al. 2011). Shim et al. report social media are 'not only changing countries, but also how the media report on events. While authoritarian governments – such as Yemen, Libya and most recently, China – aimed to control the media environment to maintain the status quo, the people strived to initiate the revolution through e-mobilization by using social media. The convenience and effectiveness of social media to reach the masses dramatically impacts the way journalists access information.' These findings are confirmed by Silva, who has reported the results of a study of user generated content (UGC) and participatory culture (Silva 2011). Her research is based on an examination of CNN's website and the role of non-professionally produced video content published on the CNN site. Research by Singer (2010) on local British newspaper journalists also shows at least some journalists have serious concerns about the potential of UGC to 'undermine journalistic norms and values unless carefully monitored' and are therefore often reluctant to incorporate UGC into the news presented online.

New journalistic roles may be emerging as a consequence of social media, research suggests. Bruns (2005, 2011) presents findings that the role of the curator has emerged in digital journalism to complement the traditional role of gatekeeper. In this role, the journalist collects or facilitates the collection of content from networked individuals (Dutton, 2009) or what some have called citizen journalists, organizes that content, perhaps in the form of an interactive map or some other visual or graphical format, presents and shares it digitally or online via the Web or for mobile tablet

▶

device, utilizing potentially advanced news crowd sourcing platforms that enable citizen analysis of that information. One unsettled issue is who bears legal or ethical responsibility in this curation model of social media journalism. In such an environment, social media can act as a disruptive force for traditional media and journalistic practices, models and norms. Social media can also exert increasing pressure to make journalism and media more transparent. That is, by engaging journalists and the public in a dialog or discourse about the news, there is pressure to make news processes and practices more transparent, such as getting news organizations to reveal their sources of news, at least when to do so would not compromise the integrity of [a] story or a source. News organizations, editors and reporters historically have often protected their sources [as] a closely guarded, competitive secret, sometimes for good reason ... Yet in the networked, mobile, digital 21st century, scoops are almost non-existent, at least for long or for more than a few fleeting seconds, and making the process more transparent might go a lot further toward building public trust and understanding in the media.

 Stop and think 9.4

1. In what ways are social media bringing about changes in the practices of traditional journalism?

2. Do you understand what is meant by the emergence of a new Curatorial role for some journalists as a consequence of the advent of new media?

Conclusion

In critically examining the possibilities afforded by recent developments in new media and through the use of social media networks in particular, the intention of this chapter was not to be in any way dismissive of the potential for citizen engagement and social change. The chapter did, however, strike a note of warning. In our 24/7, always on, media saturated world there is a real danger of being dazzled by the glitz of new media technologies and applications. However, we need to ask hard questions about what all of this is really about. Is it truly about democracy, empowerment and **citizenship**? Is it about liberating oppressed groups of people? Have these developments genuinely facilitated critical discourse about the persistently unequal relationships of power in the social world? Or are these things merely illusory? Standing back from the millions of digital exchanges which take place online each day it is not that difficult to view the bulk of this activity as being pointless narcissism.

Not all of the world's citizens reap the benefits of this apparent flattening of the boundaries between media producers and media audiences. As has been previously argued in Chapter 3, there continues to be a pronounced digital divide between the **developed and developing world** – notwithstanding the fact that the cheap labour supply in poorer parts of the world is used to produce the components needed for laptops, tablets and smartphones.

While new media and social media networks do facilitate audience agency and the spread of counter-hegemonic ideas (for those who have access), the powerful position of multimedia conglomerates remains intact. They retain significant levels of control over the production and distribution of content through old and new media. They have succeeded in colonizing, privatizing and commercializing what potentially was a public sphere. A critical take on audiences as producers in a social media or new media setting is that they are a free reserve army of labour from whom the global media giants are not slow to harvest valuable data. In conclusion, while these developments allow for greater agency in a media context by marginalized groups, stigmatized communities or oppressed people, a failure to recognize the sheer power of multimedia conglomerates and their associated interests is a failure to see the complete picture.

Chapter summary

1. This chapter has emphasized the need to adopt a critical stance regarding the ways in which new media and social media are understood.
2. The political economy perspective suggests that we think critically about the continued dominance of multimedia conglomerates in the fields of new media and social media.
3. While the potential that new media and social media have in terms of improving the democratic health of society is acknowledged, the chapter warned against adopting a naïve standpoint. Securing hegemony by the powerful in media and other settings is an ongoing process and power is not something that is ceded easily.

(Continued)

4. The chapter questioned the degree to which we can usefully consider the internet a public sphere or the true extent (and impact) of netizenship.

5. The chapter also interrogated the received understandings of audiences as produsers and citizen journalists.

Further reading

Curran, J., N. Fenton and D. Freedman (2012) *Misunderstanding the Internet*. Abingdon: Routledge. All seven chapters by James Curran and his colleagues are essential reading for media students interested in questions concerning new media, social media and power; see also N. Fenton (2010) *New Media, Old News, Journalism and Democracy in the Digital Age*. London: Sage.

Sullivan, J.L. (2013) *Media Audiences: Effects, Users, Institutions and Power*. Thousand Oaks, CA: Sage. An excellent introduction to audience studies, see in particular, Chapter 8, 'Media fandom and audience subcultures'; Chapter 9, 'Online, interactive audiences in a digital media world' and Chapter 10, 'Audience agency in new contexts'.

Online reading

Go to the companion website and read the following:

- Breen, M.J. (2007) 'Mass media and new media technologies', in E. Devereux (ed.), *Media Studies: Key Issues and Debates*. London: Sage.
- M. Meadows (2013) 'Putting the citizen back into journalism', *Journalism*, 14(1): 43–60.
- H. Ornebring (2013) 'Anything you can do, I can do better? Professional journalists on citizen journalists in six European countries', *International Communication Gazette*, 75(1): 35–53.

CHAPTER  10

Conclusion: The How and Why of Media Analysis

Chapter overview

This final chapter will assist you in the important task of undertaking critical media research. Its overarching aim is provide you with some concrete and practical advice in taking your first steps in engaging in media research. To close the circle first raised in the book's introductory chapter, there is an explicit emphasis placed on the challenges involved in undertaking research about media power and the relationship between the media and the economically and politically powerful. The chapter concludes with a renewed call to continue to ask contentious questions about the media.

Key concepts

- Research methods
- Research design
- Research question
- Literature review
- Mixed methods
- Qualitative research
- Quantitative research
- Grounded theory
- Research ethics
- Triangulation
- Production, content and reception

Introduction: This is not a methods chapter ...

This concluding chapter starts with a health warning. While it focuses on the *how* and *why* of media analysis, it deliberately does not spend time rehearsing the mechanics of specific research methods. It is therefore not a research methods chapter in the traditional sense. In earlier chapters of this book (and in the companion website) I have already highlighted many examples of the main research methods used by media and other researchers in attempting to address critical research questions. While this final chapter does contain a 'Further reading' resources section which will point you to a number of very useful key research methods books and will be helpful in your own journey as a student researcher, it does not contain the usual features of previous chapters. Rather, in conclusion, I want to take the opportunity to engage with a number of important themes which are meant to help you to think more critically and more incisively about media analysis. Our job as students of the media is not to ask questions for the sake of just asking questions. Our job is to ask critical questions which inevitably are intertwined with challenging questions concerning unequal power relationships.

In order to overcome the sometimes dismissive attitude towards media research, and media studies more specifically (regularly found in media and political discourse), we need to ask hard questions of the media. In doing so, we need to use tried and tested research methods which are reliable, systematic and representative. As indicated at the very outset of this book we are best served by adopting a **mixed-methods** approach which will assist us in addressing the complexities inherent in doing media research and analysis. This will allow for the triangulation of findings from each research method applied and make up for any shortcomings in each of those selected methods.

In common with research undertaken in other academic fields or disciplines, media research usually starts with a tentative question or a sense of puzzlement. Some examples might be: Can we ever truly measure media effect? Are social media responsible for undermining or strengthening community ties? Are media professionals dictated to by powerful interests in society? Is gender, ethnicity or class of significance in reaching an understanding of how a media text is read?

I begin the chapter by suggesting a step-by-step approach which will help you to think critically and systematically about your research topic or question. Inevitably when you are doing research you will have to investigate how other researchers have previously understood the topic under scrutiny. Using a recent example by Power et al. (2012) on how one disadvantaged neighbourhood was stigmatized in a new media setting as a case study, I discuss how to best read, review and make use of existing research findings. This is followed by some further thoughts on how you can most effectively undertake research using the **production, content and reception** analysis paradigm. I conclude the chapter by reflecting on some of the challenges which are faced by media researchers when they engage in research about the economically and politically powerful.

Staying true to the overall theme of this book I restate the need for all of us, as students, teachers, and most importantly as citizens, to continue to ask hard questions about the media.

A step-by-step approach to doing media research

It is not unusual for media students to be apprehensive about facing a research project for the first time. In the following discussion I take a simple step-by-step approach which is intended to take the mystique (and fear) out of doing critical media research. From the outset it is useful to think about your research project as being just one part of a much larger jigsaw puzzle. Try to imagine yourself contributing (even in a very modest way) to the wider body of knowledge and understanding that we have about the cultural, economic, political and social significance of the media. Doing media research for an essay, project or thesis will allow you to apply theories and methods which will deepen your insights into the workings of the media. You may feel daunted by the need to use theory or specific research methods, but their use is an essential part of reaching a critical understanding of the media. Research methods will allow you to generate reliable data from which you can attempt to answer your initial research question. Media theory will help you sharpen your analytical skills and move beyond the descriptive.

Twelve steps

Before you begin it is crucial to spend some time thinking about your research question. Being clear about what exactly you want to research will save you a lot of time and potential trouble at the other end. Think carefully about each part of your research question. You might, for example, be interested in doing some exploratory research on young people and their uses of social media. In doing so you will need to address what you define as young people; whether you are interested in a subset of young people in terms of their age, class, ethnicity, gender and/or location, and what you understand as social media. It is also important to think about the rationale for undertaking the research. Why is it of personal interest to you? What are your personal motivations for focusing on that particular topic or question? Even at this early stage you should think about how your research might connect with the pre-existing theoretical and methodological concerns which make up the wider field of media analysis. Will your research findings have any likely practical benefits for media organizations, media professionals or media audiences? Have they the potential for helping you think beyond common-sense understandings of the media? Will your findings help to shed new light on old research problems? From the very beginning adopt a sceptical stance about common assumptions that may be in circulation about the media, for example video-games cause or encourage violent behaviour, or greater social media usage means less physical activity.

Detective work

A good starting point in undertaking research is to examine how others have tried to make sense of the question heretofore. It is essential to search for existing research literature. Google Scholar is an obvious starting point. Using keywords (e.g. audience reception; media effects; media genre), the search engine will allow you to see which academic journal articles, books and authors are the most read and cited. Be wary of relying upon research findings that are available online. Wikipedia can be unreliable and many websites containing partial research findings hide the fact that they are published by particular interest groups. As a rule of thumb, it is best to rely upon findings that have been published in reputable refereed academic journals, reports and books. Be aware also of whether a piece of research has been funded by a state/government body, private organization or interest group.

Be creative (and critical)

In searching for previous research it is helpful to identify who the key thinkers are in the field. Be creative and build a map noting the main kinds of questions addressed in earlier work. Think about the main theoretical perspectives and methodological approaches used in the past. Consider the degree to which those theories and methods have been fruitful or not in furthering our understanding of the research theme in question.

The art is (sometimes) in the absence

Make it a matter of practice to try to identify the so-called 'blind-spots' of existing media research. Are there aspects that other researchers have ignored? From experience, I find it useful to think about the gaps in existing research and to think about ways in which to address these shortcomings. In a later section in this chapter I take a closer look at the art of reviewing previous research.

Unless you are taking what is referred to as a **grounded theory** approach (i.e. where theory emerges after you analyse your data), you will need to decide which theoretical model (or models) best suit your research endeavours. You will have already seen in your textbook that media analysis is comprised of particular schools/approaches/paradigms which in different ways may illuminate your understanding. Thus, political economy theory, for example, will help further your insights into media ownership structures and power, feminist theory will assist you in trying to understand more about gendered media discourses, and reception theory will give you the tools to make greater sense of how fans interpret and use media texts. Don't be afraid of using more than one theoretical approach. It is sometimes more rewarding to draw upon a mixture of theoretical lenses which will tell you more about specific aspects of your research. Thus, for example, if you were interested in the ideological dimensions of television news you might want to combine elements of framing theory and discourse analysis theory with an overarching critical theory approach (see Chapter 7, 'Media Re-presentations in an Unequal World', for an elaboration). This will allow you

Step One	What precisely is your research question?
Step Two	What are the main reasons for undertaking this research?
Step Three	What are the likely benefits (practical and theoretical) of undertaking media research of this kind?
Step Four	How much research literature already exists? Where will you find this research literature? What are the key studies? Who are the key writers in this area? How have the key writers approached the topic under investigation in your project? What are the overall conclusions and arguments of each study? What are their blind spots?
Step Five	Which theoretical perspective(s) will best inform your research? Why?
Step Six	Which methodological approach(es) will best help you in carrying out your research? Why?
Step Seven	If your work involves human subjects, define exactly which population you are going to base your study upon. How will you access the population in question? How many participants do you need to make your research representative and reliable? If your research is solely focused on media content how will you access this content? Are there costs, copyright or storage issues involved?
Step Eight	Consider whether it is necessary to do a pilot study or not before embarking on the larger research project.
Step Nine	Before you begin your research involving human subjects are there any issues here about access to the subjects in question (ethical, legal, logistical)?
Step Ten	How will your (qualitative or quantitative) data be analysed? Will you use a software package (e.g. N-Vivo, N*udist, SPSS) or analyse the data manually?
Step Eleven	Identify key findings in your data. Relate these findings to the existing research literature.
Step Twelve	Write up your paper, essay, report or thesis in which you outline your key findings and your overall argument.

Figure 10.1 **Twelve steps in doing a media research project.**

to delve into the structure of your selected texts in terms of the frames or discourses employed but to also place your findings within the parameters of a bigger theoretical debate concerning the media's ideological role.

Equally, where research methods are concerned it is essential to think carefully about which research method or methods best suit your research question and are likely to generate useful data. In designing your research you will find clues concerning methodological choices in existing media research. Observation or participant observation is more suitable than administering a questionnaire if you were interested in researching the participatory and performative aspects of fandom amongst sports fans in a public setting, for example. a bar or restaurant. Combining research methods will also allow you to capture data on different aspects of social reality. If you were concerned with learning more about the constraints which shape everyday media work, for example, a combination of face-to-face interviews, observation and participant observation with a sample of media professionals would yield potentially interesting data. Quantitative methods in the shape of surveys or questionnaires also have their place in gathering data about audience behaviour. Your choice of research method(s) should be led by the kinds of questions you wish to ask. A methodological or a theoretical sectarianism will narrow your horizons considerably. In making methodological and theoretical choices it is essential that you are aware of the implications of choosing one approach over another. Such decisions invariably have consequences for how we make sense of different media phenomena.

Before you start

Before you embark on any research project you must also give due attention to a range of practical issues. If your work involves human subjects you will need to think about how you will access participants for your study. In addition to the realities of recruiting research participants you will need to consider ethical, logistical and possible safety issues. If you are doing quantitative research you will need to think about a realistic sample size in terms of your study population. Alternatively, if you are doing face-to-face interviews, holding focus groups or engaging in virtual ethnography online, you will have to take critical decisions about exactly how many interviews or observations of online subjects you need to undertake. Exemplars (in terms of sample size, etc.) may be found in previously published research. Before you go into the field you should consider pilot testing your research questions with a small sample of participants. This will help to ensure that your study participants understand your questions. It will allow you to revise or simplify difficult questions or to remove any jargon (e.g. terms like postmodern; counter-hegemonic; high-culture) which participants might not readily understand. Be aware of the ethical aspects of engaging in research. The British Sociological Association has devised very helpful guidelines which will help in thinking about **research ethics** (see http://www.britsoc.co.uk/). Remember that people have the right to refuse to take part in a research study and even when they do consent to participate, you must protect their identities and observe guarantees of confidentiality when the research project is completed.

It is essential that you anticipate what is involved in the analysis stage of your research work. In addition to thinking about the scale of your study (e.g. the number of interviews, questionnaires, field notes, media texts, etc.) you should think about how you will analyse the data you have gathered. While small amounts of data can be analysed manually, it is more usual to make use of software packages (e.g. SPSS; NVivo or Nu*dist) to assist in the analysis. Such packages have the potential to allow you to manage relatively large amounts of data and to identify otherwise complex patterns. If you are recording and transcribing interviews, bear in mind that transcription takes a considerable amount of time. In any event, where qualitative research is concerned, the quality of the data is often far more important than the quantity of the data generated.

Once you have completed your data analysis, create a list of your key findings. Think about how your key findings relate to existing debates within media analysis. Do your findings agree with or contradict current understandings? Have your findings the potential to change the ways in which we theorize about the media?

Reflect on your overall experience of doing research. If you had the opportunity to start again would you do anything differently? Would you use the same research methods? Were you overly ambitious in terms of the scale of your project? How has the use of theory helped you think more critically about the issue under scrutiny? Do you think that further research is required? What pointers would you give future researchers?

All of these considerations will help you greatly in writing up your essay/paper/project/report. They will help you to clarify your thinking and insights into the question under study. Above all else, they will allow you to build a coherent argument and to hopefully question existing shared understandings.

How to usefully engage with existing research

I am now going to suggest ways in how you might best approach reviewing research by others. I am going to confine my comments to reviewing academic journal articles but these key principles also pertain to reviewing research findings in books, reports, online, etc. (for an entertaining and insightful perspective on how to review existing research see Shon, 2012).

1. Study the article's abstract closely. Abstracts typically contain the essence of what an article purports to be about. It should state what the author's research question is, their theoretical perspective, methodological approach and overall findings.

2. Read the article in its entirety without taking notes. Does the article make sense to you in terms of its overall argument? Can you situate the article in terms of the wider theoretical debates that you are familiar with within media analysis? Is there sufficient contextual information provided for you to understand the article's overall arguments?

3. Read the article a second time more closely. In making notes summarize the following:

   • What is the author's research question?
   • Identify the theoretical perspective from which the author is working

- What methodological approach has been used? (Note whether you think it best suits the question under study)

- Pay attention to the degree to which the author has engaged with larger theoretical debates in the field and the extent to which they have provided a summary of previous research findings by others

- What are the article's overall findings? Do you think that the author has provided sufficient (and convincing evidence) in order to support his/her argument?

- What has the article failed to examine? What aspects has it omitted?

- Is there any obvious evidence of bias in the article?

- Pay particular attention to the article's bibliography. It may prove to be a useful source of other research materials that are worth following up on as you develop your own research project.

We will now apply these general principles to examining a piece of academic writing about the media (see Figure 10.2). This will be done with reference to the study by Power et al. (2012) on the representation of a stigmatized neighbourhood in the Republic of Ireland in a new media setting.

The authors examine how Google Street View represents a stigmatized neighbourhood. While Google hold that Street View permits 'a virtual reflection of the real world to enable armchair exploration' (Mclendon, 2010), the authors argue that, in fact, Google's role in the politics of representations is far from neutral. They examine how Google Street View's practices contribute to the further stigmatization and marginalization of the neighbourhood in question. The authors question the utopian promise of new media settings and find that new media settings are just as likely as more traditional media settings to produce and disseminate representations which are ideological and classed ('Why bother seeing the world for real?' may be read in full on your companion website).

If you are thinking about analysing newspaper coverage about a specific theme (e.g. representations of terrorism, the Asian Tsunami or a presidential election) you might be considering using the on-line versions of print media stories. Be careful as sometimes the on-line versions are abridged and incomplete. They may also be missing photographs or other illustrations which may be relevant in your analysis. LexisNexis is a very useful database if you intend doing a detailed and systematic analysis of media content. This vast database will allow you to gather newspaper and magazine content using a keyword search. It's a subscription based service but it is freely available in many university libraries. The database is user-friendly and will save you lots of valuable research time. See www.LexisNexis.com.

Figure 10.2 **Practical tips on gathering newspaper and other forms of print media content.**

Do it! 10.1

Read another academic journal article or book chapter of your own choosing. Apply the same kinds of questions as above. Has this systematic way helped you to better critically engage with published research findings?

Doing production, content and reception research

This book has stressed the importance of engaging in production, content and reception research. For practical reasons there will be many occasions when it is not feasible to make use of all three approaches. The following discussion notes some of the hurdles to be overcome in using these methods either singly or in combination. The discussion is not intended to discourage you in any way; rather it is meant to help you anticipate possible problems in doing reliable media research (see also Chapter 5, 'Media Production and Media Professionals'). If you are undertaking more advanced research for a postgraduate thesis, for example, I would strongly recommend making use of a mixed methods approach.

Production research

Traditionally, production research has focused on the perspectives, experiences and work practices of specific categories of media professional in the media industries, although it can now include a much wider range of research subjects, for example citizen journalists, bloggers, fanzine creators, etc. in its gaze (see Chapter 5 for a detailed discussion on production research). Doing research on media organizations using ethnographic methods (e.g. interviews, observation and participant observation) is not without its difficulties. Access to media organizations cannot be taken for granted. Many student and academic researchers have experienced problems in getting past the gatekeepers (e.g. editors, managers) who typically control access to media organizations.

A combination of research fatigue and very busy work schedules can result in academic research being treated with a mixture of suspicion, hostility and dismissiveness by many media professionals. Equally, if you are engaged in research which is focused on asking critical questions about media professionals or the media industries, it can be a challenge to gain access to key informants. If you are dealing directly with gatekeepers it is important to state clearly what your research is about and if and where it is likely to be published or disseminated. In doing this kind of research I have found it very helpful to make it clear from the outset that I have an appreciation of how media organizations and media professionals work and that my presence will not be intrusive. If access to the media industries through formal channels is problematic it may also be possible to approach prospective participants informally. Individual media professionals and others engaged in the production of media content are more likely to be familiar with the idea of being interviewed about their work so this should work to your advantage. Equally, many of the basic qualitative methods (interviewing; observation; informal discussions) used by media researchers are similar to those employed by media professionals.

Content

Because of its accessibility a great deal of media research starts with examining media content (see Chapter 7 for a detailed discussion on content analysis). Singular examples of media texts (such as a music video, Facebook page, newspaper article or photograph) are an obvious starting point in terms of applying a critical and theoretically informed gaze. Analysing media content allows you to begin to think about the intentions of its producer, the discourses employed and the possible readings of the text. However, in a larger research project you have to give some consideration to exactly how much content you intend to gather. Are there any copyright or other legal issues to contend with in using media content? For example, securing copyright clearance from music publishers to quote song lyrics in a published piece of research can be prohibitive. Getting permission from multimedia conglomerates to reproduce a still image from a movie can be next to impossible. Pay particular attention to how much media content you need to collect for analysis. Equally, give due consideration to whether you intend to engage in quantitative or qualitative content analysis. The former is usually based on a relatively large number of selected media texts, the latter on a much smaller sample but going into far greater detail.

As a systematic and reliable media research method, content analysis will allow you to draw solid conclusions about the make-up of media content. It will help you understand more about the prominence or not of specific kinds of discourses, ideologies or frames. It will allow you to have detailed insights into the make-up of media texts and will be immensely beneficial before you engage with questions concerning either production or reception. Furthermore, if used properly, it will help you avoid the problem of inference. Analysis of media content must always avoid the trap of 'This or that discourse is present in this media text, because I say so'.

Be clear about the units of analysis you intend focusing on. Are you examining the content of entire newspaper articles, headlines or photographs? Doing quantitative content analysis requires you to have a clearly defined set of codes. In both variants of content analysis you will also need to decide whether you will use deductive or inductive codes. Inductive codes emerge from the data being analysed, whilst deductive codes are based on pre-existing assumptions. Software including N-Vivo and Atlas.ti will assist you in analysing and managing large amounts of data.

Article section	Key considerations
Abstract	Does the abstract explain fully and clearly what the article is about?
Introduction	Do the authors provide you with sufficient contextual information about the location of the study? Do they adequately explain their motivations for undertaking this research? Do they relate the specifics of their research to wider theoretical concerns about the media (old and new)?
Methodological approach	While the paper is predominantly theoretical, is the rationale for the authors' chosen methodological approach – described as 'rhetorical/structuralist' – explained properly? Could the authors have said more about how the images contained in Google Street View were analysed? Could an alternative methodological approach been used? Think about the possible implications for the article's overall findings if a different approach was adopted.
Research literature	The article discusses three distinct bodies of existing research literature – focusing on the stigmatization of poor people and the places in which they live, the impact of stigmatization, and the degree to which new media have the capacity to empower communities.
Google Street View	The article discusses the emergence of Google Street View and its operations in an Irish setting. To what extent do the authors explain the limitations and possibilities of the technology in question?
Findings	Here the article concentrates on the ways in which the neighbourhood in question is misrepresented. Is there sufficient evidence presented to support the paper's overall argument? How does the representation of this neighbourhood compare and contrast between 'old' and 'new' media settings?
Conclusion	Are the article's conclusion's convincing? How well do the authors relate their overall findings to the wider body of research literature concerning media stigmatization of marginalized neighbourhoods? Are you convinced by their conclusions?
Bibliography	Review the article's bibliography carefully. Highlight key studies that you might want to follow up on in terms of your wider reading and study.
General	In your opinion, has this article enhanced your understanding of debates concerning new media? Did you find the article easy or difficult to follow? To what degree did it explain important concepts adequately?
Think critically	If you were doing a similar piece of research would you do it any differently? Would you use different research methods?

Figure 10.3 **How to critically read an academic journal article.**

Reception

In Chapter 8 I discussed the main methods used in attempting to make sense of media reception. An array of qualitative methods (observation, participant observation, interviews (structured, semi-structured, unstructured), focus groups, journaling, etc.) can be used to try to interpret how audiences encounter media texts. Reception analysis might focus on how texts are decoded or on how audiences engage in media prosumption. While the prospect of going into the field and immersing yourself in the everyday experiences of audiences might appear to be attractive, it is essential that you plan your fieldwork carefully. As has been previously noted in Chapter 8's Toolkit, 'Researching media audiences: developing a research proposal for the Globex TV Corporation' (see companion website), it is helpful to think carefully about the kinds of questions you wish to ask of your interviewees. Make sure that your questions make sense to your interviewees and are jargon-free. Pilot testing them on a small sample of interviewees beforehand will help ensure that your questions make sense and are more likely to produce useable data at the analysis stage. You will also recall that in Chapter 8 I warned against the problem of representativeness in much qualitative audience research. For an extended research project (a thesis or an academic paper) try to ensure a reasonable sample size and do take account of the extent to which your sample of interviewees (their age, gender, ethnicity, class position) mirrors the make-up of the wider social context in which you are doing your research. Attending to such details will allow not only for more reliable research but also for potentially more interesting findings. If you endeavour to ensure that your sample of interviewees mirrors the complexities of the wider social structure then you stand to generate findings that will allow you to not only compare and contrast but crucially to explain these differences in relation to your interviewees' social position.

Keep on asking awkward questions ...

In this penultimate section I want to briefly restate the necessity for a critical approach to media analysis. *Understanding the Media* has placed great stress on the vast power of multimedia conglomerates; on the media's role in fuelling social change; on the hegemonic and discursive power of media texts; on the sometimes narrow (and ill-informed) ways in which the social world is represented in a media setting; and the relative amount of power and agency expressed by audiences. The possibilities afforded by social media have also been acknowledged, particularly in terms of concerns about the democratic health of various societies, but with a note of caution.

Even though my position regarding the media does not quite amount to a manifesto, it is governed by a number of important assumptions and concerns. We continue to live in a divided world where power and resources are not shared evenly. In spite of the hopeful possibilities opened up by social and other forms of new media, the mainstream media continue to assist in the perpetuation of unequal power relationships. Given the increasingly concentrated nature of the ownership structure of the majority of media companies/organizations, it is hardly surprising that a public sphere has failed to develop. In spite of more media content and technologies in our everyday lives we are forced to reckon with the irony that in fact we encounter a narrowing range of voices, opinions and perspectives. It is in these challenging contexts we find ourselves as students and citizens.

In reading (and using) *Understanding the Media*, my overall hope is that you will never look at the media in the same way again. My wish is that it has encouraged you, in however small a way, to move away from taken for granted or 'common-sense' assumptions and to always ask challenging and difficult questions about the media. We need to retain a healthy scepticism about what is presented to us as inevitable about the media and the wider social world. Equally, we always need to use a critical lens when engaging with the discourses generated and circulated by the politically and economically powerful. While there is, of course, room in the wider canon of media analysis for investigating popular forms of media culture (as has been demonstrated earlier in this book the popular can at times be profoundly political), our priority has to be to examine the media's role in either sustaining or perpetuating inequalities and injustices. Our task, therefore, is to keep on asking awkward questions about the media and the powerful. We can't afford to be naïve in questioning unequal power relationships. By means of using the sociological imagination (see Introduction and Chapter 1 for an elaboration) we can begin this process. In doing critical media analysis the challenge to all of us is to always ask *why* and *why not?*

Conclusion: the how, why (and what) of media analysis

Rather than dealing with the key research methods used in media research in a mechanical way, this chapter has focused on questions of how and why. In terms of the *how*, it proposes that we adopt the rigour traditionally associated with the social sciences in approaching media analysis. The chapter stresses the necessity of being systematic in beginning and undertaking a media research project using tried and tested research methods. In terms of the *why*, it proposes that if we are to ask critical questions about the media, then it is crucial that we gather evidence (data) that will help us build strong arguments – data that will help us substantiate our claims about the media's social, political and economic significance. Sound data is a prerequisite to asking hard and challenging questions of the media and of the powerful in particular. The *what* of media analysis is of utmost importance. A commitment to critical media analysis means that we should not distract ourselves by focusing solely on the make-up of popular media texts or the latest trends in social media instead the task of engaging in critical media analysis means a dedication to continuing to ask questions about the media's role in reproducing (and perpetuating) unequal power relationships.

Chapter summary

1. This chapter stressed the importance of following a set of systematic methodological ground rules in doing media research.
2. It proposed 12 basic steps which need to be addressed by student (and other) researchers.
3. In particular, it emphasized the need to take a multi-method approach in media analysis and to avoid a methodological and theoretical sectarianism.
4. The challenges involved in undertaking a combination of production, content and reception analysis research were noted.
5. It restated the necessity of continuing to do media research which challenges hegemonic versions of the social world.
6. A sociological approach offers us the best chance of engaging fruitfully and critically in our efforts to understand the media.

Further reading

The following books are really useful. I would advise familiarizing yourself with texts that are focused on media analysis specifically, as well as more general social science research methods texts.

1. Doing media research

Altheide, D.L. and C.J. Schneider (2012) *Qualitative Media Analysis*, 2nd edn. Thousand Oaks, CA: Sage.

Anderson, J. (2012) *Media Research Methods*. Thousand Oaks, CA: Sage.

Berger, A.A. (2013) *Media and Communications Research Methods*, 3rd edn. London: Sage.

Brennen, B.S. (2012) *Qualitative Research Methods for Media Studies*. New York: Routledge.

Deacon, D., M. Pickering, P. Golding and G. Murdock (1999) *Researching Communications: A Practical Guide to Methods in Media and Cultural Analysis*. Oxford: Oxford University Press.

Gunter, B. (2000) *Media Research Methods: Measuring Audiences, Reactions and Impact*. London: Sage.

Hornig-Priest, S. (2009) *Doing Media Research*, 2nd edn. Thousand Oaks, CA: Sage.

Potter, W.J. (2012) *Media Effects*. Thousand Oaks, CA: Sage.

Schroeder, K., K. Drotner, S. Kline and C. Murray (2003) *Researching Audiences*. London: Arnold.

Stokes, J. (2012) *How To Do Media and Cultural Studies*, 2nd edn. London: Sage.

2. Research methods in general

Best, S. (2012) *Understanding and Doing Successful Research: Data Collection and Analysis for the Social Sciences*. Harlow: Pearson.

Bryman, A. (2012) *Social Research Methods*, 4th edn. Oxford: Oxford University Press.

Flick, U. (2009) *An Introduction to Qualitative Research*, 4th edn. London: Sage.

Matthews, B. and L. Ross (2010) *Research Methods: A Practical Guide for the Social Sciences*. Harlow: Longman-Pearson.

Scott, G. and R. Garner (2013) *Doing Qualitative Research: Designs, Methods and Techniques*. London: Pearson.

3. Reviewing previously published research

Shon, P.C. (2012) *How to Read Journal Articles in the Social Sciences*. London: Sage.

GLOSSARY

Active Audience   The term refers to the agency or creativity of media audiences. Audiences are *see* n to be active interpreters of media texts. Recent debates about audience agency have also focused on the capacity which audiences have to be produsers/prosumers.

Agency   By agency is meant the capacity that human beings have for creativity and critical self-reflection in the face of structures or constraints (*see also* **Structure**).

Asymmetrical Relations of Power   Unequal relationships of power in the social world with particular reference to how inequality manifests itself in terms of people's position in the social structure based upon one's class, ethnicity or gender in one or other combination.

Blue Collar *see* **Working class**.

Citizenship   Refers to the relationship between citizens and the Liberal Democratic state. Citizenship implies both rights and responsibilities.

Citizen Journalism   Refers to journalism engaged in by so-called ordinary citizens. Citizen journalism has expanded significantly in the context of the spread of social media. Free or cheaper forms of media technologies (e.g. blogs, Twitter and web-based zines) have allowed ordinary people to re-circulate existing media texts or create commentaries on and/or offer eye-witness accounts of matters of public interest.

Class   The categorization of members of a society according to socio-economic status. Class is one of three key variables (the others being ethnicity and gender) used to understand inequality and social stratification in modern societies (*see also* **Working class**).

Conglomerate/Conglomeration   Large-scale corporations that operate at national and transnational levels. Conglomerates are made up of a range of corporations that have strong monopolistic tendencies and are either vertically or horizontally integrated (or sometimes both) in terms of their ownership structure. Media corporations may be part of larger media conglomerates or conglomerates of a more general nature which have economic interests outside of the media industry (*see also* **Integration, Horizontal and Vertical**).

Constructionist   Researchers interested in media audiences use the term 'constructionist' to describe the discursive and reflexive activities of media audiences.

Content Analysis   Traditionally, content analysis referred to a research method used to count the occurrence of specific phenomena – e.g. particular kinds of representations – within media texts. More recently content analysis has come to refer to either quantitative or qualitative analysis of media texts. Qualitative content analysis can involve a close critical reading of a media text – focusing for example on its discursive dimensions – rather than an attempt to count the occurrence of specific phenomena within a text.

Convergence   As used here the term convergence means the coming together or merging of media technologies and media organizations. Media organizations, for example, concerned with 'old media' and 'new media' converge through the process of conglomeration. Recent developments with the mobile or cell phone allowing live streaming of television programming or photography are an example of how media technologies can converge. Convergence is in further evidence in terms of how media operate across platforms - an online edition of a newspaper might include links to social media such as Twitter or Facebook or to email in order to share media content.

Core, Peripheral and Semi-Peripheral Societies   World System Theory sees the world as being divided into core, peripheral and semi-peripheral societies. The labour forces and raw materials of peripheral and semi-peripheral societies are exploited in order to create goods and services for the core societies in the western capitalist world (*see also* **Developing and Developed world** and **Third world**).

Counter-hegemonic   *See* **Hegemony** and **Ideology**.

Cultural Industries   According to Hesmondhalgh (2013: 4) the cultural industries 'are involved in the making and circulating of products that, more than the products of any other kind of industry, have an influence on our understanding and knowledge of the world.'

Deregulation   In some territories the state has played a strong role in regulating publically and privately owned media organizations. The deregulation of the media market has seen the state play a reduced role in regulating media organizations. Conglomerates favour a deregulated environment and have lobbied the politically powerful to ensure less regulatory involvement by the state.

Diaspora   The term diaspora originates from 'diaspeirein' a Greek word meaning the scattering of seeds. According to Karim (2007: 361) Diasporas are 'viewed as comprising ethnic, cultural, linguistic and religious groups who reside in a number of countries to which they or their ancestors migrated.'

Diasporic Media Audiences   Media audiences who are members of the diaspora (diaspora).

Deserving Poor The poor or socially excluded who are deemed to be worthy of assistance or help. The deserving poor are believed to be poor through no fault of their own and are deserving of state or other forms of support or assistance. The deserving poor are sometimes referred to as 'God's Poor' (*see also* **Undeserving Poor**)

Developing and Developed World Both of these concepts are problematic, particularly the former. The term 'developing world' seems to imply that the poorer regions of the globe are (slowly) catching up with the more prosperous parts. The notion of the developed world is also troublesome in that it masks the existence of poverty and inequality in the northern hemisphere. (*See also* **Third World**, **Core, Peripheral and Semi-peripheral Societies**)

Digital Divide A concept used to highlight the gap between the information rich and information poor. While the digital divide is most apparent between northern and southern hemispheres, the concept may also be used to understand information inequalities in the 'developed world'. The concept of the digital divide warns us to be sceptical about the widely used concepts such as the global village and the information society.

Discourse A form of knowledge.

Discourse Analysis A method of research focused on the analysis of text and talk, discourse analysis is concerned with the use of language in a social context and the relationship between language use and (unequal) power relationships.

Dominant Ideology *See* **Ideology**.

Encoding/Decoding A model of media analysis devised by leading media theorist Stuart Hall, it examines how media professionals encode meaning in media messages/texts and how these texts are possibly decoded or understood by media audiences.

Effects The effects model of media analysis stresses the power of media content over media audiences. The latter are usually constructed as being passive in the face of powerful media messages. The metaphor of the hypodermic syringe injecting its contents into the minds of audience members has long been used as a way of conceptualizing the media effects paradigm.

Empirical That which is observable.

Epistemological Epistemology is a branch of philosophy concerned with truth or knowledge.

Ethnicity Within sociology the term ethnicity has come to replace the problematic concept of race. By ethnicity we mean the shared common cultural heritage of a group. Membership of an ethnic group (and not always a minority ethnic group) can have a strong bearing on one's life-chances and opportunities. Ethnicity is one of three key variables (along with class and gender) used to understand inequality in modern societies. There is an important body of content analysis-based media research on how ethnic groups are problematized in a media setting.

Ethnography, Ethnographic   A research method that has its roots in social anthropology, ethnography seeks to understand and describe social behaviour in its natural everyday setting. The ethnographic approach uses a wide range of qualitative research methodologies such as participant observation, observation and interviews as a source of data. Traditionally, doing ethnographic work meant engaging in fieldwork for long periods of time, but a marked feature of recent ethnographic work within media analysis is the truncated nature of the fieldwork (*see also* **Participant Observation**)

E-zines   Internet-based magazines or newsletters. These are often aimed at specific interest groups.

Fans   An abbreviated form of the word fanatic which in turn is derived from the Latin word 'fanaticus' meaning a devotee or servant of the temple (See De Kloet and Van Zoonen, 2007: 324). Although it is possible to identify extreme examples of fans and fan behaviour, the use of the term fan is best seen in positive, agentic terms.

Fandom   Within media and cultural studies fandom refers to the phenomenon of fans forming an attachment to a particular star, celebrity or media genre. Fan studies are often the site of some very interesting research on what some audience members can do in their role as produsers or prosumers.

Focus Groups   A research method using unstructured or semi-structured group interviews. The groups in question might be selected on the basis of gender, age or occupation. Focus groups may be used either as a sole or supplementary research method.

Feminist   The feminist perspective is concerned with gender inequalities in modern and post-modern societies. Inequalities are seen to stem from the patriarchal character of these social systems. The feminist perspective has made a very significant contribution towards how we understand the media (*see* **Patriarchy**).

Frame Analysis   Influenced by the work of the sociologist Erving Goffman, frame analysis in a media setting examines the use of interpretative frames in constructing media content. Media professionals resort to using interpretative frames in telling stories about the social world. The agenda-setting perspective would suggest that the selective framing of news stories, for example, has an important bearing on public beliefs about matters of social, economic and political importance.

Genre In a media studies context genre means distinct types or categories of media content such as punk rock or heavy metal music; television soap operas or news programming, action movies or romantic dramas (*see also* **Intertextual**).

Gender One's gender is not the same as one's biological sex. The categories male and female are social constructs. Through the process of socialization individuals are taught that particular sets of values, behaviours and roles are 'natural' to their biological sex. The media play a hugely significant role in this process.

Globalization The term globalization is at once both multi-faceted and ambiguous. As a process globalization refers to a number of things – the restructuring of economic activities on global lines; the apparent 'shrinkage' of time and space as a result of new information and communications technologies; the increased awareness of the global in everyday life; cultural homogenization and the intensification of local identities. The media industries (and conglomerates especially) have globalized in terms of both their reach and their presence in a range of core, peripheral and semi-peripheral societies. Media globalization has resulted in the wider circulation of media texts and has given rise to new kinds of concerns and questions for audience researchers in particular (*see also* **Glocalization**).

Glocalization Occurs when media audiences appropriate, localize and hybridize globally circulated media texts. In interpreting such texts, audiences 'make their own' of them.

Grounded Theory Traditionally social research has used existing theories in order to make sense of data gathered in a research project. Grounded Theory, by contrast, allows theory to emerge from the data gathered.

Hegemony The dominance of one social group over another. Hegemony may be achieved through either force or consent. Hegemonic ideologies are those ideologies that facilitate or enable domination to take place. Counter-hegemonic ideologies are ideas that run counter to those expressed within the dominant ideology.

Hermeneutic Interpretative.

Homogenization Refers to the sameness evident in the world as a result of economic and cultural globalization. McDonaldization is one of the more obvious examples of homogenization.

Hybrid/Hybridization The term hybrid has two key meanings. Hybrid media texts may be created when their producers or creators mix the ingredients from more than one media genre. Hybridization also occurs when globally circulated media texts are appropriated by audiences and are localized.

Hyperreality According to Baudrillard, in the media saturated post-modern world it is no longer a question of us having to examine how the media represent 'reality'. Media 'reality' has become the (hyper) reality for most members of society.

Ideology At its most basic ideology means the 'Science of Ideas.' In media analysis the emphasis is on examining how the media construct and disseminate ideas that are of benefit to the dominant class or other social group. We usually differentiate between dominant or hegemonic ideologies about class, ethnic or gender relations and other counter-hegemonic ideologies evident in media content.

Information Rich, Information Poor *See* **Digital Divide**.

Infotainment The merging of information and entertainment usually in a news setting. It may also refer to the increasing tendency within more serious media content of entertainment masquerading as information.

Integration (Horizontal and Vertical) The terms 'vertical' and 'horizontal' integration refer to two contrasting styles of media ownership structure. With vertical integration a media company (usually a conglomerate) owns and controls all aspects of the production, marketing, distribution and selling of a media product. Media companies that are horizontally integrated own and control a range of media companies involved in different kinds of activities such as printing, broadcasting and ICT.

Intertextuality The tendency for media texts to make reference to or make use of some of the component parts of other kinds of media texts or genres that audiences are likely to be familiar with. A television advert for soap powder making use of some of the ingredients of a James Bond movie would be an example.

Localization The term 'localization' is used in two ways in this textbook. A key facet of the globalization process is the tendency for local identities to intensify. Globally circulated media texts may be appropriated by local audiences to fit local conditions. Global media conglomerates also engage in localization in that they will create media products to suit the characteristics of the local market in order to ensure greater market penetration and domination (*see also* **Glocalization**).

Marxist Perspective   The Marxist perspective is concerned with explaining the inequalities (and contradictions) inherent in capitalist society, in terms of media analysis, the focus is on media companies as examples par excellence of capitalist organizations and more particularly on how the media facilitate the continuation of capitalism (and globalization) by representing it as being inevitable and desirable (*see also* **Political Economy**).

Media/Mass Media   The word media is the plural of medium. When we talk about the mass media we usually mean those industries and technologies capable of communicating with large numbers of people in diverse social situations.

Media Discourses   *See* **Discourse Analysis**.

Media Globalization   *See* **Globalization**.

Media Imperialism   The terms media imperialism, cultural imperialism and US imperialism ('Hollywoodisation') are often used interchangeably in reference to the spread and global domination of western media culture. Those who are concerned about western media imperialism see it as being responsible for the wearing down of local cultures. However, those who argue from a g-localization perspective believe that local audiences have the capacity to resist, hybridize and localize globalizing forms of media culture.

Media Oligopolies   Powerful media conglomerates who dominate and control the global media industry.

Media Texts   *See* **Texts**.

Media Moguls   Powerful individuals who have a controlling interest in multimedia conglomerates. In addition to their economic power, media moguls are believed to wield considerable political influence in the shaping of state policy about media and other matters of economic and political importance.

Methodology/Methods/Mixed Methods   The means by which research is undertaken. Researchers may use quantitative or qualitative research methods. In recognition of the complexity of the social world, and the fact that no one research method is trouble free, a growing number of researchers make use of a combination of research methods – a mixed methods approach – in order to more fully understand their particular research question.

Modernity   Increasingly a contentious term, modernity refers to the era in which societies became industrialized, secular and urban. The contention arises from whether or not modernity has given way to postmodernity (*see also* **Postmodern**, **Postmodernity**).

Narrative/Narrative Analysis   A research method concerned with the narrative structure of media texts. How do individual media texts such as reports broadcast on television news programmes tell or narrate stories about the social world? What conventions are employed in explaining 'terrorism' for example?

Neo-Liberalism   A now dominant ideology which sees members of society as primarily economic rather than social actors. According to this perspective, the state should either play a significantly reduced or non-existent role when it comes to the provision of goods and services in society. In addition, capital should be unfettered as far as possible and should be free from state interference. Neo-liberal marketisation ideas have assumed a dominant or hegemonic position in the shaping of state policy in terms of how education, health and welfare are provided for its citizens. It has underpinned the de-regulation (and increased privatisation) of the media.

Netizens   Citizens who use the possibilities afforded by the Internet (e.g. social media, blogs, etc.) to discuss and debate matters of economic, political and moral importance. Netizens use the Internet as a possible Public Sphere to argue, debate and inform (*see also* **Public Sphere**).

New Media   Breen (2007: 55) defines New Media as '...recently evolved systems [...] for the delivery of content to audiences. These media differ radically from traditional media in several respects; entry is cheap, the number of practicioners is limitless, geography is not a barrier, communication is a two way process and the audience has high levels of power in terms of how and when content is consumed.'

Participant Observation   A research method most associated with the ethnographic approach. The individual researcher immerses herself in the society, community or organization under study, usually for a long period of time. Participant observation may be covert or overt. It may be used as the sole method of data collection or as a precursor to other forms of data collection such as interviews (*see also* **Ethnographic Approach**).

Paradigm(s)   At its simplest, a paradigm is a model or a framework which is used to make sense of phenomena.

Patriarchy   The control and domination of women by men. Patriarchal ideologies or discourses are ones that legitimize the continuation of male dominance in positions of influence and power.

Performative   The term performative is used in the context of fan studies to refer to the ways in which some fans act out or perform their fandom. Fans, for example, may recreate and enact scenes from their favourite film or TV programme. By focusing on what some fans 'do' we move away from simply thinking about how audiences interpret or read media texts.

Political Economy Perspective A theoretical perspective concerned with understanding how the capitalist class promote and ensure their dominant position in capitalist society.

Postmodern, Postmodernity A lively debate has ensued in recent years as to whether the era of modernity has come to pass. Postmodernists argue that modernity has been replaced by a postmodern era characterized by cultural and economic globalization; homogenization; increased fragmentation of local identities and media saturation. Proponents of postmodern theory treat the certainties inherent in more traditional sociological approaches towards understanding the social world in general and the media in particular with some scepticism. The postmodern perspective celebrates what it *see* s as the fragmented nature of postmodernity. Media reality has become hyper reality or more real than reality itself. A key criticism of postmodernism is the lack of empirical evidence to support the many arguments which state that we have moved on from the era of modernity (*see also* **Modern**, **Modernity**).

Power The term 'power' is used in two key ways in this textbook. First, in terms of the power of media texts to shape audience understandings of the social world and second in terms of unequal power relationships based upon class, ethnicity, gender or geographical location.

Production Research A research tradition focused on understanding more about media organisations and media professionals.

Production, Content and Reception A model of media research which focuses in equal measure on the production of media texts, their contents and how they are received/interpreted by audiences.

Produsers/Prosumers Traditionally, media producers and media audiences (consumers) were placed at opposite ends of the spectrum. With the advent of new media, which affords the possibility of user generated content, some theorists have begun to reconfigure audiences as produsers and prosumers.

Public Knowledge The degree to which members of the public are informed about public affairs concerning politics and the economy for example. Concerns have been expressed over the degree to which members of the public are informed by media organizations which are increasingly privatized and which have a greater emphasis on infotainment rather than issues of public concern.

Public Service Broadcasting/Broadcasters   Traditionally dominant in Western Europe, Public Service Broadcasting refers to publicly owned media companies engaged in the production and broadcast of radio and television programmes. In the face of increased competition from privately owned (and increasingly transnational) media companies, Public Service Broadcasting organizations have re-iterated their public sphere function.

Public Sphere   A space allowing discourse and debate of political importance. The public sphere is seen as an essential element in the democratization of modern societies and ideally the media should facilitate such a space. The processes of privatization, homogenization, 'dumbing down' and the rise of infotainment all militate against the media providing a public sphere for media audiences.

Qualitative Research   Researchers who are interested in questions about meaning and interpretation tend to make use of non-quantitative or qualitative research methods. Key qualitative methods include interviewing, participant observation and semiotic analysis.

Quantitative Research   The term 'quantitative' refers to research methods such as content analysis or surveys that seek to count the occurrences of specific phenomena e.g. racist ideologies within media content such as newspaper editorials or the measurement of public attitudes and beliefs about welfare recipients.

Qualitative Content Analysis   *See* **Content Analysis**.

Quantitative Content Analysis   *See* **Content Analysis**.

Reception/Reception Analysis   A model of media analysis concerned primarily with the interpretative work engaged in by audiences in their engagement with media texts.

'Reading against the grain'   *See* **Resistance**.

Regulation   *See* **Deregulation**.

Research Ethics   An ethical framework (usually set out by a professional association of researchers or educational institution) which governs the way in which research is undertaken. Research ethics should convey rights to those being research and clear responsibilities on those who are doing the research.

Research Methods   *See* **Methodology/Methods**.

Research Question(s) A clearly stated question which guides a research project.

Reflexivity The concept of reflexivity refers to the capacity of social actors for reflection, criticism and self-awareness.

Representation This form of media analysis is primarily concerned with how media texts represent (or more accurately re-present) the social world.

Resistance The ways in which audience members may reject the preferred or intended readings or meanings in a media text. The term is often used to describe how audience members reject the dominant or hegemonic codes evident within a media text. Audience members are said to be 'reading against the grain' in rejecting or subverting dominant or hegemonic ideology.

Semiotic(s) A method of analysis concerned with the functioning of signs and symbols within a text.

Socialization Socialization theory examines how we learn to become members of society. Agents of socialization include the family, peer group, the education system and the mass media. We learn from each of these agencies about norms, beliefs, values, rules and ideologies.

Structure(s) Constraints that determine or shape human behaviour. In doing media work, for example, media professionals may be constrained by rules imposed by an employer, by the laws governing broadcasting or print journalism and by audience expectations.

Social Media Media technologies and tools which allow for the creation of social networks and virtual communities. Social media enable the online sharing of a wide variety of media texts. Developments in social media underlie recent developments in Citizen Journalism (the 'Arab Spring') and the reconfiguration of some audience members as produsers/prosumers.

Sociological Imagination A term coined by C. Wright Mills to encourage us to look critically at our familiar everyday social world as if we were seeing it for the very first time.

Stigmatization Following the work of sociologist Erving Goffman, stigmatization refers to the processes by which identities are spoiled. In a media setting, for example, consistently negative media discourses might be *see* n as contributing to the stigmatization of a group of people (e.g. linking crime with particular ethnic groups) or places (e.g. stressing how particular neighbourhoods are dangerous).

Structure and Agency   *See* separate entries on **Structure** and **Agency**.

Third World   The poorer and dependent parts of the world especially in the southern hemisphere (*see also* **Developed** and **Developing worlds**).

Texts   The increased concentration within media analysis on the agency or creativity of audience members came hand in hand with an emphasis upon seeing media content as texts rather than messages. Implicit in the notion of audience members 'reading' media texts is the process of active, interpretative work in the creation of meaning.

Transnational   As used in this textbook the term 'transnational' refers to both media companies or organizations and media texts. Many media texts are increasingly transnational because they are circulated globally. Transnational media conglomerates are media companies that operate in several countries.

Triangulation   By using a mixture of research methods, social scientists are able to check the findings which arise from the use of each specific method (*see also* **Mixed Methods**).

Undeserving Poor   The undeserving poor are those categories of poor or socially excluded who are demonized and who are personally blamed for their poverty and exclusion. They are sometimes termed the 'Devil's Poor.' While many poor people have been categorized as undeserving over time, there has, in recent years been a decided emphasis on disgust reactions to the welfare class or 'chavs' (*see also* **Deserving Poor**).

Uses and Gratifications   An approach within audience studies which seeks to understand how and why audiences use the media. It examines the ways in which audiences use the media to gratify their needs to be informed or entertained, for example.

Vertical Integration   *See* **Integration**.

Working Class   The term working class is more and more difficult owing in small measure to the restructuring of work itself. Broadly speaking, the term refers to those engaged in manual work. The working class may be further subdivided into skilled manual workers; semi-skilled manual workers and unskilled manual workers. The term blue-collar is used in North America to refer to the working class.

BIBLIOGRAPHY

Abercrombie, N. (1990) 'Popular culture and ideological effects', in N. Abercrombie, S. Hill and B.S. Turner (eds), *Dominant Ideologies*. London: Unwin Hyman.

Abercrombie, N. and B. Longhurst (1998) *Audiences*. London: Sage.

Acquisti, A. and R. Gross (2006) 'Imagined communities: awareness, information sharing and privacy on Facebook', Proceedings of the 6th Workshop on Privacy Enhancing Technologies, Cambridge, UK.

Alasuutari, P. (1999) 'Introduction: three phases of reception studies', in P. Alasuutari (ed.), *Rethinking the Media Audience*. London: Sage.

Altheide, D.L. (1996) *Qualitative Media Analysis*. London: Sage.

Altheide, D.L. and C.J. Schneider (2012) *Qualitative Media Analysis*, 2nd edn. Thousand Oaks, CA: Sage.

Anatol, G.L. (ed.) (2003) *Reading Harry Potter: Critical Essays*. Westport, CT: Praeger Publishing.

Anderson, J. (2012) *Media Research Methods*. Thousand Oaks, CA: Sage.

Ang, I. (1996) *Living Room Wars: Rethinking Media Audiences for a Postmodern World*. London: Routledge.

Appadurai, A. (1996) *Modernity at Large: Cultural Dimensions of Globalization*. Minneapolis: University of Minnesota Press.

Atton, C. (2002) 'News cultures and new social movements: radical journalism and the mainstream media', *Journalism Studies*, 3(4): 491–505.

Bagdikian, B.H. (2004) *The New Media Monopoly*, 7th edn. Boston, MA: Beacon Press.

Barkin, S.M. and M. Gurevitch (1987) 'Out of work and on the air: television news of unemployment', *Critical Studies in Mass Communication*, 4(1): 1–20.

Barlow, D.M. and B. Mills (2009) *Reading Media Theory: Thinkers, Approaches and Contexts*. London: Pearson/Longman.

Barthes, R. (1973) *Mythologies*. London: Paladin.

Baxter, R.L., C. De Riemer and A. Landini (1985) 'A content analysis of music videos', *Journal of Broadcasting and Electronic Media*, 29(3): 333–40.

Bauder, H (2002) 'Neighbourhood effects and cultural exclusion', *Urban Studies*, 39(1): 85–93.

Baudrillard, J. (1995) *The Gulf War Did Not Take Place*, trans. P. Patton. Bloomington and Indianapolis: Indiana University Press.

Bauman, Z. (1990) 'Modernity and ambivalence', in M. Featherstone (ed.), *Global Culture: Nationalism, Globalization and Modernity*. London: Sage.

Bell, A. (1998) 'The discourse structure of news stories', in A. Bell and P. Garrett (eds), *Approaches to Media Discourse*. Oxford: Blackwell.

Benhabib, S. (1992) 'Models of public space: Hannah Arendt, the liberal tradition and Jürgen Habermas', in C. Calhoun (ed.), *Habermas and the Public Sphere*. Cambridge, MA: MIT Press.

Bennett, A. (2006) 'Punk's not dead: the continuing significance of punk rock for an older generation of fans', *Sociology*, 40(2): 219–35.

Benthall, J. (1993) *Disasters, Relief and the Media*. London: Tauris.

Berelson, B. (1952) *Content Analysis in Communication Research*. Glencoe, IL: Free Press.

Berger, A.A. (1982) *Media Analysis Techniques*. London: Sage.

Berger, A.A. (1998) *Media Research Techniques*, 2nd edn, London: Sage.

Berger, A.A. (2011) *Media and Communication Research Methods: An Introduction to Qualitative and Quantitative Research Methods*, 2nd edn. London: Sage.

Berger, A.A. (2013) *Media and Communications Research Methods*, 3rd edn. London: Sage.

Best, S. (2012) *Understanding and Doing Successful Research: Data Collection and Analysis for the Social Sciences*, Harlow: Pearson.

Bettig, R.V. (1997) 'The enclosure of cyberspace', *Critical Studies in Mass Communication*, 14(2): 138–57.

Bettig, R.V and J.L. Hall (2012) *Big Media, Big Money: Cultural Texts and Political Economics*, 2nd edn. Lanham, MD: Rowan and Littlefield.

Biltereyst, D. (1995) 'Qualitative audience research and transnational media effects', *European Journal of Communication*, 10(2): 245–70.

Bilton, T., K. Bonnett, P. Jones, T. Lawson, D. Skinner, M. Stanworth and A. Webster (2002) *Introductory Sociology*. London: Palgrave McMillan.

Bilton, T., K. Bonnett, P. Jones, D. Skinner, M. Stanworth and A. Webster (1997) *Introductory Sociology*. London: Macmillan.

Blokland, T. (2008) '"You got to remember you live in public housing": place-making in an American housing project', *Housing, Theory and Society*, 25(1): 31–46.

Bloustien, G. (2002) 'Fans with a lot at stake: serious play and mimetic excess in *Buffy the Vampire Slayer*', *European Journal of Cultural Studies*, 5(4): 427–49.

Boero, N. (2007) 'All the news that's fat to print: the American "obesity epidemic" and the media', *Qualitative Sociology*, 3(1): 41–61.

Boero, N. (2012) *Killer Fat: Media, Medicine and Morals in the American 'Obesity Epidemic'*. New Brunswick, NJ: Rutgers Press.

Bonné, J. (2003) '"Simpsons" evolves as an industry', http://www.today.com/id/3403870/t/simpsons-evolves-industry/

Botta, G. (2006) 'Pop music, cultural sensibilities and places: Manchester 1976–1997', in *Proceedings of the ESF-LiU Conference 'Cities and Media: Cultural Perspectives on Urban Identities in a Mediatized World'*, 121–25.

Bourdieu, P. (1996) *Sur La Television: Suivi de L'Emprise du Journalism*. Paris: Raisons d'Agir Éditions.

Bracewell, M. (2009) *England is Mine: Poplife in Albion*. London: Faber and Faber.

Brackett, D. (1995) *Interpreting Popular Music*. Berkeley: University of California Press.

Branston, G. and R. Stafford (2006) *The Media Student's Handbook*, 4th edn. London: Routledge.

Breen, M.J. (2000) 'When size does matter: how Church size determines media coverage of religion', in J. Thierstein and Y.R. Kamalipour (eds), *Religion, Law and Freedom*. Westport, CT: Praeger.

Breen, M.J. (2007) 'Mass media and new media technologies', in E. Devereux (ed.), *Media Studies: Key Issues and Debates*. London: Sage.

Brennen, B.S. (2012) *Qualitative Research Methods for Media Studies*. New York: Routledge.

Brett, R. (2011) 'Moz: art: Adorno meets Morrissey in the cultural divisions', in E. Devereux, A. Dillane and M. Power (eds), *Morrissey: Fandom, Representations and Identities*, Bristol: Intellect Books, pp. 169–88.

Briggs, A. (1991) *The Collected Essays of Asa Briggs. Volume II: serious pursuits*. London: Harvester. Wheatsheaf, 107–8.

Briggs, A. and P. Burke (2002) *A Social History of the Media. From Gutenberg to the Internet*. Cambridge: Polity.

Brooker, J. (2010) 'Has the world changed or have I changed? The Smiths and the challenge of Thatcherism', in S. Campbell and C. Coulter, (eds.) *Why Pamper Life's Complexities? Essays on The Smiths*. Manchester: Manchester University Press, pp. 22–42.

Browne, M.N and S.M. Keeley (2011) *Asking The Right Questions*, 11th edition. London: Longman.

Bruce, S. and S. Yearley (2006) *The Sage Dictionary of Sociology*. London: Sage.

Bruhn Jensen, K. and N.W. Jankowski (eds) (1991) *A Handbook of Qualitative Methodologies for Mass Communication Research*. London: Routledge.

Bruns, A. (2005) *Gatewatching: Collaborative Online News Production*. New York: Peter Lang Publishing.

Bruns, A. (2008) *Blogs, Wikipedia, Second Life and Beyond: From Production to Produsers*. New York: Peter Lang.

Bruns, A. (2011) 'Gatekeeping, gatewatching, real-time feedback: new challenges for journalism', paper presented at the Congress of SBPJ or 'Journalism and Digital Media', Rio de Janeiro, Brazil, 4 November.

Brunsdon, C. and D. Morley (1978) *Everyday Television: 'Nationwide'*. London: BFI.

Bryman, A. (2012) *Social Research Methods*, 4th edition. Oxford: Oxford University Press.

Bullock, H., K. Fraser Wyche and W. Williams (2001) 'Media images of the poor', *Journal of Social Issues*, 57(2): 229–46.

Campbell, R. and J.L. Reeves (1989) 'Covering the homeless: the Joyce Brown story', *Critical Studies in Mass Communication*, 6(1): 21–42.

Campbell, S. and C. Coulter (eds) (2010) W*hy Pamper Life's Complexities? Essays on The Smiths*. Manchester: Manchester University Press.

Caragee K.M and W. Roefs (2004) 'The neglect of power in recent framing research', *Journal of Communication*, 54(2): 214–33.

Carey, J.A. (2009) *Communication as Culture*, Revised edn. New York: Routledge.

Carroll, W.K. and R.A. Hackett (2006) 'Democratic media activism through the lens of social movement theory', *Media, Culture and Society*, 28(1): 83–104.

Castells, M. (2007) 'Communication, power and counter-power in the network society', *International Journal of Communication*, 1(1): 238–66.

Chambers, D., L. Steiner and C. Fleming (2004) *Women and Journalism*. London: Routledge.

Chambers, S.A. (2006) 'Desperately straight: the subversive sexual politics of *Desperate Housewives*', in J. McCabe and K. Akass (2006) *Reading Desperate Housewives: Beyond the White Picket Fence*. London: I.B. Tauris.

Chandler, D and M. Griffiths (2004) 'Who is the fairest of them all? Gendered readings of *Big Brother 2* (UK)', in E. Mathijs and J. Jones (eds), *Big Brother International: Format, Critics and Publics*. London: Wallflower Press.

Cherniavsky, E. (1999) '"Karmic realignment": transnationalism and trauma in *The Simpsons*', *Cultural Critique*, 41(4): 139–57.

Children Now (2003) *Big Media, Little Kids: Media Consolidation and Children's Television Programming*, http://www.childrennow.org/.

Ciolfi, L. and G. O'Brien (2013) *Magic is Might 2012: Proceedings of the International Conference*. Sheffield: Sheffield Hallam University.

Clayman SE and A. Reisner (1998) 'Gatekeeping in action: editorial conferences and assessments of newsworthiness', *American Sociological Review*, 63(2): 178–99.

Cobley, P. (1994) 'Throwing out the baby: populism and active audience theory', *Media, Culture & Society*, 16: 677–87.

Collins, R. (2002) *Media and Identity in Contemporary Europe: Consequences of Global Convergence*. Bristol: Intellect Books.

Conway, B., L. Cahill and M. Corcoran (2009) 'The "miracle" of Fatima: media framing and the regeneration of a Dublin housing estate'. NIRSA Working Papers, No. 47 March.

Corner, J. (1991) 'Studying Culture: reflections and assessments. An interview with Richard Hoggart', *Media, Culture & Society*, 13(2): 145.

Corner, J. (2000) '"Influence": the contested core of media research', in J. Curran and M. Gurevitch (eds) *Mass Media and Society*, 3rd edn. London: Arnold.

Costanza-Chock, S. (2012) 'Mic Check! Media Cultures and the Occupy Movement', *Social Movement Studies: Journal of Social, Cultural and Political Protest*, DOI:10.1080/14742 837.2012.710746.

Cottle, S. (1993) 'Behind the headlines: the sociology of news', in M.O' Donnell (ed.), *New Introductory Reader in Sociology*. Walton on Thames: Nelson.

Cottle, S. (2007) 'Ethnography and news production: new(s) developments in the field', *Sociology Compass*, 1(1): 1–16.

Cottle S. and M. Ashton (1999) 'From BBC newsroom to BBC newscentre: On changing technology and journalist practices', *Convergence*, 5(3): 22–43.

Cottrell, S. (2008) *The Study Skills Handbook*. 3rd edn. London: Palgrave.

Couldry, N. (2000) *The Place of Media Power*. London: Routledge.

Couldry, N. (2002) 'Playing for celebrity: *Big Brother* as ritual event', *Television & New Media*, 3(3): 283–93.

Couldry, N. (2009) 'My media studies: thoughts from Nick Couldry', *Television & New Media*, 10(1): 40–2.

Coulter, C. (2010) '"A double bed and a stalwart lover for sure": The Smiths, the death of pop and the not so hidden injuries of class', in S. Campbell and C. Coulter (eds), *Why Pamper Life's Complexities? Essays on The Smiths*. Manchester: Manchester University Press, pp. 156–78.

Coward, R. (2006) 'Still desperate: Popular television and the female zeitgeist', in J. McCabe and K. Akass (eds), *Reading Desperate Housewives: Beyond the White Picket Fence*. London: I.B. Tauris.

Coyer, K. (2005) 'Where the "hyper local" and the "hyper global" meet: case study of Indymedia radio', Westminster Papers in Communication and Culture. London: University of Westminster.

Creeber, G. (2004) '"Hideously white": British television, glocalization and national identity', *Television & New Media*, 5(1): 27–39.

Creeber, G. (2006) 'Television, ideology and discourse', in G. Creeber (ed.), *Tele-visions*. London: BFI.

Croteau, D. and W. Hoynes (2003) *Media Society: Industries, Images and Audiences*, 3rd edn. Thousand Oaks, CA: Pine Forge Press.

Croteau, D. and W. Hoynes. (2006) *The Business of Media: Corporate Media and the Public Interest*, 2nd edn. Thousand Oaks, CA: Pine Forge Press.

Croteau, D. and W. Hoynes (2007) 'The media industry: structure, strategy and debates', in E. Devereux (ed.), *Media Studies: Key Issues and Debates*. London: Sage.

Croteau, D., W. Hoynes and S. Milan (2012) *Media Society: Industries, Images and Audiences*, 4th edn. London: Sage.

Cunningham, S. and J. Sinclair (eds) (2002) *Floating Lives: The Media and Asian Diasporas*. St Lucia, Queensland: Queensland University Press and Lanham, MD: Rowman and Littlefield Publishers.

Curran, J. (2002) *Media and Power*. London: Routledge

Curran, J. (2012a) 'Reinterpreting the internet', in J. Curran, N. Fenton and D. Freedman, *Misunderstanding the Internet*. London: Routledge.

Curran, J. (2012b) 'Rethinking internet history', in J. Curran, N. Fenton and D. Freedman, *Misunderstanding the Internet*. London: Routledge.

Curran, J. and T. Witschge (2010) 'Liberal dreams and the internet', in N. Fenton (ed.), *New Media, Old News: Journalism and Democracy in the Digital Age*. London: Sage.

Curran, J., N. Fenton and D. Freedman (2012) *Misunderstanding the Internet*. Abingdon: Routledge.

Cushion, S. (2012) *The Democratic Value of News: Why Public Service Media Matter*. London: Palgrave.

Dahlgren, P. (1981) 'TV news and the suppression of reflexivity', in E. Katz and T. Szecsko (eds), *Mass Media and Social Change*. London: Sage.

Dahlgren, P. and S. Chakrapani (1982) 'The Third World in television news: Western ways of seeing the "other"', in W. Adams (ed.) *Television Coverage of International Affairs*. Washington, DC: George Washington University Press.

Dahlgren, P. (1992) 'Viewers' plural sense-making of TV news', in P. Scannell, P. Schlesinger and C. Sparks (eds), *Culture and Power*. London: Sage.

Davis, A. (2000) 'Public relations, news production and changing patterns of source access in the British national media', *Media, Culture & Society*, 22(1): 39–59.

Davis, H. (2004) *Understanding Stuart Hall*. London: Sage Publications.

Davis, S.S. and D.A. Davis (1995) '"The mosque and the satellite": media and adolescence in a Moroccan town', *Journal of Youth and Adolescence*, 24(5): 577–93.

Deacon, A. (1978) 'The scrounging controversy: public attitudes towards the unemployed in contemporary Britain', *Social and Economic Administration*, 12(2): 120–35.

Deacon, D., N. Fenton and A. Bryman (1999a) 'From inception to reception: the natural history of a news item', *Media, Culture & Society*, 21(1): 5–31.

Deacon, D., M. Pickering, P. Golding and G. Murdock (1999b) *Researching Communications: A Practical Guide to Methods in Media and Cultural Analysis*. London: Arnold.

Deacon, D., M. Pickering, P. Golding and G. Murdock (1999c) 'Being an observer', in D. Deacon, M. Pickering, P. Golding and G. Murdock, *Researching Communications: A Practical Guide to Methods in Media and Cultural Analysis*. London: Arnold.

Dean, J. and A. Hastings (2000) *Challenging Images: Housing Estates, Stigma and Regeneration*. Bristol: Polity Press/Joseph Rowntree Foundation.

Dedinsky, M. (1977) 'The public image of welfare', *Public Welfare*, 35(4): 12–16.

Deuze, M. (2004) 'What is multimedia journalism?', *Journalism Studies*, 5(2): 139–52.

Deuze, M. (2005) 'What is journalism? Professional identity and ideology of journalists reconsidered', *Journalism*, 6(4): 442–64.

Devereux, E. (1995) 'Are you sitting comfortably? The codes and conventions of Irish current affairs television', *Irish Journal of Sociology*, 5: 110–34.

Devereux, E., A. Haynes and M. Power (2012) 'Tarring everyone with the same shorthand? Journalists, stigmatization & social exclusion', *Journalism: Theory, Practice & Criticism*, 13(4): 500–517.

Devereux, E., M. Power and A. Dillane (2012) 'A push and a shove and the land is ours: Morrissey's counter-hegemonic stance(s) on social class', *Critical Discourse Studies*, 9(4): 375–92.

Devereux, E. (1998) *Devils and Angels: Television, Ideology and the Coverage of Poverty*. Luton: University of Luton Press/John Libbey Media.

Devereux, E. (2000) 'A media famine', in E. Slater and M. Peillon (eds), *Memories of the Present*. Dublin: Institute of Public Administration.

Devereux, E. (2005) 'Media and mass media', in A. Harrington, B. Marshall and H.P. Muller (eds), *The Routledge Encyclopaedia of Social Theory*. London: Routledge.

Devereux, E. (2006) 'Being Wild(e) about Morrissey', in M. Corcoran and M. Peillon (eds), *Uncertain Ireland*. Dublin: IPA.

Devereux, E. (2007) (ed.) *Media Studies: Key Issues and Debates*. London: Sage.

Devereux, E. (2010) 'Heaven knows we'll soon be dust: Catholicism and devotion in The Smiths', in C. Coulter and S. Campbell (eds), *Why Pamper Life's Complexities? Essays on The Smiths*. Manchester: Manchester University Press, pp. 65–80.

Devereux, E. and A. Haynes (2000) 'Irish print media coverage of the 1998 Sudanese crisis: the case of the *Irish Times*', *Media Development* 1: 20–3.

Devereux, E., A. Dillane and M. Power (eds) (2011a) *Morrissey: Fandom, Representations and Identities*. Bristol: Intellect Books.

Devereux, E., A. Haynes and M.J. Power (2011b) 'At the edge: media constructions of a stigmatised Irish housing estate', *Journal of Housing and the Built Environment*, 26(2): 123–42.

Devereux, E., A. Haynes and M. Power (2011c) 'Behind the headlines: media coverage of social exclusion in Limerick city – the case of Moyross', in N. Hourigan (ed.), *Understanding Limerick: Social Exclusion and Change*. Cork: Cork University Press, pp. 211–29.

DiMaggio, P. and E. Hargittai (2001) 'From the "digital divide" to "digital inequality": studying internet use as penetration increases', *Center for Arts and Culture and Policy Studies, Princeton, Working Paper* No. 15, Summer.

DiMaggio, P., E. Hargittai, W.R. Neuman and J.P. Robinson (2001) 'Social implications of the internet', *Annual Review of Sociology*, 27: 307–36.

Dixon, J. and M. Hyde (2003) 'Public pension privatization: neo-classical economics, decision risks and welfare ideology', *International Journal of Social Economics*, 30(5): 633–50.

Domingo, D. and C. Paterson (eds) (2011) *Making Online News: Newsroom Ethnographies in the Second Decade of Internet Journalism*. New York: Peter Lang.

Dow, B.J. (2001) '*Ellen*, television and the politics of gay and lesbian visibility', *Critical Studies in Media Communication*, 18(2): 123–40.

Downing, J. (1988) 'The alternative public realm: the organization of the 1980s anti-nuclear press in West Germany and Britain', *Media, Culture & Society*, 10(2): 163–81.

Downing, J. (2001) *Radical Media: Rebellious Communication and Social Movements*. Thousand Oaks: Sage.

Downing, J.D.H (2003) 'Audiences and readers of alternative media: the absent lure of the virtually unknown', *Media, Culture & Society*, 25(5): 625–45.

Doyle, G. (2002) *Media Ownership*. London: Sage.

Doyle, G. (2013) *Understanding Media Economics*, 2nd edn. London: Sage Publications.

D'Souza, D. (1995) *The End of Racism: Principles for a Multiracial Society*. New York: Free Press.

Dudrah, R.K. (2002a) 'Zee TV in Europe: non-terrestrial television and the construction of a pan-South Asian identity', *Contemporary South Asia*, 11(1): 163–81.

Dudrah, R.K. (2002b) 'Vilayati Bollywood: popular Hindi cinema going and diasporic South Asian identity', *Javnost: The Public*, 9(1): 9–36.

Dudrah, R.K. (2005) 'Zee TV: diasporic non-terrestrial television in Europe', *South Asian Popular Culture*, 3(1): 33–47.

Dudrah, R.K. (2006) *Bollywood: Sociology Goes to the Movies*. London: Sage.

Dunaway, J. (2013) 'Media ownership and story tone in campaign news', *American Politics Research*, 41(1): 24–53.

Dupagne, M. and B. Garrison (2006) 'The meaning and influence of convergence: a qualitative case study of newsroom work at the Tampa News Center', *Journalism Studies*, 7(2): 237–55.

Dutta-Bergman, M.J. (2005) 'Access to the internet in the context of community participation and community satisfaction', *New Media & Society*, 7(1): 89–109.

Dutton, W.H. (2009) 'The fifth estate emerging through the network of networks', *Prometheus*, 27(1): 1–15.

Dyer, R. (2001) *The Culture of Queers*. London: Routledge.

Eagleton, T. (1991) *Ideology: An Introduction*. London: Verso.

Ekstrom, M. (2002) 'Epistemologies of TV journalism', *Journalism*, 3(3): 259–82.

Elber, L. (2001) 'TV's "The Simpsons" goes global', The Simpsons Archive, http://www.snpp.com/other/articles/goesglobal.html

Eliasoph, N. (1988) 'Routines and the making of oppositional news', *Critical Studies in Mass Communication*, 5(4): 313–34.

Elliot, P. (1979) *The Making of a Television Series*, 2nd edn. London: Constable and Sage.

Entman, R.M. (1993) 'Framing toward Clarification of a Fractured Paradigm', *Journal of Communication*, 43(4): 51–8.

Esser, F. (1998) 'Editorial structures and work principles in British and German newsrooms', *European Journal of Communication*, 13(3): 375–405.

Evans, P. (1996) cited in N. Hubbs 'Music of the Fourth Gender: Morrissey and the Sexual Politics of the Melodic Contour' in T. Foster, C. Stiegal and E.E. Berry (eds) *Bodies of Writing, Bodies in Performance*. New York: New York University Press, 299–96.

Evans, E.D., J. Rutberg, C. Sather and C. Turner (1991) 'Content analysis of contemporary teen magazines for adolescent females', *Youth and Society*, 23(1): 99–120.

Fairclough, N. (2001) *Language and Power*, 2nd edn. Harlow: Longman.

Fast, S. (2000) 'Music, contexts and meaning in U2', in W. Everett (ed.), *Expression in Pop-Rock Music: A Collection of Critical and Analytical Essays*. New York: Garland Publishing Inc., pp. 33–57.

Fejes, F. and Petrich, K. (1993) 'Invisibility, homophobia, and heterosexism: lesbians, gay men and the media', *Critical Studies in Mass Communication*, 10(4): 396–422.

Fenton, N. (1999) 'Mass media', in S. Taylor (ed.), *Sociology: Issues and Debates*. London: Macmillan.

Fenton, N. (2000) 'The problematics of postmodernism for feminist media studies', *Media, Culture & Society*, 22(6): 723–42.

Fenton, N. (2007) 'Bridging the mythical divide: political economy and cultural studies approaches to the analysis of media', in E. Devereux (ed.), *Media Studies: Key Issues and Debates*. London: Sage.

Fenton, N. (2010) *New Media, Old News, Journalism and Democracy in the Digital Age*. London: Sage.

Fenton, N. (2011) 'Deregulation or democracy? New media, news, neoliberalism and the public interest', *Continuum: Journal of Media & Cultural Studies*, 25(1): February, 63–72.

Fenton, N. (2012) 'The internet and radical politics', in J. Curran, N. Fenton and D. Freedman, *Misunderstanding the Internet*. London: Routledge.

Ferguson, R. (2004) *The Media in Question*. Oxford: Oxford University Press.

Fisher, E. (2012) 'How less alienation creates more exploitation? Audience labour on social network sites', *tripleC*, 10(2): 171–83.

Fiske, J. (1987) *Television Culture*. London: Methuen.

Flick, U. (2009) *An Introduction to Qualitative Research*, 4th edn. London: Sage.

Foster, N., K. Cook, S. Barter-Godfrey and S. Furneaux (2011) 'Fractured multiculturalism: Conflicting representations of Arab and Muslim Australians in Australian print media', *Media Culture & Society*, 33: 619.

Foucault, M. (1994) 'A quoi rêvent les philosophes?, in *Dits et Ecrits vol. II*. Paris: Gallimard, p. 705.

Fowler, R. (1991) *Language in the News*. London and New York: Routledge.

Fraley, T. and E. Lester-Roushanzamir (2004) 'Revolutionary leader or deviant thug? A comparative analysis of the Chicago Tribune and Chicago Daily Defender's reporting of the killing of Fred Hampton', *The Howard Journal of Communication*, 15: 147–67.

Franklin, B. (1997) *Newszak and News Media*. London: Arnold.

Frau-Miggs, D. (2006) '*Big Brother* and reality TV in Europe: towards a theory of situated acculturation by the media', *European Journal of Communication*, 21(1): 33–56.

Freedman, D. (2012) 'Outsourcing internet regulation', in J. Curran, N. Fenton and D. Freedman, *Misunderstanding the Internet*. London: Routledge.

Frazer, E. (1992) 'Teenage Girls Reading Jackie', in P. Scannell, P. Schlesinger and C. Sparks (eds), *Culture and Power*. London: Sage.

Galtung, J. and M.H Ruge (1965) 'The structure of foreign news: the presentation of the Congo, Cuba and Cyprus crises in four Norwegian newspapers', *Journal of Peace Research*, 2(1): 64–91.

Gamson, W. (2004) 'On a sociology of the media', *Political Communication*, 21(3): 305–7.

Gamson, W.A. (1989) 'News as framing', *American Behavioural Scientist*, 33(2): 157–61.

Gamson, W.A. and A. Modigliani (1987) 'The changing culture of affirmative action', in *Research in Political Sociology III*. Greenwich, CT: JAI Press, pp. 137–77.

Garnham, N. (1979) 'Contribution to a political economy of mass communication', *Media, Culture & Society*, 1(2): 123–46.

Garnham, N. (1990) 'Media theory and the political future of mass communication', in F. Inglis (ed.), *Capitalism and Communication: Global Culture and the Economics of Information*. London: Sage, pp. 1–19.

Garnham, N. (2000) *Emancipation, the Media, and Modernity: Arguments about the Media and Social Theory*. Oxford: Oxford University Press.

Gauntlett, D. (2002) *Media, Gender and Identity*. London: Routledge.

Gauntlett, D. (2007) *Media Studies 2.0* http://www.theory.org.uk/mediastudies2.htm.

Gauntlett, D. (2011) *Media Studies 2.0 and Other Battles Around The Future of Media Research*. Kindle Edition.

Georgiou, M. (2005) 'Diasporic media across Europe: multicultural societies and the universalism–particularism continuum', *Journal of Ethnic and Migration Studies*, 31(3): 481–98.

Giddens, A. (1999) *Runaway World: How Globalization is Reshaping our Lives*. London: Profile Books.

Gillespie, M. (1989) 'Technology and tradition: audio-visual culture among South Asian families in west London', *Cultural Studies*, 3(2): 226–39.

Gillespie, M. (1993) 'The Mahabharata: from Sanskrit to sacred soap; a case study of the reception of two contemporary televisual versions', in D. Buckingham (ed.), *Reading Audiences: Young People and the Media*. Manchester: Manchester University Press.

Gillespie, M. (1995) *Television, Ethnicity and Cultural Change*. London: Routledge.

Gillespie, M. (2002) 'Dynamics of diasporas: South Asian media and transnational cultural politics', in G. Stald and T. Tufte (eds), *Global Encounters: Media and Cultural Transformations*. Luton: University of Luton Press, pp. 151–73.

Giroux, H. (2004) *The Terror of Neoliberalism: Authoritarianism and the Eclipse of Democracy*. New York, Paradigm.

Gitlin, T. (1994) *Inside Prime Time*. London: Routledge.

Gitlin, T. (1980) *The Whole World Is Watching*. Berkeley and Los Angeles: University of California Press.

Gitlin, T. (2002) *Media Unlimited*. New York: Metropolitan Books.

Glasgow University Media Group (1976) *Bad News I*. London: Routledge.

Goffman, E. (1963) *Stigma*. London: Penguin.

Golding, P. and G. Murdock (1996) 'Culture, communications and political economy', in J. Curran and M. Gurevitch (eds), *Mass Media and Society*. London: Arnold.

Golding, P. and S. Middleton (1979) 'Making claims: news media and the welfare state', *Media, Culture & Society*, 1(1): 5–21.

Golding, P. and S. Middleton (1982) *Images of Welfare: Press and Public Attitudes to Poverty*. Oxford: Blackwell.

Goldsmiths Media Group (2000) 'Media organisations in society: central issues', in James Curran (ed.), *Media Organizations in Society*. London: Arnold.

Gomes, R.C. and L.F. Williams (1991) 'Race and crime: the role of the media in perpetuating racism and classism in America', *Urban League Review*, 14(1): 57–69.

Gould, C., D.C. Stern and T. Dow Adams (1981) 'Television's distorted vision of poverty', *Communication Quarterly*, 29(24): 309–14.

Gourlay, G. (2007) '"It's got a bad name and it sticks …": approaching stigma as a distinct focus of neighbourhood regeneration initiatives', paper presented at the EURA Conference, 'The Vital City', 12–14 September.

Gray, A. (1987) 'Behind closed doors: video recorders in the home', in H. Baehr and G. Dyer (eds), *Boxed In: Women and Television*. London: Pandora.

Gray, A. (1999) 'Audience and reception research in retrospect: the trouble with audiences', in P. Alasuutari (ed.), *Rethinking the Media Audience*. London: Sage.

Gray, A. (2003) 'Fans: poachers and cultural nomads', in *Research Practice for Cultural Studies*. London: Sage.

Greer C (2009) 'Crime and media: understanding the connections', in C. Hale, K. Hayward, A. Wahadin and E. Wincup (eds) *Criminology*, 2nd edn. Oxford: Oxford University Press.

Greer, C. and Y. Jewkes (2005) 'Extremes of otherness: media images of social exclusion', *Social Justice*, 32(1): 20–31.

Griffen-Foley, B. (2004) 'From Tit-bits to Big Brother: a century of audience participation in the media', *Media, Culture & Society*, 26(4): 533–48.

Grixti, J. (2006) 'Symbiotic transformations: youth, global media and indigenous culture in Malta', *Media, Culture and Society*, 28(1): 105–22.

Gross, L. (1994) 'What is wrong with this picture? Lesbian women and gay men on television', in R. Ringer (ed.), *Queer Words, Queer Images: Communication and the Construction on Homosexuality*. New York: New York University, pp. 143–56.

Gross, L. (2001) *Up from Invisibility: Lesbians, Gay Men, and the Media in America*. New York: Columbia University.

Grossberg, L., E. Wartella, D.C. Whitney and J.M. Wise (2006*) MediaMaking: Mass Media in a Popular Culture*, 2nd edn. Thousand Oaks, CA: Sage.

Gunter, B. (2000) *Media Research Methods: Measuring Audiences, Reactions and Impact*. London: Sage.

Gupta, S. (2009) *Re-Reading Harry Potter*, 2nd edn. London: Palgrave.

Guyot, J. (2009) 'Political-economic factors shaping news culture', in P. Preston, *Making the News: Journalism and News Cultures in Europe*. London: Routledge, pp. 92–109.

Habermas, J. (1962) *Strukturwandel der Öffentlichkeit*. Frankfurt: Luchterhand Verlag.

Habermas, J. (1989) 'The public sphere: an encyclopaedic article', in M.G. Durham and D.M. Kellner (eds) (2001/2006), *Media and Cultural Studies: Key Works*. London: Blackwell Publishers, pp. 73–8.

Habermas, J. (1992) 'Further reflections on the public sphere', in C. Calhoun (ed.), *Habermas and the Public Sphere*. Cambridge, MA: MIT Press.

Hall, S. (1974) 'The television discourse: encoding and decoding', *Education and Culture*, 25: 8–14.

Hall, S. (1980) 'Encoding/decoding' in S. Hall, D. Hobson, A. Lowe and P. Willis (eds.), *Culture, Media and Language*. London: Hutchinson, 117–28.

Hall, S. (1988) *The Hard Road to Renewal*. Verso: London.

Hall, S. and T. Jefferson (eds) (1976) *Resistance Through Rituals: Youth Subcultures in Postwar Britain*. Hutchinson: London.

Hall, S. and T. Jefferson (1993) *Resistance Through Rituals*. London: Routledge.

Halloran, J. (1998) 'Mass communication research: asking the right questions', in A. Hansen, S. Cottle, R. Negrine and C. Newbold (eds) *Mass Communication Research Methods*. London: Macmillan.

Halloran, J. (1998) 'Mass communication research: asking the right questions', in A. Hansen, S. Cottle, R. Negrine and C. Newbold (eds), *Mass Communication Research Methods*. London: Macmillan.

Hansen, A., S. Cottle, R. Negrine and C. Newbold (1998a) 'Media audiences: focus group interviewing', in *Mass Communication Research Methods*. London: Macmillan.

Hansen, A., S. Cottle, R. Negrine and C. Newbold (1998b) 'Participant observation: researching news production', in *Mass Communication Research Methods*. London: Macmillan.

Hansen, A., S. Cottle, R. Negrine and C. Newbold (1998c) *Mass Communication Research Methods*. London: Macmillan.

Hanson, R. (2005) *Mass Communication: Living in a Media World*. London: McGraw-Hill.

Harding, R. (2006) 'Historical representations of aboriginal people in the Canadian news media', *Discourse and Society*, 17(2): 205–35.

Harrison, P. and R. Palmer (1986) *News Out of Africa: From Biafra to Band Aid*. London: Shipman.

Hargittai, E. (2004) 'Internet access and use in context', *New Media and Society*, 6(1): 137–43.

Harvey, D. (2005) *A Brief History of Neoliberalism*. New York: Oxford University Press.

Hastings, A. (2004) 'Stigma and social housing estates: beyond pathological explanations', *Journal of Housing and Built Environment*, 19: 233–54.

Hawkes, D. (2003) *Ideology*, 2nd edn. London: Sage.

Hawkins, S. (2002) *Settling the Pop Score*. Aldershot: Ashgate.

Hawkins, S. (2009) *The Great British Pop Dandy: Masculinity, Popular Music and Culture*. Farnham: Ashgate.

Haynes, A., E. Devereux and M.J. Breen (2006) 'Fear, framing and foreigners', *International Journal of Critical Psychology*, 16: 100–21.

Haynes, A., M.J. Breen and E. Devereux (2005) 'Smuggling zebras for lunch: media framing of asylum seekers in the Irish print media', *Etudes Irlandaises*, 30(1).

Hayton, K. (2009) 'New expressions of the self: autobiographical opportunities on the internet', *Journal of Media Practice*, 10(2&3): 199–213.

Hayward, K. and M. Yar (2006) 'The "chav" phenomenon: Consumption, media and the construction of a new underclass', *Crime, Media, Culture*, 2(1): 9–28.

Hazard, E. (2011) '"Suedehead": paving the pilgrimage path to Morrissey's and Dean's Fairmount, Indiana', in E. Devereux, A. Dillane and M. Power (eds), *Morrissey: Fandom, Representations and Identities*. Bristol: Intellect Books, pp. 19–34.

Helen, N. (2001) 'Dyke attacks "hideously white" BBC', *The Sunday Times*, 7 January, pp. 3.

Henry, M. (2004) 'Looking for Amanda Hugginkiss: gay life on *The Simpsons*', in J. Alberti (ed.), *Leaving Springfield: The Simpsons and the Possibility of Oppositional Culture*. Detroit: Wayne State University Press, pp. 225–43.

Herman, E. and R. McChesney (1999) 'The global media in the late 1990s', in H. Mackay and T. O'Sullivan (eds), *The Media Reader: Continuity and Transformation*. London: Sage.

Herman, E.S. and N. Chomsky (1994) 'A propaganda model', *Manufacturing Consent: The Political Economy of the Mass Media*. London: Vintage.

Herman, E. and N. Chomsky (1988). *Manufacturing Consent: The Political Economy of the Mass Media*. New York: Pantheon Books.

Hermes, J. (1995) *Reading Women's Magazines: An Analysis of Everyday Media Use*. Cambridge: Polity Press.

Hesmondhalgh, D. (2006) 'Inside media organizations: production, autonomy and power', in D. Hesmondhalgh (ed.), *Media Production*. Maidenhead and Milton Keynes: The Open University Press/The Open University, pp. 49–90.

Hesmondhalgh, D. (2007) *The Cultural Industries*, 2nd edn. London: Sage.

Hesmondhalgh, D. (2013) *The Cultural Industries*, 3rd edn. London: Sage Publications.

Hill, A. (2002) 'Big Brother: The Real Audience', *Television and New Media*, 3(3): 323–40.

Hill, J. (1985) 'The British "social problem film": violent playground and sapphire', *Screen*, 26(1): 34–48.

Ho, W.C. (2003) 'Between globalization and localization: a study of Hong Kong popular music', *Popular Music*, 22(2): 143–57.

Hodgetts, D., A. Hodgetts and A. Radley (2006) 'Life in the shadow of the media: imaging street homelessness in London', *European Journal of Cultural Studies* 9(4): 497–516.

Hodkinson, P. (2002) *Goth: Identity, Style and Sub-Culture*. Berg: Oxford and New York.

Hodkinson, P. (2011) *Media, Culture and Society*. London: Sage.

Holliman, R. (2004) 'Media coverage of cloning: a study of media content, production and reception', *Public Understanding of Science*, 13(2): 107–30.

Hopps, G. (2009) *Morrissey: The Pageant of His Bleeding Heart*. London and New York: Continuum.

Hornig-Priest, S. (2009) *Doing Media Research*, 2nd edn. Thousand Oaks, CA: Sage.

Howard P.N. and M.M. Hussein (2011) 'The role of digital media', *Journal of Democracy*, 22(3): 35–48

Howley, K. (2005) *Community Media: People, Places and Communications Technologies*. Cambridge: Cambridge University Press.

Howley, K. (ed.) (2010) *Community Media*. London: Sage Publications.

Howley, K. (ed.) (2013) *Media Interventions*. New York: Peter Lang and Associates.

Huang, E., K. Davison, S. Shreve, T. Davis, E. Bettendorf and A. Nair (2006) 'Facing the challenges of convergence: media professionals concerns of working across media platforms', *Convergence*, 12(1): 83–98.

Hubbs, N. (1996) 'Music of the 'fourth gender': Morrissey and the sexual politics of melodic contour', in T. Foster, C. Stiegel and E. E. Berry (eds), *Bodies of Writing, Bodies in Performance*. New York: New York University Press, pp. 266–96.

Hubbs, N. (1996) 'Music of the "fourth gender": Morrissey and the sexual politics of melodic contour', in T. Foster, C. Stiegel and E.E. Berry (eds), *Bodies of Writing, Bodies in Performance*. New York: New York University Press, pp. 266–96.

Husband, C. (1998) 'Globalisation, media infrastructures and identities in a diasporic community', *Javnost: The Public*, 5(4): 19–33.

Internet World Stats: http://www.internetworldstats.com/

Ito, T. (2006) 'Journalism in power relations and Pierre Bourdieu's concept of "field": a case study of the coverage of the 1999 group bullying murder case in Tochigi Prefecture', in *Keio Communications Review*, 28: 71–86.

Iyengar S. and D.R. Kinder (1987) *News That Matters: Television and American Opinion*. Chicago: University of Chicago Press.

Iyengar, S. (1991) *Is Anyone Responsible? How Television Frames Political Issues*. Chicago: University of Chicago Press.

Iyengar, S. and D.R. Kinder (1987) *News that Matters: Television and American Opinion*. Chicago: University of Chicago Press.

James, J. (2005) 'The global digital divide in the internet: developed world constructs and third world realities', *Journal of Information Science*, 31(2): 114–23.

Jenkins, H. (1992) *Textual Poachers: Television Fans and Participatory Culture*. London Routledge.

Jensen, J. (1992) 'Fandom as pathology: the consequences of characterization', in L. Lewis (ed.), *The Adoring Audience: Fan Culture and Popular Media*. London: Routledge.

Kahn, K.T. (2006) 'Queer dilemmas: the "right" ideology and homosexual representation in *Desperate Housewives*', in J. McCabe and K. Akass (eds), *Reading Desperate Housewives: Beyond the White Picket Fence*. London: I. B. Tauris.

Karim, K. (2003) (ed.) *The Media of Diaspora*. London: Routledge.

Karim, K. (2007) 'Media and diaspora', in E. Devereux (ed.), *Media Studies: Key Issues and Debates*. London: Sage.

Kavoori, A. (1999) 'Discursive texts, reflexive audiences: global trends in television news texts and audience reception', *Journal of Broadcasting and Electronic Media*, 43(3): 386–98.

Kerr, A. (2006) *The Business and Culture of Digital Games*. London: Sage.

Kim, K.H. (2006) 'Obstacles to the success of female journalists in Korea', *Media, Culture & Society*, 28(1): 123–41.

Kirschenman, J. and K.M. Neckerman (1991) '"We'd love to hire them, but … ": the meaning of race for employers', in C. Jencks and P.E. Peterson (eds), *The Urban Underclass*. Washington: The Brookings Institution, pp. 203–32.

Kitty, A. (2005) *Don't Believe It! How Lies Become News*. New York: The Disinformation Company.

Kit-Wai Ma, E. (2000) 'Re-thinking media studies: the case of China', in J. Curran and M-J. Park (eds) *De-Westernizing Media Studies*. London: Routledge.

Kitzinger, J. (1990) 'Audience understandings of AIDS media messages: a discussion of methods', *Sociology of Health and Illness*, 12(3): 319–35.

Kitzinger, J. (1993) 'Understanding AIDS: researching audience perceptions of Acquired Immune Deficiency Syndrome', in J. Eldridge (ed.), *Getting the Message: News, Truth and Power*. London: Routledge.

Kitzinger, J. (1999) 'A sociology of media power: key issues in audience reception research', in G. Philo (ed.), *Message Received*. Harlow: Addison Wesley Longman.

Kitzinger, J. (2000) 'Media templates: patterns of association and the (re)construction of meaning over time', *Media, Culture & Society*, 22(1): 61–84.

Kitzinger, J. and C. Kitzinger (1993) '"Doing it": representations of lesbian sex', in G. Griffin (ed.), *Outwrite: Lesbianism and Popular Culture*. London: Pluto Press.

Klein, N. (2001) *No Logo*. London: Flamingo Books.

Klein, N. (2002) *Fences and Windows: Dispatches from the Front Lines of the Globalization Debate*. Vintage Canada and Picador.

Klein, N. (2007) *The Shock Doctrine: The Rise of Disaster Capitalism*. Toronto: Knopf Canada.

Koch, K. (2010) *Passions Just Like Mine*. DVD. Urban Cowgirl Productions.

Korupp, S.E and M. Szydlik (2005) 'Causes and trends of the digital divide', *European Sociological Review*, 21(4): 409–22.

Koskela, H. (2004) 'Webcams, TV shows and mobile phones: empowering exhibitionism', *Surveillance & Society*, 2(2/3): 199–215.

Kosut, M. (2012) ed *The Encyclopedia of Gender in Media*. Sage: Thousand Oaks.

Kraidy, M.M. (1999) 'The global, the local, and the hybrid: a native ethnography of glocalization', *Critical Studies in Mass Communication*, 16(4): 456–76.

Krippendorf, K. (2012) *Content Analysis: An Introduction to its Methodology*, 3rd edn. Thousand Oaks, CA: Sage.

Krippendorf, K. and A. Bock (eds) (2008) *The Content Analysis Reader*. Thousand Oaks, CA: Sage.

Krotz, F. and U. Hasebrink (1998) 'The analysis of people-meter data: individual patterns of viewing behaviour and viewers' cultural backgrounds', *Communications*, 23(2): 151–74.

Kumar, D. (2006) 'Media, war and propaganda: strategies of information management during the 2003 Iraq war', *Communication and Critical/Cultural Studies*, 3(1): 48–69.

Larner, W. (2000) 'Neo-Liberalism: Policy, Ideology, Governmentality', *Studies in Political Economy*, 63: 5–25.

Labre, M.P. and L. Duke (2004) '"Nothing like a brisk walk and a spot of demon slaughter to make a girl's night": the construction of the female hero in the *Buffy* Video Game', *Journal of Communication Inquiry*, 28(2): 138–56.

Lens, V. (2002) 'Public voices and public policy: changing the societal discourse on welfare', *Journal of Sociology and Social Welfare*, 29(1): 137–54.

Liebes, T. and E. Katz (1993) *The Export of Meaning: Cross-cultural Readings of Dallas*, 2nd edn. Cambridge: Polity Press.

Liebes, T. and S. Livingstone (1994) 'The structure of family and romantic ties in the soap opera', *Communication Research*, 21(6): 717–41.

Linden, G., K.L. Kraemer and J. Dedrick (2007) *Who Captures Value in a Global Innovation System? The Case of Apple's iPod*. California: Personal Computing Industry Center (PCIC).

Livingstone, S. (1998) 'Mediated childhoods: a comparative approach to young people's changing media environment in Europe', *European Journal of Communication*, 13(4): 435–56.

Livingstone, S (2002) *Young People and New Media*. London: Sage.

Livingstone, S. (2004) 'The challenge of changing audiences: or what is the audience researcher to do in the age of the internet?', *European Journal of Communication*, 19(1): 75–86.

Long, P. and T. Wall (2012) *Media Studies: Texts, Production and Context*, 2nd edn. Harlow: Pearson Education

Lucas, K. and J.L. Sherry (2004) 'Sex differences in video game play', *Communication Research*, 31(5): 499–523.

Lull, J. (1980) 'The social uses of television', *Human Communication Research*, 6(3): 197–209.

Lull, J. (1991) *China Turned On: Television, Reform and Resistance*. London: Routledge.

Lull, J. (1995) *Media, Communication, Culture: A Global Approach*. Cambridge: Polity Press.

Machin, D. and T. van Leeuwen (2003) 'Global schemas and local discourses in *Cosmopolitan*', *Journal of Sociolinguistics*, 7(4): 493–512.

Machin, D. and T. van Leeuwen (2004) 'Global media: generic homogeneity and discursive diversity', *Continuum: Journal of Media and Cultural Studies*, 18(1): 99–120.

MacNamara, J.R. (2010) *The 21st Century Media (R)evolution: Emergent Communication Practices*. New York: Peter Lang.

Magistead, M. (1986) 'The Ethiopian Bandwagon: The Relationship between news media coverage and British Foreign Policy towards the 1984/5 Ethiopian famine', LMA Thesis, Sussex University.

Manco, D. (2011) 'In our different ways we are the same: Morrissey and representations of disability', in E. Devereux, A. Dillane and M. Power (eds), *Morrissey: Fandom, Representations and Identities*. Bristol: Intellect Books, 119–38.

Mansell, R. (1999) 'New media competition and access: the scarcity–abundance dialectic', *New Media & Society*, 1(2): 155–82.

Mansell, R. (2003) 'The nature of the information society: an industrialized country perspective', paper presented at the 'Visions of the Information Society' ITU Conference, 18–25 February, Geneva.

Mansell, R. (2004) 'Political economy, power and new media', *New Media & Society*, 6(1): 96–105.

Mao, Y., M.S. Richter, K. Kovacs Burns and J. Chaw-Kant (2012) 'Homelessness coverage, social reality, and media ownership: comparing a national newspaper with two regional newspapers in Canada', *Mass Communication and Journalism*, 2: 119.

Marcuse, H. (1964) *One Dimensional Man*. Boston, MA: Beacon Press.

Martino, P. (2007) 'I am a living sign: a semiotic reading of Morrissey', *International Journal of Applied Semiotics*, 6(1): 103–19.

Marx, K and F. Engels (1846) *The German Ideology*, www.marxists.org

Matheson, D. (2005) *Media Discourses*. Maidenhead: Open University Press.

Mathijs, E. (2002) 'Big Brother and critical discourse: the reception of Big Brother Belgium', *Television and New Media*, 3(3): 311–22.

Matthews, B. and L. Ross (2010) *Research Methods: A Practical Guide for the Social Sciences*. Harlow: Longman-Pearson.

McCabe, J. (2006) 'What is it with that hair? Bree Van de Kamp and policing contemporary femininity', in J. McCabe and K. Akass (eds), *Reading Desperate Housewives: Beyond the White Picket Fence*. London: I.B. Tauris.

McCabe, J. and K. Akass (eds) (2006) *Reading Desperate Housewives: Beyond the White Picket Fence*. London: I.B. Tauris.

McChesney, R.W. (1999) *Rich Media, Poor Democracy: Communication Politics in Dubious Times*. Champaign, IL: University of Illinois Press.

McChesney, R.W. (2000) 'The political economy of communication and the future of the field', *Media, Culture and Society*, 22(1): 109–16

McClendon B. (2010) *Explore the world with street view, now on all seven continents*. Available at: http://googleblog.blogspot.com/2010/09/explore-world-with-street-view-now-on.html

McCombs, M. and Shaw, D. (1972) 'The Agenda-Setting Function of the Mass Media', *Public Opinion Quarterly*, 36: 176–85.

McCullagh, C. (2002) *Media Power: A Sociological Introduction*. London: Palgrave.

McLuhan, M. (1964) *Understanding Media: The Extensions of Man*. New York: Routledge.

McManus, J. (1992) 'What kind of commodity is news?', *Communications Research*, 19(6): 780–812.

McManus, J. (1994) *Market-driven Journalism*. London. Sage.

McManus, J.H. (2009) The commercialization of news, in K. Wahl-Jorgenson and T. Hanitzch (eds), *The Handbook of Journalism Studies*. New York: Routledge.

Murdock, G. (1989) 'Critical Inquiry and Audience Activity' in B. Dervin et al. (eds) *Rethinking Communication, Vol. 2: Paradigm Exemplars*. London: Sage.

McQuail, D. (1983) *Mass Communication Theory*. London: Sage.

McQuail, D. (2000) *McQuail's Mass Communication Theory*. London: Sage.

McQuail, D. (2010) *McQuail's Mass Communication Theory*, 6th edn. London: Sage.

Meadows, M. (2013) 'Putting the citizen back into journalism', *Journalism*, 14(1): 43–60.

Miller, D. and D. Slater (2000) *The Internet: An Ethnographic Approach*. Oxford: Berg.

Miller, M. (2002) 'What's wrong with this picture?', *The Nation*, http://www.thenation.com/article/whats-wrong-picture-0#

Mills, C. Wright (1976) *The Sociological Imagination*. New York: Oxford University Press.

Mirchandani, K. (2004) 'Practices of global capital: gaps, cracks and ironies in transnational call centres in India', *Global Networks*, 4(4): 355–73.

Moores, S. (1993) *Interpreting Audiences: The Ethnography of Media Consumption*. London: Sage.

Morimoto, S.A. and L.A. Friedland (2011) 'The lifeworld of youth in the information society', *Youth & Society*, 43(2): 549–67.

Morley, D. (1980) *The 'Nationwide' Audience*. London: British Film Institute.

Morley, D. (1986) *Family Television, Cultural Power and Domestic Leisure*. London: Comedia.

Morris, L. (1994) *Dangerous Classes: The Underclass and Social Citizenship*, London: Routledge.

Mosco, V. (1996) *The Political Economy of Communication*. London: Sage.

Mosco V. and J. Wasko (eds) (1988) *The Political Economy of Information*. Madison: University of Wisconsin Press.

Mullen, M. (2004) '*The Simpsons* and Hanna-Barbera's animation legacy', in J. Alberti (ed.) *Leaving Springfield*: The Simpsons *and the Possibility of Oppositional Culture*. Detroit: Wayne State University Press, pp. 63–84.

Mulrennan, T. (2010) 'The human and exploitative side of digital capitalism: the iPod's journey along the globalisation trail', *Socheolas: The Limerick Student Journal of Sociology*, 2(2): 89–102.

Murdock, G. (1982) 'Large corporations and the control of the communications industries', in M. Gurevitch, T. Bennet, J. Curran and J. Woolacott (eds), *Culture, Society and the Media*. New York: Methuen.

Murdock, G. (1992) 'Citizens, consumers and public culture', in M. Skovmand and K.C. Schroder (eds), *Media Cultures: Reappraising Transnational Media*. London and New York: Routledge.

Naficy, H. (1993) *The Making of Exile Cultures: Iranian Television in Los Angeles*. Minneapolis: University of Minnesota Press.

Nardi, B.A., D.J. Schiano and M. Gumbrecht (2004) 'Blogging as social activity, or would you let 900 million people read your diary?', *Proceedings of the 2004 ACM Conference, Computer Supported Co-Operative Network*. New York: ACM Press, pp. 222–31.

Negroponte, N. (1995) *Being Digital*. London: Hodder & Stoughton.

Newcomb, H. (1991) 'The creation of television drama news', in K. Bruhn Jensen and N.W. Jankowski (eds), *A Handbook of Qualitative Methodologies for Mass Communication Research*. London: Routledge.

News Corporation Annual Report (2011). New York: News Corporation.

Nylén, A. (2004) 'Me and Morrissey', http://www.eurozine.com/articles/2004-08-24-nylen-en.html

Nohrstedt, S.A. (1986) 'Ideological news reporting from the Third World: a case study of international newspaper and magazine coverage of the civil war in Nigeria, 1967–70', *European Journal of Communication*, 1(4): 421–46.

Norris, P. (2001) *Digital Divide*. Cambridge: Cambridge University Press.

O'Malley, T. (2002) 'Media history and media studies: aspects of the development of the study of media history in the UK 1945–2000', *Media History*, 8(2): 155–73.

O'Sullivan, T., B. Dutton and P. Rayner (1994) *Studying the Media: An Introduction*. London: Arnold.

Oduro-Frimpong, J. (2009) 'Glocalization trends: the case of hiplife music in contemporary Ghana', *International Journal of Communication*, 3: 1085–106.

Oliveira, O.S. (1993) 'Brazilian soaps outshine Hollywood: is cultural imperialism fading out?', in K. Nordenstreng and H.I. Schiller (eds), *Beyond National Sovereignty: International Communication in the 1990s*. Norwood, NJ: Ablex.

Oresjo, E., R. Andersson and E. Holmquist (2004) 'Large housing estates in Sweden: policies and practices', Faculty of Geosciences, Utrecht University.

Ornebring, H. (2013) 'Anything you can do, I can do better? Professional journalists on citizen journalists in six European countries', *International Communication Gazette*, 75(1): 35–53.

Orwell, G. (1949) *1984*. London: Secker and Warburg.

Owen, D. (2012) 'Media consolidation, fragmentation and selective exposure in the US', in H. Semetko and M. Scammell (eds), *The Sage Handbook of Political Communication*. London: Sage.

Paek, H. J. and Shah, H. (2003) 'Racial Ideology, Model Minorities and the "not-so-silent partner:" stereotyping of Asian Americans in US Magazine Advertising', *Howard Journal of Communication*, 14: 225–43.

Palmer, C., A. Ziersch, K. Arthurson and F. Baum (2004) 'Challenging the stigma of public housing: preliminary findings from a qualitative study in South Australia', *Urban Policy and Research*, 22(4): 411–26.

Parker, A. (2000) 'Alan Parker interviewed by Barry Norman', *The Guardian* interview www.filmunlimited.co.uk

Patelis, K. (2000) 'The political economy of the internet', in J. Curran (ed.), *Media Organisations in Society*. London: Arnold.

Pavlik, J.V. (2013) 'Trends in new media research: a critical review of recent scholarship', *Sociology Compass*, 7(1): 1–12

Pecora, V.P. (2002) 'The culture of surveillance', *Qualitative Sociology*, 25(3): 345–58.

Permentier, M., M. van Ham and G. Bolt (2007) 'Behavioural responses to neighbourhood reputations', *Journal of Housing and the Built Environment*, 22: 199–213.

Permentier, M., M. van Ham and G. Bolt (2008) 'Same neighbourhood … different views? A confrontation of internal and external neighbourhood reputations', *Housing Studies*, 23(6): 833–55.

Permentier, M., M. van Ham and G. Bolt (2009) 'Neighbourhood reputation and the intention to leave the neighbourhood', *Environment and Planning*, 41: 2162–80.

Peters, S and T. Peters (2005) 'What is globalization?', http://www.topics-mag.com/

Philo, G. (1990) *Seeing and Believing: The Influence of Television*. London: Routledge.

Philo, G. (1993a) 'From Buerk to Band Aid: the media and the 1984 Ethiopian famine', in J. Eldridge (ed.), *Getting the Message*. London: Routledge.

Philo, G. (1993b) 'Getting the message: audience research in the Glasgow University Media Group', in J. Eldridge (ed.), *Getting the Message: News Truth and Power*. London: Routledge, pp. 253–70.

Philo, G. (1999) *Message Received*. London: Longmans.

Philo, G. (2002) 'Missing in action', *Guardian*, 16 April.

Philo, G. (2007) 'News content studies, media group methods and discourse analysis: a comparison of approaches' in E. Devereux (ed.), *Media Studies: Key Issues and Debates*. London: Sage.

Philo, G. (2008) 'News content studies, media group methods and discourse analysis: a comparison of approaches', in E. Devereux (ed.) *Media Studies: Key Issues and Debates*. London: Sage, pp. 101–33.

Picard, R.G. (1989) *Media Economics*. Beverly Hills, CA: Sage.

Pilger, J. (1999) *Hidden Agendas*. London: Verso.

Pilger, J. (2002) *The New Rulers of the World*. London: Verso.

Platon, S. and M. Deuze (2003) 'Indymedia journalism: a radical way of making, selecting and sharing news?', *Journalism*, 4(3): 336–55.

Postman, N. (1986) *Amusing Ourselves to Death*. London: Viking/Penguin.

Potter, W.J. (2012) *Media Effects*. Thousand Oaks, CA: Sage.

Power, M. (2011) '"The teenage dad" and "slum mums" are "just certain people I know": counter hegemonic representations of the working/under class in the works of Morrissey', in E. Devereux, A. Dillane and M. Power (eds), *Morrissey: Fandom, Representations and Identities*. Bristol: Intellect Books, pp. 95–118.

Power, M.J., P. Neville, E. Devereux, A Haynes and C. Barnes (2012) '"Why bother seeing the world for real?" Google Street View and the representation of a stigmatised neighbourhood', *New Media & Society*, published online before print, 10 December, doi: 10.1177/1461444812465138.

Preston, P. (2009) *Making the News: Journalism and News Cultures in Europe*. London: Routledge.

Proctor, J. (2004) *Stuart Hall*. London: Routledge.

Propp, V. (1928) *Morphology of the Folktale*, trans. L. Scott. Austin, TX: University of Texas Press.

Punathambekar, A. (2005) 'Bollywood in the Indian-American Diaspora', *International Journal of Cultural Studies*, 8(2): 151–73.

Purcell, M. (2011) 'Neoliberalization and Democracy' in S. S. Fainstein and S. Campbell (eds) *Readings in Urban Theory*, 3rd edn. Oxford: Blackwell.

Qureshi, K. and S. Moores (2000) 'Identity, tradition and translation', in S. Moores, *Media and Everyday Life in Modern Society*. Edinburgh: Edinburgh University Press.

Radway, J. (1987) *Reading the Romance: Women, Patriarchy and Popular Literature*. London: Verso.

Rakow, L. (1990) 'Feminist perspectives on popular culture', in J. Downing, A. Mohammadi and A. Sreberny-Mohammadi (eds), *Questioning The Media: A Critical Introduction*. Thousand Oaks, CA: Sage.

Rantanen, T. (2004) *The Media and Globalization*. London: Sage Publications.

Ray, M. (2003) 'Nation, Nostalgia and Bollywood', in K.H. Karim (ed.), *The Media of Diaspora*. London: Routledge.

Renyolds, S. (1995) *The Sex Revolts: Gender, Rebellion and Rock 'n' Roll*. Cambridge, MA: Harvard University Press.

Rideout, V.J., U.G. Foehr and D.F. Roberts (2010) *Generation M2: Media in the Lives of 8–18 Year Olds*. Menlo Park, CA: Kaiser Foundation.

Ritzer, G. (2000) *The McDonaldization of Society*. Thousand Oaks, CA: Pine Forge Press.

Ritzer, G., P. Dean and N. Jurgenson (2012) 'The coming of age of the prosumer', *American Behavioral Scientist*, 56: 379–98.

Robertson, R. (1992) *Globalization, Social Theory and Global Culture*. London: Sage.

Rodriquez, C. (2001) *Fissures in the Mediascape*. Cresskill, NJ: Hampton Press.

Rochlin, M. (2010) 'Shameless Brings Home America's Poor Next Door', *New York Times*, December 31.

Rowling, J.K. (2004) *Harry Potter and the Philosopher's Stone*. London: Bloomsbury.

Ruddock, A. (2000) *Understanding Audiences: Theory and Method*. London: Sage.

Russo, V. (1981) *The Celluloid Closet: Homosexuality in the Movies*. New York: Harper & Row.

Ryfe, D.M. (2009) 'Broader and deeper: a study of newsroom culture in a time of change', *Journalism*, 10(2): 197–216.

Sabbagh, D. (2006) 'No Tibet or Tiananmen on Google's Chinese Site', *The Times*, 25 January, http://www.thetimes.co.uk/tto/business/markets/china/article2615329.ece

Saguy, A.C. and R. Almeling (2008) 'Fat in the fire? Science, the news media, and the "obesity epidemic"', *Sociological Forum*, 23(1): 53–83.

Saltzis, K. and Dickinson, R. (2008) 'Inside the changing newsroom: journalists' responses to media convergence', *Aslib Proceedings*, 60(3): 216–28.

Scannell, P. (2002) 'Big Brother as a Television Event', *Television & New Media*, 3(3): 271–82.

Schaffert, R.W. (1992) *Media Coverage and Political Terrorists: A Quantitative Analysis*. New York: Praeger.

Schlosberg, J. (2013) *Power Beyond Scrutiny: Media, Justice and Accountability*. London: Pluto Press.

Schlosser, J. (1998) '"King" poised to beat Bart', *Broadcasting and Cable*, 128(26): 48.

Schmid, H. and C. Klimmt (2011) 'A magically nice guy: parasocial relationships with Harry Potter across different cultures', *International Communication Gazette*, 73(3): 252–69.

Scholte, J.A. (2000) *Globalization: A Critical Introduction*. London: Palgrave.

Schroder, K.C. (1999) 'The best of both worlds? Media audience research between rival paradigms', in P. Alasuutari (ed.) *Rethinking the Media Audience*. London: Sage.

Schroeder, K., K. Drotner, S. Kline and C. Murray (2003) *Researching Audiences*. London: Arnold.

Scott, G. and R. Garner (2013) *Doing Qualitative Research: Designs, Methods and Techniques*. London: Pearson.

Sebeok, T. (1974) 'Semiotics: a survey of the state of the art', in T. Sebeok (ed.), *Current Trends in Linguistics I*. The Hague: Mouton.

Seiter, E. (1999) *Television and New Media Audiences*. Oxford: Oxford University Press.

Semetko, H. and M. Scammell (2012) (eds) *The Sage Handbook of Political Communication*. London: Sage.

Shi, Y. (2011) 'iPhones in China: the contradictory stories of media-ICT globalization in the era of media convergence and corporate synergy', *Journal of Communication Inquiry*, 35(2): 134–56.

Shim, K., W. Bellar and P. Kwon (2011) 'How social media are changing news routines', unpublished paper, Syracuse.

Shoemaker, P.J. and Reese, S. (1996) *Mediating the Message: Theories of Influences on Mass Media Content*, 2nd edn. Boston, MA: Longman.

Shoemaker, P.J., J. Hyuk Lee, G. Han and A.A. Cohen (2007) 'Proximity and scope as news values', in E. Devereux (ed.), *Media Studies: Key Issues and Debates*. London: Sage, pp. 231–48.

Shon, P.C. (2012) *How to Read Journal Articles in the Social Sciences*. London: Sage.

Shugart, H.A. (2003) 'Reinventing privilege: the new (gay) man in contemporary popular media', *Critical Studies in Media Communication*, 20(1): 67–91.

Silva, C. (2011) 'User Generated Content and participatory culture: how has it taken place in CNN's website?', paper presented at the congress of SBPJ or 'Journalism and Digital Media', Rio de Janeiro, Brazil, 4 November.

Silverstone, R. (1999) *Why Study the Media?* London: Sage.

Silverstone, R., E. Hirsch and D. Morley (1991) 'Listening to a long conversation: An ethnographic approach to the study of information and communication technologies in the home', *Cultural Studies*, 5(2): 204–27.

Singer, J.B. (2010) 'Quality control', *Journalism Practice*, 4(2): 127–42.

Singleton, B. (2006) 'Hunters, heroes and the hegemonically masculine fantasies of *Desperate Housewives*', in J. McCabe and K. Akass (eds) *Reading Desperate Housewives: Beyond the White Picket Fence*. London: I.B. Tauris.

Skeggs, B. (2004) *Class, Self, Culture*. London: Routledge.

Skeggs, B. (2005) 'The making of class and gender through visualizing moral subject formation', *Sociology*, 39(5): 965–82.

Sklair, L. (1999) 'Globalization', in S. Taylor (ed.), *Sociology: Issues and Debates*. London: Macmillan.

Skovsgaard, M., E. Albæk, P. Bro and C. de Vreese (2013) 'A reality check: How journalists' role perceptions impact their implementation of the objectivity norm', *Journalism*, 14(1): 22–42

Smith, P. and A. Bell (2007) 'Unravelling the web of discourse analysis', in E. Devereux (ed.), *Media Studies: Key Issues and Debates*. London: Sage, pp. 78–100.

Smythe, D.W. (1960) 'On the political economy of communications', *Journalism & Mass Communication Quarterly*, 37(4): 563–72.

Smythe, D.W. (1981) *Dependency Road: Communications, Capitalism, Consciousness and Canada*. Norwood, NJ: Ablex.

Snowsell, C. (2011) 'Fanatics, Apostles and NMEs', in E. Devereux, A. Dillane and M. Power (eds) *Morrissey: Fandom, Representations and Identities*. Bristol: Intellect Books.

Sorenson, J. (1991) 'Mass media and discourse on famine in the Horn of Africa', *Discourse & Society*, 2(2): 223–42.

Soubiran-Paillet, F. (1987) 'Presse et delinquance, ou, comment lire entre les lignes', *Criminologie*, 20(1): 59–77.

Sparks, C. (2013) 'Global media studies: its development and dilemmas', *Media, Culture & Society*, 35(1): 121–31.

Sreberny-Mohammadi, A. and A. Mohammadi (1994) *Small Media, Big Revolution: Communication, Culture and the Iranian Revolution*. Minneapolis, MN: University of Minnesota Press.

Staiger, J. (2000) *Perverse Spectators: The Practices of Film Reception*. New York and London: New York University Press.

Stetka, V. (2012) 'From multinationals to business tycoons: media ownership and journalistic autonomy in Central and Eastern Europe', *International Journal of Press/Politics*, 17(14): 433–56.

Stevenson, N. (2002) *Understanding Media Cultures: Social Theory and Mass Communication*, 2nd edn. London: Sage.

Stokes, J. (2012) *How To Do Media and Cultural Studies*, 2nd edn. London: Sage.

Stringer, J. (1992) 'The Smiths: repressed (but remarkably dressed)', *Popular Music*, 11: 15–26.

Sullivan, J.L. (2013) *Media Audiences: Effects, Users, Institutions and Power*. Thousand Oaks, CA: Sage.

Tang, L. and H. Sampson (2012) 'The interaction between the mass media and the internet in non-democratic states: the case of China', in *Media, Culture & Society*, 34(4): 457–72.

Taraszow, T., E. Aristodemou, G. Shitta, Y. Laouris and A. Arsoy (2010) 'Disclosure of personal and contact information by young people in social networking sites: an analysis using Facebook profiles as an example', *International Journal of Media & Cultural Politics*, 6(1): 81–101.

Taylor, L. and A. Willis (1999) *Media Studies: Texts, Institutions and Audiences*. Oxford: Blackwell.

Taylor, M. (2006) 'The songs that saved my life', *Guardian*, 3 April.

Tester, K. (1994) *Media, Culture and Morality*. London: Routledge.

The Right Honourable Lord Justice Leveson (2012) *An Inquiry into the Culture and Practices and Ethics of the Press*. London: The Stationery Office.

Thomas, P.N. and Z. Nain (2004) (eds) *Who Owns The Media? Global Trends and Local Resistance*. London: Zed Books.

Thomas, R.O. (2011) 'The freak incubator: *Big Brother* as carnival', *Celebrity Studies*, 2(2): 221–3.

Thomas, S. and B.P. Callanan (1982) 'Allocating happiness: TV families and social class', *Journal of Communication*, 32(3): 184–90.

Thompson, J.B. (1990) *Ideology and Modern Culture*. Cambridge: Polity Press.

Thompson, J.B. (1995) *The Media and Modernity: A Social Theory of the Media*. Cambridge: Polity Press.

Time Warner (2011) *Annual Report*. Time Warner Inc.

Toffler, A. (1980) *The Third Wave*. New York: William Morrow.

Tomlinson, J. (1994) 'A phenomenology of globalization? Giddens on global modernity', *European Journal of Communication*, 9(2): 149–72.

Tomlinson, J. (1997) 'Internationalism, globalization and cultural imperialism', in K. Thompson (ed.), *Media and Cultural Regulation*. London: Sage/The Open University.

Tomlinson, J. (1999) 'Cultural globalization: placing and displacing the West', in H. Mackay and T. O'Sullivan (eds), *The Media Reader: Continuity and Transformation*. London: Sage.

Tracy, A.L.C.D. de, (1817) *A Treatise on Political Economy*, trans. edited by Thomas Jefferson. Georgetown: Joseph Milligan.

Tremayne, M. (ed.) (2007) *Blogging, Citizenship and the Future of Media*. London: Routledge.

Triandafyllidou, A. (1998) 'National identity and the "other"'. *Ethnic and Racial Studies*, 21(8): 593–612.

Tsaliki, L. (2003) 'Globalization and hybridity: the construction of Greekness on the internet', in K. Karim (ed.) *The Media of Diaspora*. London: Routledge, pp. 162–76.

Tuchman, G. (1978) 'Introduction: the symbolic annihilation of women by the mass media', in G. Tuchman, A.K. Daniels and J. Benét (eds), *Hearth and Home: Images of Women in the Mass Media*. New York: Oxford University Press, pp. 3–38.

Tuchman, G. (1991) 'Qualitative methods in the study of news', in K. Bruhn Jensen and N.W. Jankowski (eds), *A Handbook of Qualitative Methodologies for Mass Communication Research*. London: Routledge.

Tumber, H. and J. Palmer (2004) *The Media at War*. London: Sage.

Tunstall, J. and M. Palmer (1991) *Media Moguls*. London: Routledge.

Turow, J. (1992) 'The organizational underpinnings of contemporary media conglomerates', *Communication Research*, 19(6): 682–704.

Tyler, I. (2008) '"Chav Mum, Chav Scum": class disgust in contemporary Britain', *Feminist Media Studies*, 8(1): 17–34.

Usher, N. (2013) '*Marketplace* public radio and news routines reconsidered: between structures and agents'. *Journalism*, 14(6): 807–22.

Van Der Berg, H. and C.G. van Der Veer (1989) 'Ideologies in the news: on the measurement of ideological characteristics of news reports', *Gazette*, 14: 159–94.

Van Dijk, J.A.G.M. (2005) *The Deepening Divide: Inequality in the Information Society*. Sage: London.

Van Dijk, T.A. (1988) *News Analysis: Case Studies of International and National News in the Press*. Hillsdale, NJ: Erlbaum.

Van Dijk, T.A. (1991) *Racism and the Press*. London: Routledge.

Van Dijk, T.A. (1998a) *Ideology: A Multidisciplinary Approach*. London: Sage.

Van Dijk, T.A. (1998b) 'Opinions and ideologies in the press', in A. Bell and P. Garrett (eds), *Approaches to Media Discourse*. Oxford: Blackwell.

Van Zoonen, L. (1994) *Feminist Media Studies*. London: Sage.

Van Zoonen, L. (1998) 'One of the girls? The changing gender of journalism', in C. Carter, G. Branston and S. Allen (eds), *News, Gender and Power*. London: Routledge.

Van Zoonen, L. (2001) 'Desire and resistance: *Big Brother* and the recognition of everyday life', *Media, Culture & Society*, 23(5): 669–77.

Van Zoonen, L. and M. Aslama (2006) 'Understanding *Big Brother*: an Analysis of current research', *Javnost/The Public*, 13(2): 85–96.

Van Zoonen, L. and I. Costera Meijer (1998) 'From Pamela Anderson to Erasmus: women, men and representation', in A. Briggs and P. Cobley (eds), *The Media: An Introduction*. Harlow: Longman.

Veit-Wilson, J. (1998) *Setting Adequacy Standards*. Bristol: Policy Press.

Verstraeten, H. (1996) 'The media and the transformation of the public sphere: a contribution for a critical political economy of the public sphere', *European Journal of Communication*, 11(3): 347–70.

Viitamäki, T. (1997) 'I'm not the man you think I am: Morrissey's fourth gender', *Musical Currents*, 3: 29–40.

Vivendi (2011) *Annual Report*. Vivendi Inc.

Von Feilitzen C. and U. Carlsson (eds) (2002) *Children, Young People and Media Globalisation*. The Unesco/Nordicom/Goteburg University.

Vroomen, L. (2004) 'Kate Bush: teen pop and older female fans', in A. Bennett and R.A. Peterson (eds), *Music Scenes: Local, Translocal and Virtual*. Nashville, TN: Vanderbilt University Press, pp. 238–53.

Waisbord, S. (2013) 'Media policies and blindspots of media globalization: insights from Latin America', *Media, Culture & Society*, 35(1): 132–8.

Walker, M.A. (2005) 'Guada-narco-lupe, maquilaranas and the discursive construction of gender and difference on the US-Mexico border in Mexican media re-presentations', *Gender, Place and Culture*, 12(1): 95–111.

Warr, D.J. (2005) 'Social networks in a "discredited" neighbourhood', *Journal of Sociology*, 41(3): 285–308.

Warr, D.J. (2006) 'There goes the neighbourhood: the malign effects of stigma', *Social City* 19.

Wasko, J., G. Murdock and H. Sousa (2011) *The Handbook of Political Economy of Communications*. Oxford: Wiley-Blackwell.

Wassenberg, F. (2004) 'Renewing stigmatised estates in the Netherlands: a framework for image renewal strategies', *Journal of Housing and the Built Environment*, 19: 271–92.

Webb, D. (2005) 'On Mosques and malls: understanding Khomeinism as a source of counter-hegemonic resistance to the spread of global consumer culture', *Journal of Political Ideologies*, 10(1): 95–119.

Webster, F. (1995) *Theories of the Information Society*. London: Routledge.

Wells, A. (1990) 'Popular music: emotional use and management', *Popular Culture*, 24(1): 105–17.

Wheen, F. (1999) *Karl Marx*. London: Fourth Estate.

Wheen, F. (2004) *How Mumbo-Jumbo Conquered the World*. London: Harper-Perennial.

Williams, B. (1988) *Upscaling Downtown: Stalled Gentrification in Washington DC*. Ithaca NY: Cornell University Press.

Williams, J. (1994) 'The local and the global in English soccer and the rise of satellite television', *Sociology of Sport Journal*, 11: 376–97.

Willig, I. (2013) 'Newsroom ethnography in a field perspective', *Journalism*, 14(3): 372–87.

Wilson, K.R., J.S. Wallin and C. Reiser (2003) 'Social stratification and the digital divide', *Social Science Computer Review*, 2(2): 133–43.

Winkel, F.W. (1990) 'Crime reporting in newspapers: an exploratory study of the effects of ethnic references in crime news', *Social Behaviour*, 5(2): 87–101.

Winship, J. (1987) *Inside Women's Magazines*. London: Pandora Press.

Woltz, A. (1999) 'Surrogaat voor het leven', *NRC Handelsblad*, 2 December.

Woolacott, J. (1982) 'Messages and meanings', in M. Gurevitch, T. Bennett, J. Curran and J. Woolacott (eds), *Culture, Society and the Media*. London: Routledge.

Worth, O. and C. Kuhling (2005) 'Counter-hegemony and anti-globalisation', *Capital and Class*, 84(3): 31–42.

Yang, G. (2003) 'The internet and the rise of a transnational Chinese cultural sphere', *Media, Culture & Society*, 25(4): 469–90.

Yukl, G. (1994) *Leadership in Organizations*, 3rd edn. Englewood Cliffs, NJ: Prentice Hall.

Zuberi, N. (2001a) 'The last truly British people you will ever know: The Smiths, Morrissey and Britpop', *Sounds English: Transnational Popular Music*. Chicago: University of Illinois Press.

Zuberi, N. (2001b) *Sounds English: Transnational Popular Music*. Urbana: University of Illinois Press.

INDEX

Page numbers in italics refer to figures and plates.